KEATON

KEATON

by *RUDI BLESH*

THE MACMILLAN COMPANY

NEW YORK

FIRST PRINTING

The Macmillan Company, New York

Collier-Macmillan Canada, Ltd., Toronto, Ontario

Library of Congress catalog card number: 66-13563

Printed in the United States of America

To the memory of *Harriet Janis,*

who was *Hansi* to all who loved her

CONTENTS

ACKNOWLEDGMENTS

T HE AUTHOR gratefully acknowledges the generous help of a number of people and organizations—in interviews, correspondence, photographs, permission to quote from articles, and special screenings of films. Interviews began with Buster Keaton himself and his mother, the late Myra Keaton, then extended to Keaton's wife, Eleanor Norris Keaton, his brother Harry and sister Louise, and his two sons, James Keaton Talmadge and Robert Keaton Talmadge. Also interviewed were friends and professional associates, past and present, including the late Norman Kerry, the late Clyde Bruckman, and the late Dr. John Shuman, as well as Eddie Cline, Lewis Jacobs, William "Buster" Collier, Leo Morrison, Ben Pearson, and the late Earle Hammons. Critical opinions came from Albert Lewin and the late Dr. Jermayne MacAgy. Express thanks also go to Paul Gallico and *Esquire* magazine and to Walter Kerr for permission to quote from articles, and to James Mason for access to rare Keaton films.

The following organizations and individuals connected with them have generously assisted in many ways: George Eastman House (Rochester) and James Card, curator; the Museum of Modern Art and Richard Griffith, curator, as well as Margareta Akermark, Eileen Bowser, Joanne Godbout, and Joseph Longo; The Gallery of Modern Art and Raymond Rohauer, curator; Museum of the City of New York and Henriette Beale; the National Film Board of Canada and John Spotton and Gerald Potterton; the New York Public Library, Theatre Section; the Library of the Lincoln Center for the Performing Arts and Paul Myers; Metro-Goldwyn-Mayer; Twentieth Century-Fox Film Corporation and Mike Shapiro; VPI Productions and Jules Schweren; Modernage Laboratories and Ben Attis; Deere & Company and W. E. Goranson.

And, finally, thanks are due to Robert Markel and Alan Rinzler for discerning editing.

PREFACE

T HERE WERE TWO Buster Keatons. I met one of them
at least forty-five years ago. This is Keaton the artist, and I met
him then not in person but through his films. I recall his earliest
two-reel comedies from 1920 on. No doubt I saw him even earlier (in
1917) in the Comique shorts featuring Fatty Arbuckle. I followed his
work on through the 1920's and well into the 1930's.

In the earlier decade there were three outstanding clowns or comic
mimes in the silent films: Charlie Chaplin, Harold Lloyd, and Buster
Keaton. Even then, I was impressed by the strong differences in their
work. Lloyd could make one almost helpless with pure laughter, while
Charlot brought tears with the laughter. Keaton made you laugh, then
think. Lloyd, in other words, was pure comedy—laughter for laughter's
sake; Chaplin was laughter plus sentiment and a kind of Victorian
(or *fin-de-siècle*) poetry. Keaton was the serious one—from the
never-smiling face on to extremely personal concepts of fate, which, for
Buster Keaton, is man at the mercy of both chance and The Machine.

It was a dozen or so years ago that I began seeing the Keaton films
again, at the Museum of Modern Art. It proved far more than an
indulgence in mere nostaglia. It was, in fact, a startling experience.
Cops, The Boat, The General, Our Hospitality, The Navigator—and
all the rest—were a revelation. A third of a century since they had
been made, not they but I (and the world) had changed immeas-
urably. These early films—without sound or color—were beyond any
question more pertinent, more cogent than ever. Buster Keaton was
clearly speaking to us *today*.

The rest was simply my desire, awakened then, to meet the man
behind the artist and then, having done so, the resultant urge to get
the story told of his life, as artist and as man, against the changing
background of the worlds in which he has lived: America and the
theatre, from 1895 to today, from McKinley to Lyndon Johnson, from
Indian medicine show and vaudeville to the motion picture and on to
television.

Consenting, Buster Keaton said, "The closed book has to be opened," and laid down one condition: that the whole true story be told from the beginnings to now. He drew on his own prodigious, detailed, almost-total recall, describing situations, quoting conversations verbatim even a half century or more after the event, and helping me to fill in all gaps in interviews with other people.

During all this, a warm personal friendship grew. With my growing awareness of the depth and integrity of both the man and the artist Keaton, there came to me an unfolding revelation of how uniquely his life in both his worlds symbolizes more than half a century of our changing American scene. Perpetual, relentless outward change, within which an artist remained intact, became a sort of leitmotif, and this book grew very slowly, with later developments in Keaton's career changing it perforce. Its writing spanned a dozen years.

In its last stages, with its subject nearing seventy years of age, an inevitable urgency began to shadow its pages. Would this great, long-neglected artist live to see his just fame restored?

Buster Keaton did live to see that fame of a sudden growing, to receive many an accolade here and abroad. He did not, however, live to enjoy it for very long. On February 1, 1966, he died, a full seventy years old, on his little ranch in the San Fernando Valley near Hollywood. At that moment, this book was nearing completion, a book in the sanguine present tense, about a man still alive and active, just returned from film making abroad, and planning new projects for a still unquenched creative spirit.

With all this in mind, it seemed best to leave it as written: a chronicle of an artist still alive. And Buster Keaton, assuredly, is still alive in the timeless legacy of his films. They are *his* book, which another could never write.

If this story is not just the life of one man, with all its peripheral radiating connections, and is more a chronicle of a whole time—seven decades—as seen from a particular vantage point, this is because there *were* two Buster Keatons. Beyond the man whom time inevitably had corroded is the figure that time has burnished—the beautiful mime, the tragic clown, the artist, speaking clearly through silence.

RUDI BLESH

"This is Buster as I knew him."

—BUSTER KEATON
May 23, 1965

This was my dead-pan boy, hero of a hundred movies, Frustration's Mime, pursued, put-upon, persecuted by humans as well as objects suddenly possessed of a malevolent life and will of their own.

—Paul Gallico

Two-a-Day

Buster Keaton at one year of age.

ONE

❧❧❧❧❧❧❧❧❧❧❧❧❧❧❧❧❧❧❧❧

I N T H E clichéd old legend the actors' child was born, as the saying went, just offstage in a theatrical trunk.

Buster Keaton comes as close to the legend as anyone could. Not only the son of theatre people, he is a child of the theatre itself and has been on the stage since the age of three. By stage, of course, is meant the performing side of show business, from nineteenth-century medicine show to television, with vaudeville, motion pictures (both silent and sound), stock company, road company, and circus in between.

Though not actually born in a costume trunk, Keaton all but smothered in one in the wings, where he had been placed at the age of eleven months. With his parents onstage, the trunk lid was accidentally closed by a stagehand brushing by. Considerably later, Buster's mother, running to the trunk for a quick change of costume, found him lapsing into unconsciousness.

And it was barely offstage, and practically between acts, that Buster Keaton was born, in a boardinghouse next door to a church. The church was momentarily serving as theatre for the Mohawk Indian Medicine Company, which was merely one of the ubiquitous scores of these obscure patent-nostrum peddlers on the road at the turn of the century. It was October 4, 1895, in southeastern Kansas, in the hamlet of Piqua (present-day population circa 250), which calls itself Hay Capital of the World and whose name is a phonetic variant of the Indian tribal name Pickaway. Christened Joseph Frank Keaton, Buster was genealogically preceded by a direct consecutive line of five earlier generations of firstborn sons called Joseph Keaton.

Buster's father, Joseph Hallie Keaton (hereafter to be called Joe), was born in 1867 in Indiana on a bend of the Eel River in a settlement called Dogwalk, about fifteen miles from the city of Terre Haute. Son of a gristmill owner, Joe Keaton was a pioneer before becoming an actor, having staked out a homestead claim in the Oklahoma Land Run of 1889.

3

Buster's mother was born Myra Edith Cutler in 1887 in Modale, Iowa, a village near the Missouri River boundary line between Iowa and Nebraska. Her father, Frank Cutler, wrote, produced, managed, and emceed traveling medicine shows. It was one of these, the Cutler-Bryant Medicine Show, in which Myra was the seventeen-year-old soubrette and cornetist, that Joe Keaton joined and from which he and Myra eloped.

Accidents early became an essential part of Buster Keaton's life. Before his near suffocation in the trunk, one that occurred when he was only six months old led to the nickname Buster. Toward the end of her life—she died in 1955—Myra recalled the details. "It was late morning upstairs in a boardinghouse when Joe and I heard this sudden racket. We rushed out and—my God!—there's our baby lying in a heap down on the next landing. Somehow he'd inched out of our room and, bang, down the stairs. Harry Houdini and his wife Bessie, who were in our company, got to him ahead of us. Harry grabbed the baby up, and the confounded kid began to laugh!

"Houdini gasped and said, 'That's some buster your baby took.'

"Joe looked down and said, 'Well, Buster, looks like Uncle Harry has named you.' He's been Buster ever since. That was a good five years before the Buster Brown cartoons first appeared."

It is no wonder that accidents—both the contrary, frustrating, plan-upsetting kind and the miraculous, benevolent kind—are the basic stuff of the famous Keaton comedy. They are the warp of his life, the *basso ostinato* of his career.

Keaton himself is very conscious of this. "It was almost an accident that I ever got born," he has said.

Myra verified this with a harrowing account of mishaps during her pregnancy. "We were appearing in Perry, Oklahoma," she said. "That's where Joe's folks' farm was—his homestead claim that he gave them when he went with my father's show. It was July, and hot, and Joe and I went for a buggy ride. Suddenly a cloudburst; lightning strikes near the road, the horse bolts and I'm thrown out—six months along! Nothing happened except I got scared and muddy.

"Comes September, and me eight months gone. We're in a little Kansas burg called Cottonwood Falls. In bed in our own tent—another storm, and the wind blows the tent down on us. Joe all tangled up and frantic and me on the ground laughing. Too young to know better, I guess, but by that time I was just that sure I was going to have that baby when my season come.

"Now, late in September, and Buster expected any week, any day

—and off the stage I fall. No business there—wasn't allowed on in my condition, but it was after the show. Like a ninny I stepped down onto a folding chair; it *folded*, and down I went.

"Joe picked me up, swore a little, then said, 'Thank God! That's the third accident. Now we'll be all right.' "

However, Buster, once born, began carrying on the family tradition. His christening fall initiated a new series. Two months later the hotel, where he had been left with a chambermaid, caught fire. Someone rushed into the theatre shouting the news, and the Keatons and Houdinis leaped over the footlights and tore down the street in makeup. Not looking to right or left, they rushed into the hotel. Subsequent events read prophetically like a Buster Keaton silent-film script: Myra rescues Buster; Joe and Harry Houdini muscle their heavy trunks downstairs and outdoors; and then a fireman walks up, looks at them curiously, and says, "Fire's out, folks. Been out for ten minutes."

But Myra was thoroughly frightened by this time. It was then that she began keeping Buster offstage in the wings in the open theatrical trunk, which served as a playpen and, she hoped, a crib. Sleep he disdained. Toys held his attention for about a week. From then on he concentrated on getting out and on the stage, where all the fun seemed to be. He worked on this, developing his already powerful lungs.

In July, 1896, when only nine months old, with his precocious coordination, Buster was able to crawl, "scuttling," as Myra said, "like a crawdad on a creek bottom." With that he reached his goal.

"Heavens knows how that kid ever got out of the trunk," Myra said. "Maybe someone lifted him out to get a costume, then forgot to put him back in." Joe, standing onstage alone in ragged tramp overalls, long legs apart, was doing a blackface monolog straight out of the minstrel jokebook. Suddenly the audience began laughing.

Was that corny line that good? Joe must have thought. The audience roared again, and then he felt a tug on his pants leg. There was Buster on the floor between his father's slapshoes staring solemnly at the audience.

Joe picked him up and held him out. "This is Buster," he said.

Next day Bessie Houdini persuaded Myra to have her son's first stage appearance reenacted at the local photographer's salon. The picture was the first one to go in the album of photographs and clippings that Myra methodically kept over the years.

Then in only a few weeks came the near suffocation that topped

The first
stage appearance:
Joe Keaton
and Buster, 1896.

off that series of three and ended the use of trunk as playpen. It did
not, however, end Buster's grim campaign to get back on the stage
for keeps. By his second birthday his parents were worn to a frazzle.

"We'd be doing a melodrama," Myra recalled. "Joe would be
rescuing me—the innocent maiden—from the villain's clutches and
here would come Buster onstage. Toddle over to me piping 'Mama,'
then to Joe piping 'Papa,' and that was it. Show was over."

Myra considered the possible choices. One course: leave Buster
with the landlady of the moment, while she herself, onstage and
worried, would be blowing lines. Extreme course: bring him along,
let him toddle all over the stage and break up the show. Middle
course: tie him up in the wings and his screams would stop the
show anyway. Hobson gave a better choice than Myra had. She
strongly suspected that her son held the winning cards. But she
tried. Sticking with Course One, they muddled through until the

midsummer of 1898. Then it was that, all on one hot July day in Kansas, Buster—still three months short of three years of age—settled the whole matter. Cramming a crucial and frightening trio of accidents into a single afternoon, he won his victory and, in essence, set his future.

He himself comments: "A clothes wringer, a peach tree, and a cyclone put me on the stage. And for keeps. One way or another I've been there ever since."

Consciously taking her chances, Myra had left Buster sitting on the boardinghouse back porch watching the landlady run clothes through a wringer. Quick, active, and restless, he was at that age of inquisitiveness that psychologists call the age of discovery. In a split second he was up and over and had a finger caught between the roller cogwheels. His screams of pain almost paralyzed the landlady as she struggled to free the finger. But the cogs were jammed with flesh; the crank was immovable. Off she ran, hand to forehead, to get the parents.

Buster stood there waiting. His howling stopped. He was staring at the cogwheels, the torn finger, and the blood with a look of wonder. He had just discovered The Implacable Machine.

Myra and Joe came running with a doctor recruited from their audience. Joe took the wringer apart. The doctor said, "Part of this finger has got to come off." He took a scalpel and removed the already nearly severed finger at the second joint. Buster howled. Again he stopped suddenly and stared at the doctor. He was really looking past the doctor. He had just discovered The Accident.

Sitting on Myra's lap, he gradually quieted down. She gave him a bottle of warm milk. When Joe and Myra left to return to the theatre, he was in bed upstairs, sound asleep.

An hour later his throbbing finger woke him up. He tried holding his arm up. The pain was worse. He climbed out of bed. It hurt less. He slipped downstairs barefoot and out into the front yard.

It was midafternoon and around a hundred in the shade. An immense, still motionlessness lay like a blanket over the dry prairie. Along the southern horizon, like the level edge of a knife, a black cloud was beginning to rise.

A swarm of large iridescent green bugs was circling around a tree, their thin, dry buzzing loud in the stillness. Buster caught one between the forefinger and the thumb of his uninjured hand. It buzzed angrily, struggled, and escaped. Then he saw the ripe peaches that had drawn the bugs. He stretched on tiptoe for the lowest one. It was just beyond reach. He considered the matter carefully, found a rock, threw it at the peach, and stood ready, looking up and hand outstretched, to catch the dislodged peach as it fell. But the rock, sailing past the peach, disappeared among the leaves.

Almost instantly it was back, slashing sharp-edged down his temple a half inch from his right eye. His screams brought the landlady around the house on the full run. One quick, horrified glance at Buster and she set out on the two long blocks to the theatre, again to interrupt the matinee.

Soon she was back with the Keatons and the doctor. Buster was carried upstairs and laid on the bed. The doctor cleaned the long open gash and carefully stitched it together. As before, the boy lay quietly without flinching, staring at the doctor.

Joe was fidgeting, his mind on an interrupted melodrama and a restless audience.

Myra spoke up. "We'll have to take him with us," she said firmly. The landlady looked grateful.

The doctor looked astonished. "You can't move this boy," he said.

"Then we can't finish the show, that's all."

The doctor would have none of that. He wanted to see the rest of the concluding playlet.

"I'll keep an eye on him after I give him this warm milk," said the landlady reluctantly.

"Let me fix that milk," the doctor said. He dropped in some laudanum. "Now he'll sleep."

Ten minutes later they tiptoed out. As they started down the street, Myra handed the bedroom key to Joe. In the backyard the landlady, glancing with a worried eye first at Buster's bedroom window and then at the rapidly rising cloud bank, began hurriedly removing the wet laundry from the line.

At the theatre the playlet got under way again. *Old Pompey* was one of the more ambitious melodramas by Myra's father. Joe Keaton, outrageously burnt-corked as the old freed slave, having wandered back home out ob de cold No'th, was now painfully plodding across the dead lawn of the ruined plantation. Under a painted cutout tree (a magnolia, what else?) sat Myra in ruffled pinafore as Little Flora, impoverished only daughter of the Old Massa (alias the Old Colonel), now these many years under the Southern sod.

Joe was magnificent. His failing strength barely got the lanky six feet plus of him tottering over to four-foot-eleven Myra. There, cradled in Myra's arms, he began dying, long and agonizingly. Their tearful talk of the good old days was punctuated by his gasps, groans, and wheezes and was brought to a startling conclusion by a masterly death rattle. Amid feminine tears, masculine cheers, and the applause of all, the curtain came down.

Myra dashed off and within seconds was back for the finale in her John Philip Sousa suit of red and gold, her cornet in hand. The medicine show "doctor" seated himself at the reed organ, and Myra launched into the aria "Oh! Love for Me Thy Power" from *La Sonnambula*, which she embellished coloraturawise with trills, grace notes, and triple tonguing. She was climbing with these musical detours toward the brassy climax when the auditorium door burst open and a voice yelled in, "Cyclone! Cyclone! Hit for cover!"

The theatre emptied in seconds, the well-trained locals homing straight for their own backyard storm cellars, the troupers hightailing it down the street. Just as Joe and Myra scrambled up the front-porch steps, there was a splintering crash as the tornado lowered its funnel, ripped off half the roof, and veered away. They pounded up the stairs. The door would not open.

"Joe! The key! The key!" Myra shouted.

Joe found it, turned it in the lock. Still the door would not open. "Something's holding it!" Joe shouted.

That something was air suction. As the storm moved on, it released its hold. The door opened. They raced in.

The room was empty. "Quick!" said Joe. "He's in the storm cellar with the landlady." They ran downstairs and out the back door. Leaning into the wind, Joe half-carrying Myra, they made it to the cellar. Joe yanked the slanting wooden hatch open, and while it tore loose from its hinges and sailed away, they fell headlong down the steep steps.

There was the landlady, alone, shivering with fright.

"Where's Buster?" Joe yelled. She looked at him blankly.

At that moment, Buster was sitting in his nightgown in the dusty middle of unpaved Main Street some four blocks away. Only a few minutes before, he had been awakened by the noise: the low, ominous hum of the approaching cyclone, the rending crash of frame houses tearing apart, the eerie carillon of shattering window glass, the shouts of townspeople sprinting for their cellars.

Buster had run to his window and, just as his parents were scrambling in the front door, the vast vacuum at the tornado's eye had sucked him bodily right out the second-story window. Before Joe and Myra were halfway up the stairs, their son was sailing high over trees and houses, too amazed to be afraid, and then coasting down a slow-relaxing ramp of air to land gently in the very center of an empty street.

A cyclone leaves as suddenly as it pounces. This one was barely on its way elsewhere before the bolder locals were carefully poking noses out of sanctuaries. Meanwhile the Keatons searched the little room over and over, then the rest of the house, then back again to the room. Then they gave up. Joe was staring around aimlessly, at the floor, at the ceiling, at the ground, at the sky. Myra sat on the bed, head in hands.

The tinselly stage melodrama had been shouldered aside by real drama. Now it was despair, or close to it, with tragedy apparently just around the corner. Then, as Myra and Joe always told the story later, came the Keatonian twist.

There were loud footsteps on the stairs. A stranger burst into the room. Buster was in his arms, solemn-faced as always, but with eyes unusually bright.

"You the actor people?" the stranger asked. "Ain't this yourn?"

Joe spoke with exaggerated slowness. "Thanks," he said. "Want a receipt?"

Next day news filtered in of the full extent of the cyclone's work. Among other things, on its way far down in the southeastern corner of the state it had erased Piqua. The Keatons never returned to the little place where Buster had been born. For them it no longer existed. Nearly a half century later, a friend who had driven from New York to California mentioned that he had passed through Piqua. Buster's face lighted up. "Then," he said, "I'm not the man without a birthplace after all."

He went on to say how his true stories of those fantastic happenings had too often met with polite, ill-concealed disbelief. "I show them this missing finger and this scar here on my face, and it doesn't convince them. I never dared mention Piqua, figuring it wasn't there any more. It was the cyclone story that was too much," he continued. "But recently," he said, "*Time* magazine came out with this." He produced a clipping. The article described a cyclone at Udall, Kansas. Buster pointed a triumphant finger to the key sentence: "Barber Henry Norris went to bed, woke up unhurt in the street: 'I don't know how I got there.'"

Though the cyclone left Buster unscarred, it—and the preceding accidents—won his battle for him. As soon as his wounds healed he was onstage, permanently and legally.

Joe sent him
into a corner:
Buster in 1898.

Long-suffering Joe had exploded. "Now how the hell can—"

"Look! It's him on or me off," Myra said. "Colts are let into the
pasture."

Myra was gambling on making a deal, not only with Joe but with
Buster too. In one morning she got a costume ready, an exact miniature of Joe's: a funny little Irishman's outfit of baggy trousers, fancy
vest, and a fiery red wig with Galway sideburns concocted out of silk
embroidery floss. Little slapshoes completed the rig.

This was the deal: Buster could be onstage during monologs and, if that worked out, then occasionally during comedy; in return for this he would stay quietly ("*quietly*, I said"), all the rest of show time, out of sight but where his parents could see him, in the wings.

Buster gravely nodded his consent. Joe was unconvinced. Would the kid keep to his bargain? What could he do onstage?

Buster kept his word. The first time that Joe led him onstage he quietly stood to be introduced, bowed, and walked as directed to a corner. There he stood, solemn-faced, legs crossed, leaning against the set. Joe was not prepared for what followed. Buster kept his great dark staring saucer eyes fixed on his father, his body and arms following every movement, his lips silently mouthing all the well-known lines. Hypnotically he worked to be an actor like Joe. It was sad—and it was funny, grotesquely funny, and the audience simply went to pieces.

A born showman, Joe caught on instantly. He began directing his lines at Buster. As the audience saw them, it was Joe in front in close-up, gesturing and delivering his corny lines, and it was Joe back there too, as if seen through reversed opera glasses, too far away to be heard.

To the child the laughter and applause were a music he now could share at last. He had painfully discovered The Machine and The Accident and, astride a cyclone, The Miracle. That miracle of flight out a window, through the air, and down to the street had now led to a miracle personally more important to him. He was now part of the act; the Two Keatons were now the Three Keatons.

The fateful trio of events occurred nearly seventy years ago, and yet whenever Keaton speaks of them he verbally capitalizes them as if they had just occurred. This clues their importance in his art and his life. Even then, in his first sanctioned stage appearance in 1898 and afterward, he was not working for the rewards of good behavior. This was not what the bargain, from his point of view, meant at all. Accepting the good accident and the miracle, he was doing what he had to do—start his career. This was at the age of two years and nine months, rather young as these things go. Here and at this time came the genesis of Buster Keaton's remarkable personal myth, the tripartite sense of fate that would henceforth dominate and eventually haunt his life, a nagging sense of the accidental in all actions and events, as often tying his hands as freeing them.

Keaton's lifelong concept of The Machine is as if made for this present Computer–Pop Art Age. It is mechanism, personage, and force; it is friend and foe. As gadget in his personal life, it has ranged from costly automobiles to fantasy creations such as collapsing out-houses built in his youth and a giant automatic nutcracker he built at MGM. In his film comedies, The Machine is central, from the craft that sank at launching in *The Boat* and the mechanical ménage of *The Electric House* to the stolen Civil War locomotive of *The General*.

For Keaton, The Machine can also be The Establishment, with all its potential menace to the nonorganization man—the relentless pursuing police of films like the famous *Cops* or hostile wealth and management as in *Steamboat Bill Jr*. In real life, the management angle began with an acquiescent father bringing Buster onstage. Later it would become management—friendly, then hostile—first in vaudeville and later in the movies.

So there it is: The Machine is friend or enemy, depending—no matter what you do—on your luck. With Keaton this means the unexpected, The Accident. If it is friendly, fine. But if things go bad, and from bad to worse, then it takes The Miracle to save him. In his creative and his actual life The Miracles began propitiously enough: a wind that put him on the stage.

TWO

AMERICAN show business, the entertainment world that Buster Keaton entered as a child in 1898, though in a transitional phase, was still far from today's scene. One striking difference was that virtually all entertainment, from low comedy to grand opera, was still firsthand performance—live actors, attending audiences. However, though radio was still a quarter century away and television a half century, new inventions were beginning to lead to the prepackaging of entertainment so prevalent today.

First in turn-of-the-century popularity was the mechanical, or player, piano. Foot-propelled or motor-driven, this device was everywhere, its slotted paper rolls spreading music, from good-time sounds like ragtime and the coon songs to tearjerker ballads like "A Bird in a Gilded Cage." Edison's cylinder phonograph records and Berliner's discs were beginning to bring Sousa's band, banjo jigs, and minstrel skits to the home living room. This early, however, the primitive phonograph's low-fi and curtailed performance time did not seem a serious threat to live performance. The hi-fi stereophonic long-play disc was far in the future.

The motion picture poised a more palpable threat. It was only five years since Edison had filmed *The Sneeze* in the Black Maria at Menlo Park and two years since he had filmed the then-sensational bit *The Kiss*, involving mustachioed John Rice and singer May Irwin, artistic grandmother of all the later blues-belters from Sophie Tucker to Ethel Merman. Although the period ballad "Every Little Movement Has a Meaning All Its Own" might indicate otherwise, *The Kiss* was only a short episode. The plotted dramatic narrative film, however, was soon to come with Georges Méliès' French proto-science-fiction feature film *A Trip to the Moon*. This would be in 1902, with the concurrent advent of the separate film theatre, in the guise of the Electric in Los Angeles, first of the nickelodeons—wooden benches or camp chairs placed in vacant stores. With these—however humbly and gradually—the long reign of the movies would begin.

Still, for a long time to come, live audiences who paid admittance would directly determine the success or failure of new theatrical enterprises, from medicine show and burlesque to vaudeville turn and from musical comedy to grand opera. Even with the movies, the scene remained a buyer's market, not a seller's; the audiences volitional, not captured.

Many entertainments then holding on to mass acceptance have since more or less completely disappeared. Brass bands held forth everywhere in concerts, both local-talent and high-paid stellar, that presented cakewalks, marches, and overtures featuring the virtuoso cornetists. Then—especially, but not exclusively, in the hinterlands— there were the hundreds upon hundreds of traveling tent shows. These included frontier survivors or mementos like the "Forty-niner Camps," with cancan girls in short sequined skirts, and road stock companies that hammed melodrama from *Uncle Tom's Cabin* on. Mostly under canvas too were the medicine shows hawking "native Indian nostrums"; Wild West shows both small and large, such as silver-maned Buffalo Bill's famous company; and, of course, the sawdust rings of the traditional circuses of all sizes.

Under canvas too were the traveling carnivals with sideshows largely devoted to freaks and monstrosities, as well as the lesser-known blackface minstrels, that racial libel of burnt cork and outrageous stereotype that had begun in New York City in the 1840's. By the end of the nineteenth century, blackface minstrelsy had added both all-Negro companies and racially integrated ones to the traditional all-white productions. Far above the scuffling little tent-show minstrels, the upper-crust companies had grown to a fat, decadent opulence. Though the tight-fitted, loud-patterned trousers, vests, and tailcoats persisted, along with the plantation banjos, eccentric dancing, and the close-harmony barbershop quartets, grand opera had crept in, its arias purveyed by genuine sopranos or countertenors.

The urban scene enjoyed a wide variety of indoor entertainment, from vaudeville to stage drama, from musical comedy to grand opera, and, at the most popular or mass level, the Dime Museum. City cousins of the carny sideshows, the Museums stemmed from P. T. Barnum's famous pioneering Manhattan institution that, with pseudo-learning and culture, displayed anything from Tom Thumb to Jenny Lind. At the dawn of the twentieth century the Museums—notably Huber's on the Fourteenth Street theatrical Rialto in New York— still held on.

Today's nightclubs, more nearly preceded by the cabarets of the

First World War period, had still earlier turn-of-the-century proto-
types, ranging from the quasi-respectable saloon back rooms reached
through the "Family Entrance" and featuring the ragtime piano
professors to the supper theatres with variety—that is, vaudeville,
entertainment—and on to the roof gardens with their popping corks,
chafing dishes of lobster Newburg, dance orchestras, and stage shows.

A distinctive *fin-de-siècle* feature was the Gardens, from vine-trel-
lised outdoor beer gardens with oompah bands in lederhosen to somewhat more elegant period fixtures, well exemplified by Manhattan's
famous Niblo's Garden. Niblo's opened at Broadway and Prince in
1828 as an ornamental public garden for "promenade and refresh-
ment." By 1839 entertainment was added in the form of a "public
saloon," this being a theatre–opera house seating three thousand
that promptly premiered Donizetti's opera *Lucia di Lammermoor*.
Twice destroyed by fire and immediately rebuilt (1846 and 1872),
Niblo's was finally torn down in 1895. Entertainment gardens, however, lingered well into this century. Throughout the country, often
suburban, in groves or beside stream or lake, they offered both intra-
mural and alfresco entertainment and were summer hosts to vaudeville.

American entertainment from 1890 to 1910, was a bustling, broad,
varied panorama. Multiplex and voluminous, not centralized and
curtailed, it offered something for every level of taste and enlighten-
ment, giving the public a chance to progress in taste—from back-room
ballad to opera, from burlesque to Shakespeare. It was honestly
bought and paid for, not a prepaid, dubious gift from commerce. Its
only commercials were the local ads on the fireproof asbestos stage
curtains, and even these were raised out of sight during the show.
Paying its own way, the public could and did choose. Its ratings, un-
tainted by pollsterism, were decisive, it being far more effective—let
alone rewarding—to applaud or hiss live performers than to write a
futile letter to some corporate giant or kick in the screen of your own
television set.

Also, it was a vast training school for talent, with the same opportunities for artists as for public to begin at the bottom and rise
to the top. The thousands of theatres, large and small, cheap and
fancy, required an army of talent. Today's sudden personal hit by
an unknown and equally sudden rating-generated eclipse were both
virtually nonexistent then. Performers learned their craft, with pro-
gressive outlets to display it. Although there was a caste system, it
was not rigid. Many vaudevillians—George M. Cohan and Ed Wynn,

for example—moved into musical comedy, while musical comedy stars, such as Alice Nielsen, moved into grand opera.

Talent, technique, artistry, and showmanship together formed the touchstone, it being recognized that a piano rag required these just as much as a sonata did. The talent of those two decades fed the movies, then radio, and the beginnings of television even while these media were progressively disfranchising the audience and phasing out the training program. Finally, by mid-century, with age taking its toll, the reservoir was all but dried up, and then, as talent standards were inevitably lowered, came the hucksters' and the teenagers' day.

By 1895, when Niblo's Garden was demolished, when vaudeville was the reigning popular entertainment, and when Buster Keaton was born, the elder Keatons had already been with the medicine shows for two years. It was the bottom rung of the ladder that led to vaudeville. In the Midwest, being with the medicine shows meant a long, weary round of tramping through what only yesterday had been frontier: Kansas, the Oklahoma and Indian Territories, and the Missouri Ozarks. By 1896 the Joe Keatons and the Harry Houdinis were scuffling together with an obscure outfit called Dr. Hill's California Concert Company. Harry and Joe helped raise and strike the tent; during Dr. Hill's health lecture, they walked the aisles selling Kickapoo Magic Snake Oil and the rest of the patent medicines. They all acted in the melodramas and comedies, Houdini as heavy and Joe as comic, with tiny Myra Keaton and equally tiny Bessie

Medicine show, 1894. Left to right: The "Doctor," Myra, Joe, Bessie Houdini, and Harry Houdini; foreground: two Caughnawaga Indians.

Houdini alternating in the soubrette and leading-lady roles. Myra doubled in brass and again in reeds, pumping out marches and over-tures on the harmonium or reed organ and filling a solo spot with her side-valve cornet.

It was a gypsying, hand-to-mouth life. Some weeks they got their seven dollars per family, some weeks the till was empty; sometimes they rode in dusty day coaches sitting up all night, sometimes, as Myra recalled, "only the tents rode—we walked." But it was not an aimless life. Though Myra at nineteen and Joe at twenty-nine were already medicine show veterans, their eyes had a distant focus, set on vaudeville and the glittering New York Rialto that seemed only a stone's throw away.

It would take them a half dozen more medicine shows and three more years—until 1899—to make it. But ambition plus youth gave them energy to burn. After the grueling July and August days in the dusty parades and the stifling tent, they would sit up late playing pinochle with the Houdinis. Poor as they were, it was for "real" stakes—piles of sulfur matches or the then-worthless Confederate paper money called shinplasters. From Myra's descriptions and from the extant photographs of the participants, one can visualize them in a lantern-lit tent sitting around the card table: Houdini like a lion, long-maned and deep-chested; Joe Keaton like a prairie wolf, hungry, lean, and acrobat-quick; Bessie and Myra like sparrows, chirp-ing as the cards fell. Four kids, really; yet within a few years, they would have earned their way to the big time: Harry to become the greatest escape artist of all time; Joe and Myra to become vaudeville's maddest, most famous roughhouse act, the Two Keatons. And gen-erally refusing sleep whenever there was action, propped on a pillow in a trunk watching the game, Buster, six months old, was already studying the larceny to get him onstage with the Two Keatons. One can visualize Buster too from Myra's description of "those popping brown eyes buttoning on a sobersides face."

Soon the Keatons and the Houdinis parted to go with different shows. The financial depression that had begun in 1893 was deepen-ing. In 1896 the Democrats, through William Jennings Bryan, coined a famous slogan, "You shall not crucify mankind upon a cross of gold"; but the Republicans defeated Bryan and Free Silver, electing McKinley. Meanwhile the shaky little road shows were having a bad time. Show after show folded, and the creditors, like baying hounds, leaped on the tents and equipment. But there were lots of shows around, and the Keatons were never long at liberty.

It seemed hardly a favorable time for ambition. Yet this depression proved, as that of the 1930's would later confirm, that the best business in hard times is show business. In the very midst of hunger marches and riots, urban entertainment flourished, with vaudeville proliferating and the infant cinema taking its first steps.

In 1899 the Keatons made the big jump, in Myra's phrase, "from Kansas to the Rialto." A few long, gaslit crosstown blocks of Manhattan's Fourteenth Street, centering on Union Square and Fourth Avenue, the Rialto was the pre-Broadway heart of New York's entertainment district. Here reigned vaudeville, the new thing—still often called variety—sprung from the olio of the old blackface minstrels and just entering its most brilliant decade. Facing Union Square were the Keith and Proctor vaudeville houses, and an easy stroll away along the Rialto was Tony Pastor's Theatre. Across from Tony's was Huber's Museum, survivor of the Dime Museum era, while another neighbor, perhaps not altogether inappropriately, was Tammany Hall.

Tony Pastor had started the vaudeville saga long before. In 1875 —two years before Myra Keaton was born—he conceived the idea of traveling variety companies and then successfully booked them into theatres throughout the country. Tony broke the blackface minstrel mold to include a far wider spectrum of entertainment. His epochal innovation was made while he was still in his earlier "Opera House" at 585 Broadway, but Tony—born Antonio Pastore—even then was already a veteran. His first theatre had been a beer house at 444 Broadway, opened in the year that Fort Sumter was fired on.

When Tony took over, popular theatres were the notorious scenes of drunken brawls and murder, of gambling and open assignation. They were rough and disreputable, fully deserving the enmity of the churchgoers, who fought their very existence, while actresses in more than one clear case had fairly earned the evil repute that would cling to all actresses even into the early years of this century.

Pastor wanted no part of this. He was a modern. His were the first "clean" popular theatres in this country, with no "back rooms" and no gay upstairs with private "dining" rooms. The short, rotund, dapper Italian was actually neither idealist nor reformer. A singer first, he wanted a secure world to sing in, so he bought his own theatre to star in. He also liked money. So, as entrepreneur, he set out to prove that an orderly showhouse with good entertainment would be a more profitable enterprise than the dives of that day, the customary kind of theatre-*cum*-saloon-*cum*-casino-*cum*-bagnio. He proved it to the point of changing theatrical history.

Two decades later, amid depression, vaudeville theatres were spring-
ing up everywhere; the first million-dollar house was about to be
built; vaudeville circuits were forming, to span the continent; performers—many of them brilliant—were flocking as if from nowhere
to its stages: Marie Dressler, Eva Tanguay, Elsie Janis, Lily Langtry,
Lillian Russell, even Nazimova and Sarah Bernhardt; George M.
Cohan, Bert Williams, Leon Errol, W. C. Fields, Ed Wynn, David
Warfield, Joseph Jefferson, and many more. And, of course, Buster
Keaton.

In 1899, however, the Keatons showed no signs of coming fame
as they crept in humbly through the back door. Frankly envious of
the Houdinis, who had already made it, fired with their own hopes,
and armed with grim purpose, Joe and Myra had impetuously quit
the medicine-show scuffle to come to New York without a single
booking. They all but starved until Huber's Museum finally gave
them a chance.

Huber's, adding vaudeville to try to keep up with the times, was
a lowly spot not even to be compared in show-business prestige with
the colossal freak show that had made Phineas T. Barnum rich and
famous. Upstairs in Huber's so-called Curio Hall, together with the
perennial flea circus, was a constantly changing series of oddities such
as an alleged mermaid, a spider woman hanging to a rope web, two-
headed babies and six-legged calves, and one of nature's more widely
publicized misfortunes, the Siamese twins billed as "Libbera, the
Living Double Man."

Black art was practiced there, a medieval illusion that survives today by its occasional use on television. It is nothing more than black
on black. The entire background—walls, floor, ceiling—is a uniform
mat black that will not reflect light. Nor, given a discreet distance
on the part of the viewers, can anything equally black be seen against
it. A black cat, however lively, would disappear in this setting; a
lump of coal heaved across in midair would go unspotted by the
audience. That, of course, is the idea. The environment swallows up
an actor wearing black clothes and dull-black makeup all over, hands,
face, and all. No one knows he's there, no one sees him turn around,
and only the white skeleton painted on his back ever becomes visible.
The white dishes floating through the air are actually carried on the
unseen hands of an unseen actor. Black art was frequently used in
the early films. At Huber's the hoary hocus-pocus so deeply impressed
the four-year-old Buster Keaton that many years later he wove black-
art episodes into some of his two-reel comedies.

Joe and Myra worked downstairs on Huber's variety stage. They called their break-in vaudeville act The Man with the Table, the prop in question being an oak kitchen table massive enough to hold up under Joe's strenuous acrobatic comedy. Then thirty-two, Buster's father was lean, hard, muscular, and so long-legged that Myra called him "a pair of shears." Tirelessness, the kinetic extremes of movement, and a certain sort of frontier violence characterized Joe's attack on the table. He would dive on it headfirst, turn handsprings along its top, and then from apogee plunge head down almost to the floor before, with a catlike turn, he would land on his feet. The table was at the center of the act just as it was at the center of the stage.

Applause only drove him to near-misses more and more scary. At Huber's, Myra recalled, "Joe started doing a trick that if he ever missed, nothing saved his shins. He began jumping from the floor clear up onto the seat of a chair that stood on top of his table right at the edge. It ain't easy to jump over four feet straight up in the air. When he got tired he missed and his shins scraped on the chair rungs and the table edge. That one week at Huber's fixed him proper. To the day he died, near eighty, his legs were discolored from the knees on down.

"Six shows a day," Myra continued, "were almost more than he could stand. Our hours were from three P.M. to three A.M. But the crowd hollered for that jump, hoping he'd miss."

Myra danced and played cornet solos while Joe caught his breath in the wings. For the climax of the act, he came back on, lifted her to the chair on the table; then she held out a cigar box at arm's length for him to shatter with one well-placed kick. Joe Keaton was an all-time master of the old art of legomania, at least in the kicking department. Official measurements proved his ability to kick forward and up to a height of eight feet. Far higher went his "hitch kicks," which consisted in feinting with the left foot, then jumping high in the air before launching the right foot like the *coup de pied* of an apache in a street brawl.

All her life Myra never lost her awe of Joe's kicking, onstage and offstage. "Good Lord," she once said, "he could hitch-kick ten feet straight up and could go even higher. See that?" She pointed to sole marks on the wall near the breakfast-room ceiling. "He was seventy-five years old when he put those there, just to limber up. Joe's hitch happened so fast," she continued, "that lots of people missed it. But you better see it if he meant it for you. He never laid a hand on a man. That hitch kick could break a jaw."

But in those strenuous days in 1899, Joe Keaton was not brawling. He, like Myra, was grimly intent on climbing the vaudeville ladder to the elite two-a-day theatres. As for Buster—in a retrogression to the precyclone Kansas days—he stayed with the landlady. At six o'clock Myra rushed down East Fourteenth to the shabby rooming house, gave him supper, then back to Huber's with coffee and sandwiches. Years later she recalled those swift round trips. "What a spectacle I must have been!" she exclaimed. "A woman on the street in stage costume and powder and lip rouge was just waylaid, that's all. But I was one actress the mashers couldn't catch. I ran too fast."

Huber had flatly refused to let Buster onstage. Huber feared the watchdog group called the Gerry Society, an organization that Buster has since described as "the Society for the Prevention of Cruelty to Children, a branch of the animal one." Founded by Elbridge T. Gerry, this society existed to see that the then-new and hard-won child-labor laws were enforced. In the theatre this meant that no child under seven might even walk onstage; none under sixteen might juggle, do acrobatics or walk a wire, engage in bicycle riding, and on through a long list. Every vaudevillle act had to have a New York City permit for each engagement, and the Gerry Society stood by, eagle-eyed, looking for children.

To Buster this estimable purpose was an unfair tyranny. He moped around. New York did not look like progress to him. He wished they were back in the tent shows. Soon Joe and Myra were close to wishing so too. Huber paid them a week's salary of ten dollars. Then followed six weeks of no work, running into November and cold weather. Even to these troupers, used to getting by on seven dollars a week, survival was a grim problem. There was less than seventy-five cents left when, with Thanksgiving near, they got a week's booking at the Atlantic Garden far down the Bowery. "No money in advance," said the management. By Wednesday, halfway through the week, there was fifty cents.

"We'll get by until Saturday and to hell with 'em," said Joe, laying out the whole half-dollar for supplies. This being 1899, he got a bucket of coal and an armload of kindling, three loaves of bread, a pound of bacon, and a large bag of dried navy beans. To save coal for the small grate in their single room, all three Keatons stayed in bed until late afternoon, then each evening trudged the mile and a half to the Atlantic Garden for its single evening show, and then trudged home again, Buster on Joe's back each way.

The Atlantic was certainly not a step upward from Huber's. A survivor from the earlier, rougher days, it was a beer hall with an adjoining outdoor garden now closed for the season. The walls were trellised inside and strung with faded, dusty paper grapevines. Though the stage was bare, there was, for scenery, a lady orchestra famous up and down the Bowery for its Beef Trust proportions. It was this attraction that brought in the predominantly male audiences.

One week there and once more the Keatons were at liberty. "Liberty for what?" Myra asked bitterly. Well, for one thing (she doubtless meant), liberty to run up a rent bill until your room becomes a jail; liberty to eat less each day; liberty to share your room, and your mind, with extra guests: self-doubt, then discouragement, finally, perhaps, despair.

November passed into December. Temperatures plummeted. Early snow came. Sidewalks glared with ice. Wind whistled around corners, slipped past the edges of loose windows. The bacon was long since gone. Now there were only boiled beans and cold tap water. Sometimes outside their door Myra would find a stove log, a slab of corn bread, or half a loaf of bread, left there by a landlady who knew adversity well.

Myra stayed home with Buster while Joe tramped every day from theatre to beer hall to theatre looking for work. In the early winter darkness the tempo of his returning footsteps in the hall would telegraph the disappointing message to her. At night she darned his socks, mended his thin overcoat, then washed his one good shirt and ironed it dry.

Christmas was near when one morning, after much begging, Buster was allowed to make the rounds with his father. Myra watched them down the hall, then, going to the window, watched them out of sight, Joe with Buster riding piggyback, plodding west on the sidewalk in the uncleared snow.

THREE

~~~~~~~~~~~~~~~~~~~~~~~~~~~~~~

T HE R A P I D footsteps tapped a new message. Myra opened the door. Still halfway down the hall, Joe called to her. "We're on the big time," he said.

Inside the room, he continued the story. It had been nearly noon when they had worked around to Huber's, had been turned down again, and had walked on west along the Rialto. Suddenly, half a block away, there was a well-publicized and well-known little figure in fur coat and silk hat. It was Tony Pastor, alighting from a hansom cab in front of his theatre. Joe snatched Buster up and rushed to intercept him.

Before Joe could get a word out, Tony spoke. Glancing at the thinly clad four-year-old and then looking sternly at Joe, he unburdened himself. "If that's your kid," he said, "you've got no business taking him out in such weather."

"I want to talk to you, sir," said Joe.

"Then step inside where it's warm," Pastor replied.

The rest of the story tumbled out. Joe was a little hazy here and there—it had all apparently happened so fast. He remembered showing their one clipping—"Joe and Myra Keaton are on the Huber's bill this week"—and Pastor's brushing it aside. He remembered coffee, sandwiches, and milk suddenly appearing.

"Oh!" He interrupted his story to take a half sandwich from his pocket and hand it to Myra. Then somehow, he continued, Buster and he were on the stage, with Pastor watching from the first row. "We went through our act," said Joe.

"Like in Kansas?" Myra asked, and Joe nodded.

"And so," said Joe triumphantly, "we open Monday."

"And who is we?"

"You and I."

"Hold it," said Myra, going over to Buster, who was in the corner crying quietly.

"The goddam Gerries," said Joe, referring to the Gerry Society.

24

Buster Keaton
at two years of age, 1897.

Tony Pastor's Theatre.

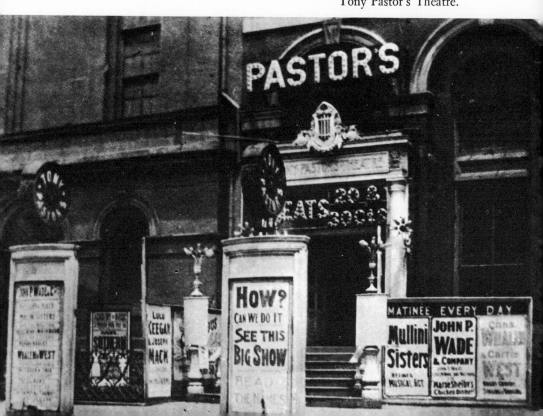

"Even Pastor can't do anything with them." Then he remembered something else in his pocket. "Look at this," he said, and held out a ten-dollar bill. "Come on, we're eating out tonight."

On December 18, 1899, the Two Keatons began a two-a-day week at Tony Pastor's intimate, galleried, jewel-box theatre, a week so long awaited that, now here, it seemed hardly real. They started, unfeatured, near the bottom of the bill. Nevertheless, on an all-star holiday program, they offered something new. The applause accorded Joe Keaton's rather hair-raising acrobatics and what Joe himself called "Myra's artistic soubrettishness" got them moved twice in the one week to higher spots on the bill. Best of all, Pastor saw to it that the Proctor Theatre manager—who had been turning Joe down for weeks—came personally to catch the act.

On Christmas Day, they went on as part of the stellar bill at Proctor's fancy Twenty-third Street Theatre. They were all the way down on the program—next to the Kalatechnoscope, which closed the show with flickery moving pictures of the surf at Coney Island.

There was a Christmas tree at home in the Keatons' room; it was decorated by Myra with popcorn and cranberry strings and an apple and an orange or two. Out of their sudden wealth, Joe gave Buster a basketball, a fairly esoteric gift inasmuch as the game itself, invented only a few years earlier, was still being seen mainly in exhibitions in the amusement parks. Even more startling was his present to Myra —a rather monstrous looking object of shiny brass that he had found in a Bowery pawnshop. He had been told that it was some kind of musical instrument. Within two months, having solved its secrets, Myra would be playing it in the act in place of the old cornet and the reviewers, as ignorant as Joe, would be calling it an oboe, a French horn, or even a clarionet (sic). Actually it was an alto saxophone, and it made Myra Keaton America's first lady saxophonist.

After a week Proctor moved the Keatons, upgrading them to his new Pleasure Palace way uptown on Fifty-eighth Street. This was the theatre that had haunted the Keaton and Houdini dreams in those Kansas days that now seemed so long ago.

But before they moved, the closing Sunday night downtown had been a real occasion. Suddenly, just before midnight, the stage swarmed with actors, stagehands, and staff; the orchestra was playing "Auld Lang Syne"; the audience was cheering; and through the thick walls remotely from outside came the clamor of fire whistles and bells. It was New Year's and something more. Never before, it seemed —even in New York—had there been such excitement. Everyone was kissing everyone else. Everyone was kissing Buster, who had sat in the wings that special night.

Nearly seventy years later, Buster still remembers it. "They were all talking about something. I didn't know what it was, but I knew it was good and thought it was mine—something to go with the basketball. They were calling it the twentieth century."

It bothered no one there that dating the birth of the new century was a current matter of hot debate among the learned. The question was: Did the twentieth century really begin on January 1, 1900? The opposing faction, in fact, would do their celebrating a year later, on New Year's Day, 1901. They seem to have been in the majority, and while those who had committed themselves earlier stuck to their beliefs, the later celebrants lightly dismissed the earlier revelry as merely a case of false labor. In point of fact, the dispute has never been settled.

For Buster Keaton, anyway, the twentieth century began as pretty much of a bust. Though he was now tacitly allowed in the wings during matinees, the action seemed even further away as he stood, immobilized, so close-by. He was not even allowed to bring the basketball to the theatre.

Proctor's gave the Keatons a running jump that carried the act through five dizzy weeks: Proctor's in Albany, the Wonderland in Wilmington, Howard's Athenaeum and then Austin & Stone's one-time rowdy museum—both in Boston—and, finally, Poli's in Hartford. Then they suddenly ran out of gas. The new century was fizzling out all around.

"On ag'in, off ag'in, gone ag'in, Finnegan," said Joe in disgust. Actually they had done extremely well for an unbooked act in mid-season. They were learning the facts of life in their brave new world. Booking had to be done well in advance, during the summer in fact. Vaudeville, after all, was variety. With the movies not yet sufficiently developed to show simultaneously in their own theatres everywhere, the vaudeville acts had to be on the move perpetually for live appearances in different theatres. Unwilling to risk last-minute booking, the theatres insisted on signing up the acts long in advance. Each week every single theatre of the thousands in the land unveiled nine to fifteen acts, from headliner down to bottomliner. Patrons might go once a week to the same theatre for the forty or so weeks of the entertainment season and never see the same act brought back. Variety was exactly that, no less. "Repeaters"—and there were a few —had to be very good and very much in demand.

Although as yet not quite in this swim, the Keatons had come too far to be downhearted. Cheerfully—if not, enthusiastically—they went back to the beer gardens, where now, at least, they could be stars and even get a little more money than the halls paid as a rule. That winter and spring of 1900 they played them all, in Manhattan, Brooklyn, and the Bronx, in Newark, Hoboken, and Elizabeth, and then when summer came they played the piers at Coney Island, Asbury Park, and Atlantic City. They got by.

With summer Joe immediately got busy with advance booking. While playing the summer parks, he wrote letters to theatre managers, enclosing tear sheets of their reviews, trying to make a practical itinerary with train jumps as short as possible. He did well. Soon he had them solidly scheduled through Christmas. Then he quit, deciding to let spring take care of itself.

With the start of the fall season, Joe placed a large expensive advertisement in the *Dramatic Mirror*. The layout included halftone pictures. One of these showed Myra standing on a chair atop a table with Joe readying to kick a shiny silk topper out of her hand—no longer the humble cigar box. Listed in the display were the future Keaton bookings:

Proctor's Twenty-Third Street ....Sept. 17–22
Proctor's Pleasure Palace ....Sept. 24–29
Pastor's (5th Time This Season) ....Oct.   1–6

> To follow: Dockstader's, Wilmington; Empire, Toledo; Columbia, Cincinnati; Olympic and Haymarket, Chicago; Columbia, St. Louis; Opera House, Chicago; Grand Opera, Memphis.
>
> Home—Dec. 24 to Jan. 6, Perry, Okla. Box 194. Open for offers after the above date.

Starting well at Proctor's, "Mr. and Mrs. Joe Keaton, the eccentric 'Tad' and the chic soubrette, made one of the pronounced hits of the bill and kept the audience laughing for fifteen minutes with original legomania and brisk knockabout work." This reviewer noted the next week that they "repeated their Proctor's hit at Pastor's."

In the wings every afternoon at Proctor's was Buster, the action still just out of reach. His fifth birthday came during the week at Pastor's. Understanding the child's bitter discontent, Tony had a backstage birthday party for him, with a towering decorated cake ordered from Luchow's. But Pastor did not quite dare to give him the only present he really wanted.

However, in less than a week, another manager in another theatre and another town would dare to do what Tony Pastor feared to do.

The Three Keatons in New York, 1900.

The stage, like Eden revisited, would open wide; life for Buster would begin at five; the Three Keatons would ride again.

It happened at the Wonderland Theatre in Wilmington, Delaware, a favorite with vaudevillians. Close to Washington, Baltimore, Philadelphia, and New York, it was a good week's schedule filler. In addition, the Wonderland boss, Bill Dockstader, was immensely popular. It was not salary, for, as all knew, Dock paid small because his theatre was small. But there was nothing small about the man. Like Tony Pastor, Dockstader was one of the old school of owner-managers, graduate performers who kept a personal contact with the actors. Soon, with big business buying up theatres everywhere, there would be no room for them.

Myra never forgot that early October week at the Wonderland. It changed the lives of all three Keatons. Her total recall begins with opening day. They were unpacking. In his accustomed way, Dockstader sat on the dressing table smoking his pipe, making talk, getting acquainted with the new act, and putting them at ease. Buster was bouncing the new basketball. It took a crazy bounce, knocking the pipe out of Dock's mouth and clattering to the floor. Buster retrieved it.

Dockstader smiled and said, "Tell you what, Buster—you round up some kids and I'll let you put on an exhibition at the matinee." Everyone laughed but Buster.

"Now you're in for it," said Joe. "The kid's eating his heart out." Then Joe explained how the Gerry Society had blocked the boy's appearance in New York. "He's only five."

"Pretty young," said Dockstader. "Roughhouse?"

"Real knockabout, but let me tell you, that kid's safer in the air than on his feet."

"Joe's right," said Myra.

Dockstader repacked his pipe, lit it, took a few draws, then said suddenly, "I'm going to give him a chance. Wednesday matinee." Answering the questioning looks, he added, "The Gerries? Forget 'em. They don't cut any ice around this town."

Dock wanted no audition; the Keatons needed no rehearsal. At show time they went on cold, and Buster and his father simply had one of their old-time romps onstage. This was the "act" that Tony Pastor had seen that cold morning months before, that went back to the Midwest days and had started when Buster was barely two. When they had first begun, Myra was frightened. She would protest after Joe had tossed the child up on a dresser top or for a long glancing slide down the wall to the bed.

"He rode a cyclone, didn't he?" Joe would say, and Buster would yell for more. It quickly became evident that the child was a born acrobat with the lightning reflexes of a cat. By three he did every comedy fall that Joe could do and was beginning to get schooling in flips and shoulder landings and was avid for more.

Myra had had no part in all this. It was strictly male roughhousing. She called it "Buster's story hour," with rueful indirect reference to the unused storybooks that Buster would not listen to. She watched the random acrobatics grow into a kind of improvised narrative in slapstick form, realizing that her son was a boy who preferred stories to be acted out.

Now, in Wilmington, she watched their "story hour" stop the show. They simply improvised. Joe started it. Picking Buster up, he walked to the footlights and said, "Father *hates* to be rough," gave him a resounding kiss on the forehead, and set him down. Buster began bouncing his basketball upstage.

"*But,*" Joe continued, "there's only *one* way to raise children. Be gentle but firm. *Never* let 'em walk over you—"

The basketball caught Joe behind the ear—as he knew it would— and down he went, rigidly, like a chopped tree. Over him, in pursuit of the ball, walked Buster.

"—like *that,*" said Joe, flat on his face. It was David and Goliath in the nursery. The theatre rocked with laughter. Joe climbed to his feet, did the rubber-leg bit, shook his head, and then seized the valise handle Myra had sewed to the back of the boy's jacket. He swung him up, back, and then straight across stage. The kid flew high in the air and disappeared in full flight through the wings. There was stony silence: they were pushing it, and Joe knew it. He pushed it a little more. Without even glancing toward the wings, he came downstage and went about some stage business.

Then, after exactly the proper number of seconds, out walked an overalled stagehand carrying Buster in his arms. Joe had given him a line, one well remembered from the day of the cyclone. "Is this yours, Mr. Keaton?" the stagehand asked.

Still the deadly silence. It was touch and go with the audience. Would they see fun or see cruelty? Then a great collective sigh of indrawn breath swept the auditorium and the "shock laugh" came. Dockstader later claimed that it raised the Wonderland roof "a whole foot."

Joe milked the laugh, slowly signing the stagehand's receipt for Buster, then stepped to the footlights and loudly cleared his throat. "I shall now," he announced, "sing that pathetic little ballad entitled 'What Right Has a Man to Buy a Collar Button When He Has a Wart on the Back of His Neck?' "

The song, like Keaton's singing voice, was only a gag. Nevertheless, the pit orchestra went into a standard vamp while Buster got busy again behind Joe's back. He was swatting imaginary flies with a standard slapstick prop, a short-handled "alley" broom. The boy's pantomime made the flies very real. Racing, stopping, turning, back-tracking, swinging wildly, then stooping to pick one up between thumb and forefinger or else stamping on it, his grotesque "chase" kept the audience howling. The laughs kept drowning out Joe's cracked baritone. Struggling with the opening measures, he would stop, bow to the applause, then patiently start in again, beginning each time with the orchestra's four-bar vamp.

A wild swing of the broom sent Joe's chair clattering from the top of the table with Buster sprawling headfirst over it. The house roared and Joe, still not turning around, bowed and started over again. Now Buster's eyes were following a fly as it zigzagged in the air, coursing erratically downstage toward Joe. Buster began tracking, his gaze riveted on the back of Joe's neck; the broom followed—*wham!*—and Joe was down again, draped over the footlights halfway into the orchestra pit. The leader pushed him back, and he sat up rubbing his neck.

"That was no fly, that was my wart," he observed reflectively. Then he did the double take, jumped up, and sent Buster flying again, clear upstage into the painted forest-scene backdrop. The great canvas bellied back like a sail in the wind, and the boy slid safely down the canvas to the floor.

The audience was at the edge of hysteria when Myra came out in her long yellow-silk sequined Floradora gown to share the final bow. Even then they milked one more laugh. Joe kicked off her wide-brimmed ribboned hat while, from the other side, Buster yanked the hidden "strip cord" (borrowed from burlesque) and down came poor Myra's dress and dignity. There she stood, deglamorized soubrette in ragged, patched pants, fancy vest, and baldpate red Irish wig, exactly like her husband and son.

Thus was born a famous headline act: mischievous son, aggravated father, and mother, the innocent bystander—the Three Keatons. Things promised to be a lot easier and safer for Myra from now on. Joe had a roughhouse partner who could keep up with him, and Myra could concentrate on the soubrette role, with dancing and tootling the alto sax. Joe and Buster would ring a thousand changes in the act for seventeen years, but from beginning to end it would remain in essence what it had always been—the same old romp that that had begun in a Kansas boardinghouse between a father and his two-year-old son.

Dockstader was waiting as they came off, Joe dragging Buster astraddle the broom. The manager looked at the boy. "Better run and take a nap," he said. "Gotta be rested for the show tonight."

The next three days Wilmington was buzzing about "the Kid." Saturday afternoon even Dock was amazed at the block-long line of schoolchildren queued up outside. He handed a five-dollar bill to a stagehand. "Go out and buy a barrel of hard candy," he said.

After the show, Buster held a children's reception on the stage, handing out candy instead of signing autographs. This initiated what for some years to come would be a popular Keaton feature. That night, as was his custom, Dockstader personally paid the acts back stage. Bowing low to Buster, he handed him a crisp ten-dollar bill. Joe made a playful grab at the money, and Dockstader shook a warning finger.

Joe laughed. "Myra'll lay it away for him," he said. "The kid'll have his own horse and buggy."

Bill Dockstader was the real founder of the Buster Keaton Fan Clubs. Only a year later this doggerel quatrain appeared in the *Dramatic Mirror:*

> Buster you're a dandy; Buster you're a brick;
> Buster you can make all juveniles look sick;
> Some day you'll be a great one, captain of the crew,
> But don't forget old Wilmington, the place of your debut.
>
> —WILLIAM L. DOCKSTADER

FOUR

~~~~~~

T H E Y were on the road and rolling, out of Gerry Society country and into the free-and-easy Midwestern and Border State cities—Chicago, St. Louis, Memphis—stopping the show everywhere, while the grapevine reports raced to the East: "Watch the Kid." Then to Perry in the Oklahoma Territory for Christmas with the elder Keatons on Joe's old homestead. It was quite a homecoming for a change. Now they came as stars.

And what a "homestaying" it became, as Myra said, waiting for offers that never came. Joe's premature cockiness in failing to complete their bookings throughout spring was bringing its inevitable result. The vaudeville ship sailed on, fully booked, leaving them becalmed in the backwaters. By February they were privately desperate, publicly humiliated. Joe began advertising weekly in the two theatrical predecessors of *Variety*, the *Dramatic Mirror* and the *New York Clipper*. Even the headline bait "assisted by LITTLE BUSTER" brought no bites. More weeks went by. Then suddenly a telegram came. Vaudeville mogul Frederick Freeman Proctor was putting the Keatons back to work—properly speaking, drafting them into service as he declared a personal vaudeville civil war.

Vaudeville was exploding into America's top-draw entertainment; vast profits were looming; certain theatre owners were making like a monopoly; the sides were being drawn for a real bareknuckles brawl. On the side of the status quo were a few pioneer independents, mainly Proctor, Tony Pastor, Percy Williams, and Bill Dockstader; on the side of the grab was, chiefly, B. F. Keith, abetted by newcomer E. F. Albee and a considerable number of opportunistic individual theatre owners not averse to the quick buck. Square in the middle in no-man's-land were the actors.

The monopoly builders' strategy was simple: control the theatres and you control booking; control booking and you control the actors; then you enter the monopolistic heaven of low wages and high prices. No theatrical guilds or unions yet existed to fight such a move.

Should it succeed, not only would all actors who refused to go along be frozen out but all resistant theatre owners as well.

To their credit, some of the owners, having once been performers, objected on principle. Anyway, riding this upcurve, they, like everyone else, were doing all right. Pastor, with one theatre, was wealthy; Proctor, who had started in the 1870's as Fred Levantine the Equilibrist, now owned six theatres. In any event, the issue was forced upon them; they were not to be allowed neutrality. Keith had quietly organized; he had set up two puppet organizations—the Vaudeville Managers' Association and its subsidiary, the United Booking Office, immediately dubbed UBO (long since defunct, with no connection with the legitimate present-day United Booking Office).

Organized piracy hid behind these organizations' elaborate pretense of helping the performer. Through them, Keith and his henchmen planned to control everything from bookings to routes and from program billing to salary. UBO's ultimatum went out: book or blacklist. It was play ball or blackball. This struck home: where you would perform, good routes without long, expensive jumps and lost time, favorable placing on the programs, the pay you got—these were professional life-and-death matters.

This witches' brew was coming to a boil while the Keatons holidayed in Perry. Meanwhile the actors began to catch on to what was happening. They began to feel covert pressure, hear whispered hints; they discovered UBO corrupting their own agents into fee splitting, found that bookings no longer came without kickbacks. Behind it all was Keith, but by the time this became clear it was already late. It was going to be hard to stop him.

Proctor decided to fight it out. He burst out with large advertisements. He listed his theatres: the Twenty-third Street, the Pleasure Palace, the Fifth Avenue (at Twenty-eighth and Broadway), and the 125th Street in Harlem, as well as his Albany playhouse and one about to be opened in Montreal. Then his appeal:

> WANTED: First Class Acts that are
> willing to play Three (3) times daily.

The actors knew Proctor was on their side. They knew that by their help in temporarily playing three-a-day instead of two-a-day he hoped to rally audience support and stand out against the Keith pressure. It was a brave but foredoomed move. Many performers rallied to him, but with the first real heat most of his theatre-owner allies defected. This left little more than his own six theatres, confined to the East and good for only as many weeks and then the acts—with all other theatres closed to them—were inevitably laid off. Keith held the aces. The fight was soon over.

It was then that the victor proved his real cageyness. He declined to punish either Proctor or the recalcitrant acts. Cruel retaliations might come in the future, but for the time being Proctor remained in business and the actors were welcomed back. But there was this change: henceforth they must book through UBO.

The Keatons were in on the battle from the first gun. Joe had immediately advertised in the *Mirror*:

> Searched and the goods found in our possession
> Sentenced to 34 days on the PROCTOR CIRCUIT
> KEEP YOUR EYE ON THE KID

Opening in Albany, they found the problem of the Kid already solved. Though every manager now wanted the famous boy, the Gerry Society would not budge. Then Proctor's general manager, J. Austin Fynes, put his legalistic mind to work and came up with a workable answer to the Gerries. First, he had Joe and Myra swear that Buster was seven years old, this being the minimum legal age for a juvenile's stage appearance—and only as an actor. Then Fynes went to the license board and pointed out that Buster's actual stage work was not acrobatics at all, at least not according to the wording of the law. In the law's own terms, Buster did not juggle, neither walked a wire nor rode a bicycle, and so forth.

"The law," said Buster himself recently, "didn't say a word about taking me by the nape of the neck and throwing me through a piece of scenery."

To the Gerry Society's discomfiture, the ploy actually worked. The Three Keatons made a ten-strike in Albany, as the *Mirror* reported. Joe promptly advertised in the favorable sheet, headlining his son:

B U S T E R
The smallest real comedian. Moved to better spots
three times in the week at Proctor's Albany house.

Next Montreal—another hit—and then New York City. The Gerries lay low, and by now the ads were reading: "BUSTER, assisted by Joe & Myra Keaton." Then at the Pleasure Palace, Buster finally burst into real fame: "a diminutive comedian who is irresistibly funny . . . keeps the audience roaring from the moment he is dragged on stage until his exit hanging to his father's leg."

The Three Keatons in San Francisco, 1901. Center: "America's first lady saxophonist."

Professional photographs were hastily taken, and the family was spread all over the magazines and daily papers. There was lanky Joe bowing; there was flouncy Myra, every small inch the Gibson Girl; and there was tiny Buster, already with that sad, puzzled look that has been his lifelong comic mask.

No wonder Bill Dockstader had written that Buster made all the other juveniles look sick. They were a *sickly* lot in those pre-Peck's Bad Boy days, a bunch of coy, simpering Lord Fauntleroys. Buster was a welcome novelty—no giggles, no dimples, no pose, just plain, sidesplitting, ridiculous fun; all of slapstick, and perhaps a little more, in one small body. And funniest of all was the unsmiling little face that immediately became his trademark. Never smiling, never moving a muscle or blinking an eye during all the horseplay, it gripped audiences strangely.

The Buster Keaton face, yesterday or today, has little to do with age or with time. It is the mask of the tragic clown. It was laughable yet faintly tragic when it was only young muscles obeying a child's will. In the beginning it was a good workman's inspiration—even, perhaps, a stroke of genius. Over the years it has become engraved in Buster Keaton's face—the seal of an artist.

The deadpan mask has always aroused curiosity, particularly since Keaton smiles freely offstage and off-camera. He himself gives the credit to Joe. It may have started, he thinks, with his concentrating on the timing of intricate and dangerous falls, but it was Joe, himself far from frozen-faced, who discovered that the laughs came when the child was serious and stopped whenever he smiled.

"If something tickled me and I started to grin," Buster says, "the old man would hiss, 'Face! Face!' That meant freeze the puss. The longer I held it, why, if we got a laugh the blank pan or the puzzled puss would double it. He kept after me, never let up, and in a few years it was automatic. Then when I'd step onstage or in front of a camera, I *couldn't* smile. Still can't."

Of course, this remains to be said: the sober face stayed on because there was a serious boy behind it. A star at five years of age, kissed and hugged by the likes of Lillian Russell and Anna Held, his head was not turned—onstage the spoiled boy, offstage the unspoiled one; an American kid who loved picnics and pop, fishing and baseball, and yet so weirdly touched by genius that he loved work even more. The five-year-old loved the roughness, loved the stage, and loved his parents. He was integrated as full participant into their adult professional life almost from the start.

Joe, ill-advisedly, tried to emulate Dockstader's poetic prowess. Joe, at bottom, was a frontier roughneck, a tough youngster who had staked out farms in the fierce armed rivalry of both the Oklahoma Land Runs, had hoboed on the freight-train rods, and had snatched Myra from a jealous father. The spats, the cane, and the topper that came later never changed him. It was this roughneck who, in those early vaudeville years, yielding to an unsuspected Victorian sentimentality, penned the classic ode that appeared in the metropolitan dailies:

TO BUSTER

And everything he did, why, just seemed to fit,
Each gesture he made with his min'ature mitt,

And the capers he'd cut was a bully good treat,
In his whirlwind endeavor to make both ends meet.

He had no promoter, no one to show him how
To make his little speech or to take his little bow,
But a kind of inspiration that seemed to hold sway,
Just a natural born talent you can't take away.

Vaudeville, not the everyday world or the world of other children, was Buster Keaton's world. Then in its full glory, it was almost as wonderful as it seemed to him. And it was fantastically strange in ways he could not grasp, precisely because it was his world.

There was indeed—and entirely apart from nostalgic memory—something of the marvelous about vaudeville. It was so magnificently irrelevant, so unpredictable, a kind of stream of consciousness of the theatre. Everything was thrown together—a dozen or more entirely different acts rushing one after the other out on the boards until the stage was as full of marvels as a vaudeville magician's silk hat: ragtime and romantic ballad; grand opera and barbershop quartet; slapstick and Shakespeare; tap dancing and ballet; legerdemain and mental telepathy; juggling, tumbling, wire walking, aerial acrobatics. It was a glorious and preposterous hodgepodge with a happy madness all its own.

It enslaved the child Buster. He went on for fifteen minutes or so twice a day with Joe and Myra. All the remaining show hours, he hung around in the wings of vaudeville theatres all over America, his eyes glued to the stage. Sixty years and more later, he still remembers it with almost-total recall.

He watched an act called Adgie & Her Lions—Adgie, beautiful, buxom, and besequined, "danced gracefully" (as faded clippings confirm) "and then disrobed fearlessly in the cage with her four Kings of the Desert." He watched Professor Fraley, a boy hypnotist only four years older than he, casting his assistant, one Miss Forsyth, all of eighteen and in pink tights, "under the fearsome thrall of a seven days' sleep." No one—including Buster—seemed to wonder how Miss Forsyth made every show while in this week-long nap.

One of Buster's favorites, though he was a little afraid of it, was the act called Powers' Hippodrome Elephants: one of the gray-skinned giants seated himself in a monstrous barber chair, a second one lathered and shaved him, and a third stood waiting with a gigantic whisk broom held in its trunk. Perhaps the elephant jokes originated here.

Another favorite was "the creature(?) called Enigmarelle writing on a blackboard and riding a bicycle." Enigmarelle, granddaddy of the robots, was straight out of H. G. Wells. Buster can recall how the operator set the metal giant going with push buttons, then took him apart—wheels, gears, levers, and all—to prove he was kosher, then did a reassembly job so that Enigmarelle could take his bow at the footlights, shift gears, and stomp offstage.

La Belle Titcomb, though as fantastic as Enigmarelle, was very definitely not sheet tin but flesh and blood. She called herself Equestrienne Extraordinaire and performed against an alpine set. With accompanying thunder-and-lightning effects, she stood on the back of a live white stallion and yodeled the "Ride of the Valkyries." Then, in a fine surrealist fantasy of sex and patriotism, a lantern slide projected the American flag on her white robes as she did a Beef Trust shimmy to make Old Glory wave and sang to her horse—with a cheerful disregard of his obvious sex—"Gee, You Are a Grand Little Girl."

Another friend of Buster's vaudeville childhood, the famous tramp comedian Harry Wills, married La Belle Titcomb. After a year he abruptly left her and gave out a statement to the press: "I should have married the horse."

Colonel Gaston Bordeverry was the sharpshooting star of Buster's day, a rifle genius who played "Comin' Through the Rye" by directing his bullets at the bull's-eye keys of a weird piano. Bordeverry too, following the taste of the day, mixed sex and mother country (or, perhaps, fatherland) in a typical wild mélange. He disrobed one Miss Leonie de Lausanne by shooting her clothes off. Perhaps he *was* a bit hasty, but his fine marksmanship is indicated by the fact that Leonie had no understudy. Then the Colonel tossed a small glass bulb high in the air, snatched up his rifle, and shattered the bulb with one shot, whereupon, out of the fragments and floating down, came a chromo portrait of Theodore Roosevelt suspended from the Stars and Stripes, which, in turn, dangled from a silk parachute, while the national anthem thundered up from the pit. What with jumping to attention while keeping their eyes on Leonie, few saw their President or their country's flag.

In vaudeville, play, if not *the* play, was the thing. So with no thought of disloyalty, Buster, with the stage freedom allowed him, could do a devastating parody of his current idol. Bordeverry, in his turn, got the treatment. A clipping Myra saved relates how "Buster Keaton introduced a burlesque on the shooting act of Colonel Gaston Bordeverry at Proctor's Twenty-Third Street Theatre that was as funny as anything the little fellow has ever done." A showman himself, Bordeverry understood Buster's motivations and was "so amused at the travesty that he loaned Buster one of his small rifles for the week."

It was in 1902 that some of the strangeness of vaudeville, and of his life in it, finally came home to Buster. Then seven years old (officially, nine), he had been in first-run vaudeville more than two years. He had, in fact, had scarcely a moment out of it if one includes theatrical hotels and boardinghouses and the ceaseless railroad trains as a part of vaudeville. Beyond the innate strangeness of this world was the strange fact that he was almost the only child in it—the rest were adults, trained animals, and, of course, robots like Enigmarelle.

In any case, it all struck home to him that year, at the Grand Opera House in Memphis. Here for the first time he saw the famous ventriloquist Trovollo and his "children," the ten carved mannequins he used. Buster was not quite sure whether they were dummies or for real. Trovollo himself confused him by habitually conversing with them offstage as well as on. Holding one in each hand, he would ask casual questions like "How did you sleep last night?" and one would flip back, "Lousy! Must we always stay in a hotel by the railroad tracks?" while the other's reply to the question "Did you enjoy lunch?" might be a rude, resounding belch.

Buster entered one of these offstage colloquies, and a four-way chat ensued. Suddenly the boy's favorite, a red-thatched, freckled moppet called Redtop, piped up, "Buster, I'd like to be your playmate." That did it. Through a handful of wood-and-sawdust dolls, a seven-year-old boy suddenly glimpsed another world, the world of children. He also conceived an overpowering desire to have Redtop for his own. He decided then and there to steal the doll, or, as he himself calls it in retrospect, "kidnap it."

He knew that after the evening show Trovollo left the ten dummies in a row against the backstage wall and under a sheet. That very night, after he had been sent to bed, he got up, dressed, and tiptoed downstairs past the open door of the sitting room where the Keatons and Trovollo and his wife were busy at pinochle. He was not aware that Trovollo spotted his getaway. Nor, as he walked quickly to the theatre, did he know that the ventriloquist was sprinting up a side street to reach the stage door first.

Tiptoeing across the stage, Buster for the first time became conscious of what every actor knows: a dark and empty stage at night is the ghostliest place in the world. He shivered, shook himself, and, squatting down, raised a corner of the sheet. He stretched out his hand.

Redtop shot bolt upright; the painted scar of a mouth flew open; out came the shrilling voice. "Don't touch me, boy, or I'll tell your old man!"

Buster has never forgotten his panic. It gave Trovollo time to crawl out from under the sheet and make his getaway. Buster could not find the stage door; he ran around in the wings, found the exit at last, then fled up the endless street to the hotel.

Myra, Joe, and the Trovollos were sitting at the card table where he had last seen them. They were looking at him and laughing. He whirled and ran upstairs.

Myra drew in her breath sharply, excused herself, and hurried after him. She found him on the bed pale and trembling. When he saw her he began to cry. She took him in her arms and said what had to be said. "Don't cry so, honey, it's only a doll. A doll with a wooden head and a stomach full of sawdust."

Buster stopped crying instantly. He was more thoughtful than convinced. Inwardly he clung to the belief formed years before, when the wringer mangled his finger, his belief in animate constructions. Eventually, in his motion pictures, this belief would emerge in the strange dual concept of machines that are alive and human beings that are machines.

But, in any event, the new world that Buster Keaton had just glimpsed, the world of other children, remained closed to him.

FIVE

AROUND 1903 there began to be rumors that Buster Keaton was a midget. Publicly ten—actually eight—years old, he was not tall even for his nonpublic age. No child, the wiseacres said, could possibly be such a phenomenal acrobat. Then, too, he dressed like an adult both onstage and off. For some time the Keatons had been fitting him with tailor-made cutaways, sack coats, long trousers, and even a derby and a cane—exactly like Joe's public garb. He had his own replica luggage too: valises and theatrical trunk, each prominently lettered BUSTER. Joe Keaton never bothered to deny the gossip. Buster knew why. "He hoped the Gerry Society might believe it and leave us alone."

Actually, Buster looked exactly like what he was, a boy, rather handsome, neat and scrubbed, his straight dark hair plastered down. Theatre critics called him electric, and the adjective was as good as any. He moved as if wired for speed, unquestionably generated magnetism, and his batteries never ran down.

But deep inside he was quiet, staring out through large unblinking eyes as if in one glance to figure out what made everything tick. His eyes missed nothing. Myra asked once, in rhetorical mock despair, "Do you even close those eyes when you're asleep?" There seemed to be two Buster Keatons: the one of quick, precise movements that always led to those sad, hilarious disasters; and the other like a skipper in a conning tower, casing the world.

His face was perpetually thoughtful and not a little strange, and his beautiful movements—there is no other way to describe them—were almost weirdly elegant in the rowdy slapstick chaos. Buster the acrobat had the natural feeling for movement that balletomanes call line. In time it would turn mob scenes and chases in his own film comedies into long swirling lines of action.

Half of any action is its timing, and what Toscanini's tempi were to symphony or a well-placed sax wail is to the blues, timing is to comedy. Joe Keaton had timing right to his fingertips, and he saw that his son got it too. That is how the "five-second ouch" came about.

"The old man would kick me," Buster once recalled, "a hell of a wallop with a number twelve slapshoe right on my fanny. Remember, we wore no pads. I rode the punches or got hurt. Now a strange thing developed. If I yelled ouch—no laughs. If I deadpanned it and didn't yell—no laughs. 'What goes?' I asked. 'Isn't a kick funny?' 'Not by itself it ain't,' said Joe. So he gives me a little lesson: I wait five seconds—count up to ten slow—grab the seat of my pants, holler bloody murder, and the audience is rolling in the aisles. I don't know what the thunder they figured. Maybe that it took five seconds for a kick to travel from my fanny to my brain. Actually, I guess, it was The Slow Thinker. Audiences love The Slow Thinker."

That same year, 1903, when June came, Joe suddenly said, "We're making enough. Let's hit Perry for a month." Buster was nearly eight, Myra was twenty-six, and Joe thirty-six, and it was the first summer vacation any of them had ever had. Buster was introduced to a new world, the real one. All day long he explored it, baseball, riding, carrying water to the field hands, and hunting with his father,

The well-dressed
young trouper:
Buster Keaton in 1901.

grandfather, and Uncle Bert. His training in the arcade shooting gal-
leries, augmented by the loan of Colonel Bordeverry's rifle, came in
handy. He got his share of the wild plains game, cottontails in the
open, quail and prairie chicken in the coverts.

During the visit, Joe's mother brought up the touchy subject of
Buster's schooling. He had had none. She was horrified. Myra promised to get the project going.

In September she bought standard textbooks and got a letter from
the New York Department of Education recommending that Buster
Keaton be admitted into public school for one week in each city
they might visit. The very next Monday, Buster started to school.
The Keatons were opening at the Bon Ton in Jersey City, so bright
and early Buster joined the morning entrance line of kids—most of
them his fans—and entered first grade. Myra was to pick him up in
the early afternoon, leaving time for him to make the matinee.

The new enrollee gave his best. The trouble was that he had got
his answers in advance from the comic school acts in vaudeville.

"What is an island?" the teacher asked.

Buster raised his hand. "A wart on the ocean."

Everyone laughed but teacher.

That afternoon Myra could not pry a word out of the boy, and
he was silent at dinner and all evening. She felt he was putting even
more zest than usual into the slapstick exchanges with Joe. Next
morning he fought like a cornered animal at returning to school.
Myra all but dragged him there.

The principal sighed when they came into his office. "Well,
frankly, Mrs. Keaton," he said, "Mrs. Casey reported what happened
yesterday, and I've concluded that school isn't going to do your
Buster much good. And to tell you the truth, he won't do the school
much good either. Now, now, he's a good boy—and bright—but he
could wreck any school in a week just sitting there."

Going home, Myra said, "Well, all right, *I'll* teach you, and by
jiminy you'll learn." Within a year she had him reading and writing
("You can sign autographs if you learn") and doing sums. Yet Myra
herself had never got beyond third grade, while Joe, after one week
of first grade, was permanently dismissed for fighting in the class-
room. Joe and Myra Keaton's practical education had come from
life and their own pride and necessities. If for no other reasons,
counting their pay would have taught them arithmetic, and the need
to scan their press notices, to read. They had not needed a school-
house. Buster, they figured, wouldn't either.

Most of all, they had learned from the people they met and particularly from the daily facing of audiences, audiences of every kind and size, degree and station. From the medicine shows on, Joe and Myra had been in tune with that feeling that comes up over the footlights from the half-dark beyond. It was the theatre's shaping force, its silence as loud as its applause. But even then, movies were beginning to be made in a secrecy almost clandestine; and soon would come radio, winging out through the lonely air from lonely studios, and the great, teeming American audiences would be split into fifty million little groups sitting alone at home.

Buster Keaton missed that shaping force when he began making movies. "You worked in a vacuum," he has said. "You wouldn't get that feeling—wouldn't touch your audience—until you sat at a sneak preview. Then you had to go back and shoot a lot of stuff over. But it helped if you came from theatre life into the movies. Personally, though, I missed the excitement. We Keatons carried excitement in our pockets. If there wasn't excitement, we found it—an accident, a train wreck, a fire—or we made it."

Then Buster remembered an opening night in 1903 at Poli's in New Haven. "The whole country," he said, "heard about this fracas. College towns were tough to play. Five hundred students crowd in and they own the house. Only a week before, at Poli's, Gaby Deslys panicked at the noise and refused to go on. When the boys discovered they were watching an understudy, they wrecked the joint, ruined the scenery, tore out a hundred seats. Yale expelled about eighty or ninety students.

"But next Monday the gang was all there, waiting. Three in the front row begin ribbing us. The old man stops and says, 'If you want to be the comics, come on up here and we'll be glad to sit down there.'

" 'Go ahead,' they say, 'you stink anyway.'

"Joe begins to come to a boil. 'One more crack,' he says, 'and I'm coming over.'

"Then Ma comes out with her saxophone. She gets a big hand, and Joe cracks as usual, 'Don't give her too much, folks. I can't hardly handle her now.'

"A Bronx cheer comes from the front row, and one of the needlers yells, 'She stinks too.'

" 'That does it,' says Joe. 'Here I come!'

"But Joe doesn't go over, not he. I do. He grabs me by that suitcase handle, pivots, and throws me right out over the orchestra pit, hissing to me, 'Tighten up.' My seventy-five or eighty pounds hit these three jerks broadside. Joe's aim was perfect. My slapshoes break the nose of one; my hips crack another's ribs. I'm back up and on with the act before the ushers and cops get down the aisle. One guy had to be carried out. We didn't stop the act for one second while all this went on. Joe signaled the curtain to stay up.

"He knew only too well that there might be a real riot. He'd had no fear of hurting *me*—I was just a handy ballistic missile. But the college boys just sat there as if stunned."

Joe Keaton, in fact, made capital of Buster's agility and resilience. As the boy grew, the roughness grew. The Gerry Society doubled its efforts to bar him from the stage, but the Keaton luck held.

Many critics of the day tried to describe the Keaton act. But, both in spirit and in fact, it was indescribable. It was never the same way twice; it threw away its clichés before they could crystallize. People came back day after day to see what would happen next, just as they followed the cartoon strips *Happy Hooligan*, *The Yellow Kid*, and *The Katzenjammers*. Monday might be twenty minutes of up-tempo mayhem relieved by "My Gal Sal" on alto sax—practical joke and counterjoke, slips, tumbles, trips, slides, and the unbelievable comic falls. Tuesday might develop into one long comic-story routine all in off-the-cuff pantomime and not a word spoken. Wednesday would perhaps unfold as recitation time, with merciless parodies of Bernhardt, Eva Tanguay, or Sothern and Marlowe's Romeo and Juliet, with the balcony and Buster falling on Joe. Thursday might be devoted to one long outrageous burlesque of some popular melodrama. Or all these things and more might be cross-stitched into a Keaton sampler of the modes of madness. Not only was it Keystone Comedy long before Mack Sennett met movie camera, it was surrealism before Salvador Dali was even born and pop art before the first Campbell's Soup can sat for Andy Warhol.

Even the dialog—though so thoroughly "vaudeville"—fitted the act, which, however mad, was based on character and on characterization. Joe might ask, "What makes you so small?" and Buster would reply, "I was raised on condensed milk"; Joe would counter, "You are very short," and Buster would flip, "If I wasn't, you would be on payday," and on such a buildup as this, Buster would take his flight into the backdrop while Joe would dedicate another crackpot ballad to his son: "I will now sing a little ballad entitled 'I Picked a Lemon in the Garden of Love, Where They Say Only Peaches Grow.'"

But why try? It was not the words but the delivery, not the action but its line and timing. The act was and remained indescribable and unique. There was only one such madly virtuoso essay in the serialization of the non sequitur, in nonsense, belly laugh, pratfall, music, dance, farce, satire, and donnybrook.

In one way only did the act never change, and it was the theatre manager's headache: chewed-up scenery, and where to bill the act. If the Three Keatons opened the program—which, being stars, they should not do anyway—the rest of the bill faced a laughed-out audience; if they played halfway down, a large chunk of the audience would leave when they finished; if at the end, nobody left—the whole house sat there yelling, "More!" As one New York critic wrote: "At 4:30 the people usually get restless; they hear the tinkle of the dinner bell in far-off Harlem or Jersey and begin to put on their things for a hasty exit. But there they sit, hypnotized by little Buster."

The Three Keatons, immune to professional competition, seemed to revise the old adage so that it read, "Three's company, four's a crowd." And then, as if to refute Teddy Roosevelt's thesis of race suicide, the threesome ran head on into its own population explosion. As Buster says, "The Pullman babies began arriving." Harry (after Houdini) Stanley Keaton was born in New York in 1904; soon he was christened Jingles (by Houdini) because of his noisy way with toys. Louise Dresser Keaton was born in Lewiston, Maine, in 1906. Within eighteen months Louise walked through an open second-story window and fell into a paved courtyard, breaking her jaw and nearly biting her tongue in two. Though she recovered quickly, this was no Keaton fun fall. Myra hired a governess to travel with them.

Louise had already, at three and a half months, tasted the Keaton excitement. At two in the morning during a sub-zero New York February, Carl Ehrich's boardinghouse caught fire. All except Buster piled out in nightgowns across the snowy street and into another house. Buster ran barefoot to the corner saloon, yelling for Joe all the way, and right through the swinging doors.

After saving the trunks and clothes, Joe began counting as in the old days. "Troubles," he said, "come in—"

"Threes," said Myra, "and shut up!"

"Don't you tell *me* to shut up," said Joe. "You'll see."

Next day he instituted family fire drills. After two months' training, the second fire came.

"We were in Sioux City," Buster says. "It's late morning. Joe's out getting the mail. Ma's taking a bath.

" '*Fire!*'

"Hah! We're trained! Throw everything on the bed, tie the bedspread corners, heave it out the window. Myra grabs a kimono, then grabs Louise; I grab Jingles. Out the window and down the fire escape. The old man runs home and gets the trunks out. And his bottle of ink. Always saved that.

"Number three came next summer—Canobie Lake in southern New Hampshire. The matinee was on at the Casino; the kids were playing in the park. Joe ran for that tinderbox called a hotel. Tried to grab all the clothes at once, pulled, and the heavy walnut wardrobe came over on him. Down he went. He wrestled out, then threw everything, trunks and all—even the ink—out the window. Then, three flights down, smoke so bad he crawled down headfirst, keeping his head low; fell against the door, and a fireman pulled him out. Ten minutes later the whole shebang caved in."

That very night Joe called another fire drill. Everyone groaned. "You never know," said Joe, "when another series will start."

Joe was talking to a reporter some years later. "We got so used to going down fire escapes," he said, "that the children cried if I took 'em out by the door."

All through the frontier and medicine-show days, Joe Keaton had been a total abstainer. Now, what with fires and other things—such as prosperity—he had taken to the convivial brew, with a very occasional shot of bourbon. It was not "lightness" or "dryness" or "low calories" that sold beer in those days. Beer was the passport to the free-lunch counter. A nickel glass and from the groaning board you could choose sliced ham or beef, rat-trap cheese or Limburger, smoked fish or sardines, pickles or radishes, rye bread or ship's crackers. Joe's favorite spot in any saloon was at the bar near the free lunch. To move into his spot while it was temporarily vacated was to ask for the hitch kick.

Nowadays after the night show it was straight to the bar for Joe and his cronies. When he overstayed, Myra awakened Buster. Whatever the town, he knew just where to go. His head would poke through the swinging doors, a few measures of "Father, Dear Father, Come Home with Me Now," and the wage earner reluctantly went home.

Occasionally he was not rescued soon enough. One night the telephone rang for Myra while she was playing pinochle with Mrs. Ehrich. "Thirtieth Street Precinct calling, ma'am. Come over and bail your husband out."

"What did he do now?"

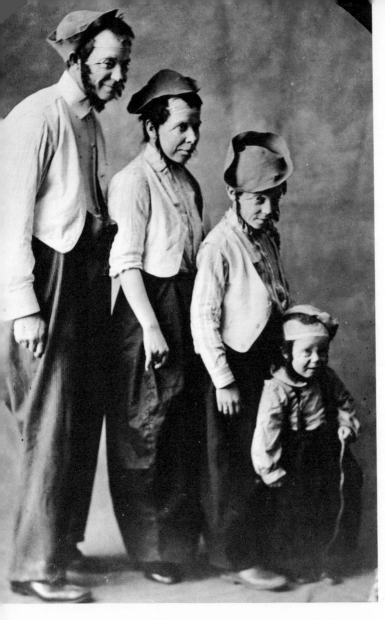

The Four Keatons.
Left to right:
Joe, Myra, Buster,
Jingles, 1906–1907.

"Kicked a guy through the big window at the Metropole."

"How much?"

"Two hundred and fifty bucks."

"Tell him this," said Myra. "I'll see him in court in the morning."

"I bid three fifty," she called to Mrs. Ehrich, and hung up.

"Well! What happened?" Mrs. Ehrich asked a bit impatiently.

"Oh," said Myra negligently, "that hitch kick again."

For all his superb physical coordination, Buster's father was a child at handling anything even slightly mechanical. Joe Keaton plus machinery was disaster. Even the simplest sort of machine was his enemy. He was by instinct antimachine, and left to him the wheel would never have been invented.

Until she learned better, Myra entrusted Jingles to Joe for daily strolls with the perambulator. Once, on the sidewalk in front of the Ehrichs', with the baby buggy parked beside him, Joe stood talking with the famous acrobat Fred Borani, inventor of a sensational diving fall that is named after him.

"Watch that go-cart!" said Borani suddenly.

The perambulator—with Jingles—had started to roll away. Joe slammed his foot hard on the front axle; the entire vehicle somersaulted; Jingles flew into Borani's arms; the go-cart handle gashed Joe's temple. It was his howl that brought Myra to one upstairs window and Buster to the other. They looked down at Joe's bloody brow and the overturned baby buggy.

"Jingles hit me," said Joe in a lame witticism.

"Well, you leave that child alone," Myra called.

It was a Boston episode that moved Myra to remove Jingles from the paternal care. It was there that go-cart and occupant got entirely away, rolling down a hill. Joe discovered it belatedly, took after it, but could not catch up. The chase ended in the center of Bowdoin Square with Joe, Jingles, and the go-cart in a wild scrimmage of horses' feet and carriage wheels. The Hub newspapers quoted Joe as arguing with the police, "Is a little exercise against the law?"

Whenever he was present at any of Joe's mechanical debacles, Buster was torn between the equally strong urges to help and to watch happily. If Myra scolded him for failing to give aid, he had only one response. "Heck, Ma," he would say, "it was going to happen no matter what *I* did."

In truth, it all accorded well with the child Buster's own philosophy of Machine versus Man.

SIX

IF JOE KEATON in those days had his troubles with The Brew and The Machine, Buster began having troubles too. The lightest of these was being coerced at a sensitive age, almost eleven, into what he called a "sissy" role. "I was Little Lord Fauntleroy because of my sister Louise," he says. "Even before she was born."

In 1906, the Keatons—now four, counting Jingles—were in New Orleans when Myra discovered she was pregnant. She broke the news to Joe by announcing in Victorian style that she was going to take time out for "another spell of knitting." Joe canceled their vaudeville bookings, cashed in their train tickets, and they sailed for New York on a coastal steamer. Even in this peaceful milieu, Buster was able to summon disaster. The last night at sea became, in the parlance of melodrama, what he henceforth called My Fatal Night.

Joe was in a big poker game and down to IOU's, with Buster kibitzing from his perch on the arm of Joe's chair. It was straight draw poker, nothing wild. Suddenly fortune smiled: Joe was dealt three aces and drew the fourth. Sighing heavily, as he had been doing all evening, he feinted at throwing in his cards, reconsidered, then sat back, checking each time the bet came to him. The other gamblers, now overconfident, were just beginning to build up the pot, when Myra appeared.

"All right, Buster," she said. "Bedtime now."

"Aw, heck, wait a second, Ma," he replied. "I want to see Dad play his four aces."

Joe let loose a string of oaths and tossed in his hand. "Take the goddamn pot, and good luck!" he said. He grabbed Buster by the collar. "*I'll* take you to bed."

Buster took this sort of misfortune lightly. He was accustomed to it. The next misfortune, however, was more galling. They had gone to New England, where Buster and Joe went with the Fenberg Stock Company, contributing slapstick turns in front of the curtain while the scenery changes were made between acts. This arrangement al-

Buster Keaton
as Little Lord Fauntleroy,
1906.

lowed Myra to stay home without traveling while the Fenberg troupe operated within a limited area. Then the Fenberg juvenile, whom Buster heartily disliked, came down with whooping cough. Fenberg put the finger on Buster.

So the most celebrated young comedian in America, at the age of eleven, became the Honourable Cedric Errol, better known as Little Lord Fauntleroy. "The vest-pocket knockabout, born with slapshoes," had to don velveteen pantaloons, red sash, and false blond shoulder-length curls. It was a colossal comedown.

"That infernal part," Buster still remembers, "was the longest speaking part in the theatre next to Hamlet. Seventy-five pages—if it was one—and no action.

"About Wednesday matinee I just got too bored. Onstage she was saying, 'Here he comes now, as if his little heart would break'—my cue—and I warble 'Dearest!' and trip over the center door fancy and do a face slide onto the stage.

" 'An accident,' I tell Fenberg.

" 'Oh?' he says.

"That night I misjudged a fall onstage and knocked the Tiffany lamp off the center table.

"Fenberg lays for me. '*Still* an accident?' he asks, with murder in his voice.

"Next came *East Lynne*, the all-time tearjerker. I was little Willie, who dies in the third act. The nurse is my mother, and I don't know it. I'm a poor little foundling, you see. But she knows *me*. This week we got a new leading lady. She came there to act, and nothing was going to stop her.

"*East Lynne* is four acts of the cryingest show ever written. The audience starts to cry in the first act, and the faucets are never turned off—sobbing all through the second act; Willie dies in the third; and for a finish, his mother dies in the fourth.

"Now, we do our quick comedy turn right after the second act— no time to change costume—so I underdress, as we say, just pulling a long hospital nightgown over the tramp outfit, powder my face a ghastly white, and climb in bed under the sheet, slapshoes and all. The curtain rises; I'm in bed, dying; and the audience reaches for fresh handkerchiefs. The leading lady works herself up and then, in a low, throbbing voice, says, 'Won't you call me Mother before you die?'

"I say, 'Sure—Mother,' go *ugh*, close my eyes, and die.

"I hear her shrieking, 'Oh, my God! He's dead!' but I don't see her coming. She zeroes in in a state of collapse, her elbows hit me in the stomach, and my feet shoot straight up in the air. There are those tramp pants and slapshoes right in the spotlight.

"Did you ever hear an audience go to pieces! They were hysterical. Laughed all through the rest of the play.

"When we leave the theatre, there's Fenberg waiting and looking like War Declared. He barely opens his mouth, and Joe hollers, 'One word to the kid, just one word, and I'll slug you. Go get that cut-rate Sarah Bernhardt and leave him alone!' "

Joe and Buster Keaton helped to kill melodrama. It was their meat long before it was the public's poison. Melodrama acts got down on their knees and begged not to be booked on the same bill with the Three Keatons.

Buster recalls with special pleasure a certain midweek at Willie Hammerstein's famous Victoria Theatre on Times Square. "Joe was onstage doing legomania alone," he says, "and I ran to the prop room, grabbed a yellow sou'wester and a lighthouse-keeper's cap, and lit a ship's lantern. Heading for the stage, I called to the electrician to douse the lights and throw a green spot on Joe.

"Then I stomp out and say, 'There's another thing you didn't know, Martin. I could have married your wife.'

"Without a second's hesitation, Joe clenched his fists and spat out the words, 'You lie! I gave you the mother, but you'll never have the *chee*ild!'

"Then I get bopped in the face, light on my fanny, and the old man falls over me. Off with the raincoat and hat and back into our act just as if nothing had happened. But the audience was killing itself. You see, I had started the famous scene from *Shore Acres* where the two brothers fight in the lighthouse."

When Harry Keaton had arrived, the papers had heralded "a new Buster Keaton." When Louise was born, *Variety*, then only a year old itself, proclaimed, "Five of a kind is a hard hand to beat." But the mold had been broken. The newcomers disliked danger, and for them the stage was not rainbow-lit. But Myra made costumes, and they made occasional appearances. Dressed alike, the five made a quaint showing (as one writer put it) "in graduated and assorted sizes, like the separated portions of a Chinese miracle box." But it was static. Nothing happened. A bow, a dance step or two, and that was all—a sort of valentine trimming, a sentimental garland on a well-loved act.

Joe never risked putting the two younger kids on in New York. Buster still had them in court often enough. Once, years before, after an appearance on Coney Island, they had been haled before the mayor by the Gerry Society counsel. He had a new dodge. Soft-pedaling the dangerous rough stuff, he harped on moral dangers, on the sad corruption of childhood. "Putting a child of tender years," he said, "into such a low, despicable, vulgar, disorderly place as Coney Island!"

Mayor Van Wyck did a double take. "What? I bicycle there myself every Sunday. I never saw any sin, only plain people having a good time. The poor are entitled to entertainment too."

The Gerries made an even stronger bid when, through political pressure, they induced the governor in Albany to look into the matter. However, the Society tipped its hand in a press release that claimed that Buster's body was a mass of deep bruises, incurred for the most part in the act. But some, they hinted, were from sadistic beatings administered offstage.

"Now we'll fix those bastards," said Joe.

At the hearing Joe insisted that Buster undress right then and there in the gubernatorial chambers.

"Where are the bruises?" the governor demanded sharply.

Society counsel turned red, then white.

Joe taunted him. "Perhaps they're covered with makeup," he said. "Shall we have the boy bathed?"

Buster laughed. The governor turned to him. "Does your father mistreat you, son?" Buster laughed again.

The governor then addressed counsel. "You are wasting the time of the governor and of the people of the state."

But the Gerry Society had the last laugh. The blow fell in December, 1907, in New York City. A Christmas benefit for poor children was slated for the old Grand Opera House on Twenty-third Street, and all the stars were participating: Lillian Russell, Anna Held, William Collier, Weber and Fields, the Foys, Bert Williams, Montgomery and Stone, and many more, including the Keatons. The benefit manager urged Joe to let his two youngest take a bow. Joe was dubious.

The manager coaxed. "They can't object to kids; it's a benefit for kids. Everyone's appearing for free, anyway."

"Well, all right," said Joe.

Next morning came five subpoenas. Even baby Louise had to be in court. The manager chickened out completely. He denied under oath having suggested—heaven spare us!—that babies go onstage. The punishment far more than suited the crime. The Gerry Society's victory was complete. The Keatons were fined two hundred and fifty dollars and the whole family banished from all New York State stages until October 4, 1909, when Buster would officially become sixteen years old. The Society was still in the dark as to his real age.

It was a heavy blow—nearly two years of exile from the top stages of America. But even wider and heavier disaster was about to fall on all vaudevillians. The theatre-owner monopoly was growing, and the performer, top man with public, was bottom man with management. Busily employed, the actors still went happily on their gypsy rounds. But it was a fool's paradise. Though wages rose higher and higher, expenses rose even higher and more swiftly. In the gay rush, however, who stopped to count what was left?

The United Booking Office ran the works, booking and routing the artists as it chose. The owners let the wages rise, getting the raises back in diverse ways. For example, UBO suddenly decreed that theatres no longer had to furnish scenery. All acts must supply their own and transport it too. Then to boost its own supposedly secret commission kickbacks, it had the commission of the actor's agent raised from 10 per cent to 15 per cent, then higher. On the heels of this chicanery came the villainous so-called Firm Contract. The Firm Contract was firm for the manager and unfirm for the actor. An act could be canceled out at any time before its third performance of the week, with no pay for the rest of the week, while, on its part, the act could not refuse to play a booking for any reasons short of injury, illness, or death. Things grew tougher by the minute. There still was no trade guild to protect the artist.

Every fellow laborer held out his hand in what had developed into a gigantic tipping racket. The gratuities demanded were considerable: two to ten dollars. If they were not paid, scenery went up wrong and was damaged, props disappeared, lights failed to work, trains were missed because draymen failed to call for sets and trunks.

The happy actors became morose. How could they strike without a union? No one with organizing ability and enough prestige came forward. Existing actors' groups were too social and too loosely organized to back any militancy. The White Rats had proved this. The White Rats was a social club of vaudeville comedians. Its convivial and honorary roster included Dave Montgomery and Fred Stone, James J. "Gentleman Jim" Corbett, Maurice Barrymore, DeWolf Hopper, Weber and Fields, and Joe Keaton, with Buster as Mascot Member No. 1. The White Rats had gone on strike in 1900 for better salaries and better working conditions for all vaudevillians. They didn't have the muscle. The strike was failing when some of the members sold out. It was a fresh, unpleasant, disheartening memory in the theatre world.

In 1917, Marie Dressler's chorus girls' strike would lead to Actors Equity, but too late by far to save the vaudevillian and vaudeville itself. There had been one successful strike, however, and only one. That was by the Four Cohans. B. F. Keith in some way doublecrossed the Cohans, or so they believed.

George M. Cohan was the family spokesman. He promptly cornered Keith in his office. "No Cohan," he said, "will ever play for you again."

"No Cohan," said Keith, "will ever play in vaudeville again."

"And this," said Cohan, "is what I suggest you do with vaudeville. . . ." And the Yankee Doodle Boy and his family were happy ever after in musical comedy.

Now more of those who could were going over to the musical

stage. A few were going into the movies. But the films paid little, the work was intermittent, and they did not name their actors. With few exceptions the film players were anonymous. To be a film actor then was to lose your name. Before 1900 the motion picture, in fact, did not have an established name of its own. Everyone tried naming the medium, with such fantastic results as Orpheoscope, Kinetograph, Kalatechnoscope, Chronophone, and Kinodrome. In those days, anyway, how pale those jerky gray shadows on a muslin sheet seemed beside the color and life of the stage.

In the growing vaudeville crisis, Martin Beck became the chief target of the wrath of the actors. Beck had been manager of the Western Orpheum Circuit. When this merged with Keith-Albee, Beck moved up into the trust's head office in the East. Surviving old-time performers still verge on apoplexy when reminded of Martin Beck's manager-booker meetings, which were held every week. They were star tribunals. The petty tyrants went down the list, act by act, rewarding "good" acts with solid, well-routed, well-paid playing time. Such acts, however, were as scarce as saints. The "bad" acts—even headliners—got layovers, bad billing, pay cuts. The meetings acted on confidential reports from the field. Provincial managers, nursing grievances fancied or real, could play absentee god at these meetings. Openly rebellious acts could be blacklisted out of vaudeville altogether.

It grew more and more like a preview of gangsterism. In 1907, Klaw and Erlanger, titans of the legitimate theatre, decided to muscle in on the Keith-Albee empire. It was a short, ugly brawl. The interlopers were not as short on theatres as Proctor had been in his doomed fight six years before. Forehandedly they tied up the Shubert chain of legitimate theatres and then began booking vaudeville into them. Their talent bait was alluring: fair employment contracts and booking. Fed up with injustices and smarting under Beck's UBO whip, many acts came over. After initial hesitation, the Keatons came over too and did eight weeks with Klaw and Erlanger, from Boston to Indianapolis.

It was substantially the Proctor story all over again. In three months it was over. But, unlike Proctor, Klaw and Erlanger were not limited to vaudeville. They remained powerful in the legit. And they definitely had thrown a scare into the trust. Before retiring from the fight, they trumpeted defiantly that they could and would repeat the raid each year, with more theatres each time, until something gave. So Keith-Albee gave: a reputed payoff to the tune of one and three-quarter million in cold cash.

This left the actors, as usual, to face the music. There was to be no amnesty now as there had been earlier with Proctor and the performers. The truants, headliners and all, were banished to the vaudeville Siberia, the second-run three-a-day Western Pantages Circuit. This spelled drastically lower salaries and, in the aggregate, weeks lost in making the long western jumps by rail. It meant headliners opening the show—the worst of professional insults. Some acts refused to go on as openers. They were through. But the Keatons stuck it out. They had been through far worse with the medicine shows. But it was an experience.

Buster recalls it vividly. "They say, 'Open the show,' we open it. It's going to hurt the other acts a lot more than us. A wild laughing act, and the next four turns look lousy. The big boys didn't give a damn—let 'em look lousy, let 'em quit. The word went down the line: 'Make it tough on all these babies.'

"So in Oakland the manager asks us, 'How long does this thing of yours run?'

" 'About sixteen minutes.'

" 'We only want eight minutes.'

" 'How in hell,' says Joe, 'do I know when we've gone eight minutes?'

" 'Your problem.'

"So I put in, 'I can fix that. Eight minutes you want, eight minutes you get.'

"I got the biggest, cheapest, loudest alarm clock I could find, the kind to wake up a battalion. When we walk onstage, I wind it, set it, and put it on the floor. Joe places a kitchen chair center upstage, about six feet in front of our own lake-scene backdrop. Then we go on with our stuff. When the alarm goes off, no matter what we're doing, we stop, I take a pose at the footlights, and the old man announces, 'And now, ladies and gentlemen, Buster will do the standing, sitting, Original Aboriginal Australian native splash dive!'

"Then I turn and run full speed—the drums are rolling; use the chair as a diving platform; off headfirst and hit that backdrop with my shoulders, my head bent under. The cymbals crash, the canvas bellies back, and I slide down headfirst. At the last tenth of a second, I put my hands to the floor, flip, and my fanny hits the floor. The public merely thought it was another Keaton gag. Only the actors got the point."

Joe smoldered. He held Martin Beck personally responsible for the Keatons' professional degradation. Backstage, in bars, on trains, everywhere, he spoke his piece. All the standard epithets and many inventive ones were used to characterize his enemy. But the campaign remained a personal, unilateral vendetta. Every local manager's orders, however humiliating, were obeyed to the letter. It was Beck, and only Beck, whom Joe wanted to get at. The spies reported, but Beck and UBO made no move. There was to be a face-to-face showdown, but it would be years in coming.

At last—mainly because the big two-a-day theatres sorely needed the banished talent—the long exile ended. This was in 1908. The following year, when Buster officially became sixteen, the Gerry Society banishment came to an end too. New York was no longer off limits to the Three Keatons. In two long years, New York, the city that forgets overnight, had not forgotten the Kid. The metropolitan dailies scareheaded the news:

BUSTER IS SIXTEEN!

As Buster grew, the act seemed to grow. Slowly, by degrees, Joe became his straight man. More and more the act was built around the genius of his slender body and his uncanny ability to convert comic ideas into visual form. In Myra Keaton's press scrapbook, the always ecstatic praise begins, at the time of the Keatons' return, to swell into something close to adulation. Terms like "the whole show," "that little genius," "Buster is unique," are to be found throughout hundreds of clippings culled from papers in a score of cities. Especially is there amazement at "his complete originality and genius for the unexpected" and at "the concentrated interest that would be remarkable at any age."

Buster even wrung a tribute from Mr. Moneybags, as the actors called B. F. Keith: "Buster is the cutest little bundle of jollity that ever wriggled into the hearts of an audience; cute from the soles of his little slapshoes to the red wig atop his wise little head."

Only a vaudeville comedian, he was front-page stuff. And perhaps the prize headline of all was the one in a Boston paper:

GIANT SNOWSTORMS CAN'T KEEP AUDIENCES AWAY FROM BUSTER KEATON

Yet even with Buster in the lineup the act laid a goose egg on its first and only trip abroad. Monologist Walter C. Kelly, the "Virginia Judge," himself immensely popular with the British, suggested a summer date in London. Joe was reluctant—he really wanted a vacation; Kelly insisted they would be a smash hit and set up a week for them at the Palace.

"You'll be over there the rest of the summer," he predicted. Won over, Joe placed a typical advertisement in the *New York Clipper*:

HEAVE HO ME LADS!
THE THREE KEATONS SAIL
ON THE GEORGE WASHINGTON JULY 1, 1909

Joe's forty-second birthday was celebrated at the captain's table two nights before they docked at Southampton. Kelly welcomed them in London at Victoria Station. Then immediately, thanks to Joe, they got off to a flying bad start. Within minutes, Joe was arguing with a cabby and had launched the hitch kick—fortunately a light, admonitory one. Repairing to a pub at Joe's request, to talk things over, Joe proceeded to lose a sharp verbal exchange with a barmaid who had refused to serve him a cocktail (she did not know how to mix it). The laughter as they left was not the kind Joe enjoyed. Joe Keaton and England were obviously not jibing.

Kelly finally settled them into a back-street hotel, they all dined, and then Joe was Kelly's guest at a club. Coming home around three in a more relaxed mood, Joe found their hostelry swinging—maids serving drinks up and down the halls, loud talk and laughter behind closed doors, and a gal throwing a sailor out of her room.

Joe burst into his own rooms, lit the gas jets, and shouted, "Heist, everybody! Up and dressed!"

Buster Keaton
at fourteen years of age,
1909.

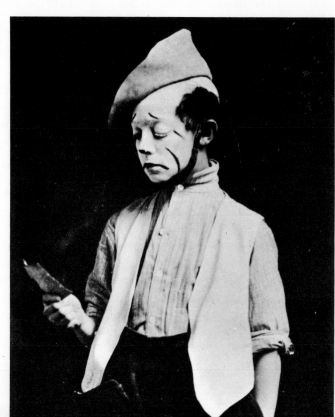

Conditioned by fire drills, the four sleeping Keatons yawned, rose calmly, dressed quickly, and walked, not ran, for the nearest exit. They walked the streets for an hour until Joe located a hotel that would conform to his basic standards.

Barely ten hours later they opened at the Palace matinee. Buster and Joe gave it everything. The act was never wilder, never rougher, never more filled with those amazing falls that an American critic once described as "fearfully and wonderfully accomplished." As if getting in his licks at England, Joe gave Buster the works. Nine-tenths of the time, the lad was in the air; the other tenth, he was on his neck. From each fresh assault he bounded up unhurt. Visually it was funny but appalling.

The only sound in the auditorium was the noise of slapstick. "Where's the audience?" Joe whispered to Buster. But Joe knew the score only too well. With the Keatons' final bow the audience came to life. Myra bowed, saxophone in hand, and the applause exploded. Buster met with cheers. Then Joe bowed, and for the first time in history—except in the medicine-show melodramas—a Keaton was hissed. Not a word was said in the dressing room. That night Joe took on a skinful.

Next morning the Palace bigwig, Sir Alfred Butt, Bart., summoned him to his office. "If you will forgive a rather personal question, Mr Keaton," said Sir Alfred, "is Buster an adopted child?"

"He's my own son," Joe replied.

The mustache quivered. Shock showed clearly through the contained British demeanor. Butt had a year-old son of his own. "Do you really," he said slowly, "do things like that to your own son?"

The audience had spoken; Sir Alfred had added the period. Joe changed tactics: more pantomime and travesty, less slapstick, no assault and battery. Buster made a hit with his impersonation of Negro comedian Bert Williams. Bert was an English favorite. As a cake-walking team, Williams and Walker had gone to London in 1899. Fresher still was the memory of the triumph of their operetta *In Dahomey*. With the original all-Negro cast, *In Dahomey* captured London, the run including a prestigious command performance for the royal family at Windsor Castle.

Buster, in his newly cracking adolescent voice, ended his skit by singing "Somebody Lied," a Bert Williams favorite. Only two years before, Bert had written special lyrics for Buster's personal use.

The Keatons closed the week in a storm of cheers and laughter. Now, suddenly, Butt wanted them to play two weeks more at the

Palace, and Scottish and English country bookings were ready for Joe to sign. But Joe was still mad at England. He curtly refused, and they sailed for home the following Wednesday. What little sight-seeing the family had done, it had done without Joe. Joe stuck with Walter C. Kelly and his private stock of bourbon.

The chief impression made by London had been on Buster: a flick of the finger or a lifted eyebrow, timed just right, could earn more laughs than a pratfall—and, a posteriori, left no bruises.

SEVEN

~~~~~~~~~~~~~~~~~~~~~~~~~~~~~~~~~~~~

I T W A S N O T a rout. It was not even a retreat. It was more a contemptuous disengagement. Now a strange anticipation hung over the return voyage. A cottage was waiting for them in Michigan. High on a sandy bluff above a freshwater lake, its rustic porches had never yet creaked to the rhythm of the summer rocking chairs. A painted sign that read "Jingles' Jungle" already hung there to welcome them. It was the Keatons' first home of their own, and the real reason for Joe's reluctance to go to England, his smoldering impatience once there, and his summary refusal to stay on.

The summer before, playing the parks around Grand Rapids, they had discovered Lake Muskegon. In two short weeks while booked nearby, they fell in love with the little lake, which opens off Lake Michigan immediately adjacent to the city of Muskegon and directly across from Milwaukee. To them it seemed an unsuspected paradise just outside the stage door. Every free moment offstage, they explored the rolling dunes, swam in the clear waters, and fried and feasted on perch they themselves had caught.

Joe voiced the consensus when he said, "To hell with working every summer." That fall and the following winter, he became an unlicensed spare-time real-estate promoter, as indicated by a 1908 newspaper clipping:

Joseph Keaton, who is with his vaudeville family at Wilkes Barre this week, is a roaming advertisement of Lake Muskegon wherever he makes a week's stand. More and more stage people are buying land at the west end of the lake and ground is being broken for a clubhouse.

It was nearly August when they arrived at Bluffton, the actors' colony that Joe had fathered. A score of cottages already edged an unpaved shoreline street. A rustic one-story clubhouse, The Cobwebs and Rafters, sat back of a new pier, the new rafters waiting for the spiders to begin work. In the next few years as Bluffton grew, sailboats, skiffs, and motorboats in increasing numbers would anchor

Lake Muskegon: Jingles' Jungle, 1911–1912. Left to right: Louise, Jingles, Buster, Myra, Joe.

offshore, and the up-to-date colony would have its own saloon, Bullhead Pasco's, with free lunch of perch fried crisp brown in Indian meal.

An amusement park sprang up nearby, but to the native Muskegonites, Bluffton was amusement enough. It was no part of the Chamber of Commerce world; the stage folk brought their own climate. It was a fraternity of old cronies: the Empire City Four, Harry Armstrong and Billy Clark (they wrote "Sweet Adeline"), Earl and Wilson, comic bellhop Paul Lucier, Big Joe Roberts of Roberts, Hays, and Roberts, and many others. The few outsiders who built there did so at their own risk.

In 1909, that first of seven Muskegon summers, Buster Keaton was fourteen years old. That summer he got his first pair of short pants. Counter to custom, he put on pantaloons at the proper adolescent age for discarding them. It announced that at last he was entering the world of children.

Until then he had had literally but one friend his own age, pretty little Elsie Janis, soon to be a musical-comedy star. When Buster and Elsie had fallen in love, he was still the Kid and she Baby Elsie. One summer day at a Midwest amusement park, they had failed to appear for the matinee. Rather worried, Elsie's mother and Myra went out looking. They found the kids in a cornfield squatting by a bonfire and roasting stolen ears of corn.

"We should have been doing better," says Buster in retrospect. "Elsie's mama seemed let down. She had feared The Worst."

However, Buster's true love right along had been a grown-up beauty, Annette Kellerman, the world-famous Australian swimming and diving star. She introduced black one-piece tights, known as Kellermans, that revealed more of the essential female shape than theatre audiences had ever glimpsed before. A natural favorite with men, Annette's modest behavior made it hard for women to hate her. For example, she always took her bows turned three-quarters away from the audience. This, of course, brought scalpers' prices for closeup seats to the left.

It was said that E. F. Albee had had a hand in Annette's sensational rise. The story—or legend—was that Albee's inspiration was born as he had a view from backstage of Annette onstage in motion. He is said to have ordered the backdrop made of mirrors. It brought a new dimension: the one hundred mirrors—count 'em—brought the audience a hundred separate back glances at a most admirable side of the beautiful Annette.

The Kellerman climax was the so-called Original Aboriginal Australian Splash, a dive into a tank onstage. She sailed straight up, high, from the diving board, doubled up like a ball with arms around knees. She hit the water in this position, and the water flew in sheets. The orchestra often ostentatiously raised umbrellas just before, and the front rows often were doused. No one minded—not even the mop-up men who followed. It was a communal excitement, firing everyone.

Buster adored Annette, and she equally adored him. In a Providence theatre, finally, he made his public tribute. It was closing night. Kellerman had just splashed. With her frank curves wet, black, and shining, she was just tripping to the footlights when an apparition streaked from the wings straight for the diving board. It was Buster, baggy pants, wig, slapshoes, and all, doing his own splash. Then he was down at the footlights, sopping wet; the audience was beside itself. Annette was as cool as she was lovely; she quietly took his hand, they bowed, and then exited together.

The theatre manager was not so cool. "What son of a bitch put that brat up to this?"

Annette was also a lady. "Such language!" she said, and stared him down.

Now Buster, having done the Original Aboriginal during the Keatons' western stage exile, was presently doing it off the Bluffton pier into Lake Muskegon for the edification of the town boys. If to them his accomplished antics intimated the strange world of theatre, then equally the Muskegon summers were to Buster holidays on the moon. It was a world, and delights, that would never become wholly his. Those long-ago summers must have been, in a special way, one of the wonders of his life. Whenever he speaks of them he seems to be turning on the lights of a faraway stage.

Buster tore into each summer day as if doubting tomorrow. He tried every athletic sport and launched his lifetime avocation of gadget building. His simplest Muskegon gadget was the Clown Pole; the most complex, the Ed Gray Awakener. Over the years, certain qualities have come to define the Keaton machine: it has brought the inventor no money and only a passing local fame; it is often, though not always, a thing of staggering complexity; and it does its job (never mind the job) with outstanding effectiveness. Its unmistakable aura is a genial, disarming madness.

Buster's first brainchild, the Clown Pole, was only an old-fashioned bamboo fishing pole stuck upright between two planks of the Bluffton pier, as if its owner had just stepped into Pasco's for a beer. It had no reel, only a line that led down to the water and a red cork bobber. However, instead of ending in the usual way with hook and bait, the line ran back underwater, around a pulley under the pier, and then up and through a window of The Cobwebs and Rafters.

The Clown Pole just stood there, none of its chicanery visible. No stranger could ever just walk by it. He would hesitate, stop, stare at the pole, while actors covertly watched him from the clubhouse. One would grasp the line inside, twitch it gently, stop, then twitch it again. The stranger would invariably seize the pole and prepare to land a fish. The "battle" would start. A crowd would gather and begin offering advice and encouragement. The upshot, of course, was foredoomed: the actor in the club yanking the pole right out of the stranger's hand, the crowd beginning to laugh, and the victim standing flat-footed and gaping. But the pole was friendly not cruel—the victim was invited inside and pinned with a wooden medal. True, he bought drinks for all.

Buster invented the Awakener for vaudeville monologist Ed Gray. Gray, a bachelor, was notably lazy. "It's a nightmare getting up," was his habitual opening midafternoon remark to the world in general. Constant ribbing about it finally spurred him to buy an alarm clock. It rang its little heart out in vain. Buster then stepped in with an invention to guarantee prompt rising with nothing dependent upon Gray's willpower, if any. Automation in an early form, Buster's brainchild almost, but not quite, anticipated the electronic computer. It had an Orwellian, *Nineteen Eighty-four* quality.

"What time shall it be?" Buster asked.

Gray went through an obvious struggle before saying, "Ten."

So at 10 A.M. each and every summer weekday, Gray's alarm clock went off—unheeded, naturally. But Big Brother was watching. The mechanism gave Gray thirty seconds to rise and turn it off, but he never did. Thereupon, hell broke loose. A lever operated by the clock started weights and counterweights of the greatest complexity all going at once: the gas was turned on and lit under the coffeepot (by a match scratched on sandpaper); a mechanical arm snatched off the sheet and blanket, if any; and an electric motor, operating through eccentric cams, made the bed rock like a foundering ship. Another day had dawned for Ed Gray. The widely discussed invention brought audiences—even occasional out-of-towners—for Gray's mechanical matins. Gathered outside the window, they weren't to be disappointed. Ed was stuck with it: he was a showman.

"You know," says Buster, "in a month or so, that infernal gadget really trained him. Sometimes he'd even get up earlier all by himself and eat. Then if he saw people coming up the hill, he'd crawl back in bed and go through all the motions. A real trouper."

Buster conceived the Clown Pole in 1909, an apprentice job. The Awakener in 1910 established him as a journeyman. The next summer, as he neared sixteen, he mechanized Ed Gray's outhouse, which commanded the treeless top of the highest dune in Bluffton. Gray welcomed this new invention. It bade fair to give him revenge on the peeping toms. Someone in life, he knew, was always being caught short; in addition, his outhouse being the colony's only three-holer, it was a sort of guesthouse anyway.

When Buster had finished his work, the privy had become a break-away prop: a tug on the innocent-looking clothesline that ran from its corner to the trim of Gray's kitchen window and the four privy walls fell outward to the ground like a house of cards. The roof, like a canopy, remained in place on four posts, but it was no help in the disaster. With the walls gone, the occupant sat enthroned in full view from any part or parcel of Bluffton. Watching Gray's Hill became a popular pursuit of August, 1911.

The story went all over the vaudeville world, and the following summer the eminent outhouse expert Chic Sale came to Bluffton to see it. He was the Keatons' guest at Jingles' Jungle, and Buster, with Joe's connivance, had prepared a welcome for him. When Sale first patronized the Keaton privy, it had been remodeled, with sound effects and a psychological booby trap. Buster had hung wooden water-closet tanks above each of the seat holes. The customary pull chains hung down from each, and each if pulled would trigger events. Conditioned reflex took care of this, neither Sale nor most subsequent guests stopping to question what business water tanks had being in a two-holer anyway.

The pulling of the chain fired a blank cartridge in a .45-caliber revolver directly under the seat plank and rang a large fire bell hidden above a false ceiling under the shingled roof. It was like a Chinese torture: subtle cruelty ruled this catastrophe. The walls did not need to fall down. From Chic Sale on, each hapless occupant dashed outdoors with pants down or skirts up, as the case might be.

The gasoline internal-combuston engine had entered Buster Keaton's life shortly before the Keatons went to England. In Macy's toy department he found a tiny but real automobile—a roadster, with bicycle wheels, weighing less than two hundred pounds. It was a Browniekar, priced at two hundred and fifty dollars, and with a three-horsepower air-cooled single-cylinder engine, it achieved eighteen miles per hour. Buster bought the floor model with no particular financial strain, as he had been earning fifty dollars a week or more for years and saving most of it. The first of his many cars, the Browniekar followed the family everywhere, shipped with the scenery and trunks.

At Bluffton, Joe immediately acquired a secondhand steam launch, which they rechristened *The Battleship*. Straight off, Buster yanked the antique upright boiler and installed a two-cylinder gasoline engine. No one showed him how; he seemed to have an instinctive kinship with machinery that was totally in contrast with his father's hostility and fear of it.

By 1912 Jingles had inherited the Browniekar, and Buster bought a big, rangy Peerless phaeton. He was then only seventeen. A year later he added a classy Palmer Singer to his automotive stable. All three cars were in Buster's name. Joe refused even to learn to drive. His hatred for machinery was broad, catholic, and inclusive, from threshing machine to sewing machine, including telephone and cylinder phonograph, and now adding horseless carriage and cinematograph.

Joe's hatred of motion pictures—he called them "flickers"—was deep and unreasoning. It cost Buster—in fact, the whole family—an opportunity to get into the new medium early. This was in 1913, the year that Charlie Chaplin joined Keystone. George McManus' cartoon strip *Bringing Up Father* was making a hit in the Hearst papers. William Randolph Hearst himself proposed that the whole Keaton clan do a film serialization of the cartoons, with Joe as Jiggs, Myra

Buster and Jingles in the Browniekar, in front of Mrs. Ehrich's theatrical boardinghouse, New York.

Lake Muskegon: Buster and Joe in *The Battleship*, 1909.

as Maggie, and the rest of the family scripted in. McManus enthusiastically agreed. Hearst, who was fond of the Keaton stage act,
was high on the idea. He offered an excellent salary, filming that
would not interfere with their vaudeville schedules, and even proposed to list the names of the Keatons as stars, an almost unheard-of
thing at that time.

Overriding Buster and Myra, Joe squelched the idea out of hand.
"What!" he said to the great Hearst. "We work for years perfecting
an act, and you want to show it, a nickel a head, on a dirty sheet?"

Crowded into the Muskegon bit—besides machinery, practical and
infernal—were sports, especially baseball. Buster and a new pal, the
young legit actor Lex Neal, conscripted enough Muskegon youths
to form a sandlot team. Buster played shortstop and utility, neutral-
izing his short stature by speed afoot, adequate hitting, and an excellent pegging arm. Occasionally he unlimbered secret weapons to
befuddle opponents, such as doing a backflip before snagging an
infield fly or turning cartwheels on his way to scoop up an easy
grounder. The big gun was the Borani, the startling, difficult headfirst
dive; it involved twisting and reversing in midair directly in the path
of an advancing runner—one second a human projectile and the next
a baseman standing smack in front of the runner, ball in hand, and
tagging him out. It made for laughs and even helped to win an occasional game.

The baseball bug bit Buster hard. He has never lost interest to this
day. In the 1920's he almost single-handedly made the Hollywood
film colony into a nonprofessional minor league of the different
studios. When he finally went with MGM on a contract pointedly
specifying "no baseball," it was L. B. Mayer himself who rescinded
the clause and asked Buster to head the studio team. During all
those lush Hollywood years, Buster would never miss the World
Series; and whenever the New York Giants won the National League
pennant, he traveled with them during the Series.

Myra kept the Jungle neat, although children flew through it like
locusts. She reveled in three months of freedom—no quick changes,
no scrubbing makeup, no catching trains; time to hang over the back
fence for a little gossip, even though it ran along such lines as "X is
leaving that act," or "Y doesn't know his wife is carrying on with that
Italian juggler," or "Martin Beck says that Z is through. . . ."

For Joe it meant fishing, poker at The Cobwebs and Rafters, a
dram or two at Pasco's, and plain rocking on the porch. By 1912 Joe
Keaton was forty-five; he had lived hard and felt older. He was aging

and hated it like hell. That fine, lean-muscled machine, honed and hardened on the frontier, was slowing down, the old endurance petering out. He was an athlete first and last, and time was stealing his cash. He was drinking more, enjoying it less.

Joe had been a rather famous beer man. For years the dailies had carried Keaton "plants"—sent in by Joe to get the act publicity—that were published with heads such as

BEER SIGN WAS
CAUSE OF SAVING
KEATON FAMILY

This particular story related how a train they were on broke down one hot summer afternoon. Suddenly Mr. Keaton spied afar off a shady oasis with a familiar sign: the foaming schooner and the price, five cents. He led his flock there to rest in the shade while he quaffed the brew. Suddenly the whistle blew and off went the train. The stranded family upbraided the father during the long hours of waiting. Little did they know! For only a few miles away their train hit an open switch, and everyone in their car met a horrible death. Moral: The Keatons' lives were saved by a glass of beer.

Every few months a seidel or a schooner in the nick of time saved the Three Keatons. City editors welcomed these tales of tidal waves at Atlantic City, collapsing theatre ceilings, burning hotels, and other disasters, and always it was Joe Keaton's harmless little glass of beer that saved them all.

But now Joe used beer only as a bourbon chaser. Bourbon told him that he was young again. There was plenty at home, bottles of Old Green River sent by the famous Kentucky distillery in exchange for Joe's "singing" of the ballad "Sailing Down the Old Green River on the Good Ship Rock and Rye." But Myra never lost count of the home stock.

So began the post-office trips that Buster still remembers with annoyance. Twice a week at noon, resplendent in spats and carrying his cane, Joe boarded ship, Buster at *The Battleship* wheel, and off they chugged on the half-hour, five-mile trip out the channel and along the Lake Michigan shore to Muskegon. Then the lengthy stops: the Continental Hotel bar, the Elks temple, and a series of Main Street gin mills. At last, the post office, where they would "pick up a letter or so, buy a two-cent stamp, and then all the same stops over again working our way home."

The sun would be low and Joe high as they docked. Buster smoldered—another afternoon lost, impressed into service on His Majesty's ship. "Shanghaied" was Buster's actual term. He pondered the matter, removed the timer from the engine, then announced that *The Battleship* was laid up for repairs. Joe nursed his bad temper for exactly a week, then requisitioned the Peerless with Buster as chauffeur. The fast land trip suited Joe. It saved saloon time. Then Buster at last got out from under. He hunted up Gallagher and taught him to drive. Gallagher—only his mother knew his first name—was a fireman, cop, bartender, general jack-of-all-trades. Like Mr. Gallagher and Mr. Shean, Joe and this Gallagher were happy doing the bars together.

In 1912, with the new Peerless as scout car and pickup truck, Buster began a clinical study of the boy-girl syndrome. Now near seventeen, he had never been one to do things by halves. So that summer and a later one resulted in two main episodes that, with his penchant for old-time movie titles, Buster subsequently named, respectively, Exiles in the Woods and The Lost Summer.

It had all begun in June, 1912, with The Lecture. Joe Keaton took Buster aside and let go—four sentences and no frills.

"Stay away from local girls or their old man will have a shotgun at you.

"Stay away from street chippies or you'll be in a hospital for life.

"When you're ready, if you need dough I'll loan you the two dollars.

"The only safe place is the best place in town, Della's."

Buster recounts the first episode. "I had a friend in Muskegon named Bob. We had the afternoon and his house all to ourselves. This local girl came over. She started fooling around. We made molasses taffy. We ate it. But she kept fooling around—cute as a bug's ear and dying for experience. So all right, let the lady have her way.

"Later on we all went out and had banana splits. Three scoops, fresh strawberries and raspberries, pineapple, chocolate, whipped cream, nuts, and cherries—all for a dime.

"We took her home then and start for Bluffton, driving slow, and talking it all over. Suddenly a souped-up Ford pulls up alongside—the sheriff and some woman.

" 'Pull over to the curb!'

" 'Whillikers,' says Bob, 'that's her mother!'

"I don't stop to think, just quick-shift down to second, step on the gas pedal, and off we go with the Model T right behind us.

We reach a place where the paving ends and the streetcar tracks leave the street. I whip the wheel over and take to the tracks. The sheriff sticks to the dirt road, and we lose him fast.

"At Bluffton we ditch the car and head straight into the blackjack woods to the cabin of a hermit we knew. He was called Beanie because he lived on pork and beans. There we hole up. After two days Beanie disappeared early one morning, and the next thing we knew we heard a klaxon blowing.

" 'That's Lex's *Dixie Pirate*,' I said. And, sure enough, there's his speedboat just offshore. We swim out, and Lex heads back.

" 'Everything's hunky-dory,' he says.

"Mom told us the rest of the story. When he lost us, the sheriff located Joe at Bullhead Pasco's. The girl's mother started speaking her piece, and Pasco jumped in. 'Hell, we all know *you*, lady,' he says. 'Who doesn't?'

"Everyone laughed, and then Bullhead says to the law, 'What kind of a shakedown is this?'

"The sheriff says, 'Holy hell!' and walks out."

Joe's dressing down did not bother Buster. But the revelation contained in Myra's story did. "I didn't know that about her mother," he said to Myra. "Honest I didn't. If I had, I never would have fooled around with the poor kid."

The Lost Summer was the summer of 1915. Buster was nearing his twentieth birthday. On the Fourth of July he spent a full day, beginning with swimming races and diving, followed by a nine-inning ball game, and ending with Buster and his friend Lex Neal pushing the heavy *Battleship* down the ways into the water. Being the stronger of the two, Buster took the brunt of this. That night he noticed something wrong. Whatever it was, it hurt—and it hurt where it shouldn't. He tossed all night. After breakfast he called Gallagher out on the porch.

Gallagher listened and then asked a few questions. "At Della Pritchett's?"

"Yes."

"When?"

"About a week ago."

"Flaxseed," said Gallagher. "Flaxseed is the only thing. Poultices."

Just then Lex appeared on his bike. Completely forgetting his three automobiles, Buster dispatched his pal to the drugstore in Lakeside, two and a half miles away. Lex raced to Lakeside and raced back with a sack of flaxseed meal.

Myra had gone visiting and was away when the first-aid squad of Gallagher and Neal sprang into action. The flaxseed had boiled over in the laundry tub and all over the kitchen floor and the poulticing was well under way before Joe noticed anything. He happened to glance into the bedroom where Buster lay sweating under a mountainous poultice. His experienced eye instantly sized up the situation.

"So," he said, "I thought I warned you about streetwalkers . . ."

Buster groaned.

". . . and told you and told you I'd send you to the best."

"That's where I went," said Buster. "But she picked me up on the street."

Joe Keaton stamped out to Bullhead Pasco's. The patrons there took the matter under advisement.

"Being so careless with our kids," said one.

"Soliciting minors on the street," said another.

"Della and that girl should be horsewhipped," said a third.

"Let's go," said a fourth.

Soon the whole crowd was in front of Della Pritchett's "house" in the Muskegon red-light district, known as the Sawdust Pile. The area at one time had been given over to sawmills, and the ground was deeper in sawdust than the finest saloon floor.

Heading the vigilantes, Joe rang the doorbell. A Negro maid appeared, then Della herself in a wrapper, her hair in curlers, eyes heavy with sleep. She glanced out, opened the door, and began to speak. "Why hello, Mr. Kea . . ." then, seeing Joe's face clearly for the first time, slammed and bolted the door. The mob thereupon laid to with rocks and brickbats, shattering the front windows. Inside, Della rushed to the telephone and got the chief of police. He came at once with a carful of cops.

"Joe Keaton!" he said. "What *is* this?"

Joe told him.

"Are you sure?"

"Christ! Don't you think I would know?"

"Why those lousy whores," said the chief. "I oughta help you throw those rocks. Just don't burn the joint down."

This showy riot started The Lost Summer. Joe considered all doctors quacks. He had known mainly the medicine-show kind. So every neighbor, every acquaintance, every friend, every local expert on home remedies or good old reliable patent medicines or herbs gathered in the dark of the moon had his or her chance. Every day a new cure. Never was a highly private illness so widely publicized.

The more medicine, the sicker Buster became. He lay pale and listless, genuine fear in his eyes. Near the end of August, Joe went fishing one day. On the lake he met an acquaintance, a doctor from Muskegon.

"Where's Buster?" the doctor asked. "Haven't seen him lately."

Joe told him the whole story.

"Let me look at that boy."

Half an hour later Buster was in the sitting room smiling wanly and saying, "I never had a dose, for gosh sakes. Strained myself shoving *The Battleship*."

"Right," said the doctor, looking at Joe. "But your friends damn near dosed you to death."

There were ten days left. Buster set out to make the most of them. Then vacation was over.

They were packed and waiting for the drayman when Joe came home, flushed, from Pasco's. "Let's rassle!" he said, as if it were the good old days. Buster hung back.

"That boy ain't got his strength back," said Myra.

But Joe persisted. Finally he became challenging. They locked arms, and the tussle began. Father and son had wrestled for fun for many years, but this time it was different. The children felt it, crowding closer to watch. Buster was as tall now as he would ever be, but Joe topped him by a head and had inches to spare in reach. Buster, however, was not yet twenty, while his father was nearly fifty.

Suddenly Joe was flat on his back and Buster was pinning his shoulders to the grass. Then the boy leaped up, face averted, and ran into the house. Joe climbed to his feet; he was wobbly and reeking of whiskey. He lurched and started after the lad.

Myra grabbed his sleeve. "Don't!" she cried sharply. "Leave the boy alone." Myra knew the score. "You've lost him," she said. *And me too*, she might have thought.

EIGHT

AFTER that first summer in 1909 at Lake Muskegon, it was as if the London difficulties had never happened. The Three Keatons roared back into action, a unique act, vaudeville's most outstanding blend of slapstick, pantomime, travesty, and madness. It was that fall that the New York banishment ended. The next five years rolled by, bright and blurred with excitement.

Because of what was to follow, Buster Keaton remembers that half decade with special pleasure. "The next five years—what years! Sending the kids off to school one by one, Jingles to that Kalamazoo military academy and, later on, Louise to a Muskegon school. That brought the three of us back together again—the original three who went through all the hard times together. Success, sure. Money, sure. But this was the *old* times.

"The things that happened! Like the train wreck that morning in Harrisburg. At least we called it a wreck when we all stopped laughing. That was just before Jingles went away to school. What a pileup in that compartment! Mom and Louise on the floor, Jingles and me out of the upper berth on top of them, and then, on top of all of us, grips, boxes, valises, saxophone, typewriter. And Joe standing razor in hand and lather all over his face where he got shoved into the mirror when the freight engine bumped our Pullman. And a hundred and fifty bucks for it. The adjuster all but begged Joe to take the check. Joe handed him a couple of passes and says, 'Catch the show tonight.'

"He came backstage after the show. He laughed and said, 'If you haven't cashed that check, hand it back. I saw your act, and no train wreck could hurt you folks.'

"A hundred and fifty bucks and a new routine for free—Joe all lathered up at a mirror with a big wooden razor; I let him have the basketball in the neck and—*bop!*—he gets his face slammed into the mirror and looks like a custard pie had hit him. Always had to remind him to go into the routine—he hated the taste of soap. So

I'd remind him out loud, and he'd crack, 'Are you trying to tell the author what to do?'

"Laughs, laughs, day and night. I remember them all.

"Those practical jokes that went on and on like movie serials. Like the trunkful of cats. Why did I ever start that? A hundred cats lived in that theatre in Buffalo, barely holding their own against the rats. So I fill the Leightons' prop trunk with assorted cats. Nice and dark and cozy, so they all go to sleep. The trunk was a part of the act, so when they open it onstage, out fly the cats, all over the Leightons, up the scenery, even out into the audience.

" 'If I know the Three Leightons,' said Joe, 'just look out.'

"We met the Leightons in nearly every theatre, but nothing happened.

" 'I like it less and less,' said Joe. 'I know those boys.'

"Then I found that knothole in the floor in Columbus. Stopped and looked at it with that alley broom in my hand and walked away. Walked back and looked at it again, jabbed at it with the broom handle and missed. Gave up and walked away again. Just then Joe started his recitation and needed a noise obbligato. So I walk over and really go to work on it. Jab and miss, jab and miss. Get into every crazy position—even on my head—to aim better but still miss. Sounded like the Light Brigade; no one could hear a word Joe was saying. He picked up the gag, stopping and starting over, doing the slow burn.

"Then he begins to really wonder, 'What the hell *is* that over there?' walks over, and I point at the hole as serious as if God only knows what's down in there. I keep missing. So I get sore, take off my coat, roll up my sleeves, spit on my palms, take the broom in both hands, sight down the handle, take aim—Joe bending over watching me—shake my head, line it up again, take a fresh aim. More of a production, for Chrissake, than Palmer lining up a thirty-foot putt. Finally I let fly. Hit the hole at last; the broom goes in up to the bristles, and I go smack on my face with my feet up in the air. A beautiful fall. After all that buildup the audience is absolutely killing itself. All over a hole in the floor!

"But *I* know what Joe has on his mind. *All right, son,* he's thinking, *now what do you do for a topper?*

"Okay, Joe, here it is. Pretend the broom is stuck. Can't get the damned thing out. Pull and yank and tug—no soap. Joe plays along, getting the drift, steps back, scratches that bald wig, then grabs me from behind around the waist like a tug-of-war at the Hibernians' picnic, and we give it all we got—the ad-lib drummer down in the pit building it up with snare rolls.

"Back and forth. We gain a few inches, can't hold it, and the broom gains it back. Back and forth, back and forth, then I whisper, 'Now!'

"Out comes the broom and down we go—a clubhouse-sandwich pratfall—drummer smashing the cymbals and the house going crazy. I remember asking Joe later, 'How did that simple gag get such a laugh?' And Joe replying, 'If you think that was simple, you're simple. It's not what you do but how you do it.'

"So now every theatre we go to we have a knothole drilled in the stage. That's where the Leightons finally came in. One waited down below stage until the broom got stuck, then he tied the end of a ball of string onto the tip of the handle. We hauled up miles of string.

"Next time out it's a live eel at the end of the string. Joe had bourbon stashed in his trunk, and he honestly thought he had snakes. Next time, no string at all but the handle all smeared with mustard. Joe wasn't easy to faze. He wiped his hands off on *me*—who else?— and ad-libbed, 'They've got everything on this broom handle, including our two weeks' notice.'

"The Leightons held on. Next time it was rope tied to the handle, two whole theatrical 'long lines,' a hundred and sixty feet. We hauled it up fathom by fathom while the orchestra segued into 'The Sailors Hornpipe.' Who cued them? The Leightons. At the end of the rope a dinky little American flag, and the ork went into 'Stars and Stripes Forever.'

"I began to sense trouble. I spoke to Joe.

" 'You turned 'em on, boy,' he said, 'but you can't turn 'em off.'

" 'Let's drop the knothole gag.'

" 'Drop it, my ass,' said Joe. 'We stick. Let's see what they do next.'

"We saw. It was at Shea's Theatre in Toronto. It was 1914, and that crack Canadian regiment, the Princess Pat, had just been cut to pieces in Flanders. Canada was in mourning. We yank the broom out, start to haul up the rope, and one of the Leightons hisses from the wings, 'There's a German flag on the end of the rope.'

"My knees grew weak. 'Let's drop it,' I whisper.

"But Joe's jaw is out a mile. It's haul away, boys. I'm thinking fast. Get down on my knees. Wait. Here comes the flag. Stamp on it. Spit on it. Desecrate it as no flag was ever desecrated. Now hold it up for everybody to see—the enemy flag!

"Holy Christ, look at it! The Union Jack! The silence sounded like thunder out of China 'cross the bay.

" 'Get off this stage—fast,' and Joe's already on his way.

"We're in the wings. I can still hear that sound. Fifteen hundred people all drawing in their breaths together. And then more silence for a little while—like a hundred years.

"And then it comes. They're laughing! The old shock laugh.

"So Joe went to the Leightons. 'Drop it guys,' he said. 'We're square.' It was Lee at Appomattox.

" 'Not scared, are you?' asked one.

" 'Scared as hell, and you damn well know it. Next time we'd be hanging by our necks up with the scenery.'

"It must have been soon after that that the act began to change. In one way it had to, of course. I'd got too big for Joe to throw around. He was fifty now; could still kick, but his aim was off. He missed my hat once in New Haven and got me in the back of the neck. I was out for twenty-two hours, Myra by the bed all the time. Concussion.

"Since he couldn't throw me any more, he began sliding me around on the floor. Like a human toboggan. That's when I told a reporter that I'd given polish to the American stage.

"The act had to change. But Joe was changing too. Not like the old man any more. Mad most of the time, and could look at you as if he don't know you. But he could become the father quick enough —those lickings onstage for things that had happened before. No more private spankings. In front of a thousand people. Finally I'd get sore, and we'd start trading. And still keep it funny.

"Funny? People should have felt the wallops we were handing out. Like the time he found the pipe in my jacket down in the dressing room and stalked out, and I said to one of the actors, 'Now I'll catch it. If you want some excitement, just watch from the wings.' What a beating, and I'm nineteen! And they always told me that my own mother began rolling her own at fifteen. And when he found the cigarettes, the tune was, 'A man smokes a pipe.' Well, we gave the comics a new routine that day of the pipe, and they've used it ever since. We got into that rhythm with our haymakers, and the orchestra went into the 'Anvil Chorus.'

"Myra told me, 'Joe's not punishing you.'

Joe Keaton and Buster, 1911–1912.

"I said, 'It *feels* like it.'

"She said, 'No, he's not mad at you or anyone else. It's old Father Time he'd like to get his hands on. Man or woman,' she said, 'some can take getting old, some can't.'

"It made it more understandable, no more standable. Anyway, like the Indian said, it went on like that for a while, then it got worse. When I smelled whiskey across the stage, I got braced.

"Yet you have to say, 'Poor son of a bitch, fighting something he'd never catch up with!' But, sweet Jesus, our act! What a beautiful thing it had been. That beautiful timing we had—beautiful to see, beautiful to do. The sound of the laughs, solid, right where you knew they would be. . . .

"But look at what happened—standing up and bopping each other like a cheap film. It couldn't last that way. Every time he got a snootful he'd sound off about Martin Beck. No matter who—agents, theatre managers, anybody—tell 'em what he's gonna do to Beck. With his mind on Beck he'd come on the stage wild. That's when I had to fasten a rubber rope onto that old basketball of mine and keep swinging it around like a hammer thrower to keep him off me. Get him running, let out the rope a little, and bop him on the fanny. There were times it was him or me, but we had to keep it funny— me on the old table like a ringmaster: 'Hup, Prince! Hup, Prancer!' Audience laughing like hell and my dad falling on his face. But still the showman, drunk or sober. He'd get up off the floor, his wind all gone, and stumble to the footlights for an ad lib: 'This is the last skit George M. Cohan will ever write for me,' or 'If we can get Nazimova, we're going to put out a number-two company.'

"You could feel it in the air—we were overdue to meet up with Martin Beck. But that tightwad manager in Providence came first. Of course, he should have furnished us strong kitchen chairs, not old ones that broke if you stepped on them. And he shouldn't have charged us for them when they broke, much less the price of new chairs. But neither should Joe have gone nuts that closing night, when he saw the deduction, and smashed up all that furniture back-stage. That gold French sofa! Boy! Did the news get to New York fast!

"That was 1915. From Providence we went straight to New York, and Martin Beck laying for us, standing in the wings at the Palace and whispering just loud enough for Joe to hear, 'Make *me* laugh, Keaton.'

"Joe snapped, 'I'll make you laugh, Martin Beck, you low-down, no-good bastard,' and took off after him. Beck ran, Joe right behind, out of the theatre and up Forty-seventh Street. The stagehands tried to grab him and slowed him down a few seconds, and he lost Beck in the crowd. It was a good thing. He'd have killed him for sure.

"As it was, he only killed the Three Keatons. We'd been sick; now we were dead. Out to the sticks—even Martin Beck didn't dare to throw so well-known an act out of vaudeville entirely. But it was the Western Orpheum three-a-day for us, and for keeps this time. We were through with the big time forever.

"Three-a-day with such a tough act wore Joe and Myra out, and got me down too—the bruises never got a chance to heal. And now Joe was so sore that it was eating him up. 'You think I've been drinking? Watch me now.'

"I don't know how we lasted as long as we did. Finally—it was in February, 1917—Myra decided to call it quits. Joe was abusing her too. We were on the train from Oakland to Los Angeles when she said to me, 'Buster, God help me, I can't take any more.'

"When we got to L.A. we swiped our trunks out of the alley back of the theatre, gave the manager some money for Joe, and ran. For Muskegon. As we say in the theatre, we left Joe with egg on his face. Left him his trunk and the old beat-up table he had started with.

"I still can hardly believe we did it. Except for Myra, I guess I'd have gone on taking it."

NINE

TODAY, almost fifty years later, Buster Keaton still recalls vividly a certain March morning in 1917 and the days that followed. On that particular Monday morning it was dark and windy, cold and full of rain. He was walking rapidly down Broadway and into Times Square. The newsboys were shouting about another ship sinking. America's entry into the war seemed very close.

Buster had left his mother with relatives in Detroit and had come to New York looking for work. Though now twenty-one, it was the first train trip he had ever taken alone. He came to an office building, entered, and caught an elevator. Then he was in the private office of Max Hart, agent for the Three Keatons.

"What do you want to do with me?" he asked. He emphasized the last word very slightly.

Hart caught the emphasis. "Where are Joe and Myra?"

"I want to work alone," Buster replied.

"What's wrong?"

"We broke up the act," said Buster shortly.

Hart did not press the matter. He knew the score already. He proceeded to the point. "Are you of age?"

"Since last October."

"Okay," said Hart, reaching for his hat and coat. "Come with me. I'm going to get you in *The Passing Show*."

The Passing Show of 1917 was ready for rehearsal. The Shuberts, as Buster knew, had already announced the signing of comedian DeWolf Hopper ("Casey at the Bat"), the famous dancing duo the Dolly Sisters, and singer Irene Franklin, justly known as the Beautiful Redhead.

Now going into its sixth annual edition, *The Passing Show* was the *Follies'* most serious competition. Bidding against Ziegfeld and relying heavily on Hart to supply talent, the Shuberts staged a lively show that, over the years, had featured stars like Trixie Friganza, Charlotte Greenwood, and (at one time) Marilyn Miller; Bernard

Granville (Bonita Granville's father), Willie Howard, and Ed Wynn. *The Passing Show* had launched a future grand-opera star too, the young baritone John Charles Thomas. The Shuberts grabbed at the chance to sign Buster Keaton.

"Rehearsals begin Friday—that's in four days," said Lee Shubert. "At the Winter Garden."

An hour later, at lunch, Buster did a verbal double take. "I'm in musical comedy!" he said.

"In *The Passing Show*, to be exact," said Hart patiently. "Your salary—as shown in the contract you signed—starts at two hundred and fifty dollars a week and climbs to three hundred dollars. Your name goes up in lights on the marquee. And the Shuberts leave your comedy turn entirely up to you."

Tuesday and Wednesday went by in a daze. To prove that he was through with vaudeville, Buster (who could easily have had passes) bought a ticket for every variety bill in town and sat with the audience. It was another first for him. Afterward, however, he would slip around to the stage door to see his friends.

Each morning he walked over to check whether the Winter Garden was still there. Late each night he sat in his hotel room, unable to sleep, thinking out a routine. He was thinking in terms of silent pantomime. This in itself was not difficult. The difficulty lay, rather, in the new circumstance of working solo. He set up obstacles, with hotel chairs and tables as props, to stumble over and get tangled up with. He would think up a task for them to interfere with; but, more important, first he must create a fate for himself by setting up its inanimate pawns. Joe Keaton was gone. Someone—better, something —had to take his place.

It was not easy, he found. In fact, it was extraordinarily difficult. It denied all his twenty-one years to date. He still remembers the struggle and how, late at night, his thoughts would turn again to his family. He had wired his good news on Monday to Myra, his last line the question "Where is Joe?" She wired back, "Congratulations and good luck." Joe, she reported, had trailed her to Detroit, but she was firm about the separation. So now he was at the deserted actors' summer colony in the cottage on the lake.

By Thursday morning Buster was like a fighter at the end of training. He rose early, went to Childs' and ordered a stack of pancakes, looked at them and thrust them aside untouched. He began walking the streets, looking at the window displays without seeing them. Unthinkingly he turned a corner, head down. Someone called his name.

Buster looked up. It was Lou Anger, an old vaudeville friend of the Keatons. He had been a "Dutch" comedian, *à la* Weber and Fields, and his wife, Sophye Bernard, the original "Poor Butterfly Girl," was presently starring at the Hippodrome on Sixth Avenue.

"I'm heading for Norma Talmadge's studio," Anger said. "Come along. Just a few blocks over on Forty-eighth."

Buster hesitated, then fell in step. As they walked, Anger explained that he was now managing the Joseph M. Schenck film enterprises, which included separate producing companies for the famous Talmadge sisters, Norma and Constance. Although many movie companies were already moving to Hollywood, said Anger, Schenck preferred to operate in New York.

"You've never been in the movies, have you?" Anger asked.

"No," said Buster. "Joe got mad at them." He told Anger of the *Bringing Up Father* offer that William Randolph Hearst had made and how Joe had received it.

"Too bad," Anger observed. "You'd be in the big money now."

Buster, however, now tended to agree with Joe's decision. In his book, musical comedy rated way above motion pictures. He was not a confirmed moviegoer. To him they seemed secondhand and derivative—a painting versus the real scene. He said so to Anger, who objected strongly.

Buster defended his thesis. "I got mad at the movies myself," he said. "Remember when they turned our pet theatre, the Victoria, into a movie house and renamed it the Rialto?"

Without waiting for an answer, Buster continued, "Joe and I went there once. And what did we see? Two of the gags we invented. Who did our 'Anvil Chorus'—the bop-trading routine? Fatty Arbuckle and Al St. John. And who did my stunt of holding my own neck in the doorway—you know, with the one sleeve rolled up so the bare arm looked like someone else's trying to pull me through the door?"

"Sure," said Anger. "You used to call it The Hidden Adversary."

"Right," said Buster. "So who, of all people, do you imagine, was doing *this* gag?"

"I'll bite. Henry B. Walthall?" said Anger, referring to the star of *The Birth of a Nation.*

"America's Sweetheart," said Buster flatly. "Mary Pickford."

Anger laughed. "The Keatons," he said, "invented gags faster than anyone could copy them. But the movies are different. We used to hit each theatre once a season. But try working up gags for a new two-reeler every six weeks."

This conversation was, as Buster remembers it, the prelude to his personal introduction to one of the gag stealers, Roscoe "Fatty" Arbuckle. For it was at this juncture, as he recalls, that Anger announced that they had reached the Schenck Studios, an old warehouse between First Avenue and Second. Anger invited him to come in and look around.

They entered and proceeded upstairs. There, in separate areas of one vast, dark, barnlike loft, three production companies were at work filming three motion pictures—a feature drama, a feature high comedy, and a two-reel slapstick short. It was a strange scene of busy klieg-light islands in the dark. But to Buster Keaton it seemed not strange at all but rather homelike. For it was little different from vaudeville; it was as if vaudeville's mad, consecutive non sequiturs were being performed all at once on a great stage at night.

In the first island Eugene O'Brien and beautiful, dark-haired Norma Talmadge were doing a scene from the stage hit *Poppy*. As Buster and Lou Anger approached, the director called a break. Anger introduced Buster all around, but with some difficulty because of the noise coming from the farthest island—a series of shouts, crashes. and bumps. The two stars complained bitterly of the racket. Their director put in a firm word. Norma, he said, had been totally unable —*totally*—to hear the violinist playing just off-set to create the necessary romantic mood to inspire the emoting. If Anger didn't do something about the noise, the director added, he might as well let the violinist go. The implication was clear: no fiddling, no feeling.

They went on to the middle island, where blonde, slender Constance Talmadge was filming a comedy called *A Pair of Silk Stockings*. The noise continued. Constance's director and her leading man, Harrison Ford, put in their complaints. Constance herself seemed unrufflled. She recognized Buster instantly and told him how often she had enjoyed his vaudeville antics. Was he going into the movies?

Winking at Constance, Anger replied for Buster. "He declared war against us years ago," he said.

They moved on, coming at last to the noisy corner. The jerry-built painted set represented the interior of an old country store, its shelves and counters piled with canned goods, bottles, dry goods, and notions. The noise suddenly ceased. The floor was littered with sprawling bodies. Someone called, "Break!" and a man stepped in front of the camera holding a slate up to the lens. On the slate was scrawled "Butcher Boy, Scene 3."

The scramble untangled. Buster immediately spotted Roscoe Arbuckle's famous two hundred and sixty pounds in the always too-short and too-tight cuffless trousers and the nondescript plaid shirt. Arbuckle retrieved his too-small gray derby from beneath an extra player. It was hopelessly smashed. Someone tossed him another.

The rest of the cast consisted of some eight to ten assorted rustic characters of the type then called rubes. Among them Buster recognized Al St. John, Roscoe's nephew. Anger introduced Buster, then turned to speak to a girl who stood nearby with a script in her hand. Slender and brown-haired, she bore the Talmadge stamp.

"Natalie," said Lou, "this is Buster Keaton."

After the introduction Buster turned to Arbuckle. "I thought you were still with Keystone."

"No," Arbuckle replied. "Mr. Schenck has just set up a company for me—a real fancy French name, Comique." He pronounced it "Cumeeky." He eyed Buster with friendly respect. "Come on," he said, "and do a bit in our next scene."

"Aw, I don't think so," said Buster. "Thanks anyway."

"Well, then," said Arbuckle, "stay and see how we work." He turned and shouted, "Twenty-minute break."

Known all over the world as Fatty, Roscoe Arbuckle was only five years older than Buster, but at twenty-six he had already had four years in the movies. He was an established two-reel favorite with Mack Sennett and Keystone when Charlie Chaplin came over from vaudeville to join the outfit. For the two ensuing years, both alone and teamed with Mabel Normand—ex-model who had begun with Vitagraph in 1909, the same year that Mary Pickford began with Biograph—Arbuckle had enjoyed a popularity fully as great as that of newcomer Chaplin. With Keystone, Fatty had made a large number of pictures, including at least twenty with titles employing his familiar nickname, such as *Fatty's Flirtation*, *Fickle Fatty's Fall*, and *Fatty and Mabel Adrift*.

Then Chaplin had forged ahead sensationally. Using as a springboard Sennett's first feature-length comedy, the six-reel *Tillie's Punctured Romance*—in which he costarred with Mabel and Marie Dressler—Chaplin jumped to the rival Essanay Company for twelve hundred and fifty dollars per week. Next joining Mutual in 1916, Chaplin was now at this time (1917) reputedly earning six hundred and seventy-five thousand dollars a year. If the figures were true, in less than four years he had eclipsed Mary Pickford as filmdom's highest-paid star.

Buster Keaton knew nothing of these salaries. He did know, however, that few names were better known the world over than Fatty Arbuckle, two words everywhere pronounced with affection. Wide-eyed, innocent-looking, monumental but baby-faced, Fatty filled a special niche in the affections of all. So although famous enough himself, Buster followed his guide with a certain respect.

"Anything special you want to see first?" Arbuckle asked.

"Yes, the camera," said his gadget-conscious, machinery-minded guest. Buster all but climbed inside it, inspecting the intricate gears and threading sprockets and, in particular, the alternating shutter, that basic invention that made moving pictures possible by photographing and stopping a swift series of separate images—rather than a blur—on the film, then screening them in the same stop-and-go way.

Then he examined the carbon arc lights called kliegs and inspected the painted white lines spreading in reverse perspective on the floor to mark off the camera range; next he saw the cutting room, where scenes were edited and spliced; finally he went with Roscoe to the projection room, where some of the "dailies," or "rushes," of the previous day's shooting were run off for him.

Foreseeably, Buster automatically loved each gadget, each technical trick. But there was more here. His mind leaped ahead to grasp the essence of a new medium: a montage of perfection, with all the mistakes left on the cutting-room floor. This was no theatre of the single night with the road in between; it was an arena for inspired patience and know-how. As the phonograph could put inspiration into everlasting grooves, capturing that most evanescent of all things, music, so the films could preserve forever the happy harlequin magic of a clown.

This, he saw, was for him. As the last frame of the last rush faded on the screen, he stood up in the darkness. The twenty-minute break had been nearly an hour. "Let's do that scene," he said.

They did four or five. Dinner was forgotten, and it was nearly midnight when they knocked off.

"See you in the morning?" Arbuckle asked.

"Oh, gosh," said Buster, "I start rehearsals in *The Passing Show* tomorrow."

Next morning Buster was waiting for Max Hart when the agent arrived at his office. He told him what had happened. "I want to stay in pictures," he said.

"Then stay in pictures you should," was Hart's reply. He took the Shubert contract from his desk, tore it in two, and dropped it in the wastebasket. Then, seized by a sudden question, he looked at Buster. "What's Schenck paying you?" he asked.

"I didn't ask," said Buster.

Buster left Hart drumming on his desk and looking at the ceiling.

"You're late," said Arbuckle as he walked on the set. Not until Saturday did Buster discover that he was working for forty dollars a week. Six months later it would be one hundred dollars, and in his last pictures with Arbuckle it would climb to one hundred and twenty-five dollars. Eventually, of course, his own films would bring him two hundred thousand dollars and more in take-home pay each year.

But it can be truthfully said that it would never really matter to Keaton. What mattered was what matters to an artist—art. On that very first day in the "Cumeeky" studio, an artist fell in love.

Scene from *The Butcher Boy*, 1917. Al St. John (holding pitchfork), Roscoe Arbuckle, Buster Keaton (far right).

The Magic Silence

TEN

〉〉〉〉〉〉〉〉〉〉〉〉〉〉〉〉〉〉〉〉〉〉

I T W A S altogether remarkable how motion pictures got made without an expert around the place. It was comedy's great good luck in those days that management felt that clowning was something best left to the clowns. Experience had shown that a two-reeler could be knocked together in an average of six weeks, with the comedians and the basic staff doing all the carpentering. Arbuckle did his own directing; the gagmen included the electrician and the cameraman; actors and propman suggested camera angles and lighting; and the story, like Topsy, just grew.

"Let's make Fatty a butcher boy," someone would suggest, or, "Let's turn Fatty loose in Coney Island," and a new comedy was on its way.

It was a freewheeling chaos that ran at a minimum of expense and in a minimum of time, a Model T made at home instead of in a multimillion-dollar factory. And yet it was the golden age of silent-film comedy, the great era of great pantomime, when Chaplin, Arbuckle, and Harold Lloyd—and in a year or two Buster Keaton and then, soon after, Laurel and Hardy—stamped their unique personalities on a master product resulting from a process almost unbelievably informal.

To Buster Keaton the process seemed as normal as it really was. For the Keaton vaudeville act, similarly, had just grown, often surprising the Keatons more than anyone else. To Buster six weeks—as compared with an improvised twenty-minute stage turn—seemed like all the time in the world to produce twenty minutes of completed movie short.

From that moment after the last of the rushes in the projection room, when his decision came, Buster Keaton was committed to films. After the sad ending of the Three Keatons, still so fresh in memory, the change of scene was highly desirable. It was better, even, than musical comedy: films were not a public stage. Creatively it was still better: in place of the set routine demanded by *The Passing*

Show, film-comedy making, as Buster had discovered, could offer the same kind of open-end raceway for inspiration that vaudeville had.

And so it was that it all came about so easily. Arbuckle never formally offered him a steady job on the payroll, and Buster never asked for one. He simply went to work and was automatically paid. He immediately began to percolate in surroundings at once so challenging and permissive. He seethed with brilliant sight gags. From the start Arbuckle implicitly entrusted him with the more intricate and dangerous falls. Within three months he was assistant director.

At the end of the second week he had sent a part of his salary to Myra at Bluffton, where she had gone to live with Joe again. She sent it back with thanks and wrote that they had rented the family's second cottage, which they had built a few years earlier. With this rent plus what they had laid up, they would be all right.

"We're getting along fine," she wrote. "Your father is quieting down and beginning to take old age a little easier. The kids miss you."

Then she added a postscript—as if hastily and away from Joe's eye: "Glad you're in the movies. Should have done it a long time ago."

Buster Keaton
as he appeared
with the Arbuckle company
in Los Angeles, 1917–1918.

For Buster in *The Butcher Boy*, fate was a long series of incredibly gooey mishaps with an old-fashioned bucket of molasses. He rang every change on the theme of viscosity plus mischance. More than thirty years later Ed Wynn and he would use this sticky saga on television, with the 1917 store interior reproduced, Wynn in Fatty's original role and Buster, older but still agile, again losing the Battle of Sorghum.

Keaton's memory dredges up another of the original sequences in this his first film. "Roscoe is weighing out sacks of flour and tying them up, when a yokel fight breaks out in the store. He's to heave a sack at Al St. John and Al's to duck. This will let it arrive special delivery to the head of the innocent bystander, who, naturally, is me.

"Now, Arbuckle, wise head, knows how hard it is to wait for a thing like that without flinching. So he uses the old way: 'When I say turn—turn.' It's to be a full-figure shot of me, and it's a six-foot throw. We're set. He says, 'Turn!' I turn and that sack exploded in my face. How that man could throw! It put my neck and shoulders where my feet had been. I did a real Immelmann turn, and the sack was my motor. It took twenty minutes to get the Pillsbury's Best out of my eyes and ears.

"Now," Buster continues, "comes the tag. A month later *Butcher Boy* is released at Loew's American down on Eighth Avenue. I don't tell anyone, but I'm personally far from sure that I'll do in the movies. So I buy a ticket, go in alone, and get an aisle seat.

"Comes that scene; the sack is in the air; I half stand up in my excitement and suddenly—*pow!*—I—that's me *myself*, not me on the screen—I'm flat on my neck in the theatre aisle. Now hear this: I got up and sat down in my seat again, *honestly*, without realizing what had happened. Then I heard Arbuckle laugh. The bastard had slipped in the theatre and sat down behind me. He waited for that scene. At the very second that sack landed on the screen, he bopped me in the back of the neck. I was bruised a bit because I wasn't set for the fall, but it did one thing: it pounded it into my head that I would do in pix."

The Butcher Boy was completed in May, and next came *Rough House*. Then it turned July, and work began on *His Wedding Night*. Arbuckle's compact, congenial crew didn't even know where the time clock was. Then suddenly they needed a map to find where their studio was. The emoters' complaints about the noise finally forced the entire Comique troupe, including Luke, the acting dog, to move way uptown to space rented from Biograph on 174th Street in the

Bronx. Actually, these big studios were owned by Select Pictures head Lewis J. Selznick; Selznick, a year earlier than this, had put Norma and Constance Talmadge under contract with Select. Then Joe Schenck had signed them away from Selznick and, as Buster says, "really signed Norma—he married her too."

In those days, talent raids were a common affair and at least a compliment to your own judgment. So Selznick now had no objections to renting space to Schenck. The Arbuckleites settled noisily into the Biograph barn, where the usual quota of emoting was going on. At that moment matinee idol Robert Warwick was doing a fancy bit of celluloid, and the imported French director Maurice Tourneur was concocting another. These qualitative evaluations are those of Roscoe's slapstick company. "Everyone there," Buster tells, "was doing drawing-room pix. Tails and evening gowns were all over the place. If you spoke American out loud, monocles dropped by the dozen."

The comedians immediately endeared themselves to their new neighbors. It was noon. Everyone, from propmen to stars and from directors to management, was in the lunchroom on the fourth floor. It was a hot August day, and all the windows were open. Suddenly came raucous sounds—a series of wild *ah-oo-ah*'s from a klaxon auto horn down on the street.

Scene from *His Wedding Night*, 1918. Buster Keaton as mounted policeman.

"That's my new Hudson Super Six!" cried Al St. John. He jumped up and rushed to a window. "Get the hell away from there!" he yelled.

He was barely back at his table when the honking began again. He ran back to the window. "If you damn kids don't get away," he shouted, "I'm coming down!"

Again the horn. For the third time St. John arose. Now he took a long running leap right out the open window. As he vanished, actresses screamed. Even the directors and the hairy-chested male leads turned white under their makeup.

Then Al's arm was noticed, hooked over the sill. It was slipping, inch by inch, until only his white-knuckled hand was left, desperately grasping the woodwork.

"Save him!" an actress cried.

No one moved. Then Arbuckle said nonchalantly, "We don't need him any more. Picture's finished."

This remark seemed to release Buster, who galloped to the window and leaped to the sill to rescue Al. St. John, meanwhile, had pulled himself partly back up. The top of his head was now visible above the sill. Keaton's rescue operations were typically bumbling and disastrous, consisting in yanking at Al's hair, ears, and neck or clumsily stepping on the hand that was keeping St. John from a four-story plunge to the street.

Women were moaning now, but everyone sat transfixed. At this moment Buster's feet slipped. He slid out of the window, disappeared, and now there were two more hands clawing and clinging to the sill.

Then—whether for real or to seize the spotlight—Warwick's leading lady chose to swoon. Arbuckle doused her with a whole pitcher of ice water. Then, standing up, he yelled, "Break!"

Immediately the two clowns climbed back through the window and calmly returned to lunch. Except for them and a few teammates, the lunchroom shortly emptied. However, manager Lou Anger stayed on. He was boiling mad and full of dire predictions.

"They can't kick us out," Arbuckle said. "Our rent's paid."

"No," said Anger, "but they can keep us out of the lunchroom." Then he asked curiously, "How did you guys do it?"

"Hell," said St. John, "we were standing on the cornice of the window right below."

Like the other comics of those rugged days, Al St. John was physically tough. Nevertheless, when one sees the hard bodily contact

Scene from *Goodnight Nurse*, 1918. Buster Keaton and Roscoe Arbuckle.

and the fabulous falls of the old two-reelers, one wonders how any-one ever walked away from such scrimmages. On one particular occasion, St. John didn't. It was during the filming of *His Wedding Night*. The situation was comic but not in the script. After one typical roughhouse, Al stayed on the floor, face down and legs doubled under. It was not acting. It was real. It took five minutes to revive him.

Arbuckle, at times, could be very practical. "All in a day's work," he said. Fatty, however, had more armor than skinny St. John. His fat was actually mostly hard flesh with muscle and sinew underneath. As Buster says, "He was hard as a brick wall and fast on his feet. No man that size ever took such falls."

Two interested people watched the rushes next morning. After this particular scene, they asked for a repeat and then for still another. Then they spotted it: an extra furtively aiming a dropkick at the head of St. John, who was already down on his hands and knees.

Al leaned over and whispered to Buster, "The son of a bitch deliberately chose me. I wonder why?"

Instead of replying, Buster turned to Roscoe. In a slow, judicious tone he remarked, "That scene looked flat."

"You think so?" Arbuckle said.

Anger chipped in. "Well, reshoot. Set's still up and the extras are all here."

In the retake a certain extra caught it from both sides. St. John chopped him with a left hook and crossed with a right, whereupon, from his stance on top of a wardrobe, Buster aimed a Borani at him. It was the extra who was out cold this time.

Arbuckle showed concern at last. "God Almighty," he said, "don't take things so serious. We're not making *The Birth of a Nation*."

It was still easy to break into the movies. Many high-school girls followed the lead of Norma Talmadge, who, it was reported, had taken two snapshots of herself to Vitagraph in 1910, was signed, and almost immediately had a good part in *A Tale of Two Cities* with Maurice Costello.

Some of the newcomers, in fact, unlike Norma, were not seriously interested in a picture career. For example, there was a beautifully stacked sixteen-year-old blonde who got a part with Arbuckle's Comique company that same summer. They were working on Coney Island.

The third day on location Anger said, "We'll go back to the beginning and shoot everything over."

"What happened?" Buster whispered to Arbuckle.

"Little Cornelia ain't with us any more," Arbuckle replied. "She came in my dressing room," he went on. "Says, 'Mr. Arbuckle, which one shall I wear?' holding two bathing suits in front of her. Drops one, then the other, and there she is in the buff."

Buster stared. "So you *fired* her. Are you nuts?'

"Nuts my eye," said Fatty. "I had enough sense to get the hell

Scene from *Fatty at Coney Island*, 1917.

out of there fast. The door knocked her mother down. She was all set to bust in. Daughter would scream. Ma would yell, 'Rape!' And here would come Pa with the shotgun."

"Oh," said Buster. It made sense, like another sentence added to The Lecture by Joe. Offscreen he and Roscoe became inseparable companions. Their evenings on the town were as often stag as with dates, but in either case they traveled in top style. Roscoe's new car was a standout even on Park Avenue.

"Where did you fall into a block-long boat like this?" asked Buster, fondling a fender.

"It was free," said Arbuckle, "or, rather, the key was free, and the car just automatically came with it." Then he told Buster how Schenck had lured him from Sennett and Keystone with a big salary boost and how they had ratified the deal without a scrap of paper but only the traditional handshake. At its completion, a key was left in the comedian's palm.

"It's for a new Rolls Royce," said Schenck.

The duo's favorite haunt was the old Reisenweber's, a café-cabaret on Eighth Avenue just below Columbus Circle. Reisenweber had music, dining, and dancing on each of its three floors. The top floor was very much in the news just then with a new music called jass (later, jazz). The five-piece Original Dixieland Jass Band had brought a new and irresistible two-beat rhythm straight out of Basin Street in New Orleans.

Trumpeter Nick La Rocca and his hot combo had just capped their Manhattan triumph by making a phonograph record that was well on its way to becoming Victor's first million-sale disc. With the jazz furore now national, everyone was jamming into Reisenweber's, while the old-line dance orks were firing fiddlers, lining up brass men, and rehearsing like crazy to catch up with the New Thing. The Reisenweber patrons were particularly delighted, it seemed, by the Dixielanders' casual use of such musical adjuncts as derby hats, cuspidors, and "plumber's friends" to wave in front of trumpet and trombone for that eerie new "wah-wah" sound. Equally delightful, too, was the warm, closely entwined sort of social dancing that the jazzmen had brought up from Mahogany Hall and the backwater Cajun bayous to go with their propulsive music.

One evening, immaculately tuxedoed, the two comedians got off the elevator on the Dixieland floor at Reisenweber's (management retained a waltz orchestra for squares and senior citizens). Fatty was recognized at once by all, and Buster by a considerable number.

Applause broke out. The two bowed. The applause grew. Both recognized it as a directive. Comedians must be funny, aging though the compulsion may be.

Arbuckle looked around. The smorgasbord table caught his eye. He grabbed an entire twenty-pound roast turkey and, with the standard custard-pie technique, threw. Gravy, grease, and all, it caught Buster full in the face. Arbuckle bowed solemnly and proceeded to a table.

Buster, however, collapsed back into the open elevator, and the operator, confused, slammed the door and shot down. Buster climbed to his feet in the descending car. The innocent-bystander bit was not a fixation with him. "Down to the kitchen," he commanded.

The kitchen was in the basement. There the scullery help scraped the worst of the grease and dressing off Buster's tuxedo, shirtfront, and face. When he could see clearly again, he spotted a baker standing by the oven. "Got a custard pie?" Buster asked. "Give me two—hot."

He hurried back upstairs. All eyes were still on their idol, Fatty, when, from thirty feet away, Buster yelled, "Turn!" and Arbuckle automatically obeyed. Buster's aim had never been better.

New York was fun, but Hollywood was beckoning. Joe Schenck and his brother Nicholas were native New Yorkers. They had made a preliminary fortune in amusement parks like the Palisades on the Hudson, and they were hard to convince. Actually, they were already old hat: the trek to the West Coast was well advanced. It was hard to find good Manhattan outdoor locations, harder to keep the crowds away, altogether impossible to control the weather.

In September *Fatty at Coney Island* was finished. "We're pulling up stakes," Arbuckle announced. "Moving to California."

Buster, who had been on cloud six with a salary jump from forty dollars to one hundred dollars a week, moved up to cloud seven. He telephoned Myra in Muskegon and said, "We're in." She and Joe decided to go on ahead to rent a family-size apartment in Long Beach. This was where the Hockheimer Studios to be used by Arbuckle were located.

At the end of September, Lou and Sophye Anger, Arbuckle, St. John, Natalie Talmadge, Buster, and assorted cameramen and technicians entrained on the New York Central's Twentieth Century Limited, westbound. It was a party all the way. From Hollywood they all drove out to Long Beach, a honking, jubilant caravan. It was nearly six in the evening when they arrived.

"Come over to my new apartment for dinner," said Buster to Roscoe and Natalie.

Their footsteps on the stairs and their voices announced them to Buster's parents. Before anyone could ring the doorbell, Joe had the door open and his hand out to grasp his son's. Myra called from the kitchen, "I'll be right out."

In a few moments she backed out into the living room. "Buster," she said, turning, "do you remember what day this is?"

It was October 4, and she was carrying a birthday cake with twenty-two lighted candles.

ELEVEN

I N 1917, California's potent Chamber of Commerce was more important to the state, by far, than either political party. Its institutional advertising far eclipsed what Florida could then whip up. In addition to her built-in advantages of natural landscaping and natural air conditioning, the Golden State had had a recent and most favorable inspection from the large national attendance at the 1915 Panama-Pacific International Exposition in San Francisco as well as at the smaller concurrent exposition in San Diego.

The California ads had the advantage of a product by and large hard to oversell, one that backed up all but the most extravagant claims. It was all, indeed, much as advertised. *Emptor*, naturally, still had to *caveat*, but nevertheless the celebrated sun did shine down on the celebrated real estate, the mountains were lofty and handsomely placed, and the Pacific Ocean did indeed wash their feet. It was like the postcards but bigger and more real.

As to climate, beyond the sun's evident cooperation, the air was not all publicity hot air. The kind that you breathed, rather than listened to, was clear and fresh, not to be soiled by smog for a long time to come. It was still scented with eucalyptus and jasmine, not factory and exhaust exhalations. And for all the millions already there, as well as the threatened depopulation of Iowa, the roar of the traffic jam had not yet drowned out the native sounds of wind and sea.

Just west of Los Angeles was a climate of another sort. Equally publicized, it was the climate of a glamour almost indefinable, a sort of magical spell that is hard to recapture or even to imagine today. It was, indeed, whatever anyone chose to call it: a climate of the mind or of the spirit, a hallucination, an American myth, a national autohypnosis. But it did exist. It was the climate of Hollywood and the movies.

When Buster Keaton came to California, not as vaudeville migrant but as resident worker, the Glamour Decade was just beginning. Else-

Buster Keaton
and Roscoe Arbuckle
in *Moonshine*, 1918.

where that decade has been called the Jazz Age because it was loud
with trumpet and sax. It has also been called the Age of the Lost
Generation. It was all these things, but, outstandingly, it was the
Age of the Movies.

It was a time of unabashed hero (and heroine) worship. Babe
Ruth, in fact—and even Lindbergh—got only the edges of it. The
full treatment went to the movies and to movie stars, the actors and
—most particularly—the actresses. Not merely distance but silence
compounded the magic. Hollywood was a Valhalla or an Olympus,
a silver-screen abode with goddesses living apart behind a wall of
silence. Their beautiful bodies were ethereal yet real, their lips
framed soundless words on a wavelength we could not hear, their
gestures stirred a different air, their noble remoteness called us to
worship.

We happily shared this gaudy daydream in those ten years from
our entry into World War I until that day in 1927 when a cork-
blackened ex-vaudevillian named Al Jolson broke the enchanted si-

lence. Alas! When the shadows spoke they became mortal. Oh, the glamour died slowly, but die it did. We still kept our love goddesses —but now, perhaps, because they were so sadly not immortal any more. Most of all, after the silence was shattered, we turned to those who were not merely mortal but even tragically so—ill-starred stars, all of them: Mabel Normand and Thelma Todd, Jean Harlow and Greta Garbo and poor Marilyn Monroe.

But in 1917 the spell was just being cast. Hollywood was laying out its celestial subdivisions—Culver City, Universal City, and the rest. Long Beach, vacation and retirement capital of Iowa, was then a Hollywood branch. Here Roscoe Arbuckle and his comic demigods promptly went to work. Two weeks after arrival they started the picture *Out West*, hailing their arrival and celebrating unmetered sunshine, rent-free plains, and oak-studded hills, where, as Buster remarked happily, "a chase can be a Chase with a capital C."

Comique had a beautiful leading lady built on petite demigoddess lines. Brunette Alice Lake had acting ability, a comic flair, and that supreme talent of slapstick days—so rare in women—the willingness to absorb physical punishment in the service of laughter.

Natalie Talmadge, for the time being, had a room in the Keatons' oversize flat. Natalie had been elevated to secretary-treasurer, a big jump in responsibility from script girl. The Comique Film Corporation operated autonomously under Lou Anger, with no interference from Joe Schenck or from a board of directors. The staff evolved plots, requisitioned funds and matériel, and rolled out a two-reel short every five to seven weeks. Joe Schenck distributed them, and Arbuckle, just like Norma and Constance in their own producing units, drew a generous salary plus 25 percent of the net. Schenck was wise: he didn't oversteer, and his units made money hand over fist.

The Arbuckle comedies poured out. *The Bell Boy*, begun in early December, was completed by mid-January. A weekend off, and *Moonshine* was started. There was no retooling between new models. There was hardly a deep breath drawn.

It was a time, for all, of gratification in strenuous doing. Buster, as Arbuckle once said, "lived in the camera." All day he devised gags and sequences and the physical or mechanical ways to make them work. At night he dreamed them. Like his father when young, Buster drew on a seemingly bottomless reservoir of energy.

Myra, now a young forty, relaxed gratefully into housekeeping, with time to roll her own Bull Durham cigarettes and to enjoy her customary single neat shot of bourbon morning and evening.

Only Joe Keaton did not share in all this. He was sick with idle-

Arbuckle's Comique company on location. Third from left, Lou Anger, then

ness. His world had begun and ended with vaudeville. He had shaken hands with old age but retained his enmity. He had moderated his drinking but retained his thirst. Mostly he missed his old cronies. Not caring either way, he strolled the pier or fished the surf.

Once in a while he came to watch a shooting, and Arbuckle would rally him. "Come on, Mr. Keaton," he would say, "play Alice's father."

Alice would chip in, "You can kick me, Mr. Keaton."

And Buster would urge, "Come on, Dad. The camera won't bite."

But Joe Keaton was already bitten, and hard-bitten. The movies were third-rate entertainment, and he had his reputation to think of. Finally, out of boredom, he agreed to accompany Myra and go along with the company on location for *Moonshine*. Perhaps the title helped him sublimate his thirst.

Keaton with Alice Lake, Arbuckle, and St. John (kneeling).

Buster devised a camera gag for *Moonshine* that was the despair of the other comedy companies. A limousine drove up and stopped, its side presented to the camera. Then the camera moved directly in front of it, the door on one side opened, and, one after another, fifty-four (count 'em) "revenooers" got out of the car. For all the eye could tell, all fifty-four had been in the car at once. It was a preposterous, delicious gag.

Another company decided to do it immediately, but they would change the uniforms and raise the ante: 108 cops would alight from a taxicab. They knew exactly how: tape off half the camera lens (to one side of the vertical center line), then have the 108 men walk through the cab and step out on the other side, which the untaped half of the lens was recording. Now rewind the film to the starting point, move the tape over to cover the other half of the lens, and reshoot the film, this time recording the side of the cab the cops had entered but now with the door closed and no one near.

The film was then developed and printed, and the whole company crowded into the projection room to enjoy the rush that would top Arbuckle's. What they saw elicited groans, not cheers. Something was wrong. The side of the car from which the men were exiting was jiggling up and down like a mad cocktail shaker; the half with the closed door was as solid as Gibraltar and Prudential.

The burned technicians ruefully figured out what had happened: when the men were moving through, the car jiggled on its springs; when, with the car empty, the other side was being shot, it stayed still.

They junked the sequence and gave up without ever discovering Buster's secret: *his* car never rested on the ground, so its springs were not in operation. Using four tire jacks (concealed behind each wheel), he had raised the car by its frame until its wheels were one inch off the road. In effect, the car body became a solid platform upon which the action, both photographed and unphotographed, took place.

Roscoe Arbuckle, no less than Buster Keaton, made movies primarily for the fun of it. He was no credit hog. And there was the remarkable setup of the company: no meddling from above. Even Lou Anger let the actors and technicians alone. No one was paid to be an expert, so real expertness, wherever it cropped up, was welcomed. It was the ideal spot for Buster Keaton's motion-picture apprenticeship.

History has treated Roscoe Arbuckle shabbily. He is remembered as a rapist and murderer—the most tragic of ironies for a man who ran out of his dressing room at a nude girl's intrusion—but the facts proved, even to his jury, that he was innocent. Roscoe Arbuckle was just what he seemed to be on the screen—a fat boy who never grew up; a person of the greatest simplicity, warmth, and generosity; a man who liked everyone and liked to be liked. This is the man whom his friend Buster Keaton remembers today. But he was soon to stand trial *three* times for one alleged crime—with most of the prosecution outside the courtroom—and it is by this that he is generally remembered today.

But that was still in the future in that early spring of 1918. The incredible new green was flowing down over the California hills like vernal honey, and Buster and Roscoe seemed to have tapped the fountain of youth. At seven-thirty in the morning they sat through the rushes, chose the takes, and decided the editing. By nine, if interiors were slated, shooting began. Otherwise cars drove to location with actors, crew, equipment, and box lunches. The cameras ground away until the sun got low, and the cameraman would say "Light's getting too yellow." This, of course, would make dark pictures. Even then Arbuckle might say, "Then let's do those moonlight scenes now." During all this time, except for the half-hour lunch break, the actors had tumbled and toiled, chases had succeeded falls in the strenuous, red-blooded stuff of silent-film comedy.

Back they went then in cars jolting over plains and mountain passes. Dinner, and Arbuckle would go to the telephone. "Buster," he might say, "*The Bell Boy* is previewing tonight at the Garrick Theatre. I'll be by in twenty minutes."

They would start the long drive to downtown Los Angeles. By the time they had got from Long Beach to Hollywood, they could see the giant searchlight beams stabbing the dark sky around a theatre still miles away. Shunning the official appearances that Anger continually pleaded for, the two stars preferred this kind of informal attendance, preferably unrecognized.

"Gonna be a hell of a crowd," Arbuckle would say. "Let's park off a ways."

Then they would sneak in through the rear door, feel their way in the dark, and squeeze into any available seats. *The Bell Boy* would already be on, and soon gigantic Fatty took a gigantic fall. Then a wiseacre would speak up. "You know he never did that at all. They have what they call doubles for all those dangerous things."

Arbuckle, not to mention Keaton, had been bugged often enough by these minor-league cynicisms. On at least one occasion that Buster recalls, after this kind of sniping from a lady directly in front, Roscoe forgot himself, tapped her on the shoulder, and whispered, "Pssst! Lady, that was no double, that was me." She turned and did a double take that would have been a credit to Fatty himself.

But there were not previews every night. Some pleasant evenings were spent booby-trapping the studio. Music boxes would go into the cameras, piano wires would be stretched just above the floor, buckets of water would be balanced above doorways, coat sleeves and pants legs sewn together, and Fourth of July torpedoes triggered into desk drawers. The whole studio became a minefield. It was open season on all.

Even studio guests enjoyed no immunity. With his penchant for titles, Buster named one luckless visitor the Yearning One. This was

A visitor at the Comique studios: Charles Chaplin with Buster Keaton; the studio owner, Hockheimer; Lou Anger at far right, 1917.

a well-favored and sharply dressed stage-door Johnny who began coming every day to watch Alice Lake. He was always standing just out of camera range, undressing her with his eyes.

"Who the hell is this bozo?" Roscoe finally asked.

"Why ask me?" said Alice. "I don't know the guy from Adam."

So next day the Yearning One got the pie. It was near the end of the Custard Pie Era, which had begun years before at Sennett with Ford Sterling and Arbuckle. It was a fine art, though a dying one: custard pies for brunets or dark clothes; blackberry pies for blonds or light clothes. The pies were real and edible but reinforced: the bottom crust was double gauge to avoid breakage in transit. And the pitching was big league.

They were walking through a pie routine before pitching and shooting: the standard ploy—Arbuckle throw, St. John duck, Keaton get pie in puss. Then Roscoe saw the Yearning One lined up perfectly just beyond Buster. A glance telegraphed the change in plans.

"Okay," said Arbuckle, "hand me a pie. One take will do it."

One take did. Arbuckle snapped, rather convincingly, "For God's sake, Buster, *you* weren't supposed to duck!" Then, turning to the spot of the accident, he began in regretful tones, "I'm so sorry, sir . . ."

But the Yearning One was halfway to the exit, scraping custard and swearing in muffled tones.

Determined to follow script and apologize to someone, Roscoe turned to Alice. "What can I say," he intoned, "after I say I'm sorry?"

The slapstick ingenue did the *Broken Blossoms* bit, everyone laughed, and they went back to work.

Although the studio was closed on Sunday, the Sabbath was not a day of rest. It was a gagsters' holiday. Something could always be dreamed up to consume energy—baseball, picnics, fishing trips to the nearby mountains, card tournaments, or Special Operations. Booby-trapping the studio would be a typical example of the Special Operation. One of the more locally famous ones involved the costly, rolling, acred bluegrass lawn that framed a prime tourist showplace, actress Pauline Frederick's mansion. Keaton, Arbuckle, and St. John got up at the crack of dawn, dressed as water-company workmen, "borrowed" a water-company truck, and moved in on Miss Frederick. Before her butler awakened and, in turn, alerted her, the shovels had divoted nearly an acre as the crew looked for a water "leak." Such was the unique climate of early Hollywood that this beau geste landed them not in jail but at Pauline's breakfast table. And the water company thanked them for borrowing the truck.

Weekday nights were conventional little affairs of dining and dancing, Buster with Natalie and Roscoe with Alice; cabaret and speakeasy hopping up and down the coast from Venice to Pacific Palisades; home at two and up at six-thirty to view the rushes.

With all these goings-on, there was time left over to go into the gravel business—nearly. The Arbuckleites had found an outdoor location in Long Beach, near the studio—a large gravel pit dug into the side of a hill. It served for many desert gully or ravine close-ups. With bushes stuck into the gravel it became mountainside scenery. All day while they shot there, work was going on just out of camera range: horse-drawn wagons arriving, loading up with gravel, and driving away.

Chatting with a teamster one day, Buster asked, "What do you get for a load?"

"Five dollars," was the reply. "Haul five-six-a loads a day."

"Hear that Roscoe?" said Buster. "What say we buy the pit? Hire drivers and wagons, sell gravel, and make a hundred dollars a day. And still have our location."

"Keen!" said Roscoe.

"A natural!" said St. John.

The directors had voted. Buster addressed the driver again. "Do you know if this pit is for sale?"

"Sure thing," he answered. "My brother-in-law, he own the pit. He sell and go back to Italy."

They pursued the matter. The property, they discovered, consisted of about twenty acres and could be bought for two thousand dollars cash. They went to Lou Anger. Five hundred apiece, they told him, and they were in the gravel business.

Lou turned on the fisheye. "Nuts!" he said. "We're in the motion-picture business. Remember?"

The comedians were outvoted but not convinced. They considered going in themselves on thirds, but Arbuckle vetoed this.

"No point in getting Lou sore," he said. "And maybe Joe Schenck too."

So gravel was out.

Then, overnight, Buster Keaton was no longer an actor. He was a soldier, drafted, assigned to the 40th Infantry, and on his way to Camp Kearney near San Diego. There he went into a three-week quarantine, in common with hundreds of new draftees, before drilling would start. This quarantine, compulsory then, was to detect and weed out any contagious diseases among the newcomers. But the

Natalie Talmadge Keaton, 1923.

quarantine was suddenly cut short. Two weeks after his arrival the whole division, contagious or not, was called into action. Buster was thrown, completely untrained, into the ranks of what had the makings of a crack outfit—which it would eventually become. He was handed a rifle and fell in for assembly.

That was that. Fate had arrived, on time and hand in hand with The Accident. The comic nightmare began.

"Forward, *march!*"

One Buster Keaton scurried to keep in step; the other Buster Keaton watched fatalistically. The first Buster was getting by—quietly, frantically imitating his neighbors to his side and front. He was number two in the rear rank of the old-fashioned squad of eight men.

"To the rear, *march!*"

The whole northbound company turned on outstretched left feet and headed south. All but Buster. He was down. The soldier in front of him, swinging around like a revolving robot, had suddenly faced him, and his fist, clutching the rifle butt, had caught Buster square on the chin.

Orders are orders: the whole company began walking over him; then a man stumbled over him, cursed, fell, and the ranks began piling up. Orders or no orders, forward movement halted. The rest is a 40th Division legend. Corporals, sergeants, even shavetails, working like football referees, untangled the pileup.

Someone fanned Buster's face. Slowly he came to, then, faintly, he asked, "Did we win?"

But the war was not being won that swiftly, in one random, profane, shotless skirmish. Hostilities were still on. They were shipping east under sealed orders. Joe and Myra had given up the Long Beach apartment and were on their way in the same direction to take Harry and Louise out of school. Natalie Talmadge, on patriotic leave of absence, was touring with actor William S. Hart selling Liberty bonds. At the very time that Buster and his buddies were climbing aboard the Santa Fe troop special, Natalie was in Bluffton at Jingles' Jungle visiting Myra Keaton. The Liberty bond troup having reached Chicago, she had gone to Muskegon for a day.

Nearly forty years later and not long before she died, Myra was reminiscing, with that occasional, detailed acuity of old age. She recalled the visit and Natalie's showing her a good-luck signet ring she had bought and was sending to Buster. Myra recalled, too, her private thoughts: *A ring will soon be going the other way, looks like to me.*

TWELVE

❧❧❧❧❧❧❧❧❧❧❧❧❧❧❧❧❧❧❧❧❧❧

M YRA KEATON'S private prophecy almost immediately
showed signs of coming true. Natalie Talmadge's tour took
her to the East Coast. Buster Keaton's troop train had preceded her.
Fate—or, perhaps, only a world war—was putting the two in close
proximity at a time of heightened feelings, a time of farewells.

Buster knew that Natalie was apt to be with Joe Schenck and
Norma at their big Long Island country house. Natalie, however,
thanks to the 40th's sealed orders, knew only vaguely that Buster was
in the East, soon to embark for France and the battlefields.

Buster's company was in line for vaccine shots—and under strict
orders to stay in line. Except, of course, "if you have to go," and for
other very special or urgent reasons, unspecified. The line was in the
open sun. It was hot. The line seemed completely stationary. Buster
fidgeted. An hour passed. He saw his topkick standing alone.

Buster practiced his line to get just the right touch of deference,
then went over. "Excuse me. Can I see my mother for a few minutes
in the YMCA Hut?"

The sergeant seemed about to bark a negative, then, looking at
the pale, sad, unsmiling Keaton face, he undoubtedly remembered
the brutal pileup on the parade ground with this sad young man
beneath it all. "Okay, soldier," he said, "fifteen minutes with Mom,
and right back in line."

Mom was a telephone in the Hut. He got through to Natalie, as
he had hoped. This left ten of the fifteen minutes. Not to waste
them, Buster drank a Coke, read the sports pages, and smoked a
cigarette before rejoining the line. It had moved six inches in his
absence.

From time to time Buster glanced covertly at his wristwatch. He
sweated out a full three-quarters of an hour, then took further
evasive action. He held up two fingers in the accepted grade-school
code denoting both emergency and degree of emergency. The sergeant
was looking away. Buster inserted the two fingers between his lips

and whistled loudly. When the sergeant turned, Buster had the fingers aloft again. The sergeant, less amiably this time, growled, "All right, *all right*—if you gotta go, you gotta go."

A quick, circuitous route took Buster past the latrine and on to the far side of the YMCA Hut. A Rolls town car was sitting there. A lot of brass were standing around, shirt-sleeved in the heat and with no signs of rank except small insignia on their shirt collars and the leather puttees or cordovan boots they were wearing. Their attention was directed at Natalie in the town car. They paid no attention to Buster as he approached from the far side, his baggy "issue" pants, OD leggings, and heavy brogans all hidden by the car. The Schenck chauffeur held the door open, Buster stepped in beside Natalie, and they were off before anyone knew what was taking place.

It was Private Keaton's first AWOL. They turned toward Long Island, heading, Natalie said, to a friend's estate for an early buffet supper.

Hours later Buster eased back into the inoculation line unnoticed. Five days later he was halfway across the Atlantic in a slow, cautious convoy. They were in submarine waters; however, Buster's dangers were not subs but his own dependable, private perils. His ship's bunk proved to be the only one overlooked in the preembarkation fumigating. In advance of the trenches, he got the frontline body lice called cooties.

His detail sergeant caught him surreptitiously scratching. "I'll not report this higher up," he said, "or we'll get a general quarantine. Take this surgical soap, go to the showers, and keep scrubbing till I tell you when."

Buster was in the shower when the submarine alarms began ringing all over the ship. He heard the rush of feet all around. Covered from head to foot with green germicidal lather, he pondered. Was it another drill? Or was it really a sub this time, and all hands to the lifeboats? The second contingency was too likely to brook any delay. Out on deck he dashed and into his place in line, clothed only in soap.

It was another drill, of course.

Then, France, and they were billeted in empty warehouses, barns, and cellars in a village south of Paris. It rained day and night. The natives believed it was caused by the artillery barrages, like a distant thunder that never let up. For the first time the war, though still far away, seemed close to Buster. It was the sound of Death stalking the pitted fields and the ruined cities.

Then, suddenly, Buster learned that even this bucolic little village, so many kilometers behind the frontline batteries, was not safe. Danger came from the rain and the unmitigated dampness. Everyone had colds. Buster, in addition, had developed an ear infection that made him for the time being almost completely deaf. But he was not allowed time to nurse either ailment. His company officers had discovered that he was not only a comedian but a crack poker player. He was invited, that is, commanded, to play nearly every night. The officers lived in an old château some distance from the troop billets. To pass the guard lines at night Buster had been given a special pass.

Late one pitch-black, rainy night, pass in hand, he was sloshing back to quarters tired but cheerful, as he had quit way ahead. He looked around for the sentry but visibility was zero. It was like walking underwater.

"Halt!" came a call from the dark.

Deaf from the ear infection, Buster splashed on. Twice more the sentry shouted. Then he clicked a shell into the firing chamber of his rifle and raised it. But the sharp metallic click had penetrated Buster's numbed ears. He whirled and threw up his hands. "Friend!" he shouted, having heard this term used in frontier and Indian tales.

The guard approached with extreme wariness, his finger on the trigger. His bayonet point was touching Buster's chest before he recognized him. Then relief touched off his anger. "Why you stupid, *stupid* bastard!" he said.

"I couldn't agree with you more," Keaton replied.

His company—both brass and rank and file—had discovered that in many ways the little private was a good man to have around. The matter of linguistics was a case in point. While everyone was beating his brains out against the language barrier, Buster could pantomime all he needed to say. On one occasion his miming produced one of the most severely rationed of all French foods, the long crisp loaves of oven-baked bread.

"I wangled this out of commissary," the top sergeant had said one day, pointing to a huge wedge of Canadian cheddar.

"Hey, look!" said Buster's corporal, "I've got some red wine stashed."

"Call Keaton," said the sergeant.

"What did I do now?" said Keaton, appearing.

The topkick explained, "We need bread."

"Wait ten minutes," said Buster, and went to the village bakery.

The following—as Keaton later reproduced it in a two-reel comedy —is substantially what happened. He entered the bakery and faced the baker, a kind man, a family man with sons in the service, and a good baker. Also a man who spoke no English.

Buster went immediately into his routine, thought up on the way over. He searched his pockets for ration tickets, found none, shook his head dolefully, and rubbed his stomach. Then he went back out the front door. In seconds he was back, but this time he tiptoed in, looked carefully all around, his eyes gliding unseeing right past the baker and clearly registering the thought, *Aha! No one is here!* He whistled softly and nonchalantly as he carefully laid a franc on the counter, partly concealed a great loaf under his greatcoat, and—this time rapidly—headed toward the door. He was halfway out when the baker called to him loudly in French. Buster turned and came back with genuine defeat on his face.

The baker, sternly it seemed, reached out for the purloined—or purchased—loaf. He placed it on the counter, then took another of equal size from the shelf, rolled the two loaves together in paper, and handed them to Buster. He was smiling broadly as the comedian hurried out.

Buster has also recalled how his miming established charge accounts for his company with the village shopkeepers. As entry wedge he chose a good-looking young woman who ran a *confiserie*. "I–O–U, I–O–U," he repeated over and over while pointing to a piece of paper that bore the mystic symbols. Then he pantomimed the whole credit deal, from the taking of the goods and the signing of the IOU to the debtor's standing in line at the paymaster's and then rushing back to wipe out his debt. For a final touch he kissed her hand and murmured, "*Merci!*" With that start, all were on tick everywhere.

"No one got gypped," says Buster. "I had to become bill collector too, but I rounded 'em up every payday before their dough was gone."

He had a little act that this village—and others where the company subsequently billeted—did not soon forget. The citizens would all be watching during assembly in the public square. After the drill ritual and the command "Compan-*ee* dis-*missed!*" the soldiers would disperse almost instantly. Then would come the Keaton ritual the town was waiting for. He would still be standing there in his spot, obliviously fixing or adjusting a tunic button. He would speak from the side of his mouth to the empty space beside him, get no answer, slowly look around. Then he would do a double take, drop his gun, panic, run a few steps. He would stop, creep back, peer around a corner, then run for his gun. Ten feet away from it he would trip and fall, slide on his face, retrieve the gun, then march smartly away.

Everyone would be laughing. Buster would bow to each side of the square, then march to the sidewalk café for coffee. It was a simple little ritual and always the same—it never varied from day to day. It seemed deeply satisfying to the villagers.

Within less than three years from this time, Buster Keaton's own two-reel comedies would begin finding their way from Hollywood to France. The French, as a whole, would welcome the newcomer and would give him the affectionately vernacular nickname Malec, by which they still know him. But in not a few villages and small towns Malec was not a newcomer but an old friend of theirs returning, one who had managed to lighten some pretty grim days.

Then, suddenly, came the Armistice.

"For God's sake!" said Buster to a sergeant. "I can't go back without even *seeing* a trench!"

"You're right," said the sergeant. He wangled a leave for them, and they took off with lunches and several bottles of wine. On the road they hitched a ride on an empty AEF truck to Amiens. From there they walked out to Abbeville, a town that had been taken and retaken, shelled and reshelled, until not a wall was standing.

For an hour or so they strolled and talked among the deserted ruins. It was past noon when the sergeant announced that he was breaking out the lunch. Buster was some paces away. He had just found an unexploded hand grenade. He took careful aim at the gun slot, or embrasure, in a concrete pillbox that stood barely five yards away. He pulled the grenade pin, wound up, and let fly. It was an easy shot, but the great pie thrower missed.

"Hit the dirt!" he yelled, and both men dived headfirst into a muddy trench that lay between them. A second later the grenade exploded. The topkick crawled out of the trench and began grimly scraping the mud off his uniform. Buster followed.

"We'll eat," said the sergeant. "*Then* we're going *back*."

Halfway through the second bottle of *vin ordinaire*, however, the sergeant began to relax. He shaded his eyes and gazed off to the south in the direction of Paris, only a hundred miles or so away. He began, audibly, to change his mind about going back to barracks.

Quite predictably, next day they were in Paris taking in the sights. Three days later they were still there, with their leaves expired. They were down to a hundred francs between them, which, even at the old-

Buster Keaton with the AEF Sunshine Players in France, February, 1919.

time valuation, left them the equivalent of less than twenty-five dollars American. They had surrendered judgment, however, in going to Paris at all. Once there, they had made no effort to reclaim it. Their next decision seemed to them eminently sensible: the hundred francs should be spent, all at once, for a magnum of the finest champagne. They shook hands on the deal and walked into the fanciest place they could find.

The wine was just being poured when the sergeant called, " 'Ten-shun!" and leaped to his feet.

An American chicken colonel was just entering. The colonel said quietly, "As you were, men." As he spoke he glanced at Buster.

Buster, saluting, looked at him. Buster gasped. It was Alice Lake's old admirer, the Yearning One. He only too evidently recognized in Buster the movie actor who—to the colonel's downfall—had ducked a custard pie on a certain day in Long Beach.

Buster moved with his characteristic quick takeoff. He was at the door when he called back to the sergeant, "Come on! Come *on!*"

With the money gone and the champagne irretrievable, the AWOL duo was in a bad spot. They had no business in Paris any-way. Both knew that it was off limits to all American soldiers except authorized personnel. They walked and hitched back to their base,

Buster Keaton back from France, 1919, with Arbuckle and St. John.

let down and apprehensive. But it was a relaxed time; the local inns were buying the drinks, and even the brass were sedated by peace. The prodigals got a tongue-lashing. Buster, by then a single-stripe corporal, got two days of KP. Everyone was eating on the town anyway.

Soon the euphoria wore off. All became restive, more and more anxious to be home. Red tape suddenly snarled a transoceanic transport system that had performed logistic miracles as long as the seas still swarmed with U-boats. While transportation stretched, gaped, and then slowly mobilized, entertainment groups were hastily organized from the ranks. Buster led one for his division. Scenery was slapped together, costumes were rigged up, and a thirty-six-piece regimental band was assigned to the troupe.

Without even time for rehearsals, the mainstay was old-fashioned burnt-cork Negro minstrelsy with its banjo skits, dances, and olio of barbershop harmony and corny jokes—a medium not only familiar and easy for untrained performers but familiar and easy for audiences. If it offered no surprises, it presented no challenges.

Buster's solo spot was a bit called Princess Rajah. Buster had known a real Princess Rajah—or at least a Hoboken gal with that stage name. When he met her she was a muscle dancer (read: belly dancer) in vaudeville. One of those well-stacked beauties with rippling parts, she had first attracted attention at the Jamestown Exposition in 1907. She went on to Huber's Museum on Fourteenth Street and then was snapped up by Willie Hammerstein for his Victoria Theatre. Rajah did a Cleopatra turn with a bunch of defanged live snakes, which, as Buster recalls, were always getting hungry and wandering out from her dressing room and slithering around the theatre. Rajah's appeal, and her career, faded rapidly after the censors removed much of the real aphrodisiac drama of her original exposition turn. This saddened the public and led one theatre critic to write: "A lot has been cut out of the middle and added to the feet and hands."

Keaton portrayed the New Jersey odalisque wearing a little bra of brass dog tags and a skirt of mess kits, knives, and spoons; Bull Durham sacks hung from his ears, and a string of frankfurters wriggled in his hands—these being Egypt's fatal asp. Going from bumps to grinds, he finally whirled madly to a syncopated brass version of "The Vision of Salome" and sank to the stage twitching in death, a frankfurter held to the bra.

Corny as the act sounds, it had something. It had Buster Keaton. The whole AEF was saying, "Have you seen Princess Rajah?" when word came from General March that he wanted to see "that snake dance." The CO passed the word down to Buster. His outfit was stationed at that time in Cabanac near Bordeaux. Cabanac is a typical small French town, with stores and cafés facing a square. Buster was sitting at a sidewalk table when the order came. He got his canvas shelter half, dumped his costume hardware into it, and walked the two kilometers (one and a quarter miles) to the general's headquarters. After the performance General March sent him back to Cabanac in the general's own armored Cadillac limousine.

It was late evening as they neared the town. Buster spoke to the driver, the driver nodded. He stopped the car, Buster left the front seat, where he had been sitting by the driver, and moved into the passenger compartment. Once there he drew the curtains.

It was payday. The square and the sidewalks were crowded with the full roster of Buster's outfit. The star-emblazoned official limousine drove slowly around the square with its horn blowing. Someone recognized it as the commanding general's and yelled, "A-tennnn-*shun!*"

The limousine stopped before the biggest and most brightly lighted café. The chauffeur hopped out and opened the door. Inside Buster counted to ten slowly, then, pack on back, stepped down. "I won't need you any more this evening," he said in a loud voice.

Buster's staunch claim is that a barrage of bottles then drove him from Cabanac and that, with his quarters locked to him, he slept that night in a field, thankful to have the shelter half for cover.

The Princess Rajah skit proved a serious mistake. It kept Buster in France performing for the brass long after his buddies had sailed. It was not until the end of March, 1919, nearly five months after the Armistice, that he finally embarked for home. Then there were three weeks at Camp Custer in Michigan before he finally got his discharge. He got to Muskegon at last for a week on the lake.

At the end of April he grabbed a train for California. The entire Comique company met him in Glendale, and a string of big touring cars tooted their way to the new Arbuckle Studios, which had been set up in Hollywood right across from the Mack Sennett lot.

In Anger's private office was Buster's trunk, standing open and full of his civilian clothes. Lou handed him a beautifully wrapped package tied with red-white-and-blue ribbon. "To our hero," said Anger with a suspicious catch in his voice.

"Open it Buster, dear," said Roscoe. "It's from all of us."

Buster removed the ribbons and tore off the paper. There was a silver box inside. He lifted the lid. With a loud bang it blew up in his face. He turned and started for the door.

"Where are you going?" Anger called.

"Back to the trenches," said Buster.

THIRTEEN

B USTER KEATON was now nearing twenty-four years of age. He had been away from the movies and in the service for one month short of a year. But he definitely objected to terms like "back from the front" as applied to himself.

"I'm back from the back," he would say, or he would speak, with deadpan face, of his "career at the rear."

He had seen none of the long, bloody, brutal infighting firsthand. But now, at home, he *was* seeing the changes that war had brought. Not in his friends, however. They seemed the same.

Roscoe Arbuckle was the same fat boy, still as delighted as ever with the peppermint stick of life—and not licking it alone, sharing it as generously as always. Natalie, the quiet one of the three Talmadge sisters, seemed glad to see Buster again. Lou Anger was still the older friend of the two-a-day years. Joe Schenck, though Buster seldom saw him, was as friendly as ever. For that matter, Schenck was a fairly rare sight to all Hollywood. He had already begun his lifelong habit of perpetual travel. Perhaps, transplanted unwillingly from the East, he never felt at home in the West. Nevertheless, in Buster's absence, he had grown even richer, and he and his brother Nicholas were quietly taking hold of many of the movieland controls.

But there were big changes in the country. National prohibition for one thing. The imperative Eleventh Commandment—Thou Shalt Not Drink (Let Alone *Look* Upon the Wine While It Is Red)— had been spoken by Congress and then ratified in a plebiscite of the sovereign states, with, however, many thousands of voters absent in the services abroad. Bootlegging had already begun; the rumrunners were busy at night; contraband trucks were being hijacked and their drivers "ventilated"; beer was being needled and eyes blinded by wood "alky." The rackets were set up, speakeasies and blind tigers were flourishing, and peephole living had begun; and the Syndicate was casting its viva voce votes in the chatter of submachine guns.

Buster Keaton
and Viola Dana, 1919.

Buster Keaton had left a free-and-easy country. When he came
back it was gone.

As for Hollywood, it was a bed of mushrooms—new movie lots
everywhere. Vaudeville's stage curtain was being rung down, and in
front of it, in big theatre after big theatre, the silver screen was being
raised.

For Keaton personally, there was the new Comique lot on Alvarado
Street where Clara Kimball Young's studio had been. And there was
Arbuckle's big newly bought house, not far away, on exclusive West
Adams Street, Los Angeles' equivalent of Pasadena's millionaire row,
the famous Orange Grove Avenue.

His first night home Buster Keaton stayed in the West Adams
manse. At his first glimpse of it he turned to Fatty and said, "I
suppose you have a butler too."

Arbuckle was embarassed. He even blushed. "Aw, heck," he said,
"I had to."

"How did you ever fall into a classy dump like this?" Buster went on.

"I damn near passed it up," Roscoe replied. "Schenck was after me to get a big place, and I was looking around. Then they told me that Theda Bara had just moved out of here. So I said, 'Leave her bedroom just as it is. I'm moving in.'"

"Has she ever been back?"

"No," said Arbuckle sadly.

That night Buster and Fatty made a foursome with Alice Lake and her friend Viola Dana. Alice was now with Metro doing legitimate parts. "No bruises any more," she said.

"Oh, we fix her up now and then," said Roscoe. "She comes back for a two-reeler once in a while."

It was the same old Alice. Viola Dana, however, was something for the books. Starting four years before with Edison, she was now getting the Metro buildup. Luxuriantly dark-haired and medium in height, she had a compact, strong, neat figure. "Beautiful" did not describe her, nor did "vivacious." Not quite the former, she was more than the latter. She created her own magnetic field. She was as animal-innocent and as alluring as a panther. Buster Keaton had never felt a presence quite like this. This feminine tomboy dissolved constraint and established the natural.

Meeting Buster, she simply said, "I like you." In those days it was a fresh phrase. Within a month the Viola Dana–Buster Keaton alliance was Hollywood's most talked-about romance.

They dined that first night at the Ship's Café in Venice, the newest movie rendezvous. But it was all new to Buster, even the crowds that now mobbed the stars and begged autographs. Hollywood was a goldfish bowl; the Chamber of Commerce had discovered the movie Golconda. Supercilious Los Angeles no longer called the film studios "gypsy camps." It too had succumbed to the grand illusion.

Abe and Mike Lyman greeted them as they came in. Abe's dance orchestra, together with Blondie Clark and Harry Richman, furnished the entertainment. Mike ran the place. The Lymans were by way of being Keaton relatives, their father having married Buster's aunt Rosa Keaton in Indiana years before.

The café was built like a ship, with large portholes for windows. The night was warm, and all the portholes were open. The Arbuckle party sat at a wall table directly below one. Outside was the parking lot.

The autograph hunters came along with the food. Course after course was whisked away while the hungry four signed the menus and cards thrust under their noses. Finally Viola absentmindedly dug at her ice cream with her fountain pen. They all laughed.

"That does it," said Buster. "Let's break it up." He leaned over and whispered in Roscoe's ear, pointing to the table percolator with a lighted alcohol lamp. "When you hear the next klaxon outside," he whispered.

Seconds later a horn tooted in the parking lot. Buster hammed a violent start of surprise, stood up dramatically, and, hand to ear, leaned out of the porthole. This whole gambit brought the seat of his pants just above his plate. Roscoe meanwhile had been examining the alcohol lamp, turning it around and looking at it as though he had never seen one before. At that moment Alice, at his side, said something or other. Turning to her he negligently placed the lighted lamp, with a loud clink, on Buster's plate. The flame was barely two inches below the Keaton backside. Buster waited, giving it the "five-second ouch," then dived headforemost through the porthole. Outside, he landed on his hands and flipped lightly to his feet as chauffeurs and lot attendants began running over.

"Is the joint on fire?" asked the first arrival.

"No," said Buster, "just a fight." The crowd dispersed; all was normal. Buster went back in. His gag had doubled the autograph hordes.

Later, as the café was closing, Buster took a ring of housekeys from his pocket. He had collected them in that day of reunions. "Where shall I stay tonight?" he asked rhetorically and with fake ennui. He fingered them one by one. "With Lew Cody? Jack Pickford? Lou Anger?"

"There," said Arbuckle, pointing to the West Adams key.

Next morning Arbuckle burst into Keaton's room. "Awake?"

"Now I am."

"Get dressed and come on."

The car was waiting in front. "Breakfast later," said Roscoe. He motioned the chauffeur aside. "I'll drive."

"Where are we going?"

"Never mind."

They whizzed out to Long Beach, past their former studios, and then onto a familiar road. They went around the turn and there was the gravel pit they had so badly wanted to buy barely eighteen months before.

"My God!" cried Buster. The old gravelly hill and the one-time quarry now bristled with oil derricks.

Scene from *A Desert Hero*, 1919. Alice Lake (Salvation Army girl), Buster Keaton (holdup man), Al St. John (against bar), Roscoe Arbuckle (bartender).

"The new Signal Hill oil field," said Roscoe.

The two men sat silently for several minutes watching the pumps at work.

Finally Buster spoke. "There went a million-dollar load of gravel," he said. "What did Anger say when they discovered oil?"

"Lou! We had him tied up for days. Wanted to jump off the pier."

"Well," said Buster, "you should have let him jump."

But movies, thanks to Anger, were still their business. A new opus, *A Desert Hero*, was beginning. Conditioned by army life, Buster was called on for even more doubling. Almost immediately a scene came up calling for Arbuckle to be kicked off a freight train, roll down a steep railroad embankment, across a dusty street, and on in through the swinging doors of a Western saloon. Once inside and still rolling, he would knock down the villain just as he was holding up the joint. The latter part, indoors, was safe and easy. It was the long roll from the freight car to the saloon that presented the problem. As planned it was to have been shot in a series of separate close-ups, one for the fall from the car, another for the roll down the bank, and so on. This would have been safe, as each segment would have been enacted separately.

Buster said, "No. For a real effect and to convince people that it's on the level, *do* it on the level. No faking. Move the camera back and take it all in one shot. Don't cut until he disappears through the doors."

"Bus is right," said Fatty.

Anger objected. "You're too heavy for that long fall. You'll get yourself killed."

"Then I'll do it," said Buster. "Give me Roscoe's clothes and some pillows. I'll guarantee to do it so the damn camera will never see my face. And don't cut until I'm through those doors."

When the dust cleared, Buster stood up, dusted off his clothes, and addressed Anger. "Do I get a bonus?"

"Bonus my eye," Anger replied. "Just count your bones."

The very next day, they were shooting in the saloon interior. Alice Lake, on loan from Metro, was a Salvation Army lass who was passing the tambourine around among the ginheads and rummies, begging for pennies. This would build up for the villain's entrance. Al St. John, the bad guy, was to come charging on horseback right through the doors, lasso Alice, sweep her up behind him, and gallop away.

Again safety reared its ugly head. "You can't do it," said Anger firmly to Alice.

"He's not thinking about me," said Alice. "He's thinking about damages to Metro."

"Shut up, Alice," said Anger. "You're going back there in one piece if I have to double for you myself." Then, alarmed by the instant murmurs of approval, he added hastily, "Give your clothes to Buster."

That week, nevertheless, they struck a bad day. None of the gags registered on their laugh meters, the cameraman and the technicians. These experts' reactions could vary from mere snickers to rolling on the ground in uninhibited convulsions of laughter. Today there was not even a snicker.

"I think I'll sign with Christie Comedies," said Buster dryly, an "in" joke referring to the company considered the nadir of film comedy. "I'm getting too good for this hick outfit."

"Call it a day," said Roscoe.

They drove silently to the West Adams house, silently waited for dinner, and then silently sat down at opposite ends of Theda Bara's fifteen-foot walnut banquet board. The butler brought on fried chicken, following up with green peas, corn on the cob, whipped potatoes, and cream gravy.

Arbuckle grunted, stood up, pulled the napkin from under his chin, and threw it savagely on the floor. "Put that goddamned stuff in picnic hampers," he said, "and get the car out."

Two hours later and a hundred miles north, Roscoe parked on a turnout on the Grapevine Pass in the Tehachapi Mountains below Bakersfield. Neither man had spoken all the way. Still silent, they ate dinner and started on. There was no discussion of route or destination. In Oakland, five hundred miles north of Hollywood, they caught the 5 A.M. milk ferry to San Francisco, checked in at the Palace Hotel, and then wired Lou Anger:

IT'S BEAUTIFUL IN FRISCO STOP COME ON UP STOP LOVE STOP STOP
ROSCOE AND BUSTER

Roscoe drew a deep breath. "Now," he said, "we have a good time. First, ham and eggs, coffee, and bourbon."

Two days later in Hollywood the crew was sitting around the set playing poker, Metro was calling for Alice, and Lou was tearing his hair. Finally he telephoned Joe Schenck.

"Let 'em alone," said Schenck.

Next day the principals appeared and plunged into finishing *A Desert Hero*; then, without a break, in five weeks they turned out *Backstage*. The two films rank among the best of the Arbuckle-Keaton two-reelers.

Buster Keaton remembers *Backstage* with the same ruefulness as their gravel-pit–Signal Hill fiasco—and for similar reasons. *Backstage* was another abortive attempt by Dame Fortune to dump gold into their laps.

"At the start of *Backstage*," says Buster, "an eccentric vaudeville dancer came to us looking for work. St. John had just left us to do his own pix at Warner Brothers. This guy looked a little like Al, so Roscoe signed him as heavy. All day long this guy's little five-year-old son—a cute little devil—hangs around, singing and dancing for us between scenes. Does this give us any ideas? Not us.

"Well, to cut it short, a few months later, Papa is resting. Just rocking on the veranda and counting his dough. His little boy is in the movies and making the gold for the family. We had hired Jackie Coogan, senior; Charlie Chaplin hired Jackie Coogan, junior. We didn't have the sense to build a pic around this kid; Chaplin did. The picture was called *The Kid*, and it was a million-dollar hit."

Buster had moved into the Hollywood Hotel to room with Ward Crane, Metro leading man known as one of Hollywood's best-dressed young men. The Keaton-Dana romance was flaming—"a collision of two starlets," one columnist called it. Buster and Viola talked of eloping but never did. Little by little the affair tapered off. Buster began seeing Natalie Talmadge again. With Buster Keaton's basically serious nature, his infatuation with Viola could hardly have been casual. Nevertheless, in Hollywood in general, a love affair could be off and a new one on within the time it took to film a two-reeler.

Several weeks after the fade-out of the romance, Buster attended a stag dinner that Roscoe gave for Joe Schenck. Lou Anger was there, as well as several Hollywood leading men, Lew Cody, Crane, and Norman Kerry. The latter, a tall hunk of actor, had previously played lead with Olga Petrova and other stars under his real name, Norman Kaiser. In 1918, when the feeling against Germany was at its height, he had changed his surname.

Schenck took Buster aside after dinner. Joseph Schenck has been described by one who knew him well in those days as a man who inspired instinctive confidence in everyone he met. Perhaps Norma Talmadge's nickname for him, Daddy, most aptly described this quality.

Joseph and Nicholas had been in the picture business since the early days and in show business in general even earlier. Their big amusement park money-maker had been the old Fort George establishment in the still-rural wooded hills of upper Manhattan, an area then jokingly called South Albany. Then the Schencks joined forces with theatre mogul Marcus Loew. Not long before Buster met Arbuckle, Joe Schenck had gone into motion-picture production. He rose with a rapidity astonishing even in the movies. Now he had just had a hand behind the scenes, it was said, in founding United Artists, in which four great names, Mary Pickford, Douglas Fairbanks, Charlie Chaplin, and David Wark Griffith, were joining in common enterprise.

Schenck talked to Keaton on Arbuckle's front porch. First he asked whether Buster planned to marry Viola. It hadn't worked out, Buster replied, adding that he was going with Natalie. This seemed to please the older man. Natalie, of course, was his sister-in-law. Arbuckle, Schenck went on to say, was now going to be put into feature-length pictures. Schenck paused. Buster was all for rushing right in to congratulate Roscoe on his good luck. But Schenck laid a restraining hand on his arm. He had more to say.

Buster, he said, was ready to do his own pictures. He would inherit Arbuckle's company, with Arbuckle moving into a new company that Schenck was setting up for him. There were more details: Loew (this meant Schenck too, though he didn't say so) was about to buy

Metro and would release the Keaton comedies with the Metro trade-mark and, of course, through the Metro distribution system. But, Schenck immediately added, Buster would make his pictures in the old, proven way, with interference from no one, great or small. Schenck said that he had rented Chaplin's old lot for Keaton, on Lillian Way, right across from Metro. How soon? Only a month or two.

The formalities were simple. They shook hands and called it a deal. Nor, so far as Buster himself can recall, were there ever any papers.

Buster stayed on at Roscoe's that night. Congratulating each other, they tossed a coin for the privilege of sleeping in the Theda Bara bed. Buster won.

Next morning at breakfast Buster said, "You've got to help me find a house."

"For you and who else?" asked Arbuckle.

"Just the Keatons," Buster replied.

By noon he had leased a comfortable bungalow on Ingram Street. He got Myra on the telephone in Bluffton. "This time," he said, "is it. Bring everyone out."

Myra sold both the lake cottages, bought a Cadillac touring car, and Jingles, now fifteen, drove them all west. When they arrived the Lillian Way studios were about ready and Arbuckle, with Buster, was completing his two-reel schedule with *A Country Hero*. In the flurry of studio remodeling, this final picture was being shot in Culver City in the Henry Lehrman Studio, which had been built originally for Thomas H. Ince.

Joe Keaton came out to the set in an elated mood. He looked at Alice Lake with a new appreciation.

"All right," said Arbuckle, "let's do the old routine. You know. Aw, come on, Mr. Keaton, play Alice's father."

Alice chipped in as before. "You can kick me, Mr. Keaton."

"Stop it!" said Mr. Keaton. "I'll play with you." Again he looked at Alice. The great enemy of the cinema had fallen.

"You're *really* going to play my father?"

"At my time of life," said Mr. Keaton, "what more can I expect?" His voice, however, lacked conviction.

"Now," said Arbuckle, "Buster and Alice will be sitting on the edge of this watering trough. They're spooning. But it's your daughter he's making up to, and you don't like it. So you grab him and kick him into the trough. Use your camera foot."

"My what foot?"

The Keatons arrive from Muskegon. Left to right: Louise, Myra, Jingles, Buster.

The "downstage foot": Joe Keaton, Roscoe Arbuckle, Buster Keaton, and Alice Lake in *A Country Hero*, 1919.

"He means your downstage foot," said Buster.

"Then why the hell don't he say so?" growled Joe.

They took their places. The camera began rolling. Joe made a practiced grab at his son, and his practiced toe found its traditional mark. With this power behind him, Buster made a beautiful Original Aboriginal straight into the water.

"N.G. Kill it," said Arbuckle. "Wrong foot. Shoot again. . . . Roll."

Joe did a jig and ended up with the wrong foot again.

"Kill it," said Roscoe. "Just relax, Mr. Keaton, we'll get it."

Joe turned on him. "I've been kicking that boy's ass," he said, "ever since he was born, and now you tell me how. But I'm going to tell *you* how: unless we reverse positions so I can use my right foot you'll never get this scene."

Buster was doubled up laughing, and Alice was giggling; Roscoe joined in. Joe glared, then suddenly began to laugh too. They switched places and got a perfect take. Buster was firmly in the drink.

But the Keaton kick, once unleashed, roared on. Two seconds later, the gargantuan Arbuckle was in the trough too, in an unscripted spot and sputtering unscripted remonstrances. But too late: the heroine, herself, felt the jarring impact of a leather sole on the rear placket of her gingham dress. She took off, wailing, to land in the water ahead of the two comedians.

"Seems a little crowded in here," Roscoe began, but Buster interrupted.

"My God, Dad!" he said. Alice was crying for real.

Joe paid no attention to either man. He lifted the soaked leading lady out of the trough, remarking as he did so, "Honey, I just put too much heart in it."

"That take will do fine," said Roscoe. "How do you like picture work, Mr. Keaton?"

Joe, his fatherly arm around Alice's shoulders, had found that it could offer its moments. "Picture work's all right, I guess," he said. "Oh, it's fine."

Coming from the elder Keaton, this was the equivalent of an Oscar for the entire industry. Actually, Joe readily grasped picture making as the Arbuckleites practiced the art. Improvisation to Joe, as to them, was a way of life.

Buster had once said to his father, "A good comedy story can be written on a penny postcard." In a sense these words expressed the facts, yet in another sense they played down the contribution Buster Keaton had already made during this apprenticeship. His previous experience with all manner of live audiences had been invaluable. To him, just beyond the camera, unseen, was the audience. He had another and exceptionally rare gift—the flair for making the incredible credible. There was a logic, however mad, supporting his wildest plotting: grant his first scene and you grant all. This logic had underlain the hilarious vaudeville nonsense of the knothole in the stage. Its motivation was perfect and believable, the universal human weakness: curiosity.

The postcard-plot theory consisted first in setting up a character (or characters) and a basic situation. The late James Agee once described it about as follows: "You have two men carrying a grand piano over a narrow one-way suspension bridge. Halfway across they meet an escaped gorilla coming the other way." For the rest of it the postcard simply laid out what another great silent-film veteran, Harold Lloyd, recently called "islands—four or five gags planned in advance . . . in between the islands you had to shift for yourself."

Up to this time, as Buster was preparing to leave Arbuckle, this had been the time-honored method from Sennett and Keystone on. Now Chaplin was beginning to reject it, and so was Buster Keaton. Buster called it "dragging gags in by their heels." He filled his postcard out —that is to say, of course, not an actual postcard but his mental

A Keaton machine. Scene from *The Garage*, 1919.

schema, scraps of paper, or whatnot—not with gags but with what he called "main laughing sequences." These were happenings—not just pratfall plus custard pie—articulated in a cause-and-effect series that boosted believability. Three of these main laughing sequences, rising climactically, sufficed for the twenty minutes of a two-reel short.

The time had arrived when the Kid, formerly of vaudeville, was about to make his own films. He had had a long, happy, and valuable training period with an early master. There is confusion with regard to the Arbuckle Comique films. Many have been lost (or, certainly, misplaced), and the exact order of their making is not certain, the order of release not necessarily being the same.

In any event, either *The Garage* or *A Country Hero* was the last picture in which Buster Keaton and Roscoe Arbuckle officially appeared together. Starting with *The Butcher Boy* of early 1917, in twenty-one and a half months of actual work—leaving out the Keaton army term—the two made from fourteen to perhaps seventeen two-reelers.

Now, in 1920, Buster Keaton was to be able to test and expand his theories with his own company and under his own direction. The way he would fill out the "postcards" might, if his theories held water, lead to some all-time comedy masterpieces.

As a matter of history, they did.

FOURTEEN

⚡⚡⚡⚡⚡⚡⚡⚡⚡⚡⚡⚡⚡⚡⚡

IF HOLLYWOOD was a gamble, Buster Keaton now at
least held the dice. His future rode on what he would throw. The
past was past. That was sure. The movies had come up and vaudeville had faded, together with the memory of its famous boy. The
Three Keatons were clippings in Myra's scrapbook. The Kid had to
make it all over again.

Not that Buster, in those years at least, thought of his life and
his life's work in the chancy terms of win, lose, or draw. He was an
optimist. Moreover, he was an artist and not a gambler, except insofar as all art is a gamble against the unattainable. Gamblers are not
really fatalists. Buster Keaton, from childhood on, had been in the
truest sense a fatalist. In that true sense, fate meant fortune as well
as nemesis. Every action and inaction of Buster Keaton's life, every
decision and procrastination, seemed to support his philosophy: you
do the playing, you even write the part, but someone else furnishes
the stage.

Joe Keaton had always done that—until Myra and Buster left him
with his trunks in a Los Angeles alley. Now, in 1920, the Joe Keaton
on the scene was less a father, more a friend of the family. But fate
is as consistent as it is persistent: now there was another Joe, Joe
Schenck.

These dispensations from above, from father or from father image,
included taking care of all the nagging practical matters, such as
financial arrangements. These details, Buster Keaton quite evidently
thought, lay outside the serious pursuit of laughter. They were offstage entirely. He gave hardly a thought to the business aspects of
his new situation. While Schenck was explaining them, Buster had
barely listened, his mind already far ahead planning new routines
on a new stage.

The exact organizational setup of the Keaton Film Company may
never be known. It was, and has remained, highly nebulous to the
outsider. Perhaps intentionally so, perhaps not. Its details were never

public. The corporation has been inactive for some three decades. Now Schenck himself is dead. And in business matters Buster's recall becomes practically nontotal. He remembers a few details. He says that he owned no shares in the producing company and that all his arrangements were verbal. His memory is of a generous Joe Schenck who would let him work as he wished, pay all the bills, and (the words are Keaton's) "*give* me a thousand dollars a week and twenty-five percent of the net."

It is to be doubted, however, that the Keaton Film Company was so casually organized as this. Its board, headed by Joe Schenck, included men like Nicholas Schenck, A. P. "Doc" Giannini (the Bank of Italy founder), David Bernstein, and Irving Berlin. In a 1925 story in the *Saturday Evening Post*, Alexander Woollcott wrote of Buster Keaton as the "patient offspring who was tossed around and bounced against the scenery [but] has since come up in the world . . . his antics now converted into celluloid on so large a scale that they have incorporated him. It is—or was—possible to own shares of Buster."

Anyway, this seems sure: Buster owned none of the shares. And this too is quite evident: a big business stood or fell with him. There were, he says, annual board meetings, which he describes as festive weekends in Atlantic City following the World Series. The Schencks would rent an entire hotel floor. So far as the company's star ever knew, the board meetings, at least on the boardwalk, were social, and social on a most lavish scale. If there were business meetings, he was not invited.

Whatever its inner structure, this overt sort of paternal setup (in which Buster functioned so well) was far from typical of Hollywood, then or since. It was so much Buster Keaton's native pattern that he never thought to question whether such an anomaly belonged or could long last in the fierce, competitive movie world. The assembly lines were then being laid out in the cinema factories. In the customary American hocus-pocus—or "ledger-domain"—tradition, an art was being subverted into a business with jungle ethics. Buster's little private heaven would last just eight years—from 1920 to 1928—no more. It was to be his one big chance as an artist—a gift from Joe. With no thought of urgency, he would make the most of his time and art: the nineteen two-reelers and the ten feature pictures (five to eight reels each) upon which his permanent reputation is chiefly based.

It seems quite evident, in retrospect, that the free-and-easy workings of the Keaton company suited Joe Schenck quite as well as Buster. All that subsequently happened strongly indicates that he too preferred this arrangement but that Hollywood decreed otherwise. Indeed, it would take strong-arm pressure to make Schenck drop the methods he had found so agreeable and profitable with the Talmadges, with Arbuckle, and with Keaton.

Buster's feature films, beginning in 1923 with *The Three Ages*, would justify Schenck's faith as well as his business judgment. Costing well under an average of two hundred thousand dollars apiece, they would gross from one and one half to two million dollars each. Like clock work—as long as his hands were free—Buster would turn out two features a year, for a spring and a fall release. Who would not be satisfied with a gross of three million dollars or more on an investment of under half a million?

The Keaton company's first publicity picture was shot on the opening day in January. It is the motley slapstick crowd looking at progress. Their backs are to the camera. They are gazing at a small bungalow on Lillian Way near the busy crossroads of Vine and Santa Monica. The bungalow, as its new sign indicates, is the Keaton office. Shoulder to shoulder, in single rank as though for inspection, are Buster, the crew he is inheriting from Comique, and two visitors,

Opening day at the Keaton Studio, January, 1920. Left to right: Myra, Jingles, Joe, Buster, Arbuckle, Alice Lake.

Alice Lake and Fatty. It is a typically sentimental Keatonesque vignette—a final reunion of the old campaigners. The Comique days were over. Roscoe was at work with Wallace Beery on *The Round Up*, while Alice had just completed *Shore Acres* at Metro.

The next day Buster came early, ready to begin his first two-reeler. But Joe Schenck, not having expected the studio to be in readiness so soon, had sent word of plans he had made to fill in the expected interim. Metro, across the way, would make a feature with the new star. After that, Buster could proceed with his schedule.

Most people would have been happy to be launched with a feature by a big studio. But not Buster. "How soon can Metro start?" he asked impatiently.

Schenck replied that they would be ready in four weeks.

"Four weeks!" said Buster, appalled at the prospects of rest. "Do you mind if I make a two-reeler while I'm waiting?"

"Why not?" said Schenck.

So Buster shot *The High Sign*. It is not a good picture. It was rushed in shooting, and for the first and only time Lou Anger scrimped on costs—he had wanted Buster to take a vacation. In addition, the player roster still unfilled, untried stock players and extras were used. Keaton cut and edited his premier solo effort, then saw he had a turkey. He stalled the release date and surrendered to the health addicts. He packed his new Buick with guns and tackle, assembled his family, and announced, "We're going to Lone Pine."

There was a reason for Lone Pine. Ostensibly it was for the wild beauty of this Sierra forest spot on the Owens River between Mount Whitney and Death Valley. Actually, however, it was because Arbuckle was there on location for *The Round Up*.

The minute they showed up, Arbuckle, without even saying hello, shouted, "Buster, come here and get shot."

In a nearby scattered stand of sugar pine, Arbuckle, rifle to shoulder, was peppering away at a band of attacking Indians.

Arbuckle's director, George Melford, called, "Cut! Stand by, everyone."

"You'll be an Indian," said Arbuckle.

"Okay, okay," said Buster, "but wait a sec till I give Dad and Jingles the guns. We want pheasant for supper."

Ten minutes later he reported in costume and makeup. "Now," he said, "I'll give you a redskin biting the dust until he chokes on it. Fifteen bucks—stunt man's pay."

Melford laughed. "Seven fifty."

"Okay," said Buster, "I do it as a half-breed." He turned to the cameramen. "Pan fast or you'll lose me."

Then he was off like a sprinter. Roscoe's rifle cracked and Buster sailed into a horizontal swan dive. He volplaned for ten feet, slid on his chest for eight, and bounced for five.

"Keep shooting!" Arbuckle yelled.

The dust slowly cleared to reveal the half-breed on his back quivering and then, with a final kick, stretching out, mouth open and eyes closed.

"Dead as a doornail," said Arbuckle.

That night Buster privately screened the working, or "answer," print of *The High Sign* for Roscoe alone.

"It's great! It's great!" Arbuckle kept saying, between belly laughs, all through the projection.

That confirmed it. Buster knew for certain just where he stood. It would make money, sure. What he wanted was something else. Something new. Though only five years apart, Roscoe and he were of two different generations.

Buster remembered something Arbuckle had said that very first week, three years before, at the old Norma Talmadge studio in New York. "They're all twelve-year-olds," he had observed. "That's the mental age of your audience."

Buster had just been questioning the appropriateness of a gag. "It doesn't seem to fit your story," he had said.

"Story?" Arbuckle's voice had risen like a siren on the word.

Buster had not been convinced. At that moment, it had reminded him of a similar remark that his father had made years before in a Jersey City nickelodeon. "All that trouble and expense for kids!" Joe had exclaimed. "Hell, they were just as happy with a magic lantern."

Supposing, Buster recalls that he had thought, *just supposing that Joe and Roscoe are right? Then why make moving pictures at all? Who wants to be in the toy business?* But he found it impossible to go along.

Now, as Arbuckle laughed with that particular guffaw of his that signaled that the "good old slapstick" was in orbit, Buster knew that this film must be destroyed.

Back in Hollywood, he said to Anger, "Throw this lemon away."

Lou looked ready to faint. "It cost twelve thousand dollars."

"It's no good at any price. It's my fault, not yours."

Anger temporized. "Let's preview it anyway," he said, "just to

Scene from
The High Sign, 1920.

keep your name going. After all, it's going to be some months before you have anything else. We'll preview it," he concluded, "then put it on the shelf. I promise you."

Reluctantly, Buster agreed. Thinking it over, he decided to slip into the preview to study the audience reaction. Old comic hand that he was, he learned something new. Aside from the general approval, *à la* Arbuckle, one reaction surprised him. Many years later he told Paul Gallico about it, and Gallico quoted him in a 1954 article in *Esquire*:

They don't like it when a comic is smarter than the audience. . . . We're making some screwball picture about Black Hand or something in which there's a high sign, the fingers crossed under the nose.

So we do a simple scene, there's a street with a corner and a guy goes by eating a banana and drops the banana peel. Then I come on the other way, turn the corner and walk into the camera. Everyone knows that I'm going to slip on the banana peel—only I don't. I walk right over the peel and give the high sign into the camera. Okay, so we preview the picture. The scene doesn't get a titter. Not a titter and nobody can figure out why. Finally I get the idea and we go back and shoot the scene over again. We do it exactly the same, only this time, after I walk over the banana peel and into the camera, giving the high sign, the camera follows me and I slip on another banana peel that I haven't seen and down I go. Yaks. The audience wants his comic to be human, not clever.

It is typical of Buster Keaton that, for perfection's sake, he would reshoot a scene for a film he never intended to release, go back and preview it again, and only then exile it to the shelf.

Metro was now ready for Buster. He was to star in *The Saphead*. This would represent the fifth title and at least the sixth version of an old theatrical property. The famous old Bronson Howard play *The Henrietta* had premiered way back in 1887. Then it became *The Millionaire*, starring William H. Crane as Vanalstyne, the Wolf of Wall Street, with Stuart Robson as Vanalstyne's son Bertie, nick-named the Lamb. Finally—prior to Metro's purchase of the rights for Buster—it had reclaimed the original title *The Henrietta*, while still further metamorphosing into a highly successful stage comedy. *The Henrietta* (actually a gold mine) was still far from through. In 1913, revived as *The New Henrietta*, the venerable vehicle carried Douglas Fairbanks, as Bertie the Lamb, onstage in New York to the theatrical hit of the year. Doug subsequently did Bertie the Lamb stories off and on in the movies. In fact, he had just finished another Lamb-like characterization in the title role of *The Mollycoddle* but now was about to go into the romantic swashbuckling roles by which he is chiefly remembered today.

Restraining itself from more sensational jobs of renaming, such as *Henrietta Rides Again, Henrietta Strikes Back,* or *Son of Henrietta*, Metro had gone to current slang for the title *The Saphead*. Buster Keaton was to be the Saphead, alias Bertie the Lamb. Indestructible, seventyish William H. Crane—the play's original star of 1887—was to play the Wolf of Wall Street for the last time, and Winchell Smith, director of the 1913 Broadway revival with Fairbanks, was to direct the Metro movie version.

By script and direction it came out society comedy with overtones of farce but without slapstick or slapshoes. Bertie—rich, pampered, tailored, manicured, dumb, and lucky—wins the girl and flabbergasts his father by a sensational killing in the stock market. The story gave Buster Keaton a character type he would use in later features of his own. The Lamb is the prototype of the penniless Southern gentle-man in *Our Hospitality*, the dapper young detective in the dream sequence of *Sherlock Jr.*, the wealthy scion of *Battling Butler*, and the college-spoiled son of an old riverboat captain (Ernest Torrence)

Scene from *The Saphead*, 1920.

in *Steamboat Bill Jr.* Bertie is also substantially duplicated—with many an added Keaton twist—in the Rollo Treadway of *The Navigator*.

The Metro film immediately ran into trouble. The original Bertie, Stuart Robson, claiming ownership of the book, held up release until October. By then, Buster had made two more two-reelers of his own. When production of *The Saphead* dragged on into summer, Buster began concurrent work on his own. All summer he shuttled back and forth across the street from Metro to Keaton, changing costumes and characters as he ran.

Finally, *The Saphead* opened at the Capitol in New York. Feature-length films got top program placement and commanded reviews that shorts could not ordinarily elicit. The film immediately invited comparisons between its new star and the well-established Chaplin, whose sensational hit with Jackie Coogan was running at the same time. Robert Sherwood wrote in the old *Life*:

> It is just as well that Charlie Chaplin did not wait any longer before releasing *The Kid*, for otherwise he might have awakened one bright morning to find that his crown had passed to the pensive brow of Buster Keaton.

The New York *Times* critic wrote:

> With Mr. Keaton as its center of gravity *The Saphead* becomes one of gayest comedies of the season—for this Keaton gravity is a bubbling source of merriment.

The frozen face, the Keaton mask, born in the medicine show and vaudeville, had scored immediately, even in the Arbuckle days, with movie audiences. Although in those days many players overacted flagrantly to overcome (they thought) the silence of the early films, Buster took the opposite course. His face went with silence. Its motionlessness and the films' soundlessness compounded each other. Its immobility compelled attention, its expression compelled sympathy. Fundamentally bewildered yet completely matter-of-fact, it was a basic human portrait. It stared unblinking and unsurprised as mad mishaps and mad triumphs unfolded like marginal notes by Mark Twain. There was something humble about that face—even when the body put on airs, as in *The Saphead*, and strutted in the fine clothes of the millionaire's son.

The newcomer was to be reckoned with. An artist had appeared. Around Christmas, 1920, a motion-picture trade journal reported:

Without parallel . . . is the phenomenal rise of Buster Keaton. In many parts of the country exhibitors make Keaton the whole show for a week, playing the Keaton feature along with a Keaton comic two reeler. *The Saphead* and *The Scarecrow* are teamed.

The Scarecrow (preceded by *The High Sign, One Week,* and *Convict 13*) is the exact opposite of the Metro feature. The two pictures are completely different, sartorially, socially, and in a comic sense, yet the two Keatons are the same. Whether as field hobgoblin or as moneyed whippersnapper, there is the same basic, recognizable comedy personality.

The Scarecrow, which was filmed in September and early October, following completion of the Metro feature, is a bit of fantasy, a kind of sublimation or distillation of slapstick. Buster plays an animated scarecrow who might have come from *The Wizard of Oz*. He is a hermit—or, if you choose, an outcast—who lives in a shack full of hilarious homemade mechanical devices. It is an unearthly little comedy, leagues away from Arbuckle's extrovert slapstick. In it is the poetry of memory: Lake Muskegon and summer, the Ed Gray Awakener, the forest hut of Beanie.

The Christmas cover of *Motion Picture World* showed a fireplace hung with stockings, in each a new star: Bert Lytell, Viola Dana, May Allison, Alice Lake, Ina Claire, and Buster Keaton. And, lest business be forgotten during celebration of the Holy Birth, there were holiday wishes to the theatre owners of America:

> May your friend, Success, come rushing
>   With extended, cordial hand;
> May your ushers wilt from ushing—
>   May your patrons have to stand.

The older stars were doing all right too. The National Star Popularity Contest revealed that Norma Talmadge led the field, followed by sister Constance, with Mary Pickford third. In the male division it was Wallace Reid, followed by Charles Ray, Thomas Meighan, Eugene O'Brien, and Douglas Fairbanks.

Comedians like Chaplin—and, soon, Lloyd and Keaton—might outgross every one of these, male and female; but there were hierarchies then as now, and the mimes of fun were not considered eligible for this simon-pure dramatic contest.

FIFTEEN

〰〰〰〰〰〰〰〰〰〰〰〰〰〰〰

BUSTER KEATON was off and running, single-hitched. He made two more shorts in 1920. He had done six of his own —and only the first a turkey—in the same number of months, add a week or two, and had crammed in a multireel feature. In order, the first half-dozen Keaton two-reelers were *The High Sign, One Week, Convict 13, The Scarecrow, Neighbors,* and *The Haunted House.* They contained a lot of variety and some accomplished fun-making. Establishing their maker as a star, they also established him in the movie world as he had once been established in the theatre world. Public and critics alike were quick to sense that Keaton was a unique and authentic personality.

Motion Picture World hailed *One Week* as "the comedy sensation of the year," predicting that Buster, "graduated from vaudeville," would "reach the peaks of funmaking. He begins where other comedians leave off. His brand new gags will set movie goers laughing until (if they wear 'em) their false teeth will drop out and their waistbands will shimmy." The slangy superlatives are dated; *One Week,* rescreened and viewed today, is not. But the trade blurb did indicate what Buster Keaton, quietly and in his own way, was beginning to accomplish.

Buster characterizes *One Week* as "a mild travesty of Elinor Glyn's *Three Weeks*—only one-third as shocking." In 1920 the travesty was timely and topical. Following her sexy, sensational *Three Weeks,* Hollywood had hired Miss Glyn to heat up subtitles. "Her prose, to say the least, was steamy," *Life* magazine recently observed, and dug up a choice period tidbit:

"Zara," he murmured hoarsely. He kissed her mouth: "Do you think I am stone?" She drew back, panting and deadly white. "Animal," she hissed, and struck him across the face.

As *Life,* in further restrospect, recalled, Elinor Glyn, by writing *It,* "was thus the inventor of Clara Bow."

Convict 13 was a family reunion far from vaudeville and far from the Gerry Society. It brought all the Keatons to the screen decked out in penal stripes. The old-time shenanigans took place on a prison rock pile. By this casting, the older son was both vindicated and shriven. It made up for the unilateral goof Joe had made seven years before by spurning William Randolph Hearst's movie offer, and it expiated the guilt that Buster could not help feeling about the breakup of the act only three and a half years before.

Buster was having trouble locating a durable leading lady. Beauties, then as now, came a dime a dozen in Hollywood. But to Buster a thing of beauty was not a joy forever if it folded under a beating. He had been using Sybil Sealey. She proved a little fragile. Then he found Virginia Fox (later Mrs. Darryl Zanuck). Miss Fox was a beauty who could give mileage. She joined the company at the start of the fifth Keaton film, then called *Mailbox*, later retitled *Neighbors*.

Not a trade blurb but an on-the-scenes report by a newspaper critic describes *Neighbors*. "Fastest and funniest of them all," he wrote. "What Buster does on that fence, over that fence, through that fence, and on the clothes lines and telegraph poles . . . is so laugh provoking that the Board of Reviews and other 'professionals' in the Metro projection room voiced their appreciation in one long continuous yell."

However negligent or trusting he may have been in business matters, Keaton was practical and demanding in production. He built an organization. From Comique he retained Lou Anger, writer Jean Havez, and cameraman Elgin Lessley, adding stock players like the former Keystoners Jimmy Bryant and Joe Bordeau. He signed Eddie Cline to share his directing duties, and sister Louise became script girl, one of the characteristic but minor Hollywood nepotisms. Buster felt that

A Keaton construction, shown with the architect. From *One Week*, 1920.

he could handle the elaborate mechanizations that were a Keaton specialty. For some time he planned his own gadgetry alone.

By midsummer of 1921 the Keaton company's baseball nine was the talk of Hollywood. One columnist claimed it had been offered a Pacific Coast League franchise. Management registered no objections, even though baseball took a lot of time. Pictures poured out on schedule, getting better—and selling better—as they went along. One newspaper writer's quip (he was a sportswriter) was that the entire Keaton employment form read as follows:

> *Please Check One of the Following Questions:*
> Are you a good actor?   Yes ☐   No ☐
> Are you a good baseball player?   Yes ☐   No ☐
> Passing Grade: 50%

Buster actually did hire good ballplayers; he went out of his way to get them and hired them away from other studios without compunction. But they had to be good at movie making too—in fact, even exceptionally good. Ernie Orsatti, former baseball pro, was one. Chick Collins, top stunt man, was another. Clyde Bruckman joined the organization in 1921, avowedly as "outfielder and writer." Havez, too fat to play, served as umpire. Louise was bat boy and water boy.

Bruckman, previously a newspaperman, was with Buster Keaton for years, then later directed Harold Lloyd and W. C. Fields. Later still, during the 1950's, Bruckman, then retired, told how he joined the Keaton company. "I was with Warner Brothers," Bruckman related. "Warners at that time consisted of Jack, Sam, and Harry Warner, Monte Banks, and a few extras and props, in an old barn of a studio at Bronson and Sunset, where the big bowling alley now is.

"Then I ran into Harry Brand, an old friend of mine from newspaper days. Now he was Buster's publicity man.

" 'Why don't you come over with Keaton?' he asked.

" 'How do I know Keaton wants me?'

"Next day Brand phoned, said, 'Come over for lunch with us.'

"I did and was hired, to start the next Monday. I went back and saw Jack Warner. 'Jack, I have a chance to go with Keaton—better job, better opportunity. I'd like to close Saturday.'

" 'Can you keep a little secret?' said Jack. 'We're all closing Saturday.'

"And, by gosh, they did—for six months or more. It took a German police dog called Rin Tin Tin to take them out of the red."

Then Bruckman described the Keaton lot. "I suppose writers should coin phrases, so here goes," he said. "We were one big happy family. And that's something you don't know until—and if—you've been in one. In such a situation, gags are never a problem. You feel good. Your mind's at ease, and working.

"I was at Buster's house or he at mine four or five nights many a week—playing cards, horsing around, dodging the issue. Then, at midnight, to the kitchen, sit on the sink, eat hamburgers, and work on gags until three in the morning. And how we'd work!

"You can't match that today, when you walk in on a supervised production, cut and dried, every cough scripted and every sneeze timed, and the bigwigs all a push button's length from the set. Joe Schenck was too big to be a bigwig. He's said—and I've heard him— 'Tell me from nothing. Go ahead, what should I know about comedy?'

"Buster was a guy you worked with—not *for*. Oh, sure, it's a cliché, like the 'happy family.' But try it sometime. I even hate to mention the playing. It sounds like a buildup. But late afternoons we chose sides and had our ball game—fights, arguments. Rainy days it was bridge in a dressing room—fights, arguments. And we made pictures." Bruckman sighed. "Harold Lloyd was wonderful to me," he said. "So was Bill Fields. But with Bus you belonged.

"Well, it's all changed, anyway. So organized and big a man can't touch it. It used to be *our* business. We acted in scenes, set up scenery, spotted lights, moved furniture—hell, today even the set dresser with paid-up dues can't move a lousy bouquet. He sits and waits until the 'green man' arrives. An actor has to fight his way onto the set through technicians, supervisors, experts, and accountants. And television has followed the same lines. So . . ." He swallowed and looked up. "Other days, other ways, as Nero said.

"Oh, we'd get hung up on sequences. Throw down your pencils, pick up the bats. The second, maybe third, inning—with a runner on base—Bus would throw his glove in the air, holler, 'I got it!' and back to work. 'Nothing like baseball,' he always said, 'to take your mind off your troubles.'

"With it all, you wouldn't believe a comedian could be so serious. He showed them all how to underact. He could tell his story by lifting an eyebrow. He could tell it by *not* lifting an eyebrow. Buster was his own best gagman. He had judgment, taste; never overdid it, and never offended. He knew what was right for him."

Clyde Bruckman paused, lit a cigarette, and went on. "You seldom saw his name in the story credits. But I can tell you—and so could Jean Havez if he were alive—that those wonderful stories were ninety percent Buster's. I was often ashamed to take the money, much less the credit. I would say so.

"Bus would say, 'Stick, I need a left fielder,' and laugh. But he never left you in left field. We were *all* overpaid from the strict creative point of view. Most of the direction was his, as Eddie Cline will tell you. Keaton could have graduated into a top director—of any kind of picture, short or long, high or low, sad or funny or both—if Hollywood hadn't pushed him down and then said 'Look how Keaton has slipped!'

"Comedian, gagman, writer, director—then add technical innovator. Camera work. Look at his pictures to see beautiful shots, wide pans and long shots, unexpected close-ups, and angles that were all new when he thought them up. But each and every camera angle calculated to help tell the story—without sound, remember, and with damn few subtitles.

"Let me tell you this, and the dates will prove it: Buster Keaton was the first to film comedy at standard camera speed. Remember the old rushing, jerky Keystone comedies? They were filmed at slow speed—which does the opposite when projected on the screen, that is, speeds the action up. They thought it was funnier—and it saved film. But no undercranking for Buster. 'The unnatural tempo,' he said, 'makes the action unbelievable. Besides, it wrecks the gag timing.' So Keaton used standard speed right from the start with his own outfit. After his first release Chaplin and Lloyd followed suit. No matter what anyone may claim, Bus was first. I was there."

"What were the actual speeds?" Bruckman was asked.

"This will be a little technical," he replied, "but here it is. First, remember that all the old speeds were only approximately uniform because the cameras were hand-cranked, not motor-driven. Anyway, old standard speed was sixty feet of film per minute, which equals sixteen picture frames per second. Comedy speed, or undercranking, was generally about forty-five feet a minute, or twelve frames a second. But in extreme cases it could be as low as thirty feet and eight frames—in other words, exactly one-half as slow as standard. In projection terms that meant action *twice* as fast as it actually happened. Because, you see, in the theatres the projector speed was fixed at standard and could not be changed."

There was a further question. "You say 'old speeds.' Are they different today?"

"Sure," Bruckman replied. "Sound made that necessary—to get fidelity. It is now ninety feet a minute. That," he continued, "makes the old comedies even worse as projected today, because the projectors are still not adjustable. Even Keaton's films, done *then* at standard speed, are now shown fifty percent too fast. There are exceptions, of course. At least two places I know of use adjustable projectors. The Museum of Modern Art in New York is one. The George Eastman House in Rochester is another."

Clyde Bruckman returned to his ad-lib profile of Keaton the movie maker. "Camera speed was only one thing. The guy's honesty was impressive. He wouldn't fool his audience. None of the easy camera tricks like cutting an action into several parts with a new camera angle for each, then splicing it all togther.

"Let me cite a couple of instances. There's a gag in Buster's first feature, *The Three Ages*. The scene was the Ice Age. Bus wanted one of the cavemen to heave a big rock at him; he would take a batter's stance, swing his war club, bat the rock back, and it would bean the other guy. Now, you do this easy by the cutting technique. One shot of the guy throwing. Next shot, the rock sailing in the air. Next shot, someone out of camera range lobs it up to Buster and he bats it. Cut again. Next shot, just reverse your second shot to show the rock sailing in the air in the opposite direction. Final shot, close-up of the rock beaning the guy. Put it all together. Easy as duck soup, not a problem in a carload; the studios do it every day. It rolls across the screen with a whoosh—*but you never saw the thing really happen*; it's a patchwork of half-truths.

"Now, Buster accepted the fact that this rock must be papier-mâché. But he wouldn't accept action trickery. It had to be continuous action, from the moment the caveman picked it up and heaved it straight through to the moment it homed back and coldcocked him. 'We get it in one shot,' he said, 'or we throw out the gag.'

"We set up the cameras for a long profile shot—this rock was going to sail for thirty feet—and we worked for hours. Seventy-six takes, all for one little gag.

" 'Okay,' said Buster, 'now they'll know it was for real.'

"The other gag," said Bruckman, "was even tougher. On the face of it, it was impossible. It was in *Sherlock Jr.* We had a pool-table shot where he had to pocket a number of balls in one stroke of the cue. The camera at high level had to show it all happen. Set up the balls, Whang away and miss. We worked an hour.

" 'You know, Buster,' we said, 'this thing can't be done.'

"This made him mad. 'It *can* be done. Give me fifteen minutes with those stupid goddamn balls.' He coated each ball with white chalk, then shot it *separately* into the proper pocket. Each ball left the line of its path on the green felt. Then Buster placed each ball exactly where the line indicated, called, 'Camera!' and took one shot and pocketed them all. Publicity men would call that genius; to Buster it was all in the day's work.

"No one ever doubled for Buster. He rides the handlebars of the driverless motorcycle in *Sherlock*, flies through the air on a tree in *Steamboat Bill*, goes over the waterfall in *Our Hospitality*.

"When he *did* use a camera trick, he did it deliberately, to make an impossible statement. Like multiple exposure. *Not* double exposure, which is a picture on top of a picture, generally an amateur accident. Multiple exposure is dividing up the picture frame into parts, taping the lens to correspond, and photographing each part separately. Keaton didn't originate this idea. It had been used for years to show an actor in two roles at once. But it was a difficult technique. It was hard to join the halves of the picture without a telltale line down the middle. It was also hard to get the separate actions to synchronize—like looking up at the exact moment that your alter ego, in the earlier exposure, said something to you.

"Buster Keaton did the multiple exposure to end all multiple exposures. It was in *Playhouse*. He did an entire minstrel show all by himself—nine Busters in blackface on the stage at once. Every move, song, and dance exactly in unison. That meant taping off the lens into nine equal segments accurate to the ten-thousandth of an inch.

" 'It can't be done,' said Lessley, the cameraman.

" 'Sure it can,' said Buster. 'We won't use tape.'

"He built a lightproof black box, about a foot square, that fitted over the camera. The crank came out the side through an insulated slot. It was in the front that the business was: nine shutters from right to left, fitted so tight you could have worked underwater. You opened one at a time, shot that section, closed that shutter, rolled the film back, opened the next shutter and shot, and so on.

" 'Keep this a secret, you lugs,' said Buster. We did. Hollywood gave up on that one. No one even tried to copy it."

Clyde Bruckman stamped out his cigarette. "I often wish," he said, "that I were back there, with Buster and the gang, in *that* Hollywood. But I don't have the lamp to rub. It was one of a kind."

SIXTEEN

⧚⧚⧚⧚⧚⧚⧚⧚⧚⧚⧚⧚⧚⧚⧚⧚⧚⧚

*T*HAT HOLLYWOOD, whose passing Clyde Bruckman so bitterly regretted, was not actually, even then, like the protected little isles where Keaton and a few other fortunate artists—Chaplin, Lloyd, Fairbanks—were permitted to work. Day by day Hollywood was becoming less, rather than more, permissive. The movies were a frontier and Hollywood was a boomtown, with its national bank already established and going. In the early 1920's it still had, as *Life* has observed, "a deceptive somnolence. The corner of Hollywood and Vine, soon to become the Times Square of moviedom, was bounded by two churches and orange trees, and the street cars from Los Angeles all stopped for a half hour at noon while conductors and motormen climbed down, sat in the sun and fished sandwiches from their lunch boxes." But the lingering rusticity was scarcely more real than a movie set's facades. It was more that big business, concerned elsewhere, suffered the hicks to linger on—for a day or so longer.

What Buster's staunch writing aide Bruckman lamented is what Keaton himself has lamented for the many long years since gold swallowed up the golden days. But there were to be, as we have said, eight of those free-and-easy, frolicsome, fruitful years in the snuggery of that little isle.

Buster had bought a large bungalow on Victoria Avenue for his family. Then it was New Year's and 1921 and time to start a new picture tomorrow. Meanwhile, Buster's social pattern remained unchanged. Nowadays Arbuckle and Alice Lake, Buster and Natalie Talmadge formed the foursome. Then, suddenly, Natalie was leaving for New York to sail for Europe. The party would include Norma, Constance, and Peg, the Talmadge sisters' mother, as well as Lillian Gish and her mother. Regretfully Buster saw Natalie off. As she waved from the departing train, he might well have been thinking of a remark Myra had made a few days before. "You're twenty-five," she had said. "Old enough to be married and a father. Why Joe and I . . ."

Buster grew restless. He worked at the new picture with almost savage energy; he nightclubbed with Roscoe and Alice, taking any girl he found handy; he played baseball almost obsessively and filled in the few remaining daily hours at handball with Ward Crane or, occasionally, a bit player and ex-vaudeville hoofer named Rudolph Valentino. Another new companion was movie actor Buster Collier, son of the stage veteran William Collier.

The current film was *Hard Luck*, then came *The Goat*, both comic variations on the theme of misfortune and injustice. The public now eagerly awaited each new Keaton film, the critics searched for fresh superlatives. Buster's honed and believably motivated slapstick was now "an extremely well-turned piece of carpentering, handled by an artist," an example of "high art in low comedy."

Now, in an unaccustomed rush, Buster began mechanizing the set for *The Electric House*. The Ed Gray Awakener was going into a housewide model, to be motorized from front porch to back, from dining to living room, and from bedroom to swimming pool.

Shooting began. On the second day, the escalator—no stairs, naturally, in an electric house—speeded up as Buster was ascending. Before he could jump clear, a slapshoe caught between the steps. Instantly he was jammed at the top. "Shut it off!" he yelled.

But before the stagehands could rush to the switch, there was an ominous splintering sound. It was a compound sound, made up in approximately even parts of the sound of a two-by-four brace breaking and Buster Keaton's ankle snapping. The slapshoe was torn from his foot. Freed, he toppled and fell headlong ten feet to the studio floor. Shattered ankle and all, he retained an acrobat's reflexes; he got his hands down to the uprushing floor and made a good shoulder roll. As he came over on the broken ankle, he fainted. The finger-chewing clothes wringer of Buster's babyhood had grown into a mayhem machine.

Here was the hard luck and here was the goat. The plaster cast would be on seven weeks and Buster on crutches. And a still harder blow: heavy work was out of the question, the doctor said, for at least five months. The star huddled with himself at Good Samaritan Hospital, and Lou Anger huddled with the Metro brass. *The High Sign*, good old lemon, was dusted off and released. Then Anger went out and proselytized the best technical man in Hollywood. He coughed up, even without complaining, the salary Fred Gabouri demanded.

"Now this electric house," said Anger, adding some choice adjec-

Scene from *Hard Luck*, 1921.

Scene from *The Goat*, 1921. Buster Keaton and Big Joe Roberts.

tives, "rebuild it. And I mean *re*build it. Don't use a part that's here. Not a nail. Not a screw. Take your time—we won't have a star for a while—and make damn sure it works, is safe, and is one hundred percent foolproof. You start tomorrow."

Meanwhile, back at the hospital, there was a lot of excitement: nurses babbling about reports of a new film, *The Four Horsemen of the Apocalypse*. In it, they said, was the dreamboat of the Western world.

"We'll see it," said Buster, with no idea who the dreamboat was. He telephoned Metro and asked for the loan of a print, then requisitioned a projector from Anger. While Keaton sat in a wheelchair, the new film was run off in the darkened solarium. All was serene until the tango scene, then the solarium was a bedlam of girlish screams. Metro had stumbled upon a brand-new star, Valentino. Next day the star came to visit Buster, and the entire hospital staff lined up in the halls to see him.

Some months before all this, Rudy Valentino had rushed to Buster with big news. Director Rex Ingram had signed him to a secondary part opposite star Alice Terry in a new picture. What sold him, said Valentino, was his dancing. The part called for a fancy tango. He knew that playing this character from the best-selling Blasco Ibáñez novel was his big chance. He was right.

When the tango scene flashed on at the public preview, the ladies in the audience all but tore the theatre down. Metro hastily called in all the prints and changed the credits to give Valentino star billing. It was news of the sensational preview that had started the nurses buzzing.

Out of hospital but still caged, Buster's restlessness grew. He became disconsolate. He moped at the studio, moped at home, dodged Roscoe's calls. Slowly the hot sun of discontent focused through the glass of loneliness, then pinpointed it all: when would Natalie be home? As if in answer, her letter came: she was back from Europe but had decided to stay on with her mother in the East. He began the bombardment—letters, telegrams, long-distance calls. "Marry me. Marry me." But Natalie wouldn't say yes and she wouldn't say no.

Then he saw the headline of a syndicated article:

KEATON-TALMADGE ROMANCE IN DOUBT

Will It Be
Butter and Eggs
Or Custard Pie?

Buster Keaton
after the
Electric House
accident, 1921.

He read on. The son of a wealthy Chicago dairyman was in New York courting Natalie Talmadge.

So! He had to shoot the works. Without a word to Natalie he packed to rush east. Swearing his family and a few intimates to secrecy, he said that his wedding with Natalie was all set. He bought train tickets and took off. Along went Ward Crane and Lou and Sophye Anger. He told no one, not even his own family, the true state of affairs. He had to do it this way. He was reaching for The Miracle.

Once on this hazardous trajectory, his control was no less than admirable. He waited until he had gone a third of the way; then, at Albuquerque, New Mexico, he secretly wired ahead: "On my way for our wedding. Please set date. Wire reply." He concluded with the trip number and that of his space. In his suppressed agitation he even forgot to include the mandatory four-letter word "love."

Then the torment, destination unknown: Paradise or Pratfall? His watch hands stuck; the train hovered, a hummingbird in limbo; the sun stopped swinging; the sagebrush shadows were airbrushed on the sand.

They crossed into Texas and were at Amarillo when the club car porter brought the wire. He and Lou were playing bridge with two fellow passengers, Nicholas Schenck and Hiram Abrams, president of United Artists.

Buster summoned Crane from the chair where he was dozing. "Play out my hand, Ward."

He excused himself. Unopened telegram in hand, he flew on his crutches for his car, his compartment. He sank onto the unmade berth and tore the envelope open. "Yes," it read, "wedding here May 31."

He closed his eyes, mopped his forehead. He heard the click of the wheels beneath the car. Then he figured the time left: ten days. At last, the date registered on his brain. It was Joe and Myra's wedding anniversary. Their twenty-eighth. Was it coincidence or Natalie's sentimental thoughtfulness? Buster Keaton has never known for sure.

He got to New York early in the week before the wedding, to find the Talmadge clan deployed in serious and well-ordered activity. At the hotel, before joining them, he looked at the crutches and tossed them into the corner. "Go out," he said to Crane, "and buy me a walking stick."

Ward returned with a gold-topped malacca from Tiffany. Mid-week, Buster got the ring. Then on Friday he and Natalie, accompanied by Constance and Mrs. Talmadge, got the license. Saturday the *Times* announced the forthcoming nuptials. Monday night Joe Schenck hosted the bachelor dinner.

Next day was the day. These long years later, Buster Keaton remembers it this way. "It was in Norma's garden—flowers everywhere; roses, I think. Ward handed me the ring without a fumble; I put it on Nat's finger without a fumble and heard this voice. . . .

" '. . . I now pronounce you man and wife.' I had Nat in my arms three—make it two—seconds and she was yanked away. I heard her mother crying. Joe, Lou, Ward, a whole gang were shaking my hand. Funny how I can remember how wet it was with perspiration and how I wiped it off on my striped trousers.

"I looked and looked and finally spotted Natalie fifty rosebushes away, talking with Anita Loos and John Emerson. Just then John Golden whistled. Our signal: the car is ready.

"I grabbed Nat and said, 'Let's scram.'

"We headed for the big entrance gates, bulling through—not *that*

The Natalie Talmadge–Buster Keaton wedding, May 31, 1921.
Left to right: John Emerson, Anita Loos, Natalie, Buster.

fast, with my ankle. But we made it. Just as we went through the gate there was music, and Nat said, 'Look.'

"Up on top of the wall was a monkey dressed as a bride, in a short skirt, doing a little dance. And a grind organ, somewhere, was playing 'The Merry Widow.'

"The limousine was there. We headed west, towards New York. It was a perfect setup for a crack, so I slid the window back and called, "California, James.""

It must be admitted, right off, that this is an artist's story. This chronicle by the usually factual Buster Keaton seems at least faintly suspect. At least, the detail of the simian ballet is almost too perfect a touch. It bears every evidence of romantic hindsight—a gilding of the nuptial lilies, the ex post facto plotting of a scene. It shows the fine hand of a master comic writer.

Things like that, however, *were* always happening to Keaton. Anyway, here is the *Times'* sober and factual account:

The marriage of Miss Natalie Talmadge, the screen star, and Buster Keaton, the film comedian, took place yesterday afternoon at the summer home at Bayside, L.I., of the bride's sister, Miss Norma Talmadge, who in private life is Mrs. Joseph M. Schenck.

It was a quiet country wedding, staged in the midst of flowers and foliage. The ceremony was performed on the piazza of the Schenck home, which was decorated with a profusion of snowballs and other late Spring flowers. Justice Valenti of the City Court officiated.

Miss Constance Talmadge, who is Mrs. John Pialoglou in private life, was matron of honor for her sister. The bride wore a simple frock of pale gray, and her sister was also gowned in gray. Ward Crane acted as best man.

The honeymoon will be spent in Los Angeles, and the bride is to appear with the bridegroom in his next picture play.

No little grind-organ monkey waltzing to Lehár here. Why did the *Times* neglect to mention this? Was it, perhaps, judged as news not fit to print? The *Times*, anyway, did err in one detail: there was no honeymoon, despite everyone's urging—not even a drive across country. Buster recalls his mother-in-law's disappointment. To Peg, a Talmadge bride without a honeymoon had one part of her trousseau missing. But it was Buster who had made the decision. Now married, he was even more plagued by the lost months. If he could not act, then, he argued, he could plan pictures and plots.

There were, of course, other plans to be made too. They sat in their compartment and talked. At this moment they seemed to share the same dream, the modest desire for a quiet life, a small house, and children. Despite his fondness for motorcars, good food, and lively friends, Buster was essentially a moderate man, especially if measured against Hollywood standards. His conservative dress, for example, made him a bird of almost drab feather in a gaudy aviary.

Already rising from seventy-five thousand dollars well toward one hundred thousand dollars a year, his income seemed certain to rise far more still; and income tax was no problem in those days. He was conscious of no real desire for a movie star's palace or for palace life. To be sure, his was a risky nonconformity. The Hollywood pattern was set: an *arriviste* life of palms, palaces, and parties.

His conscious desire was for a farm, or, in California terms, a ranch. In the homogeneous script of his own life—a script that blended life and stage as seamlessly as his own multiple-exposure films—one memory stood out almost naggingly. It was a bit of unfinished business from eighteen years before. Unlike the Wright brothers' initial turn at Kittyhawk that same year of 1903, Buster's business had had to be dropped just when it had fairly started. Perhaps, being fragmentary, it had for him the tantalizing magic of the incomplete. Buster had been nearly eight years old, and his four weeks on an Oklahoma farm, with his father, his grandfather, and his Uncle Bert, had seemed, ever since, like a door that opens a crack to reveal wonders and then closes.

Buster had been eyeing the undeveloped San Fernando Valley just north of Hollywood, where you could buy a farm—hills, live oaks, fields, springs—for a hundred dollars an acre. Not a private dude ranch but a real farm. It *was* a modest dream, at least at that moment. In only a few years, however, "roughing it" would become popular (with palominos and silver-studded Western saddles) and the stars would flock to the valley. Almost overnight San Fernando land would be fetching many thousands of dollars per acre.

Buster recalls how he broached the dream to his bride. Looking out of the train window at the endless dry sagebrush of Texas, he saw, instead, spreading live oaks and willows along fresh streams. He remembers what he said.

"We find a farmer with a wife and kids," he said. "We build 'em a cottage, and they run our farm. Give 'em a home. You can grow anything out there, Natalie. Just go down for water. We'll have an orange grove and chickens and a few choice cattle. We split the profits with the farmer. In a year or two, after it's running, we build a big, roomy ranch house of our own at the other end of the acreage. Beam ceilings, stone fireplaces. Saddle horses, pets. We're by ourselves but only a few minutes from Hollywood and an easy haul to the beaches."

The question of where to live in the meantime interposed.

"In a rented apartment," he said, then came back to his unfinished business. "We have servant quarters, a nursery, a governess' room, and"—he seemed to feel that this would clinch the matter—"we have a private baseball diamond."

Natalie was vague. She was a city girl, Brooklyn-bred. It is hard to know what "farm" really meant to her. To some in her position, it could have been alluring indeed; to others, frightening. She probably had never really known solitude or the open spaces. Anyway, she plumped for an interim deal: a nice little house in a nice little neighborhood—with paved streets.

After the hugging, kissing, and handshaking at the station in California, Buster led Natalie over to a shiny new Mercer roadster, a custom-built car of a type then known as "the rich man's Stutz."

"A homecoming present for you," he said. "Climb in."

Natalie's hand flew to her hair.

"Oh," he said, "your hairdo. Okay, let's ride in the limousine with Mom and Dad."

House hunting began immediately. Though the specifications were not his, Buster accepted them. None of the smaller ones ever seemed quite right. One on Westchester Place was big enough. It was in a limousine neighborhood. It would do.

SEVENTEEN

܀܀܀܀܀܀܀܀܀܀܀܀܀܀܀܀܀܀

I T W A S mid-June; 1921 was nearly half gone. Buster looked forward to getting back to work at last. Natalie, busy shopping and settling, would not be in the next picture after all.

The industry had just reprieved the convalescent Buster by cutting down on all summer releases. With no Keaton release now required until after Labor Day, he could make up the lost ground. Provided, that is, that the ankle, with the cast so recently removed, would let him go before the cameras. His impatience was intensified by news from Schenck. After its first twelve months of operation, the Keaton Film Company was buying the Lillian Way studios outright, for cash.

As if to help, the ankle injury cleared with a rapidity that astonished the doctors. They revised the prognosis: he could begin light work in a few weeks. From the studio point of view, however, it was going to require a new and special kind of picture story. The writing staff struggled, pondering the unthinkable, a sedentary opus for Buster Keaton.

"It's like near beer," Jean Havez complained.

Bruckman chewed his pencil, pawed his blank papers, went to the water cooler, lit a cigarette, threw it away. "Hell!" he said. "Lights! Camera! Action! What action?"

Old-timer Havez expanded the theme. "If we can't have falls and chases what's left?"

"Keep going, slaves!" said Buster only half in jest. "Think! Cogitate! Ponder! *Reflect!*" He snapped an imaginary whip, popping his lips as the imaginary thongs landed. Instantly, a memory picture flashed into his mind: *reflections*, a hundred *reflections*—the hundred mirrors Albee had dedicated to Annette Kellerman. One hundred Annettes—that's what *her* audience saw. What a vision! She had only to stand there in all her beauty—the loveliest bit of total inactivity he could recall.

That was it! "We don't need falls or chases," he said. "I'll be the entire cast." He outlined his idea: a picture swarming with Buster Keatons. "The whole picture is a visual gag. I hardly have to do anything."

That is how *The Playhouse* began. It could have been subtitled *Memories of the Theatre*.

Doubting Thomases will not believe that Buster Keaton could today recall such details, particularly, perhaps, the subtle, swift, inward flashes of the germinative idea. But those particular years of childhood and youth are exactly where his total recall lies. And for good reason: those were the golden, creative years before the door closed and a lax, tarnished, dishonored time ensued. Keaton's memory has preserved that earlier time, its vital moments embalmed like beetles in amber. It is here that the artist is most to be trusted, where recall can recapture the old insights and the strange ways they came about.

And, to push doubt to the limit, if he *has* reinvented a solution, he did not invent the original problem, and the new solution is only another piece cut out of the same bolt of goods. If the memory is creative, so was the life, and at the least we have an exact analogue of the event.

Similarly—as if to prove the point—*The Playhouse* itself is a thing that was conjured up out of memory, an inward creation from the long continuum of past and present, of then and now, in Buster Keaton's conscious and unconscious mind. It is a potent memory, fertile and patient. Keaton's past has always upstaged his present.

The Playhouse is a theatre of memories of the theatre. It is a small-town opera house. The lobby poster announces: MINSTREL SHOW TONIGHT. Buster buys a ticket and goes in. The scene cuts to the orchestra: Buster as fiddler, Buster as cellist, Buster as bassist; then, panning to the right, Buster as clarinetist, trombonist, and drummer. Now, through multiple exposure, a general shot of the all-Keaton orchestra. Cut to wings: Buster as stagehand raising the curtain.

Cut to stage and minstrel show: *nine* Buster Keatons in blackface, from Mr. Bones to Mr. Interlocutor, filling the stage. (This was the meticulously synchonized tour de force that Bruckman especially remembered.)

Pan from stage to audience: front row to back, this too is all Keaton. (Except for the front row, the Keatons are all cardboard-mounted life-size blowups of photographs.) In one of the boxes a Buster in tuxedo looks at his program, turns to a Keatonette in evening dress, and says (subtitle): "This fellow Keaton seems to be the whole show."

Shot of the program:

KEATON'S OPERA HOUSE
*** *Program* ***
BUSTER KEATON PRESENTS
BUSTER KEATON'S MINSTRELS

Interlocutor	BUSTER KEATON
Bones	BUSTER KEATON
Sambo	BUSTER KEATON
Tenor Solo	BUSTER KEATON
Asleep in the Deep	BUSTER KEATON
Comic Effusion	BUSTER KEATON
Song and Dance	BUSTER KEATON
Quartette	BUSTER KEATON
Clarionette Solo	BUSTER KEATON
Finale	BUSTER KEATON

Staff For Buster Keaton

Manager	BUSTER KEATON
Stage Director	BUSTER KEATON
Musical Director	BUSTER KEATON
Electrician	BUSTER KEATON
Property Man	BUSTER KEATON
Theatre Transportation	BUSTER KEATON
Advance Agent	BUSTER KEATON
Dances Arranged by	BUSTER KEATON
Special Instructor	BUSTER KEATON
Original Songs & Music by	BUSTER KEATON
Scenery Painted by	BUSTER KEATON
Mechanical Effects by	BUSTER KEATON
Marches Arranged by	BUSTER KEATON
Tableaux by	BUSTER KEATON

* * * * * *

Cut to auditorium: Keatons infest the theatre—dowagers and tycoons, rowdies and prisses, wives and hubbies, and whole bevies of brats sucking lollypops and spilling soda pop on innocent neighbors. Masterly chaos.

Cut to stage: the minstrels bow and do a Shuffle Off to Buffalo, clearing the stage for two new Keatons, a song-and-dance team. It's a swift dazzler, the duo rushing on from opposite wings, racing through a unison cane dance, bowing, and exiting—one running off forward to the right, the other off backward to the left. An invisible hand erases them as if they were animated cartoons.

Scene from *The Playhouse*, 1921. Left to right: Keaton, Keaton, Keaton, etc.

Cut to, cut to, cut to—it becomes more and more like a dream. The next scene shows that it *was* a dream. It is a shabby room. Buster, fully dressed, is sound asleep on the bed. A man enters, shakes him, points to the door. Two more men appear and begin removing the furniture. It is the classic eviction scene of the old melodramas, even to Buster sitting in despair, his head in his hands.

But we do not reckon with Keaton if we assume that it has *all* been a dream and that the present scene, on the contrary, is completely real. *He* cannot admit that the theatre itself is not real. Dream or no dream, the theatre must still be there. Suddenly, the furniture removed, the movers seize the actual bedroom walls, with a few quick pulls dismantling what we now see was only a stage set. The evictor was the stage manager; the moving men, stagehands; and Keaton himself, a stagehand stealing a nap.

The theatre remains, magnified; a hundred Keatons have been reduced to an assistant stagehand. This left Keaton the author with a problem: how to match all this swift, swirling fantasy through the second reel. He accomplished it simply, weaving the remaining sequences out of a "fantasy" that once had really existed, the strange world of vaudeville as he himself remembered it.

The screen now throngs not with Keatons but with memories. One of them is there in the flesh: gigantic Joe Roberts as the "heavy," playing the stern stage manager. Big Joe, friend from vaudeville and the Muskegon summers, had joined the Keaton company with the second picture and stayed on until he died. Gentle as he was, he was a most convincing menace, an adequate surrogate for Joe Keaton, a new paternal nemesis for Buster.

Onstage come the memories. First the knothole in the floor that had once so nearly gotten a Canadian lynching for Joe and Buster. Now it is Buster the stagehand sweeping the stage, spying the hole, jabbing the broom handle at it, and falling headlong on his neck. Next he reached back to 1909 at the Palace Theatre in London for a memory of a primate actor called Peter the Great. Peter, a chimpanzee, had dined in full dress, biked and roller-skated to the American ragtime strains of "Down in Jungle Town," undressed and donned pajamas, and then retired to bed. Peter the Great topped any animal act Buster had ever seen. So now, a dozen years later, Buster, furry arms trailing, bikes, dines, and then clambers up into a box to sit on a lady's lap. Now memories overlap: Buster, still as Peter the Great, takes the old Original Aboriginal dive into the painted backdrop, slides down, and flips to his feet.

That, of necessity, recalls Annette. And now she appears, as impersonated by the shapeliest extra Buster could find. As "Annette" dives, Buster is being chased (Havez got his chase despite all), the glass tank onstage is smashed, and a flood pours into the orchestra pit and out into the auditorium, a rising indoor lake. The Australian splash is played up so big, in fact, that the picture ends with Buster's escape out the entrance doors with a bass fiddle as his boat. Buster had actually furnished the "topper" for the first reel.

The Playhouse scored heavily. One of the biggest laughs came when the opera-house program flashed on the screen. The laugh requires a bit of explanation today. It was the period, 1921, of Thomas H. Ince's directorial ascendancy. Part was real, part was self-buildup, especially screen credits. These had got to the point of screenwide trumpeting: story by Thomas H. Ince, directed by Thomas H. Ince, produced by Thomas H. Ince, and on and on. The critics had been needling him for some time. One had just quipped: "Ince's new picture is to be called *Modesty Is the Best Policy*." The public had tumbled too, so now a prolonged belly laugh greeted Buster's bit of Ince's baiting. Significantly, Ince abruptly ceased the practice.

About then, Buster, incurable quipster, was being interviewed. *The Playhouse* was mentioned. "I don't deserve any credit," he said. "Thomas H. was my Ince-spiration."

When describing the picture years later, Clyde Bruckman had singled out the remarkable synchronization of the separate actions in the nine-part, individually shot minstrel ensemble. Bruckman, however, did not detail how the synchronization was achieved. Quite recently, Keaton himself explained how he accomplished it. "Actually," he said, "it was hardest for Elgin Lessley at the camera. He had to roll the film back eight times, then run it through again. He had to *hand-crank* at *exactly* the same speed *both* ways, *each* time. Try it sometime. If he were off the slightest fraction, no matter how carefully I timed my movements, the composite action could not have synchronized. But Elgin was outstanding among all the studios. He was a human metronome.

"My synchronizing was gotten by doing the routines to banjo music. Again, I got a human metronome. I memorized the routines very much as they lay out dance steps—each certain action at a certain beat in a certain measure of 'Darktown Strutters' Ball.' Metronome Lessley set the beat, metronome banjo man started tapping his foot, and Lessley started each time with ten feet of blank film as a leader, counting down, 'Ten, nine, eight,' and so on. At 'zero'—we hadn't thought up 'blast off' in those days—banjo went into chorus and I into routine. Simple," Buster concluded.

Not all people concur. One who does not is Albert Lewin, the director remembered for *The Moon and Sixpence*, *The Picture of Dorian Gray*, and other features. Being an avant-garde art collector, Lewin's pictures frequently referred to artists and the art scene, and it is both as film artist and as art collector that Lewin views the Keaton *oeuvre*. Lewin finds more in *The Playhouse* than the admitted technical originality and virtuosity, startling as these are.

A few years ago, on location in Mexico, Lewin was recalling the picture, which he had not seen again since 1921. With a memory like Buster's own, he went over the sequences. Then, however, he dwelt on "atmosphere." "An altogether extraordinary emotional effect," he observed, "came from the dreamlike, obsessive, hallucinatory repetition of that strange frozen face. It was almost nightmarish—a phantasmagoria of masks.

"There is no question," Lewin concluded, "that Buster Keaton, among other things, was a surrealist even before surrealism. Such fantasy! Not even Pirandello ever conjured up such extraordinary visions."

EIGHTEEN

T HE PACE was stepping up. Even on a protected island, Hollywood called the tune and set the tempo. Buster and Natalie were living it up as he, at least, had never expected to: cars, parties, and houses—each larger and more expensive than the one before. It was a long shakedown cruise. Or it was a series of stopovers on the grand tour. Or it was vaudeville's endless stages. No matter what it was, it was *not* home.

Buster Keaton might just possibly have done the impossible. He might have established a beachhead outside the theatre and films. It could have held home, family, friends. But by now the retreat was impossible. It was too late. It was all theatre. The play was the thing.

As the whirl began in earnest, Buster was twenty-six. He looked young, felt young. But to Myra—who came from an early-aging generation—he was already past the time of life when wild oats were decent or prudent. It looked too much like a pattern to her. She had been through that mill already with Buster's father.

"You're too old to burn the candle at both ends," she said.

But, like the poet Edna St. Vincent Millay, Buster had discovered what a lovely light it gives. He went on burning it.

Myra gave up. "You're just like Joe was," she said. "Too full of beans."

Privately, though, as Buster can recall, he more than once was troubled. The Buster back of the mask would speak. "I would take myself aside," he says, using a favorite expression, "and ask myself some questions. 'Me a big shot? Me a glamour boy?' I'd even ask my police dog. 'Captain,' I'd say, 'what are *we* doing here?' I never got a decent answer out of him. He'd whine, begin to wag his tail, then change his mind and unwag it.

"Captain was a puppy with our first house. Now he was full-grown. He began sleeping on my bed at six weeks and two pounds. He had filled out to a hundred and sixty pounds. It was his bed now. I had one corner, and that was shrinking. Though I hadn't taught him to drive yet, he went to the studio every day in the Mercer with me. He didn't like cops—especially on motorcycles."

Captain was Buster's dog—and his only. Captain wanted it that way. Lou Anger had barred him from sets during shooting after the dog had floored Big Joe as he was roughhousing with Buster. He still, however, had sat by his master's side in the projection room during the dailies. Now that was off limits too. He had assaulted Big Joe's image by a flashing leap to the screen from ten feet away.

"There," said Anger in anguish, "goes five hundred bucks."

Even Arbuckle complained, Captain having knocked him down while he was wrestling with Buster on the lawn. "My God," he said, "we can't even horse around any more. That wolf is going to kill one of us for sure."

"One of us is right," said Buster, "but not *me*."

Roscoe gave Buster a hurt look. "You, of all people," he said, "had to get a dog without a sense of humor."

The evening foursomes had resumed, Buster and Natalie, Roscoe and Alice. Neither prohibition nor all its agentry had been able to drive conviviality under cover in movieland. Cities might now be measured in status by the number and class of their speakeasies, but the blind pig never flourished in Hollywood. Screen folk wanted no part of guzzling without an audience like duck hunters in a blind. They would have liked passing out in the big Memorial Coliseum with a hundred thousand spectators allowed in free.

The beachside cafés were the next-best bet. There they lapped it up, perhaps the headiest wine being that of adulation. Through uncurfewed nights, the liquor in hip pocket, lady's handbag, or under the table, the wild fun went on. Unlike in other cities, Thursday was the big night rather than Saturday. This was because the colony dispersed every weekend—by car, Pullman, and yacht—to Catalina, Coronado, Frisco, Lake Arrowhead, Tijuana (then spelled Tia Juana), and a number of other retreats.

Thursday night now meant Mike Lyman's Sunset Inn at Pacific Palisades (successor to the Ship's Café). Lyman called these soirees "Fillum Fotoplayer Food Festivals" (unaccountably leaving out "Firewater") and dedicated them each week to a different star, with menus listing such *haute cuisine* entrées and entremets as "Mammoth Olives *à la* Roscoe Arbuckle," "Chicken *à la* Fanny Ward," and "Shrimp Cocktail *à la* Buster Keaton."

The Sunset Inn was large, and the public considered a five-dollar *couvert* cheap enough for the privilege of ogling stars and starlets, directors and top moguls, plus the free entertainment. Lyman did not pay the special entertainers—Chaplin, Lloyd, Arbuckle, Keaton, Mix, Fairbanks, and a dozen more gave their all. Even the endless traipsings of Gloria Swanson, Mabel Normand, Nazimova, or Clara Kimball Young to powder room and back were production numbers.

Baseball would be played on the dance floor with the French roll as ball and the walking stick as bat, with sides chosen up from comedians, matinee idols, bankers, socialites, and any other "in" characters.

One night Chaplin announced a benefit ballet for his old boss Mack Sennett, who sat nearby. Sennett, insulted, turned his head. He needed a benefit like a hole in the head, but he got it anyway. The ork slithered into "The Rustle of Spring" and the ballet came on. "Ballet" is not the correct term but "came on" is. Keystoners from past and present appeared, Chaplin and Charlie Murray, Ford Sterling and Fatty Arbuckle, Chester Conklin and Al St. John, Ben Turpin and Mack Swain, with added star Buster Keaton, all wrapped in tablecloths and milling around on tiptoe in an outrageous travesty on all aesthetic dancing from Loie Fuller to Isadora Duncan.

Buster Keaton and Captain.

It was not yet the day of the withering wisecrack and the put-down one-liner. It was a time of practical psychology and self-analysis at fifteen dollars per fifth of "Scotch." Another great complex-remover was the practical joke, Hollywood's second art. Some of the jokes have become legends. Somewhere in every practical joke, at one end or the other, seemed to be Sid Grauman. The late Grauman, owner of fabulous movie palaces—the Million Dollar Theatre in Los Angeles, the Egyptian and the Chinese in Hollywood—rendered a devotion to the practical joke that was absolute. Win or lose, he was for it, even as victim. "Sid Grauman," Buster Keaton once said with respect, "hated peace."

Grauman made history—of a kind—in his theatres. His brainchild was preserving actresses' footprints in cement. His idea too, it is said, was the stage prologue before the film feature—those synchronized symphonies of cancan kick and flashing thighs now purveyed almost solely at Radio City Music Hall.

But Sid Grauman's greatest accomplishment, old-timers agree, was the daylight theft of the million-dollar rug. That was a once-in-a-lifetime thing. Grauman kept his hand in with smaller, occasionally even picayune doings—like lifting Natalie's costly new fitted case from her limousine, then sending it by special messenger gift-wrapped and tagged "Merry Xmas to Nat from Sid."

Only a light jab, but the victim naturally complained to her husband, "Will you let him get away with this?" Naturally not. So, on New Year's Eve, it came about quite logically that shooting broke out between the "Pharaoh's Guards" who nightly paced back and forth, high above the heads of the movie crowds in line for tickets, on the Egyptian Theatre's parapets.

Some in line panicked—the more impressionable—(you could never tell when it would be gangsters and not solid citizens), and the Hollywood police began swarming all over the place, confirming the fears of those who had chickened out. But Grauman was already on the phone. "Congratulations, Buster," he said. His experienced eye had instantly spotted the ringers on the parapet, Bryant and Bordeau, Buster's former Keystoners.

The (reputed) million-dollar rug, a fifty-foot (reputed) Isfahan in the lobby of the Hotel Alexandria where Grauman lived, had acquired famous associations even before its theft. It had been underfoot during a strange little flurry of fisticuffs. This event—though picked up on some front pages—was reported as follows by one Los Angeles daily on its sports page:

Charles Spencer Chaplin entered wearing gray flannels and weighing 126. Louis B. Mayer entered wearing navy blue serge and weighing 198. Chaplin led with a remark to Mayer. Mayer countered with a crack. Mayer then led with his right and missed. Chaplin swung with his left and missed. Both fell down. The decision: Double TKO.

The fight, however bloodless, was not a publicity stunt. It was bona fide grudge. Chaplin was furious at Mayer for what he claimed was unauthorized exploitation of his name. Mayer's films of Chaplin's divorced wife, Mildred Harris, were being billed on theatre marquees, it was said, as follows:

Mrs. CHARLIE CHAPLIN

It is a fact that Mayer had claimed he had no control over theatre owners' actions, but then, shortly after the brawl with Chaplin, he said in an interview in *Motion Picture World* that Miss Harris "disdained to capitalize on the Chaplin name."

Thus consecrated to the offbeat and the shady, the Isfahan was now to have no peace. Grauman's plan was elegantly simple. A rug cleaner's van drove up, the men presented a cleaning order made out on the hotel's own order form, rolled up the rug, and carried it off. Time passed. The rug stayed away. The order was found to be forged. The police were called in. Reporters followed. Neither van nor cleaning firm could be found. It was headline stuff.

Weeks passed. The insurance company added its operatives to the sleuthing force. The hotel called in private eyes. The search spread over southern California. Hope diminished. It began to be believed that the rug had been smuggled into Mexico.

Then Grauman's private delight was cut short. It was being rumored that the Hotel Alexandria's manager, Grauman's friend, was to be indicted for grand theft. Sid casually invited his friend to attend the opening that night at his Million Dollar Theatre. They were just being seated in Grauman's private box when the curtain rose for the prologue. The stage was filled with dancers. The manager looked at the stage, turned away, then did a double take. He nearly fell out of the box as he yelled, "They're *dancing* on my million-dollar rug!"

"Don't be a little boy about it," Grauman replied. "I'll send it back tomorrow. You're not going to pull it out from under my ballerinas' feet."

The Hollywood climate proved itself again. Sid Grauman, self-confessed archthief, Robin Hood of the bored, was Public Hero No. 1.

"How did you stash it?" Buster asked him curiously.

"I hung it with the backdrops," said Grauman. It was a new bit of theatre lore even to Keaton. All this elaborate mischief, in fact, *was* theatre, Buster Keaton's old familiar terrain. It was vaudeville and Lake Muskegon and Childhood Before the Fall, all repackaged and gift-wrapped.

Buster relaxed—a little too much. Hollywood was more than a colony of actors on vacation. There was more to it than met the eye. It was ruled not by Momus and Comus, the Mardi Gras gods of mirth and misrule, but by a set of characters not of the stage— bankers, merchandisers, wheeler-dealers. Their real idea of fun (no matter how they might ham it up at the Sunset Inn) was a limousine ride to the deposit window. They held the purse strings.

It was not a safe place to be wholly and only the theatre's child. Chaplin, already a millionaire, had long since effectively seized the strings. With United Artists he was "rolling his own." Harold Lloyd was just about to do the same. Buster Keaton would be wise to follow suit. It *could* be done now—later on, who could tell? But Buster's wisdom was the wisdom of the artist. Besides, the paternalistic setup with Schenck, repeating the earlier, broken-off pattern, was both satisfying and reassuring to Keaton.

To all appearances it was a truly free-and-easy era. But even in 1921 its end could be foreseen. Banks were buying in, and where banks are, mergers are. Mergers would spell, for a long time to come, the end of the independents. The power war had begun years before, almost with the first flickery films. Now it was becoming a battle of giants. If money was the power, theatres (just as in vaudeville) were the weapon. Anyone with a camera could make a film. But could you show it? It was no academic question.

Joseph Schenck, it is true, was not—then, at least—a part of all this. Schenck was an old-time individualist, an independent, a lone wolf who did not run with the pack. Quite obviously he liked money and, as obviously, power. It was, it would seem, a question of means and method or, deeper still, perhaps one of meaning. Call Joseph Schenck a Victorian, if the term has any meaning left. Victoria's century was his century in large part. In any case, apart from questions of philosophy, Schenck was an open-field runner, not a power-play man. And he was secure, at least for the time being, through connections with Marcus Loew that assured him Loew's large theatre chain in which to show his films. But it was a shifting battlefield of shifty people.

The theatre question, quite recently, had in fact all but wrecked

United Artists in its very beginnings. The new biggies did not like the idea of actors making their own films. They closed all their theatres to these stars, and the new company found itself all dressed up with no place to go. This hit where it hurt—where, indeed, it could be fatal. Art or no, United Artists had come into being for one main reason: the big companies refused to pay Pickford, Fairbanks, and Chaplin the salaries to which their vast popularity entitled them.

This popularity won the battle, if not the campaign. Faced with boycott, United Artists simply threatened to give their feature films, *first run,* to all the neighborhood theatres in the country and even, where necessary, to show them in tents and vacant buildings. The threat was startling: it was "back to the nickelodeons." United Artists had the stars. For the time being the threat worked. Nevertheless, it clearly indicated what the power lever's fulcrum actually was.

Buying up theatres was both an offensive and a defensive move, and as the industry grew, it had developed in two ways. It had begun in the early days, from about 1902 to about 1913, when the functions of manufacture, distribution, and sale (that is, showing in theatres and, actually, rental) were not yet clearly defined, separated, or controlled. At that particular time, demand exceeded supply: film production did not keep pace with the building of theatres. As a result —especially since films were still easy and cheap to make—certain owners began making films for their own theatres. They thus became, in effect, manufacturer, wholesaler, and retailer in one. (Some of these men were now among the Hollywood biggies.) Once started in on making their own movies, they naturally favored their own product over that of the original people in the movie-making field. The newcomers—the straddlers—expanded their movie production and expanded their theatre chains. The seeds of monopoly were sown.

The squeeze was now on the other guys, the original producers whose product had been too scarce. Now, instead, it was a drug on the market. They had to go out and rent, buy, borrow, or build theatres for their films. The seeds of trade war were sown. The rip was already showing in the seat of a new industry's pants.

Dog ate dog. Surviving dogs formed packs. Pack attacked pack, nipping off any loners skulking around the edges. It was, in fact, a place for dogs. It was no place for the unwary or the innocent. As the cycle from production to final consumption narrowed, then finally closed, the fat dogs grew fatter, the lean ones starved to death. This would be the scene a decade and a half later, when, at last, the U.S. Department of Justice would break it up with antitrust suits

against the industry. It was not, unfortunately, within Justice's juris-
diction to ask the question "Where do art and the artist fit into all
this?" But certainly it was a germane question. It was the question
Buster Keaton did not face.

The scene and the actors change, but the play remains the same.
In the early 1920's the movies were in the position vaudeville had
once held. They were so popular that they could do no wrong. But
they were dying of cancer—or progress. However, it would take time.
Radio was barely born; television was still a science-fiction gimmick.
It was yet the movies' day onstage. No matter who owned them or
ran them, they were an entertainment monopoly per se. The public
was theirs.

But the public was not a monolith—it was multiform humanity.
It had its power blocs, its minorities, and its lobbies—for prohibition
or for free beer, for moral rearmament or for shorter skirts, for
Beethoven or for jazz.

The films' effect upon manners and morals had been perceived by
a few; the few had intimidated the press and released a propaganda
torrent. The idea of film censorship was rising. State censorship had
already begun to stop Theda Bara in her tracks. The industry itself
might soon have to take action.

For the current was running stronger. Native curiosity was now
getting an assist from militant prudery. Having snatched spirituous
liquor from innocent lips, the blue noses were now getting nosy
about the movies. The giant public spotlight already turned on Hollywood and its private lives now began to serve two purposes. The
reformers hunted for dirt. Kinsey was not yet on hand to show that
they couldn't miss, whether in Hollywood or on Main Street. The
rest of us, it seemed, stared with a kind of obsessive romanticism.
Keyhole glimpses of stars with their hair down made many a columnist's name. Most of us asked what Flossie La Belle wore, or
didn't wear, in bed. The puritans asked whom she entertained there.
It was faintly incestuous, a brooding fantasy. In his Mack Sennett
biography, *Father Goose*, Gene Fowler commented:

A weirdly powerful relationship, unspoken and unwritten, exists for a
little day between the public and its stars. Many patrons of the motion
picture look upon the dimes [!!] they drop into the box-office window as
payment in full on a solemn contract for the right to control the private
concerns of their screen favorites . . . implied . . . is a fantastic dream
marriage.

Fowler, writing in 1934, could look back upon what, more than a decade before, had developed out of this dream marriage of Joe Doakes and Flossie La Belle and/or Jane Doe and Jeffrey Princeworth. It was 1921. Suddenly the air was loud with the screams of the guilt hunters. Their first victim was the unlikeliest candidate in all Hollywood.

On Friday, September 2, the Friday before Labor Day, Buster Keaton telephoned Roscoe Arbuckle. "I just rented a yacht," he said. "Nat and I want you and Alice to sail with us over the weekend. We'll go to Catalina—just swim, fish, and take it easy."

"Gee whiz, I'd love to, but I've made other plans," said Roscoe. "I've promised to drive up to Frisco with some guys."

"Who?"

"Lowell Sherman and Freddy Fishback."

"Break it with them," Buster urged. "You'll have more fun with us."

Buster can still vividly recall how disappointed Arbuckle sounded, how he hesitated. "No," he finally said, "I can't. A promise is a promise."

It was an honorable decision but also one that Roscoe Arbuckle would regret for the rest of his life. The trip to San Francisco would end his career and indelibly stain his good name. It was a practical joke by fate, the master joker.

NINETEEN

~~~~~~~~~~~~~~~~~~~~~~~~~~~~~~~

ROSCOE ARBUCKLE and his friends partied in San Francisco over the long Labor Day holiday. Their hotel suite was the scene of a come-one, come-all open house, with wine, women, and song in the bootleg-booze–flapper–jazz pattern of the twenties. On the following Friday, September 9, a young woman died in a San Francisco hospital. Her name was Virginia Rappe. She had been a guest at the wide-open Arbuckle-Sherman-Fishback party. Two days later still, on Sunday, September 11, Roscoe Arbuckle was in a San Francisco jail—held without bail prior to being officially charged with rape and murder.

Was it rape?

"No," said practical Hollywood. "He didn't need to."

Was it murder?

"No," said his friend Buster Keaton when he heard the incredible report. "Roscoe Arbuckle couldn't murder a fly."

But this was a land where law ruled, and the law would have the final answers. And finally the law spoke. "No," it said, "no on both counts."

But over the land, in the meantime, another voice had spoken. " 'I'll be judge, I'll be jury,' said cunning old Fury."

The law thought, or hoped, that Fury didn't matter. "Acquittal is not enough for Roscoe Arbuckle," the jury said, in a remarkable legal document that the foreman read in court. "We feel that a great injustice has been done to him. . . . There was not the slightest proof adduced to connect him in any way with the commission of a crime. . . . We wish him success and hope that the American people will take the judgment of fourteen men and women who have sat listening for thirty-one days to the evidence, that Roscoe Arbuckle is entirely innocent and free from all blame."

But Fury had already spoken. Law's verdict had ceased to matter —it was null and void, irrelevant, immaterial, and incompetent. It had been seven months and three juries since Arbuckle's initial arrest.

The name of this man, even though innocent, had been too long associated with those two ugliest words of our language.

Even Fury did not have the last word. The last word was Doubt's. It was not even certain who, or what, had really been on trial in that long, troubled term of adjudication that ended on March 16, 1922. There are no pages in legal history more complex and confused than the three trials of the State of California vs. Roscoe Arbuckle. Witnesses appeared, witnesses disappeared. Witnesses swore, then reneged. Witnesses perjured themselves, made wild allegations and frightened retractions. Witnesses were publicly censured by the judge. The prosecution, at times, sounded like the defense.

From pulpit to press the ranting was slanted, consciously aimed to sway America and to destroy Arbuckle and Hollywood, the Beast and the Great Whore. Despite all, the great silent majority stood all along with the final jury. But the minority decision out of court, the screaming headlines and sermons, the whispered rumors (as nasty in the churches and women's clubs as in the alleys)—all drew the portrait that has never faded, the fat, baby-faced killer, the monster who raped and slew.

Although the Frisco drama drew ninety-four articles in the New York *Times* and reportedly sold more Hearst papers than the sinking of the *Lusitania*, it was nevertheless only a trial within a trial. The entire land was convened, a kangaroo court, to try the flesh merchants. Hollywood chickened at the first *ipse dixit*, pleaded *nolo contendere*, and threw Roscoe to the lions, a showy, easy sacrifice—a one-man purge.

Never was the panic button more quickly pressed. The instant Arbuckle was jailed, three days before even the coroner's inquest, the surrender began. At a Sunday-midnight emergency meeting the San Francisco theatres banned all Arbuckle pictures. Early next morning, September 12 (as reported by the *Times*), "Sid Grauman, long a personal friend of Roscoe Arbuckle's, withdrew his latest picture, *Gasoline Gus*, without comment or announcement." *Sic transit amicitia!*

Next day, the Famous Players–Lasky office advised everyone to continue the Arbuckle screenings and Joseph M. Schenck declared the innocence of the accused, while, simultaneously, the F. F. Proctor theatres were banning his films. To round out Tuesday, the Los Angeles Athletic Club expunged Fatty's name from the membership rolls.

By Wednesday the bomb shelters were jammed. Arbuckle was

banned from Los Angeles to Chicago to Philadelphia. Michigan's ban was unconditional and statewide. New York alone, through its Motion Picture Commission, firmly declared that it had "no right to bar the showing of any film because of the morals or personal life of the actors who appear in it."

On September 17, in a bit of local slapstick in Thermopolis, Wyoming, 150 cowboys shot up the screen where an Arbuckle comedy was being shown. A bit anticlimactic was the revelation, five days later, that the shooting was only a publicity stunt of the theatre owner.

Roscoe Arbuckle still had had no chance to defend himself or, then or ever, to face his real accusers. With his trial nearly four weeks in the offing, a new note of horror was added to the Hollywood nightmare. The immensely popular star Wallace Reid suddenly collapsed, and he was found to be a dope addict. This dope story shocked as no other has ever shocked, before or since. Another black mark went up against the modern Babylon—in fact, two, since the whispers were that Wally's addiction had begun when morphine was pumped into him to keep him at work after he had suffered a back injury on location.

The temper of the press was unmistakable. When, on Friday, September 30, Roscoe returned to Hollywood on temporary bail, the dailies reported him as being stoned by a mob at the Los Angeles railway station. Only the New York *Times* was brave enough to print a reporter's eyewitness account of the large crowd that cheered him and presented him with flowers.

One day later, when his friends gathered at his house, a typical tabloid scarehead was:

ARBUCKLE CELEBRATES
IN LOS ANGELES HOME

This was followed by descriptions of costly limousines arriving throughout the night at a mansion ablaze with lights. There was no explanation of what the comedian had to celebrate.

Buster Keaton recalls that it was an evening shadowed by a shapeless dread. "What could you say to the poor bastard? He was getting the works. A funeral would have been more cheerful. Half the people there whispered and tiptoed around, and the others laughed too loud."

Certain circumstances—plus untold conjecture and rumor—brought Roscoe Arbuckle to trial. The circumstances: Arbuckle had engaged a suite of rooms for the Labor Day holiday for himself, actor Lowell Sherman, and director Fred Fishback. The suite, a living room and two bedrooms, was on the twelfth floor of the St. Francis Hotel on Union Square. Next morning open house began. People, mostly uninvited, crowded in and out, consuming vast quantities of bellhop-supplied bootleg liquor. The exact number of these people was never determined. Some were never identified, even by name. This did not faze the State of California. This was not a whodunit but a *hedunit*.

The revelry seems to have lasted most of Sunday night. On Monday morning at about ten-thirty, actors' agent Al Semnacher telephoned Arbuckle, awakening him. He said he had driven up from Hollywood with a dress model named Bambina Maud Delmont and his client Virginia Rappe. Miss Rappe, twenty-three and pretty, was a movie actress of five years experience in bit parts.

"Come on up," said Arbuckle. He rose, bathed, shaved, and was breakfasting in pajamas when Semnacher arrived, having added two additional girls—Alice Blake, dress-model friend of Delmont, and a show girl who thereafter was referred to variously as Sadie Reiss, Zey Preven, Zeb Prevost, and Zeh Prevon.

The newcomers attacked the liquor. Other people began dropping in. The liquor attacked the people. Later, in court, Miss Delmont would admit to having had "ten drinks of whiskey" in a short period and then "doing a little dance" to the music of a windup phonograph. Men put on women's hats. The overloaded ones disappeared into the bathrooms and returned wan but ready for more. There were, in short, thousands of such parties going on at that very time all over the country, in kitchens, hotel rooms, penthouses, speakeasies.

No one noticed Virginia Rappe "staggering" from the sitting room. The time was put at about 2 P.M. Perhaps half an hour later, Arbuckle went to his bedroom to get dressed. On what then took place, his own testimony never varied. The bathroom door bumped against something; he pushed it open by main strength and found Virginia on the floor. She mumbled a request for water, gulped a glass and a half. She wanted to lie down. A *passout*, Arbuckle thought, and carried her to the nearest bed. He returned to the bathroom, dressed, and prepared to rejoin the party. It was then, he said, 3 P.M.

He heard moans and found Virginia on the floor between the twin beds. She had ripped off her dress, was clutching her stomach, and seemed to be frothing at the mouth. He stepped to the door and called for help. Maud Delmont came in. He left the girl in her care.

Sober enough to remember his duties as a host, Arbuckle returned in a few minutes to see how Miss Rappe was doing. He found Miss Delmont massaging the girl's bare abdomen with ice. He protested and removed the ice. Miss Delmont told him, angrily, to mind his own business, so he left the bedroom.

The party roared on. "Dead soldiers" were discarded, new bottles opened; bellboys came with more and with "setups"—ginger ale, glasses, ice. Everyone—even those later testifying to the most sinister goings-on—assumed that Virginia Rappe had simply passed out. In a while, however, her screams and wails became audible above the noise. Arbuckle remarked that she would have to be sobered up or taken away. Fishback prepared the traditional cure-all, a tub of cold water, and dunked the girl. She screamed louder than ever. Shortly after 4 p.m. Arbuckle called the desk. The manager himself came up. He suggested moving Virginia down the hall to a vacant room. Roscoe and Miss Delmont wrapped her in a robe, then he and the manager carried her there and put her to bed. Miss Delmont did not go along.

The party continued. Everyone forgot Virginia. The rug was rolled back, the phonograph wound up, and the "rug-cutters" went to work. (Soon this would be "Raper Dances While Victim Dies.") It was late evening before the crowd thinned. Arbuckle, Sherman, and Fishback, together with a few guests, were among the last diners in the main dining room. Next morning, Tuesday, September 6, the three drove back to Hollywood.

Maud Delmont meanwhile took a room of her own in which to sober up. This took some time. Next day, Wednesday, she found Miss Rappe still in bed. Virginia looked bad. Miss Delmont called in a Dr. Rumwell. He examined the girl and ordered her hospitalized. He and the staff concluded that she was suffering a "systemic upset from alcoholic poisoning." Two days later, on Friday, she died. Rumwell did an autopsy and found that peritonitis had been the immediate cause of death. A later postmortem disclosed a ruptured bladder. Her body bore a number of superficial bruises.

Hearing of the party, the police came in and summoned every guest they could find for questioning by them and by the coroner's office. Arbuckle left Hollywood before dawn on Saturday, September 10, bringing with him Fishback and Sherman and (at Lou Anger's request) attorney Frank Dominguez. (Later on, famed trial attorney Gavin McNab was retained to head the defense.) Rumors were already flying. Before departing, Arbuckle and his two friends issued a joint statement that no violence had been done to Miss Rappe.

Maud Delmont, meanwhile, "in a state of collapse on the 12th floor of the St. Francis," was telling a lurid tale to shorthand stenographers sent by police to her bedside. It was pure Elinor Glyn. Arbuckle, she said, had dragged Virginia Rappe to his bedroom, announced, "I've waited five years and now I've got you," and then locked the door. Virginia was "screaming piteously," and Miss Delmont had had to kick and batter the door before Arbuckle, after a lengthy wait, had finally let her enter. "There lay Virginia, helpless and ravished."

Miss Delmont's story subsequently varied materially from trial to trial, and she never did explain why all the other guests—including the girl's personal agent, Semnacher—paid not the least attention to all this. At trial, Arbuckle explained that he had locked the door for privacy while dressing and had discovered Virginia's presence only after he had found the bathroom door blocked. He later unlocked the outer door, from bedroom to sitting room, he testified, when he called for help.

When Arbuckle arrived at police headquarters, Detective Captain Griffith told reporters that the star would not be arrested unless the complete investigation should connect him with a crime. Forty minutes later Griffith's associate, Captain Matheson, had clapped Arbuckle in a cell and charged him with murder in the first degree, District Attorney Matthew Brady in the meantime having talked with Sadie Reiss (or Zeh Prevon or take your choice). Her story, never made public, was rumored to be even more lurid than Maud Delmont's. It proved even more unstable too. Two days later Sadie refused to sign the statement, although she was threatened with a perjury charge. The DA announced, "Whenever wealth and influence are brought to the bar of justice every sinister and corrupt practice is used in an effort to free the accused." This was quite evidently a smoke screen to hide a red face. It was already clear that great pressure was being brought to condemn Arbuckle, innocent or guilty, while the wealthy and influential ran like rats. In fact, Coroner Harry Kelly stated that women's groups and clergymen were hounding him to prove Arbuckle a murderer. On the basis of his findings, however, he construed the case as manslaughter, at the most, and did not name Arbuckle.

The fire-and-brimstoners thundered from the pulpit, "Arbuckle lives a life fit only for swine," and "The salacious and sensuous are dragging the youth of the nation through a sordid stream of moral infamy." The latter jeremiad cost its voicer, the Reverend Mr.

Straton, most of his congregation. More than two hundred of them resigned, saying the outburst "surpassed even vaudeville." But many clergy remained determined to destroy Fatty Arbuckle. Professor William McKeever of the National Presbyterian Board even called for "martial law in the cities until the mad, mob spirit is taken out of the movies."

For these, such a stance at least passed for a moral crusade. For others it was a chance to grab the spotlight. Movie director Henry Lehrman, for example, snatched at the calcium light in a *Times* interview. Once associated with Sennett and Arbuckle at Keystone, Lehrman had not even been in San Francisco, let alone at the fatal party. But he called for full punishment for "this user of cocaine and opium—this beast who has outraged and slain Virginia, my first and last sacred love." Hollywood, peeking out, was bewildered—it had not even known that Henry and Virginia were engaged.

Lehrman gave the best critique of his own performance. Asked by the interviewer whether he would attend Miss Rappe's funeral in Los Angeles, he replied that he was too busy with his affairs in New York. Nor was Lehrman there when a crowd of eight thousand fought to get into the services for his sacred love.

The preliminary hearings were marked by Miss Delmont's hysterical outbursts, the default of more of Arbuckle's friends, and the appearance of more and more women witnesses. The case seemed morbidly attractive to females.

Semnacher, having earlier affirmed Arbuckle's innocence, now claimed that the accused had spoken of his (not Miss Delmont's) applying ice to Miss Rappe's body and also had said that he had taken her "into a room and committed certain acts likely to have caused her injury." Three days later, when Semnacher again reversed himself, the presiding judge rebuked him as "a worthless witness."

Lowell Sherman had cut out for the East before being questioned, and he successfully evaded all attempts to bring him back. He left behind a statement affirming Arbuckle's innocence and augmented it with a fuller deposition in Chicago. Sherman, however, shortly discovered what the trial was really all about. Only a few days later, New York papers reported him as "released from his contract with a large motion picture company."

Among the new female witnesses were Alice Blake, one of the Semnacher-Rappe-Delmont contingent, and a number of hospital nurses who had attended Miss Rappe. Miss Blake's recital of violent rape by a monster was already a little late. It was discredited in advance by Zeh Prevon's statement and retraction of a similar story.

The nurses' testimony varied wildly. Although neither autopsy showed any evidence of rape, one nurse said that Virginia had told her that she had been violated, and another nurse quoted the deceased as asking, "Did they find him? Have they got him?" This closely resembled the published reports by Misses Delmont, Prevon, and Blake quoting Virginia as saying, "I'm dying, he killed me," or "He did it." Rumwell, on the contrary, testified that when he had talked with Virginia shortly before her death, she had said that she had been drinking and could not remember what had happened.

Attention was drawn to the fact that in all the accusations, the attacker was never named. It was always "he"—the immemorial Adam. Then Nurse Jean Jameson was called and threw a bombshell. Virginia, she said, had confided to her that she had been ill for "many weeks with a certain ailment," for which she had blamed a Hollywood screen director. She had named the director. He had not been at the St. Francis party.

Doctors then cautiously testified that syphilis (the "certain ailment") *could* have caused the bursting of the bladder and in turn led to peritonitis. They strongly doubted it, however. Asked specifically whether physical violence might have precipitated the bursting of the organ, the medical men said that it was possible, then carefully added that a fall could also have done so and caused the bruises as well.

The state's case had become a mare's nest. It was collapsing before it could come to court. Even tabloids like the New York *News* were admitting

ARBUCKLE CASE WEAKENS

Emboldened, the defense moved for dismissal. The motion was brushed aside. Police Judge Sylvain J. Lazarus, who was presiding, was bluntly frank. "We are not trying Arbuckle alone," he declared. "We are trying our present day social conditions, our present day looseness of thought and lack of social balance."

California was feeling its sovereignty. Reducing the murder charge to manslaughter, it impaneled a theoretically unprejudiced jury (the defense had expended its challenges on the first prospective panelists questioned), and trial began. The prosecution paraded witnesses to the stand for a month. Even the press had to admit that the accused was the most consistent of all the witnesses and that the prosecution was seriously damaged by some of its star testifiers. For example,

Miss Rappe's housekeeper, Irene Morgan, volunteered that she had frequently cared for Virginia after the actress had drunk to excess. She added that Miss Rappe had on occasion cried, screamed, and doubled up in seeming pain while tearing off her clothes. This last unsolicited tidbit disposed most effectively of the torn dress that Miss Delmont had removed from the Arbuckle bedroom and kept until the trial. Miss Delmont's surprise exhibit lost its relevance in the light of this testimony.

The prosecution then proceeded to nail down its rebuttal of its own point. Another witness, subpoenaed by the state from Chicago, was called to testify to Miss Rappe's good reputation. This witness had worked with the deceased at a department store in the actress's premovie days. She was impelled to recall that on at least three occasions Virginia had torn off her clothes and screamed. On one occasion, she had ruined an evening dress from stock; on the second, she had been taken to the store infirmary; after the third, she had been discharged from her job.

Testimony and cross-examination ended; opposing counsel summed up; judge charged jury. The panel was out for an interminable time and finally requested that it be discharged as hung. A court official tipped off the press that "the balloting favored acquittal throughout." The foreman later stated that "one of the two in the minority refused to consider the evidence at any time and said . . . that she would cast her ballot against Arbuckle and would not 'change it till hell froze over.' "

The foreman told reporters, "It seemed to us that the prosecution's case was an insult to the intelligence of the jury. It asked us to substitute conjecture for facts."

A new trial was set for January 11, 1922. Meanwhile the state's star witness, Bambina Maud Delmont, faced the law herself and was convicted on December 18 of bigamy. She was sentenced but placed on probation to allow her to testify at the second Arbuckle trial.

The motion-picture industry had thoroughly panicked. It now began the wholesale (and probably illegal) procedure of writing retroactive morality clauses into existing actors' contracts. United by adversity, Hollywood got together on the old question of self-regulation and film censorship. Will Hays, incumbent Postmaster General under Harding, resigned to head the new Motion Picture Producers and Distributors Association, thenceforth called the Hays Office. With wide powers and a position strongly akin to that of Judge Kenesaw Mountain Landis, so-called Czar of baseball since the 1919 Black Sox scandal, Hays too became known as Czar. Many actors, many films felt the power of Hays and the Hays Office. It was here that the expression "giving him/it the office" originated.

The second trial was barely under way when still another film-capital sensation broke: the unsolved murder of director William Desmond Taylor. It smeared two women stars with completely un-proved scandal. One was Mary Miles Minter. The other was Mabel Normand, so long associated with Arbuckle in the Keystone years.

Gene Fowler observed in the Sennett biography:

It mattered not that some of the world's best detectives and a host of officials agreed that neither Mabel nor Mary could have committed, or even witnessed, the crime. The habitual witch-burners came screaming into the public squares to rant against the sins of movieland. Down with the Arbuckles and the Normands.

Was Arbuckle's second jury affected by this scandal? Although it too was hung, now it was ten to two for conviction! Amazed, the New York *Times* commented that the two juries might have been from two different races of beings. The case for the prosecution, the *Times* added, had been even weaker the second time out.

The third trial began March 16, six months after Arbuckle's arrest. A verdict by a jury of his peers had really ceased to matter. Public sentence had long been under way. The state now produced some seventy witnesses. Roscoe found himself actually in two separate trials. More successful than the State of California, the United States confiscated Fatty's beloved Rolls Royce for illegal transportation of intoxicating liquor. Stripping off the upholstery, however, had un-covered no cocaine.

To Arbuckle the loss of the car was a fleabite. While the trial was on he was given a leather-bound checkbook as a birthday present. "If I write a check for one dollar," he remarked, "I'll be in still an-other trial." By the end of his third and last murder trial, the Ar-buckle defense expenses totaled one hundred and ten thousand dollars.

The last jury was out six minutes: one minute for deliberation, five for preparing a statement. This was the statement we have al-ready examined. The *Times*, with good reason, called it "a unique document of legal literature."

The jury tried faithfully to say to the people, "For God's sake, lay off Fatty Arbuckle." Yet if one fact about the whole confused affair *is* clear, it is this: the American people never sat on the case of Roscoe Arbuckle—they were sold a bill of goods.

One week after Arbuckle's acquittal the Hays Office officially banned all his comedies and barred the comedian from ever again acting in films. Hays stated, "After consultation at length with Nicholas Schenck, representing Joseph Schenck, the producers, and Adolph Zukor and Jesse Lasky of Famous Players–Lasky Corporation, the distributors, I will say that at my request they have canceled all showings and all bookings of the Arbuckle films."

It was as predictable as it was unjust. Hays could not betray the scandal that had put him in lifetime clover. Asked to comment on the statement by the jury foreman, Hays refused.

"Does this mean that Arbuckle is out for good?" he was asked.

"You know as well as I," Hays replied, "the purposes of our organization—'to attain and maintain the highest moral and artistic standards.' "

Not everyone, by a long shot, thought that they were being attained and maintained by compounding injustice. In 1924, Gilbert Seldes, acute observer of the 1920's scene, wrote in his *Seven Lively Arts*: "It seemed . . . in 1922 that . . . if a moving picture actor was declared innocent, he was barred from the screen."

In all Hollywood only Buster Keaton still tried to help Roscoe Arbuckle. He opened his purse—no one will ever know how much money he gave his friend. More practically, he pleaded with Joe Schenck to let the exiled star become a director. Schenck objected. Fatty's name, he said, was anathema—or a shorter, simpler word to that effect.

"Then I have a name for him," said Buster. "Call him Will B. Goode."

Schenck had to laugh. Eventually Roscoe got his directing chance. Schenck cleared it with Hayes and changed the suggested *nom de guerre* to William Goodrich.

After the last trial and the ensuing Hays fiasco, Buster Keaton, talking with Natalie, summed up an era's ending. "Things will never be the same again in Hollywood," he said. "Nor anywhere else."

The Crest of the Wave

TWENTY

~~~~~~~~~~~~~~~~~~~~~~~~~~~~~~

I F, W I T H success, Buster Keaton's perpetual fatalism had been fading, Roscoe Arbuckle's ordeal, from its almost fortuitous beginning to its almost foreseeable finale, would certainly have revived it. As it was, it simply confirmed it anew.

What gripped him, as always, was the way that random events or willed actions could equally bring about the same ending. Like the branchings of the highroad in O. Henry's *Roads of Destiny*—no point in getting hung up picking one: take any road from one to three— they all end up at the same place anyway. And in the same events. Buster found himself comparing his father with Arbuckle. *Joe had it and threw it away. Roscoe had it and it was taken away. There may be a difference,* he thought. *If so, I don't see it.*

Perhaps it was only coincidence or his own normal artistic development, but it is true that certain comedies that Buster Keaton made during his friend's seven-month ordeal show a new depth and a more determined emphasis on fate. Yet such is the comic genius that these same comedies loosed laughter everywhere.

In fact, having gotten a belly laugh with the program listings in *The Playhouse,* Keaton was now about to get what some old-timers claimed was the longest sustained laugh the theatre had ever known. It came with his eleventh two-reel comedy, *The Boat,* which was begun about a week after Arbuckle's arrest. The laugh, like an organ point of risibility, accompanied the prolonged disaster of the launching of the craft from which the picture takes its name.

Buster Keaton built two pictures around oceangoing vessels. Many prefer the six-reel film *The Navigator* of 1924 to the 1921 short *The Boat.* It is mainly a matter of taste: one is a novel, the other a short story, but the theme is the same: man adrift in a boat on the endless sea. It is the grandest, simplest theme of all, from the Ark to the *Argo* to the tossing rowboats of Dunkirk. Others, however, believe that it is in *The Boat* rather than in *The Navigator* that we find the real Buster Keaton. Their preference is based less on the choice between shorter and fuller statement and more on the question of endings. That the first is about the flimsiest of homemade craft and the other the grandest of ocean liners is beside the point. The point is not the length of the stories, not the craft, not even the voyage, but the destination—where will voyage and voyagers end?

The real answer of Buster Keaton, both artist and man, is "Nowhere." His answer to the question "Where?" is the question's echo. It broods over every voyage, large or small. It is not so much "Is this trip necessary?" as "Is this trip going anywhere?" For voyaging is inescapable—it is life, it is time. In *The Boat*, the question is left honestly unsolved: "Nowhere" is both answer and nonanswer.

In *The Navigator* Buster bows, mockingly maybe, to the happy ending. The voyage in *The Boat* is from somewhere to nowhere; that of the liner in *The Navigator*, from somewhere to somewhere else. The two-reel comedy *The Boat* was successful, but *The Navigator* was one of the top-grossing comedies of its time. If the pudding's proof is in the eating, there it is: give us Americans the happy ending any old time.

Before the building of the boat begins, there is a happy little home: a bungalow with a family of four. Then Dad constructs a yacht in the bungalow basement—and disaster ensues, to go on and on and then to end in stalemate. Dad is Buster Keaton. As the picture opens he has just finished the yacht. It is ready to be launched. Dad puts wife and two little sons (this was before Buster's own two sons were born) in the family Model T, hitches a towrope to the boat's bows, lets out the clutch, and hauls away. The yacht edges out, squeezing through the too-narrow basement door; its flaring sides begin tearing out the house foundation, and then the craft is clear.

Good!

Good? Just wait. We watch the Ford towing the boat away. Then we—and the family—glance back. The house is trembling. The Ford stops to let all gaze back, transfixed. The bungalow shudders from rooftree to foundation and collapses. Home is gone—a heap of debris in its place. The four stare at the ruins, then stare at one another—all with the same Keaton deadpan—and drive on.

The launching ways are reached; the boat is set in the cradle; it is ready for christening.

Good!

Just wait. Having skillfully maneuvered the yacht into place, Dad will now park the Ford. His foot touches the wrong pedal—reverse—and in one fated second he has backed off the pier and into the drink. A moment later he bobs up soaking wet and scrambles to land. Now car is gone. They stare blankly at its watery grave, then at one another.

Now began the long laugh that rocked the theatres in 1921. Swinging a Coca-Cola bottle, Mom says, "I christen thee *Damfino*." The bottle does not even break. Instead, it leaves a deep, ominous dent in the hull.

Slowly, with Buster standing in the bows, the *Damfino* starts down the ways. Slowly she keeps on, nearer and nearer to the bosom of her native element. Now her stern is sinking and the water begins washing forward over the deck. She doesn't stop—on and on—now her stone-faced skipper is going under; the water is to his knees, to his shoulders, and his ship, the proud *Damfino*, settles down on the bottom of the bay.

It seemed to take hours, and through all the slow-unfolding catastrophe, the laughter grew and grew, to reach its hysterical crescendo with the boat's engulfment. The laughter rolled in breaking gasps and howls on through the blank interchange of looks and the slow fade-out; it echoed through the slow fade-in of a subtitle:

YOU CAN'T KEEP A GOOD BOAT DOWN

With these words the last gasping echoes turned into a vast sigh of relief. Final disaster had been sidestepped. The next shot shows the *Damfino* salvaged, raised, repaired, and in commission. Her flag is flying. The family of four, all in officers' uniforms, are on deck. To sea!

The happy ending? Don't you believe it! Mischief's chain continues. It becomes clearer and clearer that the boat's slangy moniker

Launching the *Damfino*.
Scene from *The Boat*, 1921.

means not "damn fine" but "damned if I know." All day long, as the craft passes through the long straits that lead to the sea, things break off and members of the family fall off. A low bridge tears away the whole gallant superstructure—bridge, masts, and funnel. The nail that is used to hang a picture on the cabin wall goes right on through and water spurts in. Ad infinitum. *Dal capo al fine*, it is a virtuoso performance, a *fugato* of ineptitude and mischance, Keaton's cadenza in the concerto of hard luck.

The sun is setting as the boat reaches the open sea. We've made it! Good! We'll go below for dinner. How homely but festive at table —an occasion after all: our first meal on the great Pacific Ocean!

Then comes the storm. The boat rocks, dishes slide to the floor. Leaks spring everywhere, water gushes in. Dad rushes to his short-wave sending set: SOS! SOS!

The signal reaches a coast-guard cutter. The captain radios back, "Who are you?"

Dad taps back, *"Damfino."*

"Well, if they don't know, who the hell does!" the captain exclaims irritably. "Some practical joker. Stay on course."

There goes the last and only chance of rescue. The *Damfino* is foundering, with only a bathtub for a lifeboat. They paddle away in pitch-black night, tossing on mountainous waves. Then Junior pulls out the drain plug. The bathtub starts to sink.

Then, suddenly, it stops sinking. The waves subside. The water is calm. One by one, Dad first, they cautiously put out a foot, then a leg, then step into the water. It is not even knee-deep. Once more the four deadpan faces exchange a blank look. Then Mom's lips frame a soundless question. The subtitle flashes it on:

WHERE ARE WE?

Dad answers. No subtitle is needed; it is easy to read his lips: "Damned if I know!"—or "Damfino!"

And off into the darkness they go, wading nowhere through a universe of mud and knee-deep water.

The Boat is as great a laugh-getter today as ever. Its Homeric theme, tuned to laughter, cannot stale. Audiences still find its ending funny. Yet it is a haunting ending, not a happy one.

Keaton's developing methods of story construction are especially traceable in a story both factual and absurd such as *The Boat*. Its story is not a string of gags in the old Keystone manner; rather, each ridiculous accident is part of an unfolding narration, each makes the

Where are we? *Damfino!* Scene from *The Boat*, 1921.

next more believable and increases the nagging sense of inevitability that is both so funny and so troubling. With these shorts, Buster Keaton's work—both plot and performance—was now indeed becoming, as a reviewer had just written, "high art in low comedy."

Buster recalls that some of *The Boat*'s laughs were in the filming, not the film. Gabouri, the new technical-effects man Lou Anger had hired, seemed infected by the Keaton syndrome. His own maiden voyage was not auspicious. He built two separate *Damfinos*, outwardly alike, but intended for two different purposes. One was designed to sink at launching, the other to float. The gremlins that slept in the Keaton Studio at night decreed otherwise. No. 1, though loaded with scrap iron, refused to sink. Its bottom kept falling out and dumping the iron to the bottom, whereupon the empty shell would shoot up like a cork.

Each time this happened the location rang with laughter, Elgin Lessley and crew, Buster and cast all rolling on the ground. Gabouri sweated and swore. Finally, patience gone, he faced the recalcitrant hulk. "Goddamn your miserable waterlogged soul, you're going to sink!" He gave up on the scrap iron, fastened steel cables below the waterline, ran them to a winch that was turned by a donkey engine, and No. 1 sank by main force. All hands cheered.

Gabe relaxed. But the gremlins didn't. No. 2, built to float, was determined to sink. "This can't happen to me," said Gabouri, although it already had. All through the voyage, No. 2 kept taking on water and listing, until finally a crew had to stay belowdecks manning jury-rigged pumps.

"It's your ordeal by water," Buster said.

Anyway, his ordeal over, Gabouri made Buster a solemn promise. "Someday," he said, "I'll get you a boat that *is* a boat, one that will sail if you want it to sail and sink if you want it to sink." Three years later he made good that pledge. The new boat was the ocean liner of *The Navigator*.

The next picture, *The Paleface*, marks the end of 1921. After *The Boat*, with its crystallization of fate into the symbols of ship and sea, there was a new drive toward visual truth in both action and photography. In *The Paleface* are Keaton's first serious attempts at applying documentary techniques and point of view to the filming of comedy. He does this without losing sight of comedy's first aim: to create laughter. *The Paleface* is an exceptionally funny picture, shaped with Keaton's deep sense of the utterly ridiculous. It is lighthearted, completely unshadowed by Nemesis. As if reacting sharply against the fatalism of *The Boat*, Buster in the new picture invokes his own lifelong personal defense against adverse fate, namely, The Miracle.

The Paleface casts him in a new variant of the role of the well-

Scene from *The Paleface*, 1921.

intentioned innocent: a butterfly-chasing entomologist who wanders straight into an intertribal Indian war. The saving miracles include his six-hundred-foot slide down a mountainous gravel slope, his escape from a burning cabin by devising asbestos underwear, and, finally, his adoption by the tribe as Little Chief and his marriage to the chief's daughter, Little Squab.

To combine fantasies like these with documentary photography was no small feat, though one aided greatly by Keaton's own ideas of reality, which, though pragmatic, derive from a childhood and youth lived in vaudeville. *The Paleface* signally proves how the photographic realism of documentary techniques can heighten the credibility of the almost incredible. It also made picture making even more dangerous for Keaton. In his visual lexicon, documentary photography, to be of intrinsic value, must show what is really taking place—no camera tricks, no half-truths, no stunt man doubling for him. Pursuing this policy would from now on involve Buster in more and more physical hazard.

The long, accelerating slide on gravel was one such hazard. It was executed by the star himself and photographed in one continuous shot. Even more obviously dangerous (and, hence, thrilling and persuasive to see) was his sensational flight over a suspension bridge spanning a deep mountain chasm. Perhaps ten to twelve feet long, this bridge consisted of two parallel stretched wires that originally had held a solid floor of barrel staves laid crosswise and edge to edge. Only half of the staves remained. Facing his Indian pursuers, Buster crawled rapidly backward. Using both hands with flashing speed, he picked up a stave at a time in front of him, then deposited it behind —like a human Caterpillar tractor laying his track as he went—thus constantly bridging the void himself but leaving no bridge for his pursuers. As he eased off on the far bank, he had picked it clean of staves.

But some of the subtle essence of the Keaton comedy sense is revealed by the net accomplishment, in terms of escape, that accrued from this accomplished and highly dangerous flurry of action: *it is all for naught; he does not get away.* Having gone over the bridge backward, he steps off the bridge to the embankment and right into the arms of more hostile tribesmen, who have only that instant arrived on the other side of the chasm.

But we were speaking not of screen dangers from actors made up as Indians but of real dangers to flesh and bone involved in risky stunts. Characteristically, this Keatonian escape fiasco leads, with

Keatonian logic, immediately to another escape maneuver—also really performed—one even more dangerous in actuality. Captured, he wrenches loose from his captors, whirls, and, as if instinctively, dives for the bridge. But there *is* no bridge; he has just stripped it bare of staves. His dive arches on, headlong, down into a very real, very deep chasm. The camera, without cutting scene, pans down to follow his dive to its end, a plunge into a mountain stream. Documentary photography thus revealed honest, continuous action and really hair-raising danger, for the chasm was a full sixty feet deep. It goes without saying that there was no safety net.

A mime by nature and by training, Buster Keaton thinks in visuals. Silent pictures suited him. They were opportunity, not limitation. His silent films, from his first to his last, were the talk of the industry because of the small number of subtitles they needed to explain their action. With Keaton, action alone is almost complete communication. There are times, in fact, when it is complete. With him, action can also be almost incredibly beautiful, in a very pure kinetic sense—that is to say, not action *for* something but action in itself. In 1922, with *The Paleface*, Keaton—going on still further from documentary clarity and verisimilitude—began to reach for kinetic line. He sought it for expressiveness. In bringing that, it also added aesthetic value. In *The Paleface* we see Keaton's first use of large masses of people in long swirling lines of action, beautifully activated rhythms that, within five years, would culminate with the sweep of armies in *The General*.

Enrico Guazzoni had done it first in the Italian film *Quo Vadis*. That was in 1912. David Wark Griffith was the first American director to use crowds with that kind of rhythmic sweep and majesty, in 1915 in *The Birth of a Nation*. After Griffith, other directors had manipulated crowd movements in serious dramatic films. But Buster Keaton was the first (and virtually the only one) to apply the method to comedy. It is rather remarkable to have done so at all. It underlines Keaton's ineradicable sense of comedy as serious and of the theatre as the really real thing.

These various aspects of realism come to the fore in the very next picture, *Cops*, conjoining with the fatalism temporarily exorcised in *The Paleface*. Begun while the third Arbuckle trial was nearing, *Cops* —both in title and in substance—almost certainly betrays Buster Keaton's growing sense of the hopelessness of Arbuckle's predicament. It is only on the surface that *Cops* is a replay of the old Keystone theme. It is much more, more even than man adrift on the sea but consoled by his family. It is man completely alone and fleeing before his fellow men. It is fate operating through accident and misunderstanding, nullifying good intentions, canceling hope, bringing ruin. In the police en masse against the lone individual, Keaton found the perfect embodiment of his hostile machine–man concept, of fateful accident without saving miracle.

It sounds as if we are talking about Kafkaesque tragedy—something senseless, absurd, and irremediable. And indeed, in part, we are. *Cops* is certainly the most serious (indeed, tragic) and possibly the greatest (or most thoroughly achieved) of all the Keaton two-reelers. It is a simple story, simply told, with implications on many levels. In brief: it is one man against the police; it is man against fate; it is fate worked out through the machinelike hostility of man toward his fellow man; and it is fate inside the individual, in the ineradicable patterns of his own stupidity, so that it is man against himself.

Although no miracle comes to save Keaton, *Cops* itself is something of a miracle: the Kafkaesque tale is yet an unforgettably funny tale, a pure evocation of the world of Buster Keaton, as uniquely Keaton as *The Gold Rush* is uniquely Chaplin. It is a picture full of what Gilbert Seldes has called Keaton's "enormous, incorruptible gravity . . . intense preoccupation . . . hard sense of personality."

In *Cops*, Buster himself, acting with the best of intentions, fetches disaster down upon his own head. So vehement, so vindictive, so utter is this final disaster that one can readily accept the idea of "roaring, destructive, careless energy" that Seldes ascribed to the workings of slapstick. So fatally fitted into the chain of his ultimate destruction is every move that Buster makes that one is reminded of art historian Dr. Erwin Panofsky's description of Keaton the comedian as "imperturbably serious, inscrutable, and stubborn, who acts under the impulse of an irresistible power unknown to himself, comparable only to the mysterious urge that causes the birds to migrate or the avalanche to come crashing down."

In *Cops*, as Seldes wrote, "thousands of policemen rushed down one street; equal thousands rushed up another; and before them fled this small, serious figure, bent on self-justification, caught in a series of absurd accidents, wholly law-abiding, a little distracted."

This whirl of mass action, Keaton's first comedy essay in utilizing the grand manner of *Quo Vadis* and *The Birth of a Nation*, caught every knowing eye at the time. Particularly so because of Buster's personal use of it: preceding the swarming screen and sweeping action was a lonely moment of empty space and no action. This is the moment *before* the cops pour down the street, the moment when fate hangs in the balance—and there, down at the far end of the long avenue, stands the policeman's quarry, all alone, poised but motionless, in a Di Chirico-like perspective of ominous space. It is a disturbing moment, haunted with almost too many possibilities. Whatever may or may not follow—escape or capture—this moment holds its own complete meaning, that of the essential loneliness of the individual. Here in this dissolving moment, Buster Keaton found the perfect visual symbol he would use in film after film.

A museum director, the late Dr. Jermayne MacAgy saw this visual symbol as uniquely Keaton. "Buster Keaton's portrait," she said, "is not a close-up. It is Buster in a great empty space, facing you from far, far away. There he stands motionless for that one moment, waiting for his fate."

The simple story of *Cops* is that of an easygoing youth, getting nowhere in particular, whose girl, the mayor's daughter, issues him an ultimatum: become a big businessman or you lose me. He sets out. Suddenly he has capital: a policeman's wallet—in his hands by innocent mischance. He does not know the man or where to find him or even that he is a cop. (Already the *gendarmerie* is entering his life.) He goes into business: he pays a sharpster, who does not own them, for a horse and wagon that are not for sale; then he pays a con man, who does not own it, for a houseful of furniture. The real owner, naturally, is a cop.

Buster now sets out in the wagon he thinks he owns, aiming to sell—at a handsome profit—the furniture he thinks he owns. Then he will be what his girl wants him to be—a success. It is the American dream.

The American dream quickly begins turning into nightmare. He and his wagonload of furniture somehow stumble into the midst of the annual police parade. Unable to get out of the line, he is swept along the crowd-lined avenue toward the reviewing stand in front of the City Hall. There stands his girl with her father (the mayor) and all the other dignitaries. Just as he approaches, the scene cuts to the roof of the City Hall. Up there, out of sight, a group of anarchists are lighting a bomb. They toss it over the parapet. It lands on the wagon seat beside Buster. Oblivious, inattentive, absorbed as usual, Keaton lights a cigarette with its burning fuse and carelessly tosses the bomb to the sidewalk right in front of the reviewing stand. The blast catapults him into the air, shatters the wagon, tips over the reviewing stand, and flattens the marchers like rows of tenpins.

Scene from *Cops*, 1922.

Scene from *Cops*, 1922.

A quick shot shows the people on the stand upset and shaken but not injured. The wagon, however, is upset and the furniture scattered over the pavement. But his problem is much more immediate. It is survival. New York's Finest, to the man, are after him.

It is thousands after one; the pursuit swirls through the city; the lines of action spread into panoramas; the tempo quickens—and then abruptly the chase ends as Buster flees into a great open doorway, his pursuers on his heels. It ends because, as the camera pans to the sign above the door to show, he has fled into Central Police Station. Pushed by unseen hands from within, the great doors close. The scene fades.

Another fades in: Slowly the great doors open; a policeman backs out, a great bunch of keys in one hand. Slowly, carefully, he closes the doors again, turns a key in the lock, tosses the keys into a garbage can, and turns. It is the face we all know.

Seldes wrote of this figure, "Quietly, quietly locking the huge doors behind it. *It*," Seldes repeated, "it, yes, for by that time Keaton has become wholly impersonal."

A symbol, yes, but not yet impersonal. Only a final defeat can do that to him. So far, against all odds, against the law's myriad myrmidons, against fate, he has seemingly triumphed. Flight, capture, and escape were all gratuitous delays of his only real objectives: success, then marriage. At this very moment *she* walks by. He turns to her. She tosses her head and walks on. His shoulders slump. Fishing in the garbage, he retrieves the key and opens the door. In the flash of an eye a dozen grasping hands drag him inside. The doors close.

There is left only the final shot: a simple tombstone. Carved at the top, a finial slightly askew, is Keaton's little porkpie hat. Engraved on the tombstone are those final words: "The End."

The cops did not win. Fate did. But, even then, it was not overt disaster. Fate, rather, moved a final piece, checkmating hope. It was the victim, as if made mad by the gods, who then destroyed himself.

Had there been an epitaph on the little stone, it might well have read: "He Did the Right Things. He Thought the Right Thoughts. Wha' Happen?"

He was the boy Alger didn't write about.

The memory of *Cops* that Buster Keaton most likes to tell concerns the old swaybacked nag that pulled the wagon.

"Onyx," he says, "was my costar. Bruckman, for some cockeyed reason, named him Onyx. I can't recall why we didn't rent a horse. Anyway we bought this old-timer.

"There was a scene—before we stumble into the parade—where Onyx slows down and can't pull the heavy load of furniture any longer. I'm to unharness him and lead him out from the shafts. Then it's to cut and show me, bit in mouth, between the shafts pulling the wagon. Then pan back and show Onyx up in the wagon riding.

"It was a good idea except that Onyx wouldn't go along with it. We wasted a day trying to get him up in that wagon. He wouldn't walk up a ramp, refused to be hoisted in a veterinarian's bellyband, snorted and kicked whenever we came near. We finally gave up and shot the scene with me pulling the wagon alongside of the horse. Not as good a gag, but it had to do. That finished the Saturday shooting.

"Monday morning we saw the reason for it all. Onyx had a brand-new colt standing by her when we came to the studio. *Her*, I said.

"Bruckman was just opening his mouth to say something. I could feel the word forming in his mind. I beat him to it. 'The baby's name,' I said, 'is Onyxpected!' "

TWENTY-ONE

F OR Buster Keaton, Onyxpected, the foal that only his dam
expected, ushered in a year of signs and wonders. Straight off,
it was found that Natalie was expecting. This discovery did no less
than precipitate changes of some moment in the movie industry. At
that time the Talmadge clan was box office second only to the Pick-
ford-Fairbanks royal couple. Norma and Constance were always at
or near the top, while Buster and Harold Lloyd shuttled back and
forth right behind Chaplin. Now, it developed, Natalie Talmadge
Keaton was not to birth her baby without handmaidens from her kin.

It was a distaff decision. With the Norma Talmadge, Constance
Talmadge, and Buster Keaton companies all founded and headed by
Joe Schenck, and with all the principals in-laws, it was a tight combine and one that, from the outside, looked like a benevolent patri-
archy. In point of fact, however, it was more nearly a matriarchate.
The real clan ruler was Mrs. Talmadge, who, as mother and mother-
in-law, could pull rank on them all. Peg Talmadge was an agreeable,
motherly lady but one also thoroughly conscious of her position.

After shifting Roscoe Arbuckle to Hollywood five years before,
Schenck had kept the two sisters' companies in New York. After
Natalie's marriage, Peg Talmadge commuted back and forth between
the East and West Coasts. She, as well as Norma and Constance,
had been pressuring Schenck to move everything to California. Now,
with Natalie expecting, the heat was really on.

"The moment the women heard the news about Natalie," says
Buster, "Joe didn't have a Chinaman's chance." So in January, 1922,
he began preparing for the move.

"Peg came right on out and moved in with us, and the girls
rushed their current pictures through. They were converging on us
like homing pigeons all that early spring. By April the walls were
bulging. Nat had said, 'This Westchester Place house will be big
enough for anything.' Perhaps it wasn't Sanforized. It had certainly
shrunk."

The three sisters went house hunting, Peg took stabs at it, and even busy Buster helped. With the concentrated search, *the* house was soon found and rented. It was on Westmoreland Place, a house with a ballroom filling the third floor, a vast house that looked almost cottagey set back on its extensive grounds.

The invincible sisterhood escorted young wife and husband into this find, settled them—and themselves—firmly into the various ells and wings. Housewarming began and never stopped; Connie was learning to ride a bicycle in the ballroom or racing about in a new Mercer roadster that matched Buster's; friends filled the great halls at all hours; Peg was busy trying to direct the gestation of her first grandchild. "It was not exactly a rest home," says Buster.

Once in a while Papa Joe Keaton and Mamma Myra would appear. Most of the time, however, they waited on the sidelines in the Victoria Street bungalow that Buster had given them. There did not seem to be much for them to do.

No one could be perfectly sure what the expectant father thought about it all. His perfect manners could not always be taken at their face value—the face, after all, was the famous dead pan. Peg had a certain respect for her son-in-law. In the book she wrote in 1924, *The Talmadge Sisters*, she tells how he looked "straight out of his serious brown eyes in an almost disconcerting fashion. Any vacuous politeness, or banality, or hypocrisy seems to be instantly killed under that direct, straightforward stare."

It became an acute problem to keep on schedule at the studio and yet play host nearly every night. While his physical energy, as always, seemed adequate, nevertheless, for the first time, his creativity dropped off under the strain. The next two comedies show it. After eleven straight good ones (not including the initial effort, *The High Sign*), *My Wife's Relations* (despite the promising allusiveness of the title) and *The Blacksmith* are like early Keystones, little more than good slapstick, plus the Keaton comic personality.

Temporarily, at least, Joe solved these difficulties by filming on location at Truckee, near Lake Tahoe in the snowy High Sierras of northern California. There, anticipating Chaplin's *Gold Rush* by three years, he did *The Frozen North*. With the setting, however, all similarity between the two pictures ends.

Where *Cops* and *The Boat* are intensely personal documents, *The Frozen North* is an artist's tour de force of fantasy and, in addition, a travesty on a famous Hollywood actor. In both respects it is delightful. Relieved from domestic pressures, Buster "took it off the top." The comedy opens with one of the most wildly improbable bits of all Keatoniana: Buster emerging from a Manhattan subway-exit kiosk that stands alone in the midst of a snowy wilderness—strolling out as casually as if stepping into Times Square. Then the story unfolds, a burlesque by a master of travesty on William S. Hart, the dour, horse-faced, and horsey hero of the Westerns. The Keaton who had lampooned every hammy melodrama in vaudeville and stock has a field day doing a takeoff on Hart's thespian peculiarities and on the highly stylized and fairly absurd conventions of the celluloid horse opera of the 1920's.

"I didn't name Hart," Buster says, "but I was Two-Gun Bill all the way through. He didn't speak to me for a year."

Buster was a bit nonplussed by Bill Hart's reaction, being accustomed to the vaudevillians' tolerance. Yet he might well have anticipated a personal kickback of some degree, for Hart, as strong and silent as the next wrangler, had added many touches to the cowboy pattern. He was unique as a cowboy who could weep. He was the sensitive type—a kind of poet in chaps. And here was Buster in the saloon weeping in his beer. "When I saw that girl in another's arms, I cried. But I was having trouble with the glycerine tears and could only cry from one eye. So I took my finger and moved some glycerine over to the other eye."

Bill Hart had cleaned up the rowdy, roistering frontier and made it fit for women and children. He virtually originated the sexless, ascetic, he-man sort of horse opera. He never kissed the girl, though he threatened to up to the last moment, keeping her and the audience in suspense as he fought the battle with his baser self. Perhaps that is why he always lost her and never did graduate from his lone bed on the lone prairie. And, of course, he never stole, so he could hardly have enjoyed Buster's holdup of the Klondike saloon. Not only did he heist the illegitimate mazuma, but, in addition, at his command "Hands up!" all hands obeyed, even those shyly concealing ones of the famous bare-skinned calendar beauty September Morn, who hung framed behind the bar. Buster had had this choice bit of pop art specially copied from the Chabas painting but with mobile arms.

"I know Hart didn't like it a bit," says Buster, "but a lot of people had been waiting for it to happen."

With *The Frozen North* finished and the Keaton company back in Hollywood, Buster's bustling, highly populous, and somewhat unreal home life came suddenly into focus when his first son was born.

Scene from
The Frozen North, 1922.

Soon the baby was at home in his crib in the nursery, with Captain on guard day and night. Each new visitor had to be separately introduced and undergo his screening as a security risk. Now it was the police dog's turn to try to function in two separate and demanding worlds. He lost weight and grew nervous worrying about Buster while guarding Buster's son. He had nightmares and his ears twitched. Almost hourly all night he padded softly into the master bedroom, sniffed around, looked longingly at the foot of Buster's bed, then dutifully padded back to the infant's crib. His special hell came each morning when Buster vaulted into the Mercer studio-bound. Captain ran back and forth between car and house in an agony of indecision until Buster was gone, then for the next hour lay in the nursery, sighing throatily.

The baby's birth had revealed the overlooked fact that Joe and Myra Keaton were grandparents equally with Peg Talmadge. For a little moment the outnumbered Keaton men were supreme and were allowed to name the child. The name, of course, was a foregone conclusion. Joe loved to escort visitors to the crib. Captain would growl; Joe would push him aside with his foot. Growling a bit louder, Captain would nevertheless make room. Joe would then clear his throat in the old footlights manner and announce, "This is the seventh first son of a Keaton to bear the name Joseph."

The first announcement, however, as well as the first reference to sevens, had come from Buster at the hospital and appeared in the Los Angeles newspapers:

Joseph Talmadge Keaton, born Friday evening, June 2, 1922, at exactly 7 minutes past 7 P.M., weighing exactly 7 pounds and born with 7 lungs.

Joseph Keaton VI
and Joseph Keaton VII.

The picture under way when Joseph Talmadge Keaton was born is titled *Daydreams*. Coming on the heels of two of the most slapstick of the Keaton comedies, it is an unexpectedly sad, rueful, self-deprecatory little film. As such, however, it indicates a maturing comedian essaying the visualization of feelings as well as physical events. *Daydreams* succeeds in the attempt, using an interesting device that might be called parallel scening. Another anti-Alger opus, the floundering attempts of its country-boy hero to make good in the big city are contrasted as the pitiful failures they really are with the glowing scenes that his hometown sweetheart pictures to herself as she reads his glowing letters. *Daydreams* ends with Buster once more the quarry of the law, the streets again swarming with its minions. But no miracle intervenes here, not even a temporary stay of execution as in *Cops*. There is not even the quasi-victory of resignation.

Deliciously funny, *Daydreams*, as dual in feeling as it is in scening, is at the same time as utterly pessimistic as a story can well be. Keaton at this time was well on his way to making the American film public eat the unhappy ending and like it too. Essentially, there can be little doubt that themes like those of *The Boat*, *Cops*, and *Daydreams* express Buster's own deeply underlying feelings of apprehension and inadequacy. Such themes—whether expressed as failure or as fate or as both—are not merely constantly recurrent in his work but, even more, also inform his whole basic comedy personality.

Disaster is also the theme of the picture that followed. The mechanisms in *The Electric House*, having once in actuality maimed Buster, now in playacting finish him off for good. This harping theme was becoming only a little short of obsessive, as if failure and disaster were the Grail. It was as if Buster Keaton's lifelong stage role of underdog and butt of mischance had at last pervaded his basic thinking. If so, for it to move on into the events of his actual life would be only a short step.

Certainly, anyway, there had been four comedies with the same basic theme in less than a year. Destroyed by the elements in *The Boat* and by his fellow men in *Cops*, betrayed by his own hopes in *Daydreams*, he was now to be annihilated by machinery or, if you prefer, by a house, for the Electric House is both. And, to go a step further, house is home. It is likely that Buster Keaton tells a great deal in his art.

The original 1921 footage, made before the escalator accident, had been destroyed. Fred Gabouri, doubly determined following the fiasco of his sinking and nonsinking boats, had made a journeyman's test out of the push-button house. Now a new picture would be made from scratch, with its story unchanged.

The House, first brainchild of a just-graduated, just-married correspondence-school electrical engineer, is finished and ready to market. The mechanized bungalow is to be the beginning of a successful career. Big Joe Roberts, wealthy prospective purchaser, is on his way to inspect the marvel. If he is impressed, he will order hundreds as a real-estate promotion. Buster, once again Horatio Alger, Jr.'s would-be heir, is on his toes and primed to put over the big deal. Big Joe arrives.

All the rest is creeping disaster. Every contrary, illogical, exasperating, ridiculous way in which gadgets can go wrong is exploited, right through to the final sequence at the swimming pool. And what a pool! Olympic-size, electrically heated, chemically softened, infrared purified, and even perfumed. And everything instantaneous—no waiting around.

At the moment, for demonstration purposes, the superstatus natatorium is empty. "The pool fills in thirty seconds," says the inventor. "You just push this lever."

Presto! Niagara sluices in—the pool is brimful.

"It empties just as fast." He reaches for the lever, his foot skids on the splashed pool rim, and he falls against the lever. Having thus effectively but prematurely reversed the controls, he topples into the instantly emptying pool, is swept along, and in mere seconds reaches the gigantic drain at the end, to be sucked in and away.

The scene cuts and fades in on the seacoast. The camera zooms in, then centers on a rocky arch from which water is pouring into the Pacific. We zoom in still closer. Out on a murky stream comes that pale mask of a face, those wide staring eyes. The porkpie hat loosens its hold and floats away. The face grows larger and larger. It fills the screen in close-up. The field of vision rises. At last, over the grotto arch, we see a sign:

LOS ANGELES SEWER

Outrageously funny as this closer is, it is doom, unequivocal and explicit. Fate and Buster Keaton make a great writing team. Their surprise endings are especially effective. Yet Buster's own favorite memory from *The Electric House* concerns a gentle little gag involving animals. It occurs at luncheon, which was the inventor's hospitable method of demonstrating the workings of the dining room. The table is fastened at one end to the wall between dining room and kitchen. In the wall are cut two small arched openings at table-top height. From one issues a toy electric-train track that runs around the table just inside the place settings and then goes back through the other archway.

In the kitchen, completing its loop, the track runs around a serving table. There the cook loads the flatcars of the miniature freight train with the dishes of each course and then presses a button to alert Buster. Pushing the button by his plate, he then brings the train out into the dining room, stopping it, in turn, in front of each diner, who lifts off the dishes intended for him. To the gratification of all, the device works perfectly, delivering each course from soup to entrée and then removing the dishes.

In the meantime we have had glimpses of the family cat and her litter ensconced at one edge of the serving table in the kitchen. Now, as the cook turns away to get the desserts, the mother cat strolls off. Left alone, the kittens climb into the flatcars. Tabby, strolling on, steps on the signal button that rings the "ready" buzzer at the head of the dining table. Buster pushes his "start" button and out comes the train loaded with cat. Oblivious as usual, Buster stops the train at Big Joe's place, saying as he does so, "Here is your dessert, sir."

In those relaxed, free-flowing, productive years, one film quickly led to another. So now, abruptly, in the way he had, Buster Keaton

veered from the fate motif to pure mnemonic theatrical fantasy, as
he had done earlier in *The Playhouse*. The new film was *Balloonatics*. It has the feel of a retreat, or a respite, from reality. For his
leading lady he used Phyllis Haver, a Mack Sennett bathing beauty
of impressive, slightly Amazonian figure. In fact, she towered a full
head above the comedian. *Balloonatics* was a final comic fling for
Miss Haver, who, following the lead of Gloria Swanson, was about
to move into dramatic parts.

Balloonatics carries Buster around an amusement park and, luckless as usual, through the Tunnel of Love and, by the unfathomable
Keatonian logic, into the basket of a runaway balloon. Drifting on
the winds of the same logic, the balloon takes him to Phyllis—an
outdoor girl camping alone—deposits him, then disappears. He is
the first Adam in her alpine, brookside Eden, and most unwelcome.
But Buster sticks. He's lonely, and there's no place to go, anyhow.
He tries to be a good provider, but his hunting stinks—he's too sym-
pathetic with the animals. Then, suddenly and by sheer accident, he
knocks out a bear and saves her life.

The Amazon melts into a woman, and off they go down the honeymoon river in a canoe, reclining under a canopy like that of Cleo's
barge, wrapped in each other's arms. Time ceases to exist as they
blissfully float along. But the watchful camera moves ahead along
the river to show what awaits: a sheer waterfall down which the
river plunges to the plains a thousand feet below. It is sure disaster,
especially with a Keaton aboard.

Nearer and nearer floats the canoe, its wrapped-up lovers still unconscious of their plight. Its prow is at the brink. They kiss. And—
strangely, strangely, straight out into space glides the canoe; as if
on the ghost of an unfallen river, it sails into the open sky.

The camera view widens and we see that the canopy of the canoe
has hooked itself to the land anchor on the basket of the lost balloon.
It has just been hanging around until it could be of real service.
The picture fades out, in pure lunacy, with the embracing lovers—
Nature Girl and Nature Boy—navigating the sky in a canoe. They
never saw the waterfall. They've never looked around since. They're
up there, somewhere, still.

It seems a pity to cross-examine such a fairy tale. Yet it is hard
to escape the fact that in Keaton's stories it is only in fantasy that
fate stays its hand. In every story Keaton says something—whether
by intent or not does not much matter. Here he appears to be saying, in effect, "Don't look now, but a miracle just saved me."

Strangely enough, right at that moment Joe Schenck was readying another miracle in the rolling Keaton career. Buster would be halfway through his next picture, *The Love Nest*, when he got the news: he would start making full-length feature comedies. The Keaton Studio, after thirty-one months of operation and the production of nineteen two-reel shorts, would suspend operations. In early March, 1923, it closed its doors to prepare for the new schedule.

Keaton's films, so far, had been phenomenally successful. Now, in Schenck's judgment, the new star was being wasted in shorts. Two-reelers were flooding the market. In barely thirty months, the little hat, the slapshoes, and the sad frozen face had become famous—perhaps because, with all its passive immobility, that pale mask projected our own feelings. Perhaps, by very dint of its stoic non-expression, it encompassed the human gamut, from curiosity to amazement, from befuddlement to overhasty judgment, from complacency to terror, from fatalism to stubborn, doomed determination, from hope to despair.

Nor was Buster a famous mime only in this country. He already had received the popular accolade of affectionate nicknames all over the world. He once listed a number of these:

> France: Malec
> Spain: Zephonio (later, Pampliñas)
> Poland: Zybsko
> Czechoslovakia: Prysmyleno
> Liberia: Kazunk
> Cochin China: Wong Wong
> Siam: Kofreto
> Iceland: Glo Glo

Then he commented, "No one as yet has given me authentic translations, but I imagine that most of these terms of endearment signify null and void, and their combined meaning, if totaled up, would equal zero."

Zero, certainly, had not been the profits from the pictures that had brought the frozen face to so many countries and had inspired such an array of nicknames. Buster believes—and it seems probable —that his stockholders had divided several million dollars in something like twenty-eight months of production time. He calculates from his bonuses over that period.

Now, instead of the former eight shorts a year, it would be two features, one for spring and one for fall. In length, they would run from the five reels of *Sherlock Jr.* to the eight of *The General.* Of course, many features ran far longer than this, particularly the later epic dramas and musicals.

There was more than prestige for a star involved in feature films. It was for very sound reasons that Chaplin and Lloyd had moved into feature production. "We all had to," says Buster. "Schenck said it was the only way to get big rentals. The exhibitor, anyway, was often featuring our two-reelers over his main film. So why not make him pay for it? It would more than double the rentals—would mean twenty-five hundred dollars and more a week from each theatre. Multiply that amount by several hundred theatres, just in this country alone. And don't forget how much longer pictures ran than they do nowadays." In those days, in point of fact, good features were shown and reshown for years. In Europe the cream of the Keaton silents—with dubbed-in sound tracks—are still being shown and still command crowds.

"As for me personally," Keaton continues, "feature stories meant something else again. We were knocking ourselves out dreaming up new stuff every six weeks—and gambling each time. A couple of duds in a row and you could slip way down the ladder. With six months —four times as long—to each film, you could give it all you had. And," Buster added, "I had begun to want longer stories. A challenge, yes, but also room to develop the thing. To wring it out. To really say it."

Schenck raised his star's weekly salary from one thousand dollars to two thousand dollars, and a little later to twenty-five hundred dollars, while continuing the 25 percent bonus on the net. His optimism proved well founded. Up to 1928 (Keaton estimates)—a half decade during which costs rose rapidly—Buster's features, despite expensive production, cost on the average only two hundred and ten thousand dollars each. And (his bonuses indicated) they outgrossed the phenomenally successful two-reelers. "Some of them," he says, "hit the one-million mark, some climbed to two million." An important point, incidentally, to bear in mind is this: the stock-in-trade was not sold but rented, thus remaining the manufacturer's property.

The Keaton Studio reopened in late March, 1923, and for more than a month everyone worked on story sequences and gags for the initial feature. Though the resulting film is strongly Keaton, the story credits go to Clyde Bruckman, Joe Mitchell, and Jean Havez. Having once—in *The Playhouse*—lampooned Ince for hogging credits, Buster Keaton was no game for that sort of trap. Buster was remarkably

To coin a phrase, "One happy family," 1923. Joe Mitchell, Clyde Bruckman, Keaton, Jean Havez, Eddie Cline.

objective toward his work, lacking the hunger for personal glory. Either he was unaware of the full importance of his part, from germination to development, from gags to story, and from production and direction to acting, or else he chose, as in his pantomime, to play it down.

Bruckman, however, once took pains—years later—to point it out. "One of Buster's great abilities," he said ,"was his judgment of materials in advance. Honestly, he made us look like green hands. He seemed to sit apart—outside himself—and just look at things. Not only the material for others in the picture, but for himself. I have damned seldom seen him go wrong."

Bruckman went on to mention Buster's flexibility. The stories, Clyde pointed out, were important only so far as they went—almost, but not quite, the "postcard plot." Impressed by Keaton's improvisations, Bruckman called the plot as "important as a tune to a jazz band, and no more." A story conference, he said, was one thing; that unique time and space in front of the grinding cameras, altogether another. There intuition replaced logic. Thought and feeling became art.

"The cameramen," said Bruckman, "knew one thing: never stop cranking until Bus said, 'Cut!' Anything might happen. Once into action, it would unfold in his mind, developing as he went along, germinating from a gag to a scene, from a minor scene to a master scene.

" 'Well,' we would say after a long scene that no one had dreamed of had been filmed, 'well, what do we do now with such and such a sequence? How the devil does this fit with it?'

" 'Hell,' Bus would say, 'don't you see? We don't need it now.' "

The essential Buster Keaton was formed in the two-reelers. Looking back at the films he made up to the end of the winter of 1922–1923, immediately preliminary to the changeover to features, we can differentiate between two main types of Keaton stories and essay a comparison of their basic meanings. "Fact" and "fantasy" might be the most basic terms—these two approaches were constantly played off against each other, both between separate films and within individual pictures. On the side of fact would be *The Boat*, *Cops*, and *The Electric House*, and on the fantastic side would be *The Scarecrow*, *The Playhouse*, and *Balloonatics*. Combining fact and fantasy in approximately even amounts would be *The Paleface*, while *The Frozen North* (even with its subway kiosk in the snowy tundra) is not completely fantasy, having as its core of reality its lampooning reference to William S. Hart.

And yet the pictures both bear out and deny such easy distinctions. Keaton is not so easily pigeonholed. All his films are essentially fantastic, and their reality stems from their star's subtle persuasion of our belief. Buster Keaton's own world (it may well be believed), though unified, is not our world. The real to him is the make-believe to us—medicine-show melodrama, circus sawdust, vaudeville tinsel, the calcium-light glare on the improbable. Then, as we concentrate on the fantastic rather than the factual, we find the two essences shuttling equivocally back and forth, until light becomes shadow, and shadow light.

But still our nagging belief in the Keatonian reality persists—of course it does, because *this* is the way life really is. Life is real, life is earnest? Phooey! Life is absurd! Long ago, Calderón put it a little more gently: *La Vida Es Sueño*. Today the gloves are off in such writings as Samuel Beckett's *Waiting for Godot* and Eugène Ionesco's *The Chairs*. And there, of course, is where Keaton's meaning connects with both past and present. His film comedies were perhaps the first examples of the Theatre of the Absurd. Although this is beyond doubt true, Keaton still is not so easily pinned down. For playwrights like Beckett and Ionesco and contemporary novelists like Joseph Heller and Thomas Pynchon (to single out only a few) dress man the absurd in the clothes of absurdity. Some of Buster Keaton's stories are actually more realistic as expressions of life's more often covert than overt absurdity than are the works of writers like these, because, like Camus and Sartre (and long before them), Keaton often gave us the absurdity beneath life's realistic surface. It would be, on the other hand, the fantastic half of the Keaton *oeuvre* that foretold Ionesco and his school, all those who argue the disjunctive meaninglessness of life, its lack of true causality, and hence its absurdity. Only in a rare opus like *Balloonatics* does Keaton follow this method. Far more often, with him, event follows event with precise, impeccable, remorseless causality—*and yet the whole is absurd.* Keaton does not propound absurdity—he lives it or stumbles over it.

And all this, of course, is why Buster Keaton at his best is both tragic and outrageously funny. If life is absurd, that is man's disaster. And man's wit is the light that glances off his meaningless life.

TWENTY-TWO

B USTER KEATON'S first feature comedy was *The Three Ages*. Preparation of story, sets, and mechanical props was completed by the end of April, and the filming, which took less than three months, began in May.

Although the story skirts the essential problems of long-story writing, it is an interesting idea. Technically it stems from D. W. Griffith's epic *Intolerance*, the twenty-odd-reel allegory of 1916. Using at least as many stars as reels—including Constance Talmadge and, in a bit part, Natalie—Griffith had traced human intolerance from ancient Babylon to the present. Keaton now traced human love (in parallel sequences) in three ages—the Stone Age, imperial Rome, and the 1920's.

Buster was quite aware what it was that he was really doing. "Cut the film apart," he says frankly, "and then splice up the three periods, each one separately, and you will have three complete two-reel films." He was making a cautious approach to his first piece of long-story construction.

Joe Schenck, after setting up the Keaton Studio for features, had sailed to London with Norma and Constance to pick the winner of a highly publicized English beauty contest. British girls vied for the prize—second lead in Norma's next picture, which was to be *Within the Law*. The Schenck party returned to Hollywood with the winner, Miss Margaret Leahy, and her mother. Miss Leahy got the full Hollywood treatment of fanfare and fetes.

Then to work. The very first day, it became apparent that the English beauty simply could not act. She could not even be coached in the mechanics of walking, standing, and sitting down. On the third day, Norma's director, Frank Lloyd, gave up: either the contest winner left the picture or he would leave it.

Schenck was both shocked and boxed in. He wanted Lloyd. Privately, having seen Miss Leahy perform, he didn't want her in Norma's picture. But the situation was delicate: the contest prize had no escape clauses, and if Miss Leahy and her mother were to sue for breach of contract they had a perfect case. Then Schenck found an out. It was said by some—and might well have been true —that he got the idea from his mother-in-law.

Peg Talmadge certainly watched over her daughters like a mother hawk on the nest. A remark that she had once made, as quoted by Buster himself, had made the Hollywood rounds. It had happened at a dinner party.

"I don't let my daughters marry actors," Mrs. Talmadge had said, in a Right is Right and Wrong is Wrong way.

"But Peg," Buster had exclaimed, "you let Natalie marry me!"

She smiled indulgently. "You're not an actor," she said, "you're a comedian."

This was now Schenck's line. When Buster objected to including the English girl in *The Three Ages*, Schenck retorted, "Comic leading ladies don't have to act." Buster knew better. He renewed his objections. Schenck marched on. *The Three Ages* would triple its gross in England with an English heroine, he estimated. Buster gave in, being no good, anyway, at the sort of tussle that was the Hollywood diet. He inherited Margaret Leahy.

He still shakes his head recalling what they went through. "The scenes we threw in the ash can!" he says. "Easy scenes! We got a good picture—we could have had a fine one. But, my God, we previewed it *eight* times! Went back and reshot scenes like mad."

It was more important to Buster than it proved to be to Miss Leahy. After this film she retired from pictures, married well and presumably happily, and settled down in the orange groves.

The Three Ages combines farce, broad burlesque, and considerable social satire. Its basic plot is the rivalry of the Adventurer (Wallace Beery) and the Faithful Worshiper at Beauty's Shrine (Buster Keaton) for the hand of the Girl (Margaret Leahy), who is the daughter of the Big Shot (Big Joe Roberts).

The story is divided into four sequences, each being acted out consecutively in the three successive periods of history before proceeding to the next sequence. At the end is a short epilogue. The four sequences are: first, the rivals calling on the girl; second, both courting her; third, challenge and contest of the rivals; fourth, foiling the villain, or winning the girl. For example, the two rivals call on the girl in the Stone Age, then in imperial Rome, and then today, after which the story proceeds to courtship.

The film is a whirlwind of incidents, starting with the two rivals' first appearance: troglodyte Beery atop a mammoth; Faithful Worshiper, bedecked in skins and with a tangled thatch of hair, pacing the back of a dinosaur like a captain on the bridge.

From the start it looks like an uneven contest, with Beery looming over his diminutive rival. Generally speaking, too, Buster is quite aptly his usual inept, blundering self. In a typical gag, a towering cavewoman, resenting his advances, pushes him off a boulder. (Blanche Payson, six foot three and formerly a policewoman, New York's first, was specially hired for this bit.)

But in each real crisis there comes The Miracle. But with a difference: now (as if Buster Keaton had begun to believe in the mounting success of his film career) the miracles are actually allowed to spring from his own actions. Item: in the Stone Age he wins the girl by launching himself in the air from a catapult to seize her from the towering rock where she is captive. Item: in Rome he wins the race by fitting his chariot with sleigh runners (a snowstorm having blanketed the Imperial City) while Beery's chariot flounders far in the rear. Then, still in Rome, he rescues and wins the girl, whom Beery has kidnapped, in a real flame of action. In one long continuous series of physical feats, he seizes a spear, leaps from a balcony onto the back of a horse, gallops to the Beery villa, and pole-vaults, with spear as pole, to the balcony of the room where she is held. He rides off with her to happiness. Item: in the Modern Age, he is in jail for supposed bigamy, as a result of Beery's machinations. All the Keaton acrobatic athleticism goes into his escape and the feat that follows—a meteoric flight and a startling fall down a skyscraper light well, crashing through window awnings. Bedraggled, he appears in the traditional nick of time at Beery's wedding to the girl. These scenes are worthy of the athletic, romantic Doug Fairbanks.

But, though Keaton is now willing to grant miracles to his own efforts, he still must sell himself short—in each age. Dragging the girl away by the hair, he must stumble and fall. As the Roman slaves lift the couched litter to carry the couple to their wedding, the floor must fall out, to leave them sitting on the ground as the slaves walk on. And running from the church, happily married at last, he must lose her in the city traffic. The course of true Keaton never runs smooth.

The epilogue of *The Three Ages*—Keaton calls it the tag—is in three brief period scenes: Buster coming out of his home cave, followed by wife and nine fur-clad kids; out of his home villa, followed by his connubial matron and five little togas; and out of his home bungalow, followed by wife and one Pekingese.

From the production standpoint the picture is notable for a tech-

Scene from *The Three Ages*, 1923. Margaret Leahy and Buster Keaton with young extras.

nical innovation in the scene showing Buster riding the dinosaur. He was first filmed pacing back and forth on a white plank against a white sheet, with side lighting to erase shadows. (Note that this is the old black-art principle of black on black in reverse.) The resulting shot showed him apparently pacing in the air. This was all in the upper half of the picture frame, the first part of what would be a dual multiple shot, in horizontal rather than in lateral halves. Just as in the multiple shots of *The Playhouse*, Lessley now rolled the film back to the starting point and proceeded to shoot the lower half. And here came the innovation: the dinosaur, which was now separately photographed (to appear solidly beneath Buster), was an animated cartoon.

According to Bruckman, queried subsequently, this was the first combination of live action with simultaneous cartoon action. "It was Buster's idea," Bruckman said. "Having put Beery on an elephant, we were wondering, 'How do you top an elephant?'

"Buster said, 'Remember *Gertie the Dinosaur?'*

"We looked blank, and he said, 'The first cartoon comedy ever made. I saw it in a nickelodeon when I was fourteen. I'll ride in on an animated cartoon.' Then he figured out how to work it.

"We were flabbergasted. Jean Havez finally looked at him with

that fat John Bunny squint and said, 'This guy's memory isn't ele-
phantine, it's dinosaurian!' "

The Three Ages auspiciously launched Keaton in features. For
contemporary American audiences, in addition to the timely 1920's
satire, the chariot race constituted a riotous burlesque on the famous
race in Lew Wallace's *Ben Hur* as earlier enacted on the stage by
two great Bills, William Farnum and William S. Hart. (The MGM)
epic that starred the veteran Francis X. Bushman and made a new
star out of Ramon Novarro was not made until 1926, three years
later than *The Three Ages*.)

In England, exactly as Schenck had predicted, huge audiences
turned out to see "that nice English girl who won the contest." A
London newspaper heralded the premiere:

Attended by a royal party headed by the Queen Mother, the opening
in London next week of Buster Keaton's first feature comedy, *Three Ages*,
will be the most brilliant compliment ever paid an American film. Besides
Queen Mother Alexandra, there will attend Princess Alice, the Earl of
Athlone, the Duke of Northumberland, the Duchess of Devonshire, and
the Countess of Limerick. Also, there will be a private screening for the
royal newlyweds, the Duke and Duchess of York.

When the filming of a picture began, Keaton always set the writers
to work on a new story, conferring with them at night, squeezing in
the time, somehow, amid the ceaseless parties at home. *The Three
Ages*, following heavy previewing and revisions, was barely in the
shipping cans when the next plot, developed from a Havez idea, was
ready. Its title, *Southern Hospitality*, was soon changed when it was
heard that a film of the same name was under way elsewhere. Havez'
story became *Our Hospitality*. The writers, privately concerned with
the toll Buster's social life was exacting, wanted the location scenes
to be shot first. They suggested the High Sierra country near Lake
Tahoe, which in summer is at its best.

Buster agreed. He immediately began planning an outing to include all the Keatons and Natalie and the baby too. Natalie immediately objected. The baby was too young. Buster pointed out that
he was nearly fifteen months old. He would be safer at home, Natalie
insisted.

"With Captain?" Buster laughed and reminded her of one of the
big police dog's more spectacular ministrations. They had been sitting in the drawing room, Buster and Natalie, Peg and Constance,
and little Joe, just beginning to crawl, was on the floor. Captain was
watching him, cocked ears and wrinkled forehead betraying his worry.

Twice the infant, after a yard or two of progress, had collapsed on his face. The third fall was more than Captain could stand. With a low, anguished growl the dog lunged with that terrifying swiftness of his, seized the baby's entire neck in his great jaws, and held him up.

The women screamed, Captain looked at them sideways, and Buster jumped for the dog. Before he could reach him, however, the baby had his hands back in position, Captain had released him, and he was crawling away. Buster picked the child up and brought him to Natalie. There was not even a pink spot on the wet little neck. No bird dog ever lifted a duck more gently.

Having recalled the incident to make his point, Buster waited for Natalie's answer. It was no, firmer than ever. Buster went to the studio and huddled with Havez, Bruckman, and Mitchell.

That night at home he casually remarked, "Our little Joe has a part in the new picture."

Natalie stared at him, looking a little stunned. Buster pressed on. "Just one scene and you can bank a hundred bucks for him."

Buster still was not through. "And you, Nat," he said "are my leading lady."

TWENTY-THREE

〜〜〜〜〜〜〜〜〜〜〜〜〜〜〜〜〜〜〜

T HE CARAVAN arrived like an army land convoy. Buster's big new Packard led the touring cars that carried actors and technicians, and equipment followed in trucks—cameras, lights, makeup, costumes, props, commissary, and kitchen. Like an infantry detachment, they deployed into an ordered camp on the banks of the Truckee River. This short but good-sized stream, which wanders placidly through nearby Reno swallowing the divorcées' castaway wedding rings and meanders into California, here and there rouses itself to a foaming rage that echoes like thunder in the narrow gorges. The Truckee is a mercurial river that fishermen treat with respect.

Here are the lofty California alps, the high Sierra Nevada of the Spanish name that promises eternal snow. It is a region of mile-high valleys and meadows, land of a long-renowned beauty, with Lake Tahoe a blue sapphire at the center of snowy peaks that tower to twelve thousand feet. The Truckee-Tahoe Valley, lying at an altitude of better than six thousand feet, is a great basin of crystalline clarity, one lifted in an upper remoteness from the world. In July and August the sunlight shafts down obliquely over the surrounding peaks, cool with high reflections of granite and snow.

This was Tahoe and the Truckee as they were in midsummer, 1923. In those premotel days, beautiful Tahoe's perimeter, half in Nevada and half in California, had not yet become seventy crowded consecutive Miracle Miles of gas station and gift shop, supermarket and roulette palace, honky-tonk and garage, hostelry and hamburger stand. And Tahoe itself, blue-black in its ancient watery crater depths, was of an unmatched clarity and purity not yet soiled by society's clogging wastes.

For Buster, it was Muskegon and far more. Even today he can recall that Tahoe summer magic. It brought an illusion of wholeness, of two worlds merging at last. There had been, perhaps, too many breaks in his past, but especially two: the Oklahoma summer when the door to childhood had opened, then closed; and the Los Angeles incident that had separated the Three Keatons. As they drove into their riparian campground under its towering sugar pines, his father and mother, his brother and sister, his wife and child all together with him in the one car, it seemed to be a mending he had needed, a reconciliation of disparates into the one real thing.

How easily they all seemed to settle into the grateful routine, on through the day from that sacred dawn hour when Joe and Jingles and Buster came back with the wriggling rainbows and they all sat down to cook and eat them right out of the sizzling pans. Time, somehow, turned back to write Natalie and little Joe into an earlier, happier history. It couldn't be, but it seemed to be.

The river's voice was endless. Within its sonorous circle all things seemed possible—even belief. There, Buster Keaton believed. He believed in the unbelievable present. He believed in the unbelievable future. He even, for that little while, believed in himself—not in the old self-imposed role of the underdog winning through defeat, but in himself winning by himself. It was a bright interval. At its center, it held Natalie with him.

So *Our Hospitality* is more than a funny picture, though it is very funny indeed. It is unique in the work of Buster Keaton as a story completely without bitterness. In it, for that bright interval, is that encompassing belief, the belief in life. Fate still frowns, weaving her complex toils around the small comic figure; but even she drowses, drunk with summer, her old menace muted.

Our Hospitality is real Americana, persuasively nostalgic. Set in the period between 1810 and 1831, it is an imagined legend of a vanished American scene—like the thousandth telling of an old, old tale.

"Let's do the Hatfield-McCoy feud," Havez had said.

"Great!" Buster had exclaimed. Then he had laughed and said, "But let's call 'em Canfield and McKay. That gang might come gunning for *us*."

Then they just had fun. Buster let his black hair grow to the luxuriant romantic length one sees in the limners' portraits of the Federal period. The costumers had a field day, amazed at how handsome this famous funnyman could look in the old-time greatcoats, brocaded waistcoats, and the tall, flaring, plush top hats. Old prints were conned, locations chosen, and sets built, with far more care than "serious" films received.

"If we do it," Buster had said, "we do it right."

Our Hospitality is the only film with three generations of Joe Keatons in it: Joe V, Joe VI, and Joe VII. Buster's father has an

During filming of *Our Hospitality*, 1923. Three generations of Joe Keatons.

important role in the early part of the film. His fifteen-month-old heir appears briefly in the prologue playing John McKay (Buster) as an infant. The script called for him to cry. He bawls. Later on, Schenck asked curiously how they had got his nephew to cry, adding that he hoped they hadn't jabbed him with a pin. Buster grinned. "We simply kept him past his feeding time."

The prologue takes place in 1810 in an imaginary town in the Shenandoah Valley. It is played big, overgestured and overemoted like the film dramas of the 1920's. The wealthy Canfield clan, headed by the Old Colonel (Big Joe Roberts), rule the valley. The impoverished McKays—decimated by Canfield gunnery—are all but extinct. Only three survive: a young man, his wife, and their baby son. Then, one stormy night outside their half-ruined cabin, the father is shot down by a young Canfield. Next morning his widow rises at dawn and escapes by stagecoach with the child. This ends the prologue.

The main story begins twenty-one years later (1831) in New York. The introductory subtitle reads:

BROADWAY & FORTY-SECOND STREET, NEW YORK

This, the turn-of-the-century scene of many a Keaton vaudeville triumph, is shown as it looked long before, at the dawn of the indus-

Traffic jam, Broadway and Forty-second Street, 1831. Scene from *Our Hospitality*, 1923.

trial age. The set, reproduced from an old print, shows a rural cross-roads hamlet in farming country. An ironic Keaton touch indicates the onset of New York's traffic problem: he comes racing up on a proto-bike, only to be held up by the local constable to let a horse and wagon pass across. The bike is actually a Gentleman's Hobby-horse, the granddaddy of all bicycles, a two-wheeled contraption with no pedals that is propelled with a striding motion of the feet on the ground. This too is from an old print. Keaton himself is John McKay, now grown to a rather pampered, foppish young manhood.

His mother, who brought him to safety, has since died. John has been brought up by an elderly aunt, and today he attains his majority. His aunt tells him his history: he is the last of the McKays; the ancestral estate in the Blue Ridge Mountains is his to claim. But she does not tell him of the age-old Canfield-McKay feud. She sees him off in New Jersey on the newfangled steam railroad, a string of converted stagecoaches drawn by an antediluvian locomotive of the Stephenson type—boiler and firebox on wheels, with open platform where the engineer-fireman (Joe V) stands. Her last words of advice to her nephew: "Watch out for the Indians around Trenton."

The next sequence is the long struggle through the mountain wilderness to the Shenandoah Valley. John McKay shares a coach with a beautiful young stranger (Natalie Keaton). This sequence is dominated pictorially by the breathtaking landscapes and in comedy by the locomotive and its engineer. Joe is very funny, the locomotive equally so. In one scene the locomotive jumps the bumpy track to meander through a meadow (Joe is frying eggs on the fire), and the passengers remark, "Roadbed a bit smoother here." Later, the iron horse slams full speed into a tunnel presumably far too low to accommodate the towering smokestack. But, in the new Keaton mood, no disaster ensues: the tunnel is actually bottle-shaped, and the smokestack glides through the part corresponding to the neck of the bottle.

As the rushes began arriving in Hollywood the writers were appalled. It began to dawn on them that they had made a straight man out of the star and thrown the comedy to Joe and the locomotive. Bruckman and Havez telephoned Buster for instructions.

"Relax, I knew it all the time," said Keaton. "It won't spoil the picture. I played against Joe for seventeen years."

It is a journey through the mad, mad, mad world of Keaton—from bottle-shaped tunnel to the cowcatcher fitted with whisk brooms to sweep the rails clear of grasshoppers, from the track that Joe bends to detour around an immovable donkey to the track that is permanently humped over logs too laborious to move, and on to the bearded old conductor who blows his bugle in the tallyho jump seat high at the end of the last coach. And there are the gentle Keaton touches too: his little dog padding along unseen beneath his master's coach right to journey's end; the lovely stranger asleep, her head on Buster's shoulder as he holds her protectively, carefully easing the bumps, lest she awaken.

Coming into the depot, she says, "You must come and have dinner with my family, John."

The Canfields meet her. She introduces him. At the surname McKay, the men's eyes widen, then narrow. But she repeats the invitation, and John McKay, still unaware of the feud, accepts.

"This evening, then," she says as they part.

McKay then sets out to find his ancestral home, which he mentally pictures (and the screen shows us) as a porticoed plantation manse amid magnolia blossoms. At last he finds it, the shack, now caved in and vacant, where his father had died. When he sees it, the imagined mansion again fills the screen for a second, then explodes in a cloud of dust and flying Ionic columns.

When he arrives for dinner at the Canfields' bona fide mansion the problem of Southern hospitality arises. Colonel Canfield takes his three sons aside. "As long as a guest is under our roof," he says, "he is protected by the code of chivalry."

McKay overhears. Their sworn enmity, whatever its reason may be, dawns on him, and he grasps his immediate problem. To stay alive he has to stay in that house. Once out the door unarmed and he's a dead pigeon. He stalls and stalls. The Canfield girl begins to realize the deadly trap she has unwittingly baited. Everyone is fidgeting behind the elaborate courtesy. It approaches the breaking point. McKay excuses himself and goes into the back service hall behind the grand staircase. There he finds a long servant's dress and a sunbonnet.

Seconds later it is apparently one of the Canfield servants who trails past everyone, through the entrance hall, and out the front door. The "servant" is halfway to the entrance gate, when one of the Canfields glances out. The hastily donned skirt is accidentally hitched up behind, revealing McKay's trousers. His detector shouts, the guns roar, and McKay, vaulting the picket fence, takes to the woods. After a long chase in the twilight, he escapes.

Time has passed. John and the Canfield girl are going to elope. She waits in a rowboat at the river's edge. He is making for the rendezvous when the Canfield men pick up the scent. A new chase begins, through woods and up into the Blue Ridge. John becomes trapped by a rockslide on a cliff ledge a hundred feet above a deep mountain lake. Unthinkingly, he calls for help and gives away his position.

Thirty feet overhead, a Canfield boy hears and replies. He offers to throw down the end of a rope, planning that the rescue will promptly turn into an execution. After tying one end around his own waist he tosses down the loose end, which McKay then secures around himself. Just as he is cinching the knot, his perfidious rescuer loses his footing on the precarious edge. Dirt begins falling on McKay, then small rocks, and suddenly the Canfield boy hurtles past, plummeting to the lake. The rope whips taut, McKay is jerked from his feet, and he too falls lakeward.

The following shot is one of the most spectacular bona fide scenes ever photographed. A long view straight down to the lake, it shows the tandem fall of the two men at either end of the stretched rope, from the start of the fall all the way down to the surface of the water. The sheets of water are still rising from the Canfield boy's dive when McKay hits.

The succeeding close-up through the crystal-clear Tahoe water shows McKay far down in the depths. He is coming up with the rope still around his waist. His enemy, having untied himself, is close behind. McKay climbs ashore and races for his waiting sweetheart in the rowboat. They shove off and almost immediately find them-

Just before the leap. *Our Hospitality*, 1923.

The leap begins. *Our Hospitality*, 1923.

selves in rapids. The boat capsizes and they are thrown clear. The girl is swept away, with John swimming in desperate pursuit. The chase has suddenly proliferated—McKay is now a pursuer but with a far different quarry.

Now comes a swift and breathtaking series of events. McKay is still trailing her, when suddenly she is swept over a waterfall ahead. As he nears the edge himself, he seizes a long floating log with a broken branch projecting from its downstream end. This branch reaches the brink first and hooks itself around a tree stump that is wedged among the rocks at the brink; in the racing current, the entire log pivots up into the air like a gigantic lever, with John clinging to the rising end. It looks like sure disaster—the log swings upright like a mast, then continues on, out—far out in the air beyond the edge of the falls—and down. Down, down, it goes. But the wedged end remains fast—it works like a hinge; and when the log is straight out and horizontal, like a gigantic bowsprit, it stops and remains steady.

John looks down and sees her, soaked but safe, huddling on a tiny, inaccessible ledge of stone, halfway down the falls and off to one side.

Consider their position: she trapped on a tiny ledge; he trapped at the end of a virtual mast. He looks around: from the brink of the falls there seems to be no escape—unscalable rock walls block either end, and no one could swim upstream in such a torrent. If he lowers the rope to her and pulls her up, she will only be trapped in a new position. How can he at one and the same time escape from his position, free her, and enable both of them to reach safety?

There is only one solution, and it is an extremely risky one. He knots the loose end of the rope around his horizontal log. Then he stands and hurls himself headlong out into space—in a direction exactly opposite from the ledge where the girl is crouched.

The rest is mechanical but wonderful: rope and rescuer become one mechanism obeying the laws of dynamics. The slack takes up and suddenly McKay and his rope are a thirty-foot pendulum swinging down and around with blurring speed. Passing the ledge at the bottom of the pendulum's arc, he sweeps her into his arms and they swing up and land high above on a lip of rock a scant foot to one side of the edge of the falls. From there they can scramble to safety.

It is shining action. Few films can show a moment as thrilling, and it all but stands alone as one that was done without fakery by the star himself. (A lightweight dummy stood in for Natalie on the ledge.) A desperately dangerous, wildly exciting feat done in the full dynamic dimension of one continuous filmed sequence, it leaves audiences, today as yesterday, limp and breathless.

The two lovers now flee on foot. Past the falls they encounter a minister in a buggy. They climb in and drive away. The scene dissolves into an upstairs room in the Canfield mansion. Through the door we see the minister standing. Just then the Canfield men arrive on the run, derringers in hand, and shoulder into the room. The camera follows, and then at last we see John and the girl in a corner kissing. They have just been married.

So there goes the feud. Colonel Canfield strikes a noble pose. "The time has come," he says, "to bury the hatchet."

He leads off, laying his gun on the table that holds the Bible. One by one his sons follow suit. John McKay watches narrowly until all are disarmed, and then, through a final fade-out, he busily removes the arsenal hidden on his person, in pockets and stuck under his belt, six-shooters, derringers, knives, and finally, stuck in a boot and hidden by a trouser leg, the hatchet.

But this one time—whatever the final laugh—Buster Keaton is not throwing it away. It was not luck, it was not accident that carried him through those harrowing moments at the waterfall's edge.

No estimate of *Our Hospitality* is complete without mention of Elgin Lessley's camera work. Its clarity and beauty, altogether exceptional then, are uncommon even by today's standards. Shots such as the views of the locomotive silhouetted on a mountaintop against the towering summer clouds are of particular beauty. Among the many things that keep Keaton's best silent films modern—despite the lack of sound, color, and wide screen—Lessley's photography must be included.

Buster made a truce with fate that summer of *Our Hospitality*. Fate, not he, broke the truce—or, at least, nature stepped in to play several roles not in the script.

First, there was Natalie. Three weeks after they began shooting in the mountains, she discovered that she was pregnant. Toward the end, it became a race with time.

"Before we finished that picture," Buster remembers, "we didn't dare photograph her in profile. Joe Schenck said, 'Never use Natalie in another picture. You could break this company.'"

Next came Joe Roberts' stroke. He was hospitalized in Reno and recovered enough to go on. Near the end of the filming of the studio shots back in Hollywood, he suffered a second stroke. Feeling toward

Big Joe Roberts
in *Our Hospitality*, 1923.

Big Joe as he did, Buster was ready to junk the picture. But the fifty-five-year-old trouper insisted on completing the job. In the last few scenes, although he gamely covers up, his feebleness can be seen.

A month after the final retake, Big Joe Roberts died. He had been with Buster three years, in every film from the second one on, twenty films in all. With his passing, Buster lost a great heavy. He lost too a friend from his childhood days in vaudeville, one who could share his memories of the stage and of summers at Lake Muskegon, one who had played pranks with him and manned the Clown Pole, the big star of the high jinks at the old Cobwebs and Rafters, "dressed," as Buster always remembered, "like Buster Brown. My God, he'd scare an audience half to death, like Man Mountain Dean romping around with a lollipop." Perhaps even more, still, than a friend, Buster had lost one-third of an image, one of the three Big Joes in his life. With Joe Keaton and Joe Schenck, Joe Roberts had made up a kind of tripartite paternal figure upon which he had come to rely.

But even then, up there by Tahoe, nature was not through. Buster nearly became a victim of the Truckee River, which all those weeks had been giving them trout and serenading their meals and their slumber.

"For that scene in the rapids," he recalls, "the one where I'm trying to catch Natalie—someone doubled for her in those shots, of course—we picked the best rapids from a pictorial point of view, a two-hundred-yard stretch where the water moves fast and white. I'm supposed to grab onto a sixteen-foot log and float out into the bad water.

" 'Can you hold on to the log?' Gabouri asked me. I said, 'Yes.' So he put a holdback wire around the log, ran the wire out about sixty feet, and then anchored it tightly around a baseball bat. There were three men holding that bat.

"The idea was to shoot this close up to establish the action while they keep me from getting swept away. Then we'd go into a more distant profile for long stretches of milder water, where they can control the log and me.

"Fine, we're shooting, then the wire goes *pop*, real soft, and—*bang!*—the log and I are in the rapids, and off to hell we go. I hear the guys yell and start into the rocks and underbrush along the river. But I'm thinking about myself—think fast or forget it. I sure as shooting have to shed that log or it will beat me to death against the boulders. So I kick loose and sprint ahead. Can't look around, but I know that log is right on my tail. I'm hitting boulders now with my hipbones and knees, and a couple I hit so hard on my chest that I go clear up out of the water and over. The main thing is to keep from whirling. I'm fighting for breath and trying to remember how long the rapids are and how much of them are left.

"It starts to quiet down, and I think, *I've made it!* Then suddenly I'm in foam a foot deep. You don't breathe very well in foam, and you sure as hell can't swim on top of it. I later found that there was three hundred yards of that foam ganged up at the end of the rapids. It was a bend in the river that saved me. I couldn't have made ten yards more. I grabbed some overhanging branches, pulled myself out, feet still in the water and just lay on my face fighting for air.

"All of that took maybe a minute and a half, two minutes. It took Ernie Orsatti, Chick Collins—the stunt man who had begged to do this sequence for me—Gabe, and the rest nearly ten minutes to fight through the underbrush. I don't suppose they knew what they would find.

"First thing I asked was, 'Did Nat see it?' She was sitting there crocheting when we started the scene.

" 'I'm afraid she did,' said Gabe.

"Then I asked Lessley, 'Did you get it?'

" 'Both cameras. It's all on film,' he said."

Gabouri offered to resign. Buster put a wet arm around Gabe's shoulder. "You'll never make another mistake," he said. Gabouri never did.

Our Hospitality—seven reels, the Keaton Film Company's second feature comedy—was released on November 20, 1923. It scored an outstanding success. It cost two hundred and eight thousand dollars and grossed around a million and a half.

Here in our country it is seen upon occasion at a museum or a college. At a showing a few years ago at Cornell, the students cheered after the waterfall scene, and as the lights went on they gave a resounding standing ovation to an actor most of them had never seen before.

Our Hospitality has also left a memento in one of our great public institutions. Buster Keaton not so long ago took his present wife to see it. "I was playing Washington," he says, "in the stage show *Three Men on a Horse*. I said, 'Eleanor, I've got something to show you.' We went to the Smithsonian, and there it was—the Gentleman's Hobbyhorse, our replica of the first bicycle ever made. There hadn't been one left in existence, so we built it from an old print.

"Somebody from the Smithsonian," Buster continued, "saw it in *Our Hospitality* and wrote us asking for it. So we shipped it on."

TWENTY-FOUR

〰〰〰〰〰〰〰〰〰〰〰〰〰〰

R ETURNING from a personal tour abroad, Mary Pickford and Doug Fairbanks brought news. Their popularity in Russia had astonished them. They had expected a polite reception but got an ovation. It had previously been assumed that Russia did not duplicate America's worship of its movie heroes and heroines, a deduction stemming from Russia's brief rentals of our films. But the Fairbankses found American films—old and new; good, bad, and indifferent—being shown all over the place.

"There's something rotten in Russia," said Fairbanks. And he was right. The Reds were renting foreign films just long enough for the state laboratories to make copy negatives, then were printing and screening the "state-owned" copies. Doug and Mary further reported that although they and Charlie Chaplin were the top stars here, Buster Keaton outdrew them all behind the Iron Curtain. Presumably this was because he was a doomed rather than a successful capitalist. And sad about it too.

Buster liked his new schedule of two films a year. It left breathing space, especially for the World Series. With *Our Hospitality* premiering in New York, he and Natalie went to watch the Yankees take the Giants in six games, mainly because of Babe Ruth's triple, double, three singles, three homers, and eight walks. Outfielder Casey Stengel's three homers couldn't save the Giants.

Following the Series, Joe Schenck, as usual, took over a floor of an Atlantic City hotel for the annual Keaton Film Company board meeting. Back again in Hollywood there was, Buster says, "another directors' meeting." The Talmadges were once more in residence *chez* Buster, supervising the arrival of another baby. What with bridge parties, dinner parties, just plain parties, redecoration of the nursery, and the start of a new Keaton picture—not to mention a parlormaid's theft of Constance's thirty-thousand-dollar emerald ring —things, he says wryly, "were approaching normal." Then it was Christmas and completely normal, raining presents at home and the usual carnival in the studios—in Buster's phrase, "a ten-acre office party—gin, jazz, and Jezebels." Soon the studios would become fortresses, with guards even at the postern gates. But then anyone could walk in and out at will, and even the extras mistered no one—it was "Hello, Buster," "Hi, Doug," "Good morning, Mary."

"Each year," says Keaton, "the production boys hopefully prepared schedules for December twenty-fourth: shoot scenes all day. Hah! From the opening bell the madhouse was on—milling all over the lot, through the sets, hopping all over town from studio to studio. Grips, cameramen, electricians, with stupid little presents, mobbing with stars and directors. Freeloading, yakking it up, and lapping it up. Carruthers cooked for two days—ham, turkey, duck, pie, cake—on Christmas Eve in my shack, you helped yourself. Carruthers stayed behind his bar serving drinks."

Carruthers' real name was Willie Riddle. Returning from the war, nearly four years before, Buster had tasted the Riddle cooking in a Santa Fe dining car. He hired him, and Riddle was his "cook, valet, wet nurse, errand boy, and secretary" until 1933. He held forth in the Keaton dressing rooms, especially the kitchenette, keeping a snack table and bar open at all hours.

When Willie Riddle first came to Hollywood, his own name had struck him as inadequate. "Willie this, Willie that," he had complained. "*Willie!*"

Buster searched for an imposing name; he got it out of his own sixth year, a Robert Hilliard vaudeville playlet of 1901, *The Littlest Girl*. Hilliard had been Carruthers. Now Willie stepped into the role.

Barely five weeks after Christmas, there came the second Keaton son. Robert Keaton was born on February 3, 1924, as healthy and as handsome a baby as Jimmy had been. Things had been changing. The Talmadges, Natalie included, had refused to call the firstborn Joe or Buster. It was, by common distaff consent, either Jimmy or, reprovingly, James. Now, with Bobby's arrival, there came still another change.

"By this time," Buster says, "having got two boys our first three years, frankly, it looked as if my work was done. I was ruled ineligible. Lost my amateur standing. *They* said I was a pro. I was moved into my own bedroom."

Banishment from the connubial chamber, however, was only the newest change in a long series that had begun right after marriage. Momentarily forgotten in the idyllic weeks by the Truckee River, this newest development seemed to bring the whole process more into focus.

Natalie and Buster Keaton with their two sons.

Buster Keaton was glimpsing—just glimpsing—the fact that life is *not* a play. You don't act it, you live it. And that, it had begun to appear, would take some doing; husband, son, father, host, *bon vivant*, businessman, actor, public figure—it was the proverbial treadmill, turning faster and faster.

"There were the houses, for example," Buster says. "I had stupidly thought that wandering was over—that a house was where you lived. No. Wrong again. A house is where you move from—just a landing field. We had taken off from Westchester Place and made a landing at Westmoreland. Now we were to take off again.

"Well, to be honest about it, even to me, rent was money down the drain. So *we* found a big tile-roof deal with lawns and clipped yews, for only fifty-five thousand dollars cash, on Ardmore Avenue. But we didn't have that kind of dough in the bank. No bonuses coming in for months, and the two grand each week just kept the cars, house, and parties running.

"But Joe Schenck stepped in—says southern California real-estate is the thing. I'll loan you the full amount. The Ardmore house was wonderful. We were there a year—well, ten months—refueling. Then, before taking off for Muirfield Road, we sold Ardmore. Thirty thousand bucks clear profit. Not much I, or anyone else, could say to that.

"The Muirfield place was bigger, better, fancier—hell, why argue? We bought it and began housewarming. That meant—for me, anyway—two o'clock to bed and up at six, grab breakfast, and off to work

"Soon our wing tanks were full and engines revving up again at the end of the runway. Muirfield was only a ready-made job, somebody else's hand-me-down. Now the deal was: roll your own. I was still in no spot to win a point. Now there was one hundred five thousand dollars in the bank—pay back Joe Schenck and still have fifty grand. And then, a month early, here came the bonus check, ninety thousand dollars. So we were square with my brother-in-law and still had one hundred forty thousand dollars. To cap it, Schenck then upped me to twenty-five hundred a week, take-home.

"Looked like we'd be building. So Peg rented us a house she owned on Plymouth Street, and we sold the Muirfield shanty. For a big profit, natch. I began to figure—who wouldn't?—this is nice work if you can get it. And we had it. So I went out on my own and snagged onto a couple of nice vacant plots in Beverly Hills. Buy, take a long breath, and then sell. This thing could be as big as the Signal Hill oil field Roscoe and I didn't buy. I was hooked.

"However, the women were complaining about the Plymouth Street cabin. So I quietly designed a house—Gabe helped me draw it up down at the studio—a real little ranch house, and not *that* small. Then I built it, all on the q.t., on the smaller one of the Beverly Hills pieces, a nice hillside plot. It had to be all done, with every stick of furniture in place and ready down to the last light bulb, before I'd casually drive by with Natalie and stop. She'd say, 'What a dream of a house.' And I'd say, 'Nat, it's yours.' Final sequence. Fade."

It was well into 1925 when Buster Keaton drove Natalie by to see the house he had built for her. "It's yours, Nat," he said. He remembers the occasion only too vividly. How she stared, her mouth a tight line. How silently she sat. How he took her from room to room, talking like a real-estate salesman. How she followed him from basement to attic and finally said, "Too small. Where would you put the servants?"

He thereupon did a hasty thing. The ranch house, well designed, well located, and handsome, would have sold easily at a good profit over cost. Actually, with landscaping but less the new furnishings, it had been built for only thirty-four thousand dollars. It was paid for, clear of mortgages. But the whole affair rankled. Buster showed it to the Eddie Mannixes—Mannix, then managing the Norma and Constance Talmadge companies for Schenck was soon to become an important MGM executive—and the Mannixes loved it. They paid the cost plus a mere 10 percent, Buster says, and promptly moved in. And stayed put.

The low cost of the house and the low price it fetched seemed merely to confirm Natalie's low opinion of the place. So now, at last, *the* house would be built, and built as she wanted it. The site would be the other Beverly Hills site, more than three acres of beautiful hillside, and it would be a place that could lift its turret and preen its red-tiled wings in the company of the Fairbankses' Pickfair and all the other movieland castles. It would have salons downstairs, banquet hall, billiard room, private projection room, and upstairs would be five bedrooms and rooms galore for governess, maids, cook, butler, chauffeur, and gardener. It would have tall date palms, a brook that you could turn off and on and stock with trout, and a swimming pool big enough for community use. It would be on the postcards the tourists would mail: "Buster Keaton's Italian Villa." It would take a year and three hundred thousand dollars to build and furnish.

Far as it was from Buster Keaton's own first, modest dream, the Italian Villa would nonetheless bring the pride a castle brings. Showing it to guests, he would always say, "It took a lot of pratfalls, my friends, to build *this* dump."

Obviously the prideful remark was a double-barreled one—almost, one is tempted to say, mildly schizophrenic. And it certainly was true, as Buster Keaton himself well recognizes, that the wholeness that had seemed to enter his life during that summer at Tahoe had quickly vanished. There was no doubt that he now was being called upon to live two lives, only one of which was the real Keaton's.

Buster I and Buster II.

"Me and my understudy, Buster II," he says. "Buster II could do anything—play and never get tired, be rich and handsome, never grow old. And write checks until the cows came home." That was the real Keaton speaking, the child who was perhaps wiser than the man often seemed to be. That was still the child of twenty-five long years before, the child who, behind the serious face, watched all while loosing laughter. It was still the "wise little head with the red wig" that had won hard-boiled old B. F. Keith, the vaudeville mogul. It was like the child in all of us, except that in Buster Keaton's particular case, it was the child in the complex makeup of a genius, the child who dreamed up symbols and then fitted them to the tune of the belly laugh.

It was the child, therefore, who—for all his seriousness—was observer and dreamer both. It was the child in Keaton who, some three years before the Italian Villa housewarmings began, had conceived the picture called *Daydreams*, with its sad yet pitiless little story of fact versus dream, of wish fulfillment and wish denial, and of final failure.

Even more autobiographical in essence than usual, *Daydreams* is the sad odyssey of a small-town boy in the big city, flopping every day but covering up in each letter to his hometown girl.

"I'm cleaning up in Wall Street," he writes. The girl reads the letter, then the scene fades into *her* dream: the boy at a gigantic desk, surrounded by ticker tape, manipulating mergers, cornering markets, piling up millions. Then—no fade-in but a sharp cut of scene—we see the reality: it is Wall Street, right enough; but the sad little figure is slapshoeing along with his alley broom, sweeping the street.

Next he writes: "I have become a Shakespearean actor. The daydream (his and hers): a frozen-faced Hamlet holding Yorick's skull —"Alas, poor Yorick!" The brutal truth: one of the extras in the stage mob, tripping over his spear.

Flash by flash, scene by counterscene, reality gives the lie to dream, shaming reality.

Then comes the final chase, as inevitable in silent comedy's stylized baroque as counterpoint in Bach. Buster once again, as in *Cops*, innocently gets entangled with the police. Down long streets the action swirls to a pier. He sees the ferryboat leaving the dock. With a prodigious broad jump, he reaches the deck, arises, and puts thumb to nose in defiant salute to his pursuers. Then he realizes the horrible truth: the ferryboat is *coming in!*

The cops now leap the narrowing gap to the deck. Fore and aft, above and below goes the chase. The boat loads, the whistle blows, the paddle wheels begin to turn; like Charon on the Styx, the ferry resumes its endless shuttle.

No one who has seen the film will be apt ever to forget the final scene. Faster, faster, and faster still the hero climbs inside the great whirling paddle wheel to which he has finally fled; faster, faster yet he scales the rods that hold the paddles, trying to keep above water. The down-sweeping blades try to drag him under; he fights to keep clear but disappears in the deep. After the classic five seconds, the sad, set face appears above the foam. Then, having almost surely been lost, he now is climbing up again. Under again, up again, faster and faster. . . .

With an agonizing slowness the scene fades out. The figure, merely a last dark shadow, is still moving, still climbing with the same quiet desperation. If you once saw *Daydreams*, you know for a certainty, nearly a half century later, that somewhere, somehow that frail figure of futility, half-drowned, half-alive, is still climbing up a wheel that will turn forever.

Scene from *Daydreams*, 1922.

TWENTY-FIVE

≈≈≈≈≈≈≈≈≈≈≈≈≈≈≈≈≈≈≈≈≈≈≈

IN 1924, at about the time Bobby Keaton was born, Buster began his third feature comedy. His first, *The Three Ages*, ranges from burlesque to satire. The second, *Our Hospitality*, is—in the best sense of the word—romantic. *Sherlock Jr.*, the third, is—again, in the best sense—magical. It is so both in its general tone and in its use of the stage illusions that had enthralled the boy as well as the camera magic that bewitched the man. *Sherlock Jr.* is both the shortest and one of the finest of the Keaton features.

It is easy to miss much of what a picture like *Sherlock Jr.* has to offer. Its appearance of almost childlike naïveté lulls us like a Rousseau jungle painting. We may miss both art and artist in the fairy tale. The simplicity of its stories (for it has two) can conceal the complexity of its structure and divert us too from its piercing appraisal of life and its witty comment on the very medium itself—the motion picture. Its psychological implications may also elude us because clothed in everyday situations.

Being more playful, *Sherlock Jr.* does not register with the unequivocal impact of *Cops* and *The Boat*. It is, however, a more mature work of art than either earlier picture. Insofar as it represents Keaton's retreat from the increasing fragmentation of his personal life back into the safety of childhood and the theatre, it is important autobiographically. It is necessary, however, again to point out the complexity of Buster Keaton, both artist and man. Thus, here the retreat from the situation is at the same time an analysis of the situation from which he is retreating. It is, in other words, a retreat into his art, the metamorphosis of an unbearable situation into creative symbols.

As is well known, Pablo Picasso did this very thing when, in 1953–1954, he had to face his advancing age. He had left women; no woman had ever left him. Then suddenly—when Picasso was seventy-two years old—Françoise Gilot did the unforgivable. Left alone, during the next nine and a half weeks Picasso poured out a series of 180 drawings, later published as *Picasso and the Human Comedy*. In these he himself for the first time appears as an old man. The series is therefore not only a confession but also a reassertion of the artist and the man—and a triumph over the defaulter as well.

The two situations, of course, are analogous only up to a point. Picasso has always had his art. With Keaton, the time would come when the opportunity to create motion pictures would no longer be his.

Picasso's drawings stand on their own as art, without reference to his own life. And so, it can be said, does Keaton's *Sherlock Jr.* As such, it is something of a landmark in cinema. The artist discovered the visual means to express highly metaphysical ideas. For example, he develops into a complete story-within-a-story the short dream-sequence idea he had earlier essayed in *The Playhouse*. With the utmost clarity, by an extraordinarily imaginative device, he shows us exactly when the dream begins: the dreamer rises like a transparent ghost from the sleeping body. This, remember, is a silent picture. There is no voice of unseen narrator to bridge the mystifying transition from sleep to dream by saying, "And so he slept and dreamed." But Keaton disdained to use even the silent picture's equivalent of narration, the printed subtitle. Keaton the cinematographer seemed always able to find the visual to express the idea. And the motion picture was then—and is still, despite sound—essentially a visual medium.

Buster Keaton, when he chose to be, could be both complex and subtle. This visual symbol is a case in point. It shows us, to begin with, the invisible, inward transition from waking to dreaming. But it also shows us meaning: which is the more real, the nickelodeon projectionist's prosaic life or his romantic dream? Keaton makes the projectionist's dream into a picture being shown on the nickelodeon screen. He lets the projectionist (in his dream) walk straight into the screen and become a part of this inner motion picture, this picture-within-a-picture. Thus, with the greatest subtlety, he makes us accept the outer story as real (and thus, in effect, all cinema), because we must accept the outer motion picture as real in order to postulate the inner one as unreal, that is, dreamed. This is more than visual semantics; it is graphic epistemology. It is also metamorphic magic. And true metamorphosis—it is as seemingly reversible in either direction as Keaton's own life might well have seemed to him at this particular time.

However, at this moment in *Sherlock Jr.*, he irreversibly fixes it:

Scene from
Sherlock Jr., 1924.

once the dreamer has walked down the aisle of the theatre and right into the screen, he is suddenly involved in the cutting from scene to scene of a plot he does not yet understand. He must (and forthwith does) change into another person in order to become a part of *this* story. With this startling but simple device, we not only are told that this is a different world but are given *en passant* Keaton's ironic comment on the all too often overused cinematic device of quick cutting from scene to scene—what he has called the "homeless camera."

Keaton was and is, first and always, a comedian. To make us think, he must make us laugh. Besides, he has a horror of the pompous and the obvious. Had Keaton made a long, solemn picture, very avant-garde, very realistic (and of course very sexy), along the story lines of *Sherlock Jr.*, it would, beyond any question, long ago have been hailed as a serious message. Keaton did not do the serious picture because he is too serious and because he is an artist. His art is the art of the clown.

And he worships clarity. In *Sherlock Jr.* he announces his intentions with his first subtitle: "Do not try to do two things at once and expect to do justice to both. This is the story of a boy who tried it." He tells us this is a fable and then defines fable: "A short story to teach a moral."

The boy, of course, is Buster Keaton, expressly in this film but equally in real life. In the outer story he has no specific name, nor do the other characters. He is the Boy, they are the Girl, Her Father, and the Sheik. In the inner tale, which is the Boy's dream, he alone of the four has a name: Sherlock Jr., the World's Greatest Detective. Kathryn McGuire is the Girl, Joe Keaton is Her Father, and Ward Crane is the Sheik.

The outer story is this. The Boy is projectionist and janitor of a small-town nickelodeon. His two ambitions are to win the Girl and to become a great detective. His rival in love is the Sheik, a Jazz Age city slicker ("lounge lizard" or "tea hound"). The Sheik gets in his dirty work. He steals Her Father's watch, then pins the theft on the Boy. Consulting his correspondence-school textbook, the Boy orders everyone searched. In his own pocket is found a pawn ticket: "Watch and chain, $4." It was planted there, of course, by the Sheik. The Boy is given the heave-ho by Her Father, and he returns to the nickelodeon to project the matinee movie. While it is running, he falls asleep. As he sleeps, the mystery of the theft is solving itself. When the Girl reclaims the watch, the pawnbroker fingers the Sheik.

Meanwhile, however, the Boy begins to dream. This will be the inner story. At its conclusion we shall be back in the projection room to witness the Triumph of Right. The outer story is very short, no more than prologue and epilogue to the dream. (So much for Keaton's own view of the relative importance of actuality versus dream, daily life versus theatre, reality versus art.)

Now for the inner story. The Boy has started running a film called *Hearts and Pearls, or, The Lounge Lizard's Lost Love*. He looks through the projection-booth porthole. On beyond the audience he sees a rich living room on the screen. There are three actors with their backs to the audience—a young man, a young woman, and an elderly man in the act of placing a string of pearls in a wall safe.

The Boy sits down on a stool, yawns, and falls asleep. Immediately he stands up, as transparent as a ghost. Leaving his solid, sleeping body on the stool, he looks again through the porthole. At that instant the three actors turn around. Their faces slowly change from what they were and metamorphose into the Girl, Her Father, and the Sheik.

Ghostly Boy shakes sleeping Boy but cannot awaken him. The transparent dreamer walks to the door of the booth and peels a shadowy porkpie hat from the solid one hanging on the hook. He descends to the auditorium, losing transparency and gaining corporeality as he does so. He walks down the aisle, up over the apron, and right into the screen. The effect is uncanny: one moment he is still in the theatre, the next he is in the movie.

Having walked into a movie plot, he is the immediate victim of whatever way the scenes happen to be cut. As he sets foot in the living room, the scene cuts and instantly he is outside at the entrance door. He knocks—cut—and then falls off the steps. The steps have disappeared. He is now in a garden. Then, just as suddenly, he is in an empty street. He starts walking and is in the mountains, his foot over a precipice. He turns and runs—into a group of lions in the jungle. The lions leap up snarling, then are gone—he is in a desert, almost instantly being nearly run down by a train rushing out of nowhere. The hummock of sand he falls back upon is suddenly a rock, and sea waves are breaking over him. He dives—into a snow-bank in a Far North forest. He leans on a tree, the tree vanishes, and then he is back in the garden.

The garden disappears, and with it the Boy. The real movie and the dream movie have both rejected him. He doesn't belong. When he returns he will no longer be the Boy but his own dream of himself, a great detective.

But will he return? We see the living-room set again with the three original actors. Our vantage point is that of the nickelodeon audience, and our view, like theirs, shows the screen framed by the proscenium arch and the upper part of the orchestra pit. What will happen now in the screened action? Will it go forward or backward? In other words, does the Boy up in the projection booth dream on or wake up?

Preceding any further action, a visual symbol answers the question. The nickelodeon screen begins to expand, wider, higher, until it fills the entire picture frame of the film. The theatre—audience and all— has disappeared. Now the play—that is, the dream—is the thing, the whole thing.

The action among the three actors goes on. The pearls are missing. The Girl's Father telephones the World's Greatest Detective, Sherlock Jr. He comes, in silk hat and with cane. Making light of the matter, he says, "Don't bother to explain."

Sherlock Jr. lives a charmed life. The deadly traps laid for him by the thieves—the Sheik and his accomplice, the butler—boomerang on their guilty perpetrators: the Sheik is nearly beheaded by a battle-ax rigged over an easy chair intended for the detective, and the butler nearly drinks the poisoned wine. The third trap, counted on if all else should fail, is a pool ball filled with dynamite. One tap on that ball and the joint blows up.

The Sheik engages Sherlock in a game of rotation pool. Suspense-fully it runs out to the last ball. Each time the young detective raises his cue the villain dashes from the room. The balls click, there is no blast, and he creeps back for his shot. Shot after shot, the balls skim a hairbreadth from the lethal 13. Then Sherlock slams the 13 in. There is no explosion—we discover that the omniscient detective had substituted an unloaded ball.

Now, as Sherlock Jr. gets to the heart of the crime, two old stage illusions save his life. On the first occasion he dives through a magic box. He has trailed the thieves to their headquarters. His valet, Gillette (a kind of servitor Watson), hands him a round cardboard box and lid. The box is about four inches deep and thirty inches in diameter. We watch Sherlock arrange a woman's dress in the box and replace the lid.

The thieves and two accomplices are in the house. Sherlock, outside, sets the box upright in an open window and then walks over to the front door. He is promptly spotted and is yanked inside. As the thieves prepare to do away with him for good, he gets hold of the pearls and whirls to escape. He does not, as the thieves expect, make for the open door. Instead he veers and dives headlong through the window in which he has placed the magic box. Outside, with the pearls, he strolls away undetected by the pursuing thieves.

How this is accomplished is made clear by an extraordinary pictorial device that, to be implemented, required the building of a house with a detachable end. Just as Sherlock Jr. reaches for the pearls, the camera moves outside the room interior for an exterior shot, a distant diagonal view that takes in the end, corner, and front of the house, including the entrance door and the window that holds the magic box. The camera remains at this angle while the action, unseen, continues inside and then, after a few seconds, the end of the house vanishes and we have a cutaway view, as on a dollhouse. Thus (the camera not having shifted during this fantastic develop-

Scene from *Sherlock Jr.*, 1924.

ment) we can now view interior and exterior simultaneously and so see the detective dive headlong directly through the box, land on the ground outside, and spring to his feet. Sherlock Jr. goes into the box a man and comes out a woman, walking away in bonnet and crinolines while the gang mills around in blind confusion.

Thus, as on a dual stage, Buster Keaton bared in one clear, continuous shot the secret workings of an old illusion in order to make equally clear that he was playing the gag, cinematically speaking, dead on the level. Though clearly a magician's trick, it is no easy camera trick.

Belatedly the gang discovers the ruse, and the chase is on. They are on the detective's heels as he runs toward an old barn. He seems cornered at last. But an even more spectacular illusion saves him once again. This time he seems to dive right through a man and a door. The faithful Gillette, disguised as a female peddler, stands in front of the closed barn door. Gillette is holding in front of him a street peddler's tray, open and with its lid (like that of a valise, and draped with men's neckties) up and leaning against his chest. Sherlock comes on the dead run. Gillette points urgently to the tray. Without slackening speed, the young detective dives (so far as we can see) right through the upraised lid and right through Gillette's chest and the solid door behind him. One instant Sherlock is outside, the next he is behind the closed door of the barn. It is the vanishing act deluxe.

Keaton does not give away the secret of this illusion in the film, and it is all but too complicated to describe. It involves a hidden trapdoor in the barn door directly behind the tray lid and what *seems* to be Gillette's chest. Actually, however, Gillette is suspended in a horizontal position shoulder-high off the ground—head, shoulders, and arms *outside* the barn; torso, legs, and feet *inside*. He wears the peddler's dress over only arms and shoulders, the rest of the costume hanging down, with dummy ankles and feet, like a curtain in front of the barn door and its trapdoor workings. Keaton actually did dive through the tray lid (that is, it hinged back and down at the push of his outstretched hands), but he did not dive through Gillette or the barn door, only its small trapdoor.

In recent times, Buster reenacted this scene on the Ed Sullivan television show.

The rest of the Sherlock saga is the final chase, one of the best that Keaton ever devised. Far from surrendering, the gang is fleeing to the lonely mountain-cabin hideaway where the Girl is held hostage. Gillette, now in motorcycle cop disguise, takes his master on the handlebars of his vehicle and then, under way, promptly falls off and is left behind. Sherlock, totally unaware that no one is steering, rides at breakneck speed through some genuinely hair-raising sequences. Among these is Sherlock's swift traversal of an excavation ditch with the diggers leaping out ahead of him like jacks-in-the-box. Even more sensational and dangerous is his lightning-swift crossing of a forty-foot gap in a broken aqueduct across the roofs of two moving vans at the exact moment they meet and pass in the gap. As usual, no doubles for Buster Keaton, and well the audiences knew it.

When, finally, he looks around and makes the chilling discovery that he is alone on the motorcycle, he is promptly catapulted right through the window of the very room of the very cabin where the Girl is. They leap into the Sheik's car, which is parked outside. The gang, having been outdistanced by the motorcycle, now drives up and the chase is reversed, along a narrow, winding sea-cliff road. Sherlock ends it, and the gang, by an accurate heave of the dynamite-loaded 13 ball, which he has been carrying in his pocket all along.

They are free. Then, almost immediately, they are sinking in the sea. The quick scuttling of victory comes about in this way. At a blind intersection in the road at the water's edge, they meet a truck. Sherlock Jr. steps on the brakes; they lock; the chassis stops dead still, but the car body—they in it—sails over the truck and into the sea.

Presto! The young detective raises the convertible top up to its halfway, vertical position, and in the spanking breeze, with the top as canvas, they sail away. But, like the *Damfino*, this impromptu boat is doomed to sink. As Sherlock hands the Girl the pearls and she embraces him, it founders. He is swimming with her in tow as the scene fades.

This ends the dream sequence, the movie-within-a-movie.

Back in the nickelodeon projection booth, the Boy, horizontal on the stool, his eyes closed, is making swimming motions. He falls to the floor, wakes up, and rushes to the projection-room peephole. *Hearts and Pearls* is nearing its end. That other movie, in which he had been so deeply involved, is gone. The ghostly Boy, the invincible detective, all the thrilling drama and sweet romance are no more. It is back to life.

The Girl enters, too excited to knock. "We've made a terrible mistake," she says. She is shy, he at a loss. Something romantic should happen here. What is it, and how do you do it?

He looks out at the screen. *Hearts and Pearls* is moving toward the clinch. Its hero turns the shy heroine to him. Good. The Boy turns the Girl. Next? The hero slips a ring on the heroine's finger. The Boy does likewise. Then comes the long, slow kiss. The Boy, now a little beyond his depth, manages a quick peck. Then *Hearts and Pearls* fades into its epilogue: the hero sitting at home holding twins on his lap while the heroine, rather ominously, is busy knitting. This is really deep water. The Boy scratches his head and looks directly at the camera with the full, inerasable, everlasting puzzlement of that famous frozen face. *How do you do* that? he is obviously wondering.

Beyond all its many allusions to many things, its questions posed, and its symbols from Keaton's own life transformed into signs more universal, *Sherlock Jr.* is a gay picture and a magical one. Even by themselves, the gaiety and the magic would be enough.

TWENTY-SIX

~~~~~~~~~~~~~~~~~~~~~~~~~~~~~~~~

BUSTER KEATON'S next picture is funny but not gay, explicit rather than magical. It belongs with his factually oriented work rather than with his fantasy. *The Navigator* is generally considered one of the masterpieces of silent-film comedy. Certainly its theme—man at the mercy of The Machine—is even more pertinent today than it was in 1924.

The Navigator inevitably invites comparison with Chaplin's *Modern Times* of 1936, even though the two artists are so different in point of view and method that comparison can only be inconclusive. Chaplin's personality elicits sympathy from the opening scene. Keaton wins it only by degrees as, a pampered young millionaire, he is being compelled to face up to life. Chaplin is the underdog to begin with, Keaton only when The Machine makes him so.

But it goes deeper than personality. In the assembly line's mechanized jungle it is Chaplin the human being who is hero. Keaton, on the contrary, shares the role, facing a hostile costar, The Machine. His is no romance impeded but not deterred by machinery; it is, rather, a precarious wooing that hinges on his duel with a mechanical enemy.

It is clear that here in *The Navigator*, Buster Keaton will finally strip his theme to its bare essentials; he will pose his problem with a deeper, more hopeless irony. This is the full-scale crystallization of his obsession. He comes to grips with it at last.

It was only by chance that the picture was ever made. Fred Gabouri had been lent to First National as technical man for *The Sea Hawk*, starring Enid Bennett and Milton Sills. He was sent up the northwest coast to hunt for the old, out-of-commission clippers that survived in a harbor here and there. They would be bought, then towed down the coast to San Pedro, seaport of Los Angeles, and there dressed up to look like Elizabethan war vessels.

Buster and his three writers were chewing their pencils, casting about for a new plot, when Gabe burst in on them.

"I told you a long time ago," he said to Keaton, "that I'd get you a real boat. Well, I've got you a real honest-to-God ocean liner. You can do anything you damn please with her—sail her, burn her, blow her up, sink her."

The four were looking at him, mouths wide open. Buster asked, mildly, "Don't the people care?"

"Hell," said Gabouri, "they want to get rid of her—sell her or rent her. Gonna be junked. Only thing"—he paused—"you gotta move fast. In twenty-four hours they move in with the blowtorches."

"She's rented," Buster said. "Clyde," he said, turning to Bruckman, "go with Gabe and send a wire. Sign my name."

Two days later the SS *Buford* would be leaving the estuary between Oakland and Alameda, then through the Golden Gate, ready for action and bound under her own steam for San Pedro.

After Gabe and Clyde were gone, the others sat for ten minutes, no one speaking. Then out came the "postcard." Jean Havez said, "I've got it. I want a rich boy and a rich girl who never had to lift a finger, always someone to wait on 'em—houses full of butlers, maids, valets, chauffeurs. I put these two beautiful, spoiled brats—the two most helpless people in the world—adrift on a ship, all alone. A dead ship. No lights, no steam."

Bruckman returned while Havez was talking. Clyde had the dour, hopeless face of the comedy writer. Now, however, his eyes lit up. "What a prop for Bus," he said, "an ocean liner!"

Bruckman had once tried to describe to a visitor what it was that Keaton did with props. "He can take a ladder," Bruckman said, "a pail—hell, a stick!—and have you rolling on the ground."

Bruckman, who never had seen the vaudeville alley broom and the knothole, had nevertheless seen an older Buster up to his old tricks. He put his finger unerringly on the Keaton secret. "He does something"—the writer grasped for words until he got it—"he makes the thing *alive*."

In much later years Bruckman often reminisced about *The Navigator*, particularly the plot that had developed out of Havez' basic idea. "In that particular period of the 1920's," he once said, "we were trying to shake the pattern of the final chase. A hard thing to do, it was set in the public mind. 'The chase,' Buster was always saying, 'is just one form of climax. It works so well because it speeds up the tempo, generally involves the whole cast, and puts the whole outcome of the story on the block.'

"In *The Navigator*," Bruckman would always conclude, "we didn't have another liner to chase the one we had. We had to try to come up with another climax."

With their noses pointed to a good story, the conferees had relaxed. Havez triggered a belly laugh. "Can we dunk the boss *this* time!" Everyone laughed. The whole staff had a superstitious belief that immersing Keaton ensured a successful picture.

The ship, however, would not be dunked. To ensure that, Buster had rented her rather than bought her. Sink her? "I'll say not. No, it's not the money." He reminded them of the Rolls Royce he had beat up in *The Blacksmith* only two years before. The scene, considered surefire, had met a cold, hostile silence. "You guys remember *that* dud," he said. "If we sink a beautiful ocean liner, they'll hiss. You could do it in a tragedy, where it's serious, or in out-and-out farce, where it doesn't *really* happen, but you can't do it in comedy like this. Those same people who wished *they* had a Rolls would be wishing they could inherit a liner just like I had, or even just take a trip on one."

In one of those later-year discussions of *The Navigator*, Buster Keaton was talking with Bruckman. "Havez' basic idea was good," he said. "Marooning a rich boy and a rich girl on a derelict ship. Of course, it took some figuring to get us both aboard separately and the ship set adrift and still keep it believable. But we did.

"There we were, in the dead of night, floating out to sea—neither one of us knowing the other was on board. There was a lot of discussion, remember, should we be strangers or not? My idea was that we should know each other and have a mutual problem. Marooned together—or shanghaied by fate, you might say—the problem would really be sitting in our laps. Only then, you see, we'll have a bigger problem—no two-bit problem who marries who, but just staying alive on a derelict ship."

"Life," said Bruckman.

"Yes," said Buster. "So we worked it out. I'm Rollo Treadway, a really useless young millionaire who can't even shave himself. I've proposed to this girl. She wants no part of me, my money, or my position. Doesn't need any of it. And there we are, neither one knowing the other's on ship, drifting off to nowhere in the dark."

Buster began reliving the story. "Well," he said, "it's morning. I wake up, go out on deck. See no one. Go to the dining saloon. No one there—no passengers, no waiters. I think I'm the first one up— sit and wait. No one appears. Go to the kitchen. Not a soul. It's gradually dawning on old Slow Thinker that he's on a deserted ship.

Meanwhile the girl is in a panic, looking all over to find someone alive on board."

Then he described the intricate and beautifully timed shipwide scramble of the two, searching for fellow beings through the compartmented maze of an ocean liner, or, as Bruckman called it, "a *Buford* built for two." Rollo's telltale cigarette butt, tossed from above, is the girl's first clue that she is not alone. Then follows an eerie, merry-go-round circling of the promenade deck, starting as a walk and accelerating into a crazy, panicky footrace, a pursuit of each by each in which footsteps are audible but neither is ever in sight of the other. It is a phantom race, with nameless fear as an added starter.

Keaton turned to Bruckman and laughed. "You see, Clyde, we got in a chase after all."

Then they get confused by the labyrinth of cabins and passageways and run aimlessly up and down stairs. "If you had done that to Adam and Eve," said Buster, "there would be no human race."

The girl ends up in the machine shop on the orlop deck, while Rollo is on the topmost deck resting in front of a ventilating funnel. His hat is sucked in, he dives after it, and disappears. He plummets down, on through the vent in the machine-shop ceiling, crashes on the workbench, and at last they are together.

Before she can speak, he is out with it. "Once more, dear, will you marry me?"

"When I'm cold and hungry," she says, "you ask me to marry you."

They take over in the galley. It is a famous scene, from the six coffee beans boiled in four gallons of seawater through the opening of cans with meat cleaver and auger and on to Rollo's disastrous attempt to retrieve boiled eggs from a gigantic caldron. The ship offers no culinary equipment under community size, certainly none scaled for two, whether in love or not. Their first breakfast puts another roadblock in the path of romance.

A coast-guard cutter appears on the horizon. It comes nearer. Rollo figures out that they must run up a signal flag. Which one? "That pretty yellow one," she says. The cutter sees the quarantine signal, thinks smallpox or cholera, and turns tail and runs. By then the liner is already drifting past the three-mile limit and into international waters.

Interspersed with such vital happenings as these are the juicy gags, the misadventures of a twofold innocence verging on idiocy: they fall off the liner and rescue each other; there is a hard-to-handle deck

Scene from
The Navigator, 1924.

chair that all but puts them both in irons, at least in effect; they
accidentally set off the fireworks they find aboard; and there is the
horror-touched moment in the first-class saloon when a phonograph
—needle nudged into groove by the rocking of the ship—booms out
in basso profundo: *"Danger is near thee—many brave hearts are
asleep in the deep!"* Yet the context elevates the gags into moments
that illuminate the plight of the human being in the Machine Age.
They are funny—and very frightening.

Unschooled to begin with, the two live and learn. Their predicament turns into their salvation. They mechanize the kitchen to cook
things in twos in kettles built for hundreds. They create twin beds,
with a wall of steel between, in two of the unused boilers in the
engine room—"foolproof bundling," said Bruckman.

The food stores are endless, the days balmy and cloudless, with
not even a clock to toll the time. They drift, no longer caring, lost
but content in a steel Eden, on a floating iron island of peace.

But the world is out there. Summoned by the happiness of two
lost children, hostile man appears, while The Machine, once friendly,
turns against them.

They are floating past a cannibal island, well out of javelin range,
when the rudder breaks and the ship begins drifting into shore.
Rollo Treadway, by now a young man of some skill and considerable mettle, goes down in a diving suit to make repairs. But the
cannibals are already under way in war canoes. Here is the climax
that Keaton and Bruckman wanted in place of the old-style chase.

Rollo races to complete repairs, while the aborigines race to board
the ship. His dilemma: he must leave the girl unprotected, but at
the same time only her hands on the air pump stand between him
and suffocation. The cannibals seize her before he can finish; the
hose is cut; Rollo is still trapped underwater as the natives dance
around their victim back on the island. The end seems in sight.

Suddenly a weird figure rises from the sea, a twentieth-century tribal god in mask and armor. It is simply Rollo walking up out of the depths in all the diving paraphernalia. The cannibals take to the jungle. The girl flies to kiss her hero on the blank glass face of his diving helmet. Rollo topples over backward in the water, but his still-inflated diving suit makes him into a human raft. She straddles him, employs her hands as paddles, and they make it back on board. The cannibals, however, peering from the trees, discover who this god of the sea really is, and the siege is on again. Out they come, into their canoes, then once more they are swarming aboard the ship. The end *has* come.

"The real end," said Bruckman reminiscently.

"Yes," said Buster, "the real end."

Hand in hand, boy and girl dive into the sea and sink out of sight, sealing the end.

But then, suddenly, something gigantic comes up, bearing them back above water as though it were a rescuing hand. It is a conning tower, and the submarine to which it belongs rises until its decks are just awash. The hatch opens, they fall inside, and it closes as the natives began hacking at it, stone hatchets futilely assaulting steel. The submarine dives.

Inside, the girl kisses Rollo square on the lips. He falls back against a control lever and the submarine begins to whirl. People and furniture tumble like dice in a box. The Machine—nudged by Keaton —has the last word.

"The story really ended when you two dove in and sank," said Bruckman.

"Oh," said Buster "it was in the books for us to die all right. But not in the jokebooks. We were making a comedy, remember?"

Bruckman nodded. As he sat opposite the comedian, his dour face and Keaton's tragic mask were twin portraits of the spirit of comedy.

The Navigator was the biggest money-maker of all the Keaton company's films. During its initial release period it grossed around two million dollars. It cost only two hundred and twelve thousand dollars, despite unexpected expenses. A moderate twenty-five thousand-dollar rental for the *Buford* covered ship, crew, and fuel. The most expensive single item, as it turned out, was the underwater sequence. The *Buford*'s own stern was not used in this scene. A full-size mock-up was made, and the cameramen worked in a specially constructed glass diving bell. All of this was in the budget.

The sequence was planned for the public swimming pool in River-side. This pool was only nine feet deep at the diving end; consequently, the *Buford's* propeller being twelve feet high (and the mock-up likewise), permission was sought and granted to extend the concrete pool walls up to twenty feet temporarily. When the pool was then filled, its bottom buckled and collapsed under the added tonnage of water.

Into the emergency budget went the item: "New swimming pool for Riverside, California," and the company moved to Catalina, off Avalon. The equipment was all in place and cameras ready, when in swarmed schools of fish ready to mate and the waters assumed a milky hue.

"By this time," Buster says, "Lou Anger had a tic."

So it was pack up and off to good old Tahoe, where the water was known to be clear, all for one short sequence. It was a five-hundred-mile trek and early in the season. Snow still lined the summit passes. So glacial was the water that Buster could stay down only a few minutes at a time and then had to be hauled up and revived with straight bourbon. Then the extreme cold began impeding the photography. Due to the cameramen's body heat, the glass windows of the diving bell fogged up on the inside. So the bell had to be refrigerated inside by ice piled in the corners. But this also refrigerated the cameramen, who then had to be pulled up with Buster for bourbon. Finally, arctic outfits—fur parkas and gloves—had to be requisitioned for the cameramen.

"By that time," says Buster, "*I* had the tic."

TWENTY-SEVEN

I F Buster Keaton's film profits were on the upswing, so were his in-law problems. Following *The Navigator's* autumn premiere, the World Series for Buster, and the Fifth Avenue shops for Natalie, 1925 came in with the big family stir over houses that would lead to the Italian Villa. Then Joe Schenck, stepping out of his passive-executive role, bought a play for his brother-in-law to make into a movie.

Buster recalls the incident. "A certain local screwball sold himself to Joe as a great director and also sold him a story—a Belasco show called *Seven Chances*—twenty-five thousand dollars. The money wasn't much, but the show! I had seen it in New York—1916 for heaven's sakes—and it was a flop then. Closed in a week, if I recall.

"So this *nouveau* big shot," Buster continues, "casts the picture, hires extra writers, and orders sets. In a week or so, the bills start coming in. Lou Anger blew his top—'This guy goes—now!' I said, 'How about Joe Schenck?' Lou hollered, 'Joe Schenck, Joe Schmenck!' and that was that. Except we still had the story. The type of un-believable farce I don't like. We made it anyway and got a fair picture. But when it came down to the finish, where my brides-to-be are chasing me—my God, we actually hired *five hundred* women, every shape and every size, and bridal outfits on all of 'em—well, hell, I can outrun 'em. And even if they catch me, how can you end the picture? Can I marry all of 'em? Not even in Utah. Can I fight 'em?

"So we're crippled. Can't get in any good chase gags, can't end it with any kind of climax. So we simply decided to fade on the chase. And do you know, three little rocks saved me! Our fade-out was on me, running down the side of a hill, all those weirdos after me. A real dud, and we knew it. However, we previewed it. Medium laughs, a few giggles through all that chase. Then suddenly, just be-fore the fade, a real belly laugh.

"I whispered to Bruckman, 'Now what the hell caused that?' He didn't know, so we ran the ending slow at the studio. There it was.

Waiting for the bride. Scene from *Seven Chances*, 1925.

The brides arrive. Scene from *Seven Chances*, 1925.

I had accidentally dislodged a rock. It started to roll after me. On its way, it knocked a couple more loose and there were three little rocks chasing me.

"Havez piped up, 'Like I alluz said, rocks is funnier than women.'

"So we went back and milked that gag. Gabouri laid it out. He built a hundred and fifty rocks of papier-mâché on chicken wire, from baseball size up to a boulder eight feet in diameter. We found a longer ridge, and Gabe triggered them in sequence. We assembled the gals again, a hundred feet back, and used a starter's gun. On your marks, get set, *bang*! I only had to kick the first little one and then keep going. And the key words are 'keep going' because it built up to an avalanche right on my heels. So naturally I stumble—if it's not in the script, I stumble anyway—and the big one knocked me twenty feet in the air. Lessley never stopped cranking. When I staggered up and staggered on, it was for real."

The chase in Keaton's second 1925 feature did not please him either, but it is an excellent film and in some respects a great one. *Go West*, in fact, is still a favorite in Italy, where they go to the same grand operas year after year and figure they can do the same with horse operas. Italians consider *Go West* a Western, and small wonder if one considers the no less laughable plot of the Puccini opera *La Fanciulla del West*, or *The Girl of the Golden West*.

The Charge of the Light Brigade, as Bruckman called the five hundred husband hunters in *Seven Chances*, had focused attention on the perennial comedy problem: the right leading lady. It was no walk-on (or sway-on) part, no simple pitting of a glamorous perfect thirty-six against buffoonery. She had to play straight, feed the comedian, keep out of his way, keep out of the props' way, and upon occasion take a fall. It had little dignity, less glamour—and with Keaton, precious little romance. That long, last, lingering clinch was always getting lost in a chase or, worse, a throwaway. It was no juicy part, yet she had to have looks, intelligence, fortitude, paid-up insurance, and a grasp of the art as Keaton underplayed it. So far, in five years and two dozen films, Buster had not yet found her.

They were discussing the problem at a rainy-day story conference. Suddenly Buster said, "I think I'll hire a cow." His tone brought everyone to attention. "A Jersey cow," he said. "A cow called Brown Eyes." He was serious.

Havez spoke in his slow, quiet drawl. "Cows are scarcer than actresses around Hollywood," he said, "but we can find one. However," Havez continued, "I deeply misdoubt you can train a cow even as good as an actress. They give the milk, kick the pail over, and they're through. The cows, I mean."

"Get the cow," said Buster. "I'll train her."

A new picture was jelling. It would be *Go West*, the last Keaton feature to bear the old Metro imprint. After that, it would be Leo the Lion's outfit, Metro-Goldwyn-Mayer.

Brown Eyes was found, and Buster began to train her. "Within ten days," he announced, "I'll have her following me everywhere. Now just leave us alone."

He patiently hauled her around by a halter rope. Meanwhile he started a friendship. In a day or so the rope was a smaller one, then it was a length of cord. On the tenth day, everyone was watching. Brown Eyes now fell in step right behind the slapshoed comedian with no visible implementation of the trainer's will. At the sounds of surprise, Buster pointed to a fine black cotton thread tied around his elbow and leading to Brown Eye's neck.

Despite all the byplay, there was an orthodox leading lady, billed above Brown Eyes (although her marquee billing was below), as shown by the cast of characters:

Owner Diamond Bar Ranch	Howard Truesdale
His Daughter	Kathleen Myers
Foreman	Kay Thompson
Brown Eyes	Herself
Friendless	BUSTER KEATON

Scene from *Go West*, 1925.
Buster and Brown Eyes.

Scene from *Go West*, 1925.

Friendless is a jobless ne'er-do-well in a Midwestern village. He hoboes his way out to Arizona—"barrels out west," Buster says, and the term is exactly right. He has hidden in a freight car partly loaded with barrels, which come unstacked en route and give him a terrible beating—a multiple "chase" reminiscent of the Hugo story of the unlashed cannon loose on the warship deck. Finally, to protect himself, Keaton climbs into one of the barrels, which then immediately rolls out the side door, bounds down the railroad embankment, unstaves itself on a boulder, and deposits him smack on the seignorial acres of the Diamond Bar Ranch.

Though the greenest greenhorn ever to hit Arizona, he gets a job and then a friend. He becomes a cowboy (or, at least, that was the foreman's idea), and he meets Brown Eyes. Brown Eyes is limping; Friendless removes a pebble wedged in the cleft of her hoof. Brown Eyes licks his hand; the Great Love dawns. Then he meets the ranch owner's daughter. She falls in love with Friendless. "Now there," says Buster, "was a triangle."

Then the crisis: Diamond Bar must sell its cattle and, what is more, get them all the way from Arizona to Los Angeles pronto or the mortgage on the ranch will be foreclosed. What is still more, the neighboring ranchers, for their own reasons, are determined that the sale shall not go through. And what is even still more, Brown Eyes is to go!

Friendless tries vainly to hide her. Then the ranchman's daughter intercedes with that old Western generosity that could penetrate even the heart of a damsel in love. "Let him have her, Pa," she cries. But Pa says no. Brown Eyes is rounded up with the rest.

With the cowboys perched atop the freight cars as guards and the cattle loaded, the freight train departs. A few miles farther on it runs into an ambush laid by the neighboring ranchers. Gunfire drives the Diamond Bar hands off the freight cars, but the train starts up and makes a run for it. At the last second, however, the engineer, having just opened the throttle, is shot and killed. So off steams the train with 350 head of cattle and not a human aboard—except one. Friendless has sneaked into Brown Eyes' car. Here the situation is actually worse than on the derelict ship in *The Navigator*, because there the victims at least knew what they were up against. Here, however, as a runaway train runs through signals with a near wreck at every rural crossing, Friendless remains totally ignorant of the true situation.

The train has bulled blindly through Arizona, over the Colorado, and through southern California before reality dawns on Friendless. He then sprints over an almost endless string of boxcar roofs to the locomotive cab and brings the train to a stop in the Los Angeles freight yards.

The boss had said, "If I don't sell these cattle I'm ruined." So Friendless opens all the doors and the whole vast herd piles out into the business district. The scenes that follow must be seen to be believed: Friendless and Brown Eyes bellwethering hundreds of steers through crowded downtown streets; traffic piling up; pedestrians fleeing, even up any handy telephone pole; straying dogies milling around drugstores, poking into barbershops and Turkish baths, and browsing

"Next!" Scene from *Go West*, 1925. (Joe Keaton in barber chair.)

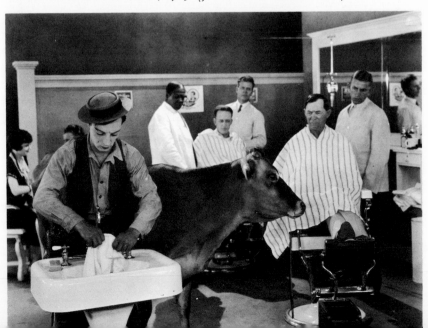

—if that's the term—through department stores. *Urbi et orbi*, the Diamond Bar bulls have "arrived."

This was the "chase" that disappointed Keaton. The steers, he felt, moved too slowly. "We didn't dare speed them up," he says, "or we would have had a real stampede."

Actually, he seems to underestimate a very real accomplishment. The *threat* of stampede, constantly felt throughout these scenes, is tremendously effective. The whole bellowing, seesawing, stomping, stop-and-go cattle drive through such unlikely terrain adds up to a slow but devastatingly suspenseful sort of climax that is resolved only when Friendless at last delivers the herd to the stockyards. But it is a happy ending for Friendless too. The owner and his daughter drive up just as the cattle are being consigned, and Brown Eyes is the cowboy's reward.

It is needless at this point to comment upon the essential strangeness of a picture like this. It inheres not merely in strange physical juxtapositions such as cattle in a Turkish bath but in subtler and deeper confrontations: those of meaning—the serious and the ridiculous; of climate—the mundane and the fantastic; and of essences— the real and the unreal. As in all Keaton's pictures, it is part and parcel of one of the strangest imaginations among the makers of movies, work that comes, as James Agee once observed, "from far inside a curious and original spirit."

It was spring. *Go West*, the fourth Keaton feature, was complete. The Italian Villa, the house for Natalie, was under construction. Buster was dashing to and fro at all hours from his Hollywood studios to the Plymouth Street house in Los Angeles or out to the Villa site in Beverly Hills.

Buster Keaton was now thirty, his energy to all appearances undiminished. More than anything, he seemed unmoored, a bit distracted, as he did on the screen. To one or two intimate friends he appeared to be searching for something he could not find. Those close to him at this period sensed his loneliness, how his life seemed uncentered in any vital way. In a sense, it was surprising that this was so, that his film work, into which he poured such intensive creative concentration, did not suffice. Perhaps it was something for which nothing could serve as sublimation. Now he seemed to seek rather than shun distraction, pursue rather than avoid complication. Whatever it was—whether or not he was hunting for some wholeness that life, in vaudeville and movies, in childhood and youth, had failed to give—Keaton, as his friend Buster Collier observed, was "spreading Keaton very thin."

The distractions, such as his card playing, were mainly rather trivial. Yet for him, as for many creative personalities, in a pinch it was not the importance or unimportance of the activity but the activity itself that counted.

Bridge was becoming a time stealer. Buster had been introduced to the game five years earlier by film executive Hiram Abrams on the train carrying Keaton east for his wedding. Buster himself recalls that Abrams had insisted that he join a game and then had twitted him for every misplay. Buster, nervous anyway (what with his broken ankle and the uncertainty about whether Natalie would marry him or not), had finally tossed in his hand in uncharacteristic anger.

This incident spurred him to learn the game. For the next year he played bridge alone, sitting with books at his elbow, playing and analyzing each of the four hands. On his second try, he was no longer a novice. Abrams again was on the other side. The game took place in a Los Angeles country club, and the stakes were high. Buster played faultlessly, he and partner winning with ease. He recalls how, like tennis victor vaulting the net, he was suddenly on his feet and shaking Abrams' hand. "We are friends everywhere," he had said, "except at bridge."

Bridge became a major obsession, ranking with baseball. Eventually Keaton was competing on even terms with the best. One or two of his plays are to be found in the bridge manuals. Ever since, the game has taken a lot of his time. But in those early years it did not bring Natalie any closer. "She wasn't interested enough," he says, "to concentrate on cards."

It would seem that there were beginning to be other distractions too, as his friend Buster Collier, rather diffidently, told just a few years ago. Collier, a stage child himself, had known Keaton since the vaudeville days. In Hollywood they had become frequent companions. Collier, although several years the younger, had got into movies first, playing the bugle boy in the Triangle feature *The Bugle Call*. That had been in 1916, when Collier was only twelve.

Speaking of these newer distractions in his friend's life, Collier chose his words carefully. "Gals," he said, "used to go for Buster. Clean-cut. Quick. Athletic. That great smile—worth a million dollars because they never saw it on the screen—his nice language, his thoughtfulness, his wonderful dancing. Yes, the gals took a second look at Buster Keaton."

Collier became reflective. "That came along," he said, "a little later on in his marriage. I don't think that Buster was fundamentally— Let me say, I think that Buster was reassured by it. I can tell you this: he was susceptible to flattery." Collier hesitated. "No, not flattery, but he sure needed affection. Affection kept him going, I'm sure of it. Kept him from building up a wall around himself. At least then."

Distractions, dalliances or divertissements, problems and all, Buster Keaton went right into a new picture. Almost as if to show Schenck how to find plays, he bought *Battling Butler*, a successful Broadway comedy by Stanley Brightman and Austin Melford. Buster himself directed his film version. He borrowed Sally O'Neill from Metro-Goldwyn, where she had just starred with Constance Bennett and Joan Crawford in *Sally, Irene, and Mary*. Sally O'Neill was a real dark-haired colleen, small enough to make romance with Keaton plausible. He also used Snitz Edwards, an actor even shorter than himself, one with an unforgettable face, quizzical, bird-eyed, and wizened. As Alfred Butler's valet, he played against Buster straight and with a tempo nicely adjusted to the natural Keaton pace, which begins pictures slower than other comedians and often ends them twice as fast.

There are two Alfred Butlers in the play. One, a millionaire's son, is hunting and fishing at the behest of his valet, who wants to make a man of him. A complete novice at all manly sports, Alfy is marvelously inept at it all. The valet, instructing him from textbooks, only compounds the confusion. They are camping in the Kentucky mountains, quartering in a vast tent complete with kitchen, bath, indirect lighting, a sofa, and a master's bed with eiderdown mattress. The other Alfred Butler is a hard-nosed pug, world's heavyweight boxing champion. The champ is in training in the same region.

The hillbillies mistake the rich Alfy for the boxer. The champ, amused, lets it ride. Then, however, he catches Alfy with his wife in an apparently compromising situation. He brushes off all explanations and sets up a grudge fight at Madison Square Garden—ballyhoo, tickets, public, and all—in which he will annihilate little Alfy.

Alfy, meanwhile, has his own reasons for accepting the challenge. Far from having been involved with the pugilist's wife, he has fallen for Sally, the mountain girl. Egged on not only by his valet but by his own pride as well, he is suicidally bent on going through with it to prove his manhood to Sally.

That puts the fat in the fire. Sally is going to New York just to see

Scene from *Battling Butler*, 1926.

her lover fight. After he wins they will be married. So it is on to the bitter end.

It is only a few weeks until the fight. The valet procures new textbooks and engages trainers and sparring partners. It's all hopeless. There is no fighter in Alfy. The worst palookas flatten him as soon as he steps into the ring. Even his valet begins to have serious misgivings.

The great fight comes at last. It runs along true to form. Buster Keaton does not imitate the wonderful, deft ballet of Chaplin in his famous film *The Champion*. This is brutally, almost heartbreakingly different, not fantasy at all but the facts of the case. Alfy takes a savage beating at the hands of a sadistic, vengeful mauler. It is a scene to turn any heart cold with terror and pity as we watch him, small and completely defenseless, walking into rib-cracking punches, tapping and flailing, grotesquely inept, stumbling, falling, and climbing back for more.

And then The Miracle. It too is not fantasy but the real thing. The champ, in effect, defeats himself. It is the kind of thing that, as Buster himself says—referring perhaps equally to his real mishaps and triumphs—"*could* happen to anyone." Sad, beaten, bloody Alfy Butler, a man in a nightmare, thinks of the mountain girl sitting out there and witnessing all this. And suddenly, from somewhere out of the black fog of pain comes anger—blazing, mad, red anger.

The world's champion is standing there, hands on hips, laughing. He is wide open. The awkward, puny demon is on him like a flash.

At last the wild punches carry weight. The champ is wobbling. The champ is down. The champ is out.

The foppish little rich boy is champion of the world. And he doesn't even care—his mountain girl is in his arms at last.

Battling Butler is based on a kind of Harold Lloyd formula but with a Keaton starkness. It was a very successful film. Its thoroughly American theme and background pleased audiences. Being really American, it pleased the British too, racking up a record at the Empire in London.

Clyde Bruckman was surprised and deeply impressed by *Battling Butler*. The absolutely straight dramatic acting in the final sequences opened his eyes. "My God," he said years later, "it was a really *dramatic* fight, not a comedy fight. Yet it stood up in a comic picture —one of the best closings of any Keaton film. You're all in there rooting for this little guy against the world's champion."

A few days after *Battling Butler* was finished, Bruckman had dropped by Keaton's house. "I've got a story for you," the writer said, pointing to a book he had brought.

Buster read the title, *The Great Locomotive Chase*; the author's name, William Pittenger; and the date, 1868. "I'll read it," he said. He opened the book that night in the quiet of his bedroom. At dawn he was just finishing the book, that stranger-than-fiction eyewitness story of a Civil War incident in which a handful of Union raiders, operating behind the Confederate lines, tried to steal a locomotive and nearly got away with it.

While he shaved, the book propped in front of him, Buster read the last lines, written by one of the raiders himself:

The next day we returned to Chattanooga and then, lingeringly and reluctantly, parted to our several homes in distant states—probably to meet no more till the general roll-call above!

Unconsciously perhaps, the author, three words from the end, had chosen an adjective that was also the name of the celebrated old locomotive that he and his fellow conspirators had risked death to steal, had seized, had almost escaped with, and then had lost. Anyway, her name was The General, and *The General* would be Buster Keaton's next and many think his greatest picture.

TWENTY-EIGHT

~~~~~~~~~~~~~~~~~~~~~~~~~~~~

"**I**T IS painful," Pittenger wrote in *The Great Locomotive Chase*, "for me to recall the adventures of the year beginning April 7th, 1862." Yet he was "confident that this story, faithfully told, will give a more vivid picture of the spirit, feeling, and awful earnestness of the Civil War than any more general history." So, despite "the memory of days of suffering and nights of sleepless apprehension," Pittenger sought "to do justice to brave men who perished in a manner ignominious in form but not in reality" and "to place romantic and almost incredible events, for which there will soon be no living witness, upon a basis of unquestionable certainty."

The raiders—William Pittenger was one of a band of twenty men —set out from Shelbyville, Tennessee, under the leadership of James J. Andrews, a Union spy. Disguised as Southern civilians, they penetrated enemy territory to Atlanta, three hundred miles south, where they boarded a northbound train, ostensibly as passengers. Their object was to steal the train and run north to Chattanooga, there to join their commander, General O. M. Mitchell, burning bridges and cutting telegraph lines on the way, thus destroying or crippling a vital portion of the Confederate communications.

The Andrews raid was astoundingly successful up to a point. At Big Shanty, a few miles north of Atlanta, they seized the train while passengers and crew breakfasted in the depot. They fled in the locomotive (The General) and three empty boxcars, having uncoupled and left the baggage car and coaches blocking the track. They were racing in the clear. Then they ran into unforeseen delays, having to wait on sidings for several southbound specials to pass. The original crew thus gained time to requisition another locomotive (actually several, the final one being The Texas) and set out in pursuit, picking up military reinforcements on the way.

This was *The Great Locomotive Chase*, The Texas hot on the tender of The General, a chase that ended, only nineteen miles short of the Chattanooga rendezvous, with the raiders' forced abandonment of the prize, their scattered flight and capture, the hanging of some and the long imprisonment of others. Thrilling reading but hardly, one might think, the material for slapstick comedy.

But Buster Keaton was no longer a slapstick comedian. Clyde Bruckman had seen him change that last sequence of *Battling Butler* from the comic scene it had been on Broadway into sheer spine-tingling drama. This man could make something out of the book he had given him. Bruckman was an old hand. He had instantly grasped the possibilities of a chase in which one Civil War locomotive pursues another, and he saw a comic gold mine in the effect of putting an engineer's cap above Keaton's great sad face.

Buster Keaton was growing from picture to picture. He was changing, and in the process he was transforming the traditional idea of "low" comedy in the films. Once he had worked strictly for laughs. Then gradually his fate-ridden character had taken on other dimensions. In the eyes of the world, the little man who was trouble's bait became as real as life. And that is what it was. There is no mistaking the evidence—in private as well as professionally: the character took hold of Buster Keaton himself. There had been a long and clear time in which it could happen, a lifetime so far—from that July day in 1898 in Kansas, the day of the clothes wringer and the cyclone, the day of The Accident and The Miracle.

For all the vicissitudes and changes, Keaton and character were of a piece. With that integrity and hard sense of personality that Gilbert Seldes has remarked, Buster Keaton had consistently developed as artist and as man. And with him, to a remarkable degree, it is impossible to separate the two.

Now, at this stage, laughs had become in a sense secondary—at least in the sense that easy laughs would no longer do. The character had to tell his story, a real story told so that all must believe. Now, neither thoughtless nor thoughtlessly provoked, laughter wells up from a deeper place. There might have been half a lifetime instead of only three years between *The Three Ages* and *The General*. In that brief span an artist came of age.

After that night of reading *The Great Locomotive Chase*, Buster raced to the studio. "It's a picture," he said to Clyde, "and I want you to help me direct it." All bent to the task; Pittenger's true story was tailored to Keaton. Having soaked up the "awful earnestness" of the graphic pages, Buster threw out mere gags as fast as they were thought up. "The whole picture is a chase," he said. "That's enough."

A serious mood descended on the laughsmiths. "Now, no shortcuts," said Keaton. "It's got to be so authentic it hurts." It must be staged on the original Alabama-Tennessee terrain.

Gabouri went there and reported that no narrow-gauge track was left in the region. "Can we use regular gauge?" he wired. They could not. Then he wired: "General in Chattanooga depot. Taking measurements." Then he was back and off to the Oregon lumber country. "Terrain ideal," he wired. "Plenty narrow gauge. Have two locomotives." He brought back location photographs, sketch maps, and a lumber company's permission to film on their virgin timberland. Then he dispatched a crew to convert the locomotives into exact outward replicas of The General and The Texas.

"How's the story?" Gabouri then asked.

"Set," said Buster.

"Good. Now work fast. Telephone the governor up there and you can get the whole damned Oregon State Guard for the war scenes."

It was already June. "Well," the governor said, "I don't know." He hesitated. "We have two regiments going into camp in two weeks."

"We'll pay them a salary on top of yours," said Buster.

"All right, they're yours."

Keaton turned to Gabouri. "Rent two thousand Union uniforms and two thousand Confederate uniforms and equipment."

Later that summer he was glad to have two militia regiments on the payroll. They put out a forest fire. It was a bad one, and The General had started it. Gabouri, for reasons both of efficiency and

Buster Keaton
in *The General*, 1926.

of safety, had advocated installing war-surplus Liberty motors in the two locomotives. But Buster was thinking of authenticity and particularly of a real firebox for the close-ups in the engineer's cab. He insisted on burning wood and heating up real steam. Sparks from The General's smokestack set off the holocaust. Suddenly it was a real battle, but the soldiers got the fire out. It could have blackened the entire area.

Sadly Lou Anger entered the emergency item: "To timber burned. $11,751.00." "Actually," he said, brightening a little, "it should read: 'To one captaincy for Buster Keaton.'" The governor had given him an honorary commission for directing the fire fighting.

Not even a Keaton story had ever moved so directly and simply. It tells itself visually. *The General's* eight reels require fewer than fifty subtitles, largely concentrated in the early exposition. It should be remembered that silent pictures relied on titles to clarify what was going on. It was far from uncommon for a feature drama to employ as many as three hundred.

The story technique in *The General* impressed the industry. Director Albert Lewin, thirty years later, recalled that the story went from beginning to end without a break in time. Actually, although a director's tribute to Keaton's story construction, this is not quite true. There are a few time breaks, but the action nevertheless flows like unbroken narrative.

Keaton altered the historic accuracy of Pittenger's book without qualms but to good effect (something, incidentally, that Walt Disney did not attempt thirty years later in his film *The Great Locomotive Chase*, from Charles O'Neill's retelling of the story in the book *Wild Train*). Keaton's changes are creative ones, relating the essence of the tale to his own character; and the authenticities of costume and locale, of locomotives and their track are homages less to history than to credibility.

Buster's role is John, The General's engineer. "There are two loves in his life": the camera profiles the beautiful old locomotive and its train of five coaches, then moves in close to show John at the throttle. His hair is long—to his shoulders—and his Windsor tie is caught by the wind. The camera pans almost caressingly along the engine, lingering on each detail: the polished brass bell, the florid letters of the name, the kerosene head lamp, the flaring cowcatcher. This is one love. The other is Annabelle Lee; a tintype of her hangs inside the cab.

Buster Keaton went further with the story than Pittenger and his-

Scene from *The General*, 1926.

Scene from *The General*, 1926. (Parker's cavalry in the background.)

tory went, in the truest sense amplifying, not distorting, truth. To history's factualities is added the catalytic leaven of personality—he loves the locomotive. So it is right for him to pursue her (as she vanishes down the long rails), on foot, on handcar, on bicycle, and finally in her sister engine The Texas, into Union territory. For, as history did not quite do, he lets the thieves reach their rendezvous with the Northern general.

As the picture opens, John is in Annabelle Lee's parlor when the call to arms comes. Fort Sumter has just been fired on. Annabelle's father and brother rush to enlist. John takes a shortcut to the recruiting office and has applied and been rejected before they reach the long volunteer line. "You are of more value to the South as an engineer," he is told. Not even knowing that he has applied, Annabelle and her family jump to the conclusion that he is a coward. John is too proud and too hurt to explain.

Time has passed. The war is on in earnest. Annabelle Lee boards John's train (refusing to speak to him) to visit her wounded father. At breakfast in the depot at Big Shanty, she discovers she has left her purse in her luggage. She climbs into the baggage car at the very moment that the Northerners are seizing the train. The baggage car is left coupled to The General, and Annabelle Lee is carried off. Soon discovered, she is bound and gagged.

John pursues his locomotive all that day through one thrilling (and seriocomic) sequence after another. That night, in Northern territory, he arrives in the darkness at the Union headquarters encampment. There he finds both his loves. First snatching Annabelle Lee, he then reclaims The General, heads her south, and steams at full throttle down the line. Now it is not only in direction that the chase is reversed—the Northerners have The Texas and are hot after the locomotive they had just successfully hijacked. John rides his engine like a jockey in the stretch, Annabelle Lee lending fluttery, uncertain assistance.

Escape had involved a rough hand-to-hand fracas in and around the locomotive cab. There is a high-ranking Union officer stretched out unconscious on the floor of the fuel tender. Going for wood, they keep stepping over him. John's concentration on staying ahead is so absolute that he fails to grasp that he has a hostage of the highest value. His unconscious prisoner is none other than General Thatcher, the Union field commander. John misses even more: as they roar through the countryside, he does not see a whole Northern corps on the move. It is General Parker's cavalry.

Through Keaton heroics and Keaton luck, John just hangs on to his lead over the pursuing Texas. Ahead lies the Rock River Bridge, which is to be the junction of Parker's cavalry and Thatcher's infantry corps, coming on the pursuit train. This, at least, John knows. Concealed the night before in Thatcher's headquarters, he had overheard the plans. He reaches the wooden Rock River trestle. With the engine halfway across, he stops and sets the bridge afire. Then he steams on, full speed. Just behind him is The Texas, with Thatcher's Thatcherless troops, while, just visible on the horizon, Parker's horsemen are galloping to the junction. John rushes to Confederate field headquarters.

He warns the commander of the impending surprise attack. The Southerners leap into action, heading for the high riverbanks at the bridge. The village is suddenly empty. John is standing all alone at the far end of the dusty square. It is the classic lonely shot—the Keaton "portrait." Yesterday he had stood alone at Big Shanty, in the relentless deep perspective of the converging steel rails, gazing after a vanishing locomotive. Now here he is once more, and once more left behind, standing far away in a frame of space, in a Confederate uniform grotesquely too large, gazing after an army that had refused his services.

Then he is angry—and desperate. He finds a sword, buckles it on, runs after the troops. He stumbles, sprawls in the dust, leaps up, runs, runs, runs.

Parker is already at the bridge; Thatcher's troops steam in from the north. Junction is effected. The fire, meanwhile, is eating into the trestle. Unaware that the Confederates have dug in in concealed positions on the far bank, Parker shouts to The Texas' engineer, "That bridge is not burned enough to stop you. Go on. My men will ford the river."

The train starts out over the bridge. The Texas negotiates the burning section. Her cowcatcher is over solid ground. And then the span collapses, a swift-descending V, and with agonizing slowness the doomed engine slides back, down the slanting rails, and into the deep water. She rolls over on her side, an engine dying, a great machine gasping out its breath in clouds of steam that rise higher than the high riverbanks.

The cavalry is in midstream, committed. The riders apply the spurs. The foremost start up the steep embankment. Then from behind rock and tree comes withering rifle fire. Cannon shells hit and burst in the river. Horses rear and fall, and their riders float or thrash in the water. It is the beginning of a rout.

On the brow of the bank the Confederate general, sword in hand,

Death of a locomotive. Scene from *The General*, 1926.

directs the ambuscade. Beside him, short and stumbling, in long, trailing gray trousers, is John, waving his sword and echoing the commands. It is his war at last.

His opportunity comes. Union snipers have just picked off the last member of a gun crew. He loads and aims the idled fieldpiece, ignorantly pointing its muzzle up like a mortar. He fires it.

Enter The Miracle. Aimed both up and awry, the misdirected shell lobs high and far upstream, away from the action. There it lands, breaching the dam of a great reservoir. A wall of water roars downstream, wiping out Parker's struggling cavalry.

The battle is over. The victors return to the village. No one has even noticed John. He trudges off to his locomotive. On the floor of The General's tender, a live general, Thatcher, is just coming to. John marches him off to headquarters and turns him over to the Confederate commander. Thatcher hands over his sword.

Now, at last, the Southern general sees John, although the youth has to accidentally discharge a revolver to attract his attention. He stares at the dusty gray tunic John is wearing. "Is that your uniform?"

John shakes his head. "No, sir, I had to wear it to get through our lines."

The general says sternly, "Take it off immediately."

John removes the tunic. The officer snatches it from his hands, then turns to an aide and takes a tunic from the aide's arms.

"Put it on," he says to John, then turns to the clerk. "Enlist the lieutenant."

It is the same clerk who at the outbreak of the war had rejected John. He repeats the old question: "Occupation?"

The answer no longer is "Locomotive engineer." Now it is "Soldier."

Lieutenant John's return to Annabelle Lee can be felt only as intentional anticlimax. Whatever he had had to prove had been to himself and has been proved.

This is *The General*. Its rich diversity of incident—sad, bumptious, heroic—makes up a cinema masterpiece. Its photography can be compared with that of Mathew Brady. The swirling lines of action that had begun years before in *The Paleface* and *Cops* became a sweep of armies on the move in this picture. This is the film that, twenty-seven years after its issue, would share honors with the new Chaplin film, *Limelight*, in London during Elizabeth's Coronation Week. It is the only film from a long list at the Museum of Modern Art's 1955 United Artists Festival that had to be repeated. It deserves the further honor of never being retired again, of being shown anew to each generation. Its setting is timeless, and as a work of art it comes close to being a new genre: a romantic-historical period dramatic comedy. If there are opposites in that definition, Buster Keaton's film reconciles them. It is, besides, a depth study of personality.

Buster Keaton would likely not relish being called a poet. But poetry is where you find it, and it is in *The General*. Time has not staled it. Time, indeed, has not yet destroyed the locomotive that plunged through the burning bridge. Rusting drive wheels and toppled boiler, she still lies where she fell, in a river near Cottage Grove, Oregon, still luring tourists to the spot.

The General was released December 22, 1926. Hollywood's holidays were the wildest, costliest yet. One columnist wrote: "This season they are sending Cadillacs instead of Christmas cards." The Buster Keatons were in the Italian Villa. Buster's brilliant career, observers agreed, had a firm footing. He was riding the crest of the wave on a gilded surfboard. The Villa was the permanent badge and warranty of his artistic and worldly success.

The party that had successively celebrated five earlier mansions still went on. The two Busters—Keaton and Collier—broiled steaks for cookout guests on the lawn; Norman Kerry and Lew Cody cast for trout in the brook or tossed grain to quail in the aviary; films were shown in the private projection room; Doug Fairbanks dived from higher and higher perches on the pergola to the pool until Buster would take up the challenge; Paul Whiteman and Bix Beiderbecke played gold-plated jazz for the Charleston in garden and house; custom cars roared in and out around the driveway's palm-edged curve.

The house on Westmoreland Place.

The house on Ardmore Avenue.

The house on Muirfield Road.

The Italian Villa in Beverly Hills.

Life, like insomnia, fed on itself. When a party died down, a limousine would come honking through the palms and festivities would start all over. Or, from next door, Tom Mix, ex-U.S. marshal from Oklahoma, would slip through a secret gap in the hedge shouting for sanctuary from a mate who, he always claimed, was a faster draw than he. "The man," he would say to Buster, "needs whiskey," and later, his nerves quieted, he would sneak back to his own castle, with its dining-table fountain that jetted blue, green, and pink water.

Granted the necessity of parties, Natalie had rightly held out for size. Big as it was, even the Villa could hardly hold the guests. It barely held the tons of furniture and knickknacks Natalie had acquired. Clyde Bruckman recalled the moving-in day, when "whatever Natalie didn't know what to do with, she'd say, 'Take it to Mr. Keaton's room.'" Clyde laughed, remembering how "Buster yelled for us to come upstairs. 'Look,' he says, 'no floor,' and damned if he couldn't walk all around the room—bed to dresser, chiffonier to desk to chair—and never touch the floor."

The Keatons' palace was built at last. There was life to be lived, and it was being lived. There were also films to be made. And between the two, a dark, narrowing chink of sleep, where the strength to do it all would flow back. It always had.

It was noticeable—except no one noticed—that the famous stone face was losing its glow, that the lines were biting deep. The famed blankness was freezing over. Whoever saw it thought only that Keaton was becoming funnier and funnier. No one seemed to notice, either, that he drank a little more—no passouts, nothing rowdy, just a quiet step-up day by day.

The Italian Villa had cost almost a third of a million dollars. But that, Buster might well have said, was only money. It was the hidden costs that hurt.

TWENTY-NINE

I N H O L L Y W O O D nothing stood still, especially the
solid, firm business and financial organizations being set up
permanently every day. Now Joe Schenck was yanking the release
of the Keaton films away from Metro-Goldwyn-Mayer. Metro had
had him; then, when Metro grew into MGM, came the disappearing
act, even though Joe Schenck's brother Nicholas was heading the new
company. Despite this and despite the fact that Metro-Goldwyn-
Mayer might soon become a titan, it was not to be given *The General*. Instead, United Artists would release this plum. The reason
was simple: Joe Schenck had just assumed the presidency of United
Artists.

The General and its two Keaton successors, *College* and *Steamboat
Bill Jr.*, would bear the seal of the independent producing and dis-
tributing company that Chaplin, Pickford, Fairbanks, and Griffith
had founded. This could not have been to MGM's liking, since the
Keaton films were uniformly profitable. MGM, just getting on its
feet after a shaky start, needed profits. Still ahead was the time when
it would be a giant, spreading scores of arts and crafts and employing
up to 4,700 persons on its 187 acres in Culver City. The forty-acre
heart of this celluloid farm had been a wheat field donated to Thomas
H. Ince by the realtor Harry Culver to get Hollywood off the ground.
That was in 1916. Two years later Sam Goldwyn bought the ex-wheat
field and held on for a number of years before selling to the new
company, stipulating that his name should be in the middle of the
name of the firm, which he did not even join. Thus was Metro-
Goldwyn-Mayer born.

MGM would soon, with the coming of sound, have a symphony
orchestra, fed by what it claimed to be "3,500,000 items of music in
a music library second in size only to the Library of Congress."
Everything at MGM was equally titanic: the makeup department
smeared greasepaint on "1200 persons in an hour," and wardrobe
dressed "5000 actors for a single day's work." Its giants were the tallest
and its midgets the smallest in the history of the world.

However, MGM had started with a colossal liability: the gigantic motion picture *Ben Hur,* being filmed in Rome. As *Cleopatra* would be (nearly forty years later), *Ben Hur* was a money sponge. More than a million dollars (of 1920's money) had already been poured into this epic, and the end was not in sight. Boldly, MGM junked the whole thing, began from scratch again with a new director and cast, and, in 1926, came up with a solid hit. But the *Ben Hur* nut had not yet been won back when Keaton went to United Artists. It is not unlikely that Nicholas Schenck made up his mind then and there to get Buster Keaton back someday.

For better or for worse, Keaton himself, of course, stood apart from all the wheeling and dealing and concentrated on picture making. In the spring of 1927 he gave his own twist to a theme Harold Lloyd had used two years earlier in *The Freshman.* The Keaton opus, his eighth feature comedy, is *College.*

New names begin appearing in the credits. The story is by Carl Harbaugh and Bryan Foy, directed by James W. Horne. The cameramen are Jennings and Haines (who had photographed *Battling Butler*). Another new name (in a new capacity) is that of Harry Brand, supervisor.

Buster Keaton is Ronald, a high-school honors graduate who loves his mother, his girl, and his books. His valedictory at graduation, "The Curse of Athletics," is a thesis on brain versus brawn, sparkling with gems like "Future generations depend upon brains and not upon jumping the discus or hurdling the javelin," and "What have Ty Ruth and Babe Dempsey done for science?" Ronald goes to Clayton College and begins starring scholastically. But his girl, who has entered Clayton too, falls for a handsome athlete. Unless Ronald too becomes a brawn boy, he has lost her. He closes his books, studies war, and gets nowhere. He is run down by hitters; he high-jumps three feet and broad-jumps five; he lets go a discus that nearly scalps the dean; he flies through the air hanging on to the hammer. Keaton was never more fumbling or more maddeningly, masterfully maladroit.

His three-letter rival is making time, and the girl is slipping fast. Ronald, to cap it all, is now summoned by the dean to account for his scholastic slump. Ronald blurts his problem, the dean understands. He maneuvers Ronald into the varsity crew as coxswain. Here, at least, his puny size and weight will actually be an advantage. Before he can fall out of the racing shell, the big race with Clayton's traditional rival is at hand. Clayton has a good crew. The two rivals start even and are running even, with or without Ronald's help. Then the Clayton rudder tears loose. Ronald snatches it out of the wake, fastens it behind his fanny, sits far out over the stern, and steers with a sort of slow shimmy. He raises the stroke; his oarsmen make up the lost distance, put their backs into it, and win by an inch.

While the crew is dunking the cox in the water to celebrate the victory, the little hero's rival completely blows his stack, carts the girl off, and locks her in his dormitory room. With this dire development, Ronald blasts off the pad. Getting to her, he conquers the physical hazards that had been defeating him: broad-jumps a campus pond, hurdles a long row of bushes, and pole-vaults through the second-story window of the room where his girl is captive, bops the villain, and flees with her in triumph.

A well-earned relaxation from the exacting major effort of *The General, College* is a romp, its open-faced, unshadowed fun as old as college and as new as the freshman class. How, it may fairly be asked, does Keaton's triumph differ from Lloyd's? Briefly: Lloyd wins by the divine right of the American go-getter; Keaton, not inevitably at all but by a miracle—love suddenly releasing his powers, freeing him from all his shackling inhibitions, timidities, and inferiorities. Behind the granite face is tenderness, and behind the tenderness is a philosophical and psychological attitude. Harold Lloyd, the comic, as Gilbert Seldes long ago observed, is "a man of no tenderness, of no philosophy . . . there is no poetry in him . . . [no] overtone or image." Seldes also remarked (in the course of a comparison of the three great silent clowns) that "Chaplin never makes fun of himself." Buster Keaton, on the contrary, can and does—even in triumph. A strange mixture of a man, with both passivity and warmth, frozen noncommunication and tenderness, doddering and determination, cowardice and courage, idiocy and brains, good luck and foul—like Everyman.

The Buster Keaton world *is* Everyman's theatre, and in that context his pictures are basically morality plays. In Keaton's comedies, if anyone suffers it is Keaton. Keaton is He Who Gets Slapped. As an index to character it might glibly be written off as the projection of a persecution complex. This is too easy. His life does not support it. Keaton believes in himself, but only, it would appear, in that lifelong role of under underdog, odds-on loser, the winner only through fluke, fortune, or fate. It is the role that got him onstage before kindergarten age, kept him there, and brought him fame and satisfaction.

His self-portrait has developed from his earliest image of himself—the boy who has half a finger in a clothes wringer or who is in midair sitting on a cyclone. It is, it must be admitted, next thing to being born on a spaceship. The Keaton mythos is one more of being mastered than of being master. It is a pain-or-pleasure process in which the deciding factor is luck, the trickiest of all bets. If it brought him the good things in life, it could as easily—as in his pictures—bring him the bad.

The personal Keaton has had a lifelong problem. It concerns reality. Teleology (or "Who runs things around here?") is only part of Keaton's lifelong problem. More basic, if that is possible, is the question "What world are we talking about?" Buster Keaton's early excursions into the world outside the theatre, as in the Lake Muskegon summers, were pleasure outings, not business trips. He took the theatre with him, like his clothes. Off the stage he is the outlander. Reality is a strange role that doesn't "play" right. Fundamentally, he will never be able to figure out why. It is his problem, his unanswerable question, his wheel that turns forever.

The problem is so ingrown and basic that in life Keaton is like a baseball player in a game where someone has changed all the rules. Hollywood was that kind of baseball game, but Joe Schenck was the friendly umpire who slanted the decisions for Buster. It couldn't last: the game was bigger than the umpire.

Keaton first felt the cold air of the real Hollywood when Lou Anger, his old friend and business manager, left the company. "It all started," Buster recalls, "with Schenck taking Lou Anger from me. He wanted him to go around the country finding new theatre locations for United Artists. Great—a promotion for Lou. Schenck said, 'Who shall we make manager?' I said, 'Why not take my publicity man, Harry Brand?' So that was okay.

"But once he was in the job he suddenly turned serious. He was grim. He was watching the dailies—how much is spent on this, how much is spent on that? He worries, he frets, he begins losing sleep. He felt he had to do something, like a guy that has to tear down a car that's running perfectly.

"I'd finished cutting *College*, previewed it, and run the sample print to test the printing. You know, some scenes too light, some too dark—have to be evened up. Then we went to Sacramento to film *Steamboat Bill Jr.* While we're there, just getting under way, *College* is released, and we all went to the Senator Theatre to see it. The credits flash on: Joseph M. Schenck Presents Buster Keaton in *Col-*

lege. United Artists Release. Written by, directed by, et cetera. And then, a separate title: Supervised by Harry Brand.

"I all but jumped out of my seat. It had gone into the prints after I had okayed the sample. It had been done quietly and with Schenck's permission. The prints—two hundred and fifty of them—were all distributed. The thing couldn't be changed.

"Now perhaps it sounds like conceit on my part. But besides my own feelings, there were two things. One was the question of interference. A bad thing to get started. The other thing was, the public was already beginning to laugh at this stupid supervisor deal, which had then been going on in Hollywood for about six months. Supervisor was only a job maker, a nothing job, just a title—but it *did* get a guy's name on the screen. Anger never bothered with screen credit. He knew his job and did it. Within two or three years supervisors were laughed off the screen, but at this particular time every new guy getting into the game was becoming a supervisor."

The facts bear out Keaton's statement and show his dates as approximately accurate. For example, in the Los Angeles *Record* for June 30, 1930, a columnist wrote concerning an impending remake of a famous old picture: "Leonard Goldstein says *The Spoilers* should have an all-supervisor cast."

"For some people credits are like candy," Buster went on. "I had laid the laugh on Ince years before with my *Playhouse*. But they just never learn. Why even Mervyn LeRoy, one of our old and good directors, had a radio sign-off credit: This is the So-and-So Show, starring Mary Livingston, Jack Benny, Don Wilson, Kenny Baker— and on through the cast—*through the courtesy of Mervin LeRoy!* Jack Benny teed off on that one. He ran an imaginary Kentucky Derby, with Don Wilson doing the description of the race, winding up with, 'And here they come, folks. They're crossing the finish line, with Malicious in the rear, by courtesy of Mervyn LeRoy!'"

Coming back to the matter at hand, Keaton said, "Well, I was badly upset by this deal in my own picture. But, I thought, *There's no point in battling Brand. I'll wait and see Schenck.*"

In Sacramento, Buster went on to film one of his finest pictures, one that, like *Our Hospitality* and *The General*, is a piece of Americana vignetted with laughter. Its locale is the Mississippi River of the side-wheeler days. *Steamboat Bill Jr.* is a kind of Mark Twain piece, a happy folklore melodrama about the bitter rivalry of two riverboat owners; it has romance and danger, even a cyclone.

Keaton thanks supervisor Brand for the cyclone. Work was just beginning, when, Buster says, the word came: "Cut out all flood sequences. Use cyclone instead." According to Keaton, Brand had convinced Schenck that flood scenes would hurt the feelings of victims of real floods (this was during a bad flood period in Mississippi). Buster objected. "How about that cyclone that has just killed all those people in the Middle West?" But wind replaced water just the same.

It was more than paper work. "It cost us twenty thousand dollars extra," Buster recalls. "Easily forty thousand dollars, actually, counting the lost time. Sets to be rebuilt, gags and sequences to be replanned, wind machines to haul up from Hollywood." The delay was far more costly than Keaton remembers. It was probably nearer a million dollars, the delay robbing him as it did of a fall release. As it turned out, *Steamboat Bill Jr.* was not released until very late the following spring. There was no new Keaton film for the fall of 1927, the first theatrical season without one.

However, to give Brand credit in retrospect for at least one result (if not intention): Buster Keaton had often been dunked in films, but he had not been blown through the air since the cyclone day in Kansas. The cyclonic climax of *Steamboat Bill Jr.* is surely one of the most fantastic dithyrambs of disaster ever committed to film.

Keaton, as usual, demanded the last iota of authenticity. Research and care went into building the hypothetical Southern town of River Junction on the Sacramento River levee at the edge of California's capital city. Even the name shows awareness: the location was in actuality just below the important junction of two rivers, the Sacramento and the American. Search continued until two old riverboats of the proper type were found. In the actual filming of what is little more than a passing episode during the tornado sequence, Buster laid his own life on the line in order to "make it for real."

In *The Navigator* he had come to grips with the man-versus-machine theme; now he faced the father-son theme—which, for Buster Keaton, was getting close to the core of things. For in this picture he, as Willie, or Steamboat Bill Jr., would let himself triumph over his father, Steamboat Bill (played by Ernest Torrence). But, this being Buster and not the Oedipean Sigmund, it is no crude victory of power, id, or ego. It is a son's triumph over a father's misunderstanding.

Great, hulking, beloved Ernest Torrence, rawboned and shagbrowed, is fighting to keep afloat, which is to say, to keep his old riverboat, the *Stonewall Jackson,* going against the newfangled mod-

Scene from *Steamboat Bill Jr.*, 1928.

ern competition. Go-getter J. C. King, local bank president and local everything else, has built a beautiful new steamer, has modestly christened her *The King,* and has announced his intention to "run Steamboat Bill and the *Stonewall Jackson* right off the river." It is more than a personality clash, different as the two men may be. It is the rockbottom American hatred of the new for the old.

The eyes in the gnarled old face, framed in the pilothouse window, glint like stars seen through the crown of an oak tree. "I'll run on this river," says Steamboat Bill, "if I'm the only passenger on the boat." It is not steamboatman J. C. King but banker J. C. King, custodian of mortgages, who smirks back.

Bill's only son is on his way to River Junction. His father hasn't seen him since he was a baby. He grew up in the East, went to Harvard, and has graduated.

"I'll bet," says Steamboat Bill to his mate, "he's bigger'n me. Let's go to the station to meet him."

In June, 1928, when this subtitle flashed on, all Buster Keaton fans involuntarily shuddered—here was the usual ghastly preparation for the first disastrous entrance. And it *is* a disaster.

In the crowd at the depot they miss each other, but the audience couldn't miss Keaton. This time he outdid himself. Willie is an apparition to give pause even to a mother: bell-bottom trousers,

Scene from
Steamboat Bill Jr., 1928.
Center, Buster Keaton;
right, Ernest Torrence.

blanket-patterned sweater, polka-dot bow tie, and striped sport jacket; a beret on his head, a wisp of mustache on his upper lip, a ukulele under his arm. Willie jostles a perambulator. The baby begins to cry, and to soothe it Willie goes into a little skipping dance, strumming the uke and singing. It is the lullaby Brahms didn't write.

Steamboat Bill looks over, askance. He can't and won't believe it. He turns away. But his mate reads the name on the valise: William Canfield, Jr., Boston. Bill's other troubles fade beside this new calamity. But it is his. It is here. And, what's more, it says it is going to help Daddy win that river war.

A girl steps off the train. "Why, Willie Canfield, what are you doing so far from Boston?"

"My father's here."

"So is mine, and you'll love him."

It is inevitable that she will turn out to be banker King's daughter, inevitable that boy and girl will fall in love. Bill struggles with the apparently hopeless. He could use a son. He orders the mustache off and the beret thrown away; he takes Willie shopping for clothes a man can wear. They fit Willie, but Willie doesn't fit them. Making a man of Willie and putting an end to this infatuation with Kitty King begin to seem hopeless. Bill hands him a ticket. "Back to Boston you go."

However, before Willie can leave, Bill has finally tangled with King, has been arrested, and is in the lockup. Willie decides he will spring Dad. This adventure ends in fiasco, with Dad still in durance vile and Junior in the River Junction hospital.

All this while skies have been darkening and wind accelerating. Abruptly, a cyclone roars into River Junction. Automobiles career into the river; King's Fish Palace Café blows into the racing current;

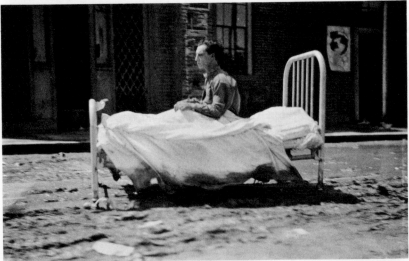

Scenes from *Steamboat Bill Jr.*, 1928.

the steamer *The King* strains at her ropes. The whole town is blowing away like Piqua, Kansas, where Buster Keaton was born. Now the entire hospital—walls and roof all in one piece—flies up into the air. Willie, on his hospital bed with an ice bag on his head, goes for a ride. The gale blows him down the street, through a livery stable, and then turns the bed over.

And now comes what is surely the high point of Buster Keaton's long career of courting death for real. He stands in the street facing the camera while the wind howls past (the cameras had to be weighted down with concrete). Behind him is a two-story building. Suddenly its entire front loosens; it comes down whistling, like a gigantic flyswatter. If ever a sight spelled death, this is it. He stands there motionless, preoccupied, not aware that a building is falling on him. Now it is inches from his head. Now he is completely out of sight and surely crushed. And then, as the great timber rectangle smashes into the street, there he stands, characteristically unmoved. The open center second-story window has passed—narrowly, exactly —around him.

With that sublime Keaton unawareness, he walks away, then glances over his shoulder. Grasping what has happened, he is seized by that all-consuming Keaton terror. He leaps like a racing car into a full sprint—and another falling building misses him by inches. Effecting these scenes involved a critical operation in exact positioning, exact designing, exact timing.

"The clearance of that window," Buster has said, "was exactly three inches over my head and past each shoulder. And the front of the building—I'm not kidding—weighed two tons. It had to be built heavy and rigid in order not to bend or twist in that wind.

"The whole gang except Gabe fought me on that one. 'You can't do it.' Bruckman threatened to quit. My director, Chuck Reisner, stayed in his tent reading *Science and Health*. First time I ever saw cameramen look the other way. But Gabouri and I figured out all the details. We knew it would work."

At this juncture in the story, only Willie is left in River Junction proper. The water and the wind have swallowed up all else. Willie slides and tumbles, picks himself up, fights on. Here is the lonely shot, over and over, one scene after another. It becomes more and more dreamlike. Here is scene cutting with purpose and meaning. It is a refrain as haunting as the repeated words of an old spiritual— "Gone, Gone, Gone."

Willie stumbles onto the stage of an empty theatre. A ventrilo-

Scenes from *Steamboat Bill Jr.*, 1928.

quist's dummy, swaying in a corner, frightens him, as Trovollo's little puppet had frightened Buster in actuality those long years ago on a Memphis stage at night. Then, mistaking the painted backdrop for the real river outside, Willie dives into it, as did the Kid in those last sad days of the Three Keatons. And still the empty stage holds him. He steps up on a table and an old, remembered magician's trick begins operating. A circular curtain (as in a shower stall) drops around him, then slides quickly up again. He has vanished—then he crawls up out of a trapdoor in the tabletop.

Then he is out of the theatre and into a dark and windy nightmare of falling houses. He catches hold of a tree, clinging with arms and legs around its trunk. Then, dreamlike, he is sailing through the air (that old Kansas miracle of levitation), still wrapped around the tree —roots and all—and he is flying far out over the river. Then down they go into the racing water.

The jail, meanwhile, has slid into the current and is slowly sinking. All alone in there, Steamboat Bill is tearing at the bars on the window of his cell, racing to escape as the water rises inside. Willie is climbing up the *Stonewall Jackson*'s paddle wheel and onto the deck. A house is floating by. Someone on its roof is calling for help. It is Kitty King. Willie lifts and heaves the *Stonewall*'s anchor; its flukes catch on the eaves of the house; like an aerialist, he goes over the tightening anchor line and grabs her. In her terror she wraps her arms around his neck with such strangling force that his hold loosens and they both go into the water. Fighting the current, he tows her to the *Stonewall*'s deck.

The magical metamorphosis is under way. A fumbling, frightened dolt is being lifted out of himself into swift and shining action. It is impossible, illogical, unbelievable—but the magic works, and we believe.

He has just got Kitty to safety, when another cry for help is heard. The jail is just alongside, so deep in the water now that Steamboat Bill is swimming in his cell with his face to the ceiling just above the water. Willie—perhaps at this point we should begin to call him Steamboat Bill Jr.—runs to the helm and steers the old *Stonewall Jackson* bow on into the jail, slicing it in two. Old Bill—who, like most sailors, cannot swim—is floundering. Down from the pilothouse, leaping from deck to deck, comes Willie to save his father. The rough old river dog, who had been so bitterly shamed by a namby-pamby son, suddenly has one to be proud of. Ernest Torrence, wonderful old veteran that he was, gave it all he had. His eyes shining, he mauls his son affectionately, one huge paw tousling his hair.

Scene from *Steamboat Bill Jr.*, 1928.

Then they see the nearly submerged pilothouse of the once-proud steamer *The King*, her owner about to drown. Willie pulls him in too. With all hands, friend and foe, accounted for, Willie unaccountably dives into the river once more. He swims off out of sight. A minute later he is back with a well-soaked minister in tow. He is indispensable for the wedding that, as the picture fades out, we are sure will follow.

Steamboat Bill Jr. actually had two variant endings. Director Reisner had the same brilliant idea that, sooner or later, seized every expert. "Buster," he said, "I want you smiling as you swim into camera with the minister."

"Oh no you don't," said Buster.

Reisner would not give up. "It's a natural gag," he maintained.

"All right," Buster finally said. "But we'll shoot it both ways, then preview with the smile."

The audience took offense. It was worse than Cal Coolidge smiling, and no more believable. A groan of disappointment rose in the theatre.

"Even the ash can groaned when we dumped it there," says Buster of the offending scene.

By this time, however, Buster Keaton had more serious things to think about. He had taken his complaint about Brand, as he had planned, straight to Joe Schenck. Buster had his arguments ready, and they were good. "It's bad on the face of it," said Buster. "For example, Doug Fairbanks comes on, and you say, 'Douglas Fairbanks supervised by Joe Doakes.' You belittle Fairbanks. Fairbanks, not Doakes, is what you're selling."

Schenck was listening. Buster pressed on, "One man writes it, another man directs it, and a star acts it. Those three people are responsible for every great picture that was ever made. In some cases one man is all three—Chaplin."

Schenck replied that supervisors were the modern thing; all the big studios were doing it.

"Maybe they are, and they can be wrong," said Buster. "It's not going to last long. The whole damned thing's a bad joke."

Schenck shook his head firmly.

Then Buster went the whole way. "There'll be no more supervisors," he said, "in the pictures Buster Keaton makes."

There was a long silence. Schenck's reply, when it came, was so quietly spoken that Buster had to lean over to hear it. Buster Keaton, Schenck was saying, was not going to make any more pictures.

Here it was again, it seemed: that closing scene without the smile.

And Then ...

THIRTY

⟨⟨⟨⟨⟨⟨⟨⟨⟨⟨⟨⟨⟨⟨⟨⟨⟨⟨⟨⟨⟨⟨⟨⟨⟨⟨⟨

I T W A S Buster Keaton's turn to listen. He sat in silence as Joe Schenck went on. Buster was making no more pictures. No, Schenck corrected himself, what he meant was no more Schenck-Keaton productions. The company was being dissolved.

"Why?" Buster's lips were dry and tight.

Schenck did not elaborate. Instead he proceeded to the next step. Keaton was going on MGM's payroll. Once on this topic, the older man seemed to relax. He grew voluble: more money, bigger opportunities, better pictures; a big staff to work for you—stories and production, cutting and editing, everything. You can't miss. My brother Nick will take care of you like his own son.

Buster just sat there. There seemed nothing to say in the face of such finality. Schenck quickly outlined the plans. Buster was to start with MGM right away. There was a settlement—Keaton remembers it as only a few thousand dollars—for all his interests (never written down or clarified anyway), including possible reissues of his pictures, nineteen two-reelers and ten feature films, pictures that by all obtainable reliable estimates must have grossed around twenty million dollars in less than eight years. The stockholders kept the films. Keaton was a free agent.

It was all familiar—a scene from a Keaton comedy—this conference with his old booster and benefactor. His face went automatically blank. He fell into his part. Not a muscle moved. But hold it! It was life—not a movie. Buster can still recall, even today, how at that moment his thoughts turned, as if against his own will, to a theatrical trunk left in an alley behind a theatre. Here went the last of his Joes.

Long after the one-sided interview, Buster Keaton was puzzling over it. He is still puzzling—and still feeling the dazing, almost physical impact of the unexpected blow.

"So many times," he has said, "I've thought it all over. Hell, I knew I was a money-maker. And not a big spender. Why, Christ, my

297

pix cost a couple of hundred grand—Fairbanks couldn't make one under a million. It wasn't that.

"I thought of this: Joe Schenck was still an independent. I don't know if it was human nature, greed, or power, but the big companies were out to kill the independents. Motion pictures were becoming the finest trust you ever saw. So I thought, *Perhaps they're after Schenck*. He was too big to knock down, but maybe his brother Nick at MGM said, 'Look, Joe, it's hurting the business.' Could be. In fact, within two more years Joe left United Artists and quit independent production entirely. Norma and Constance didn't succeed in sound pix. Joe went on and became head of Twentieth Century-Fox. But if that was his real reason, why didn't he tell me? We were friends.

"One thing: I had only one picture in 1927, with the delay caused by Brand on *Steamboat Bill Jr.* Also, Joe's own United Artists gummed up its release. Let it out only to their few theatres and took the shine off. Then the other big theatres wouldn't touch it, and it went straight down to the neighborhood houses. That may easily have cost us three-quarters of a million. But Joe Schenck was always a reasonable man. Would he blame me for that?

"But there it was: me for Metro-Goldwyn-Mayer. Just like the draft. Everyone seemed to know that it had happened. Chaplin said to me, 'What's this I hear? Don't do it. They'll ruin you helping you. They'll warp your judgment. You'll get tired of arguing for things you know are right.' I knew Charlie was leveling. Worse, I knew he was right. Harold Lloyd said it, only in different words. 'It's not your gang. You'll lose.'

"So I thought, *I'll shoot for a miracle*. I dashed to New York to see Adolph Zukor, head of Paramount. 'I want to make pictures for you,' I said, explaining that I was free.

"Zukor looked at me and shook his head. He said that he—Paramount—had signed Harold Lloyd. He wouldn't cut the ground out from under his new star. I thought to myself, *What kind of sense does that make? What the hell—Chaplin and I have both been releasing with United Artists*. But there was no talking him out of it. I left by the same door I came in by: Keaton goes to MGM.

"I went back to my hotel room to think it over and began brooding instead. I got myself thoroughly mixed up, and then I made a mistake, just like in my comedies when I do just one little thing wrong and from then on I'm in the soup up to my neck. Here I decide to ride all my winnings on one throw of the dice—I went to see Nicholas Schenck! I was flustered. It was all too much like my own scripts. I should have sat down and thought everything over. I should have just waited, whether I thought or not. Let people come to me. Metro-Goldwyn-Mayer plus Will Hays plus Joe Schenck couldn't have made me do something I never had signed to do. I was successful, I was famous, I was free. Hell, I was sitting pretty and didn't have enough sense to know it.

"This was still before the stock-market crash. There was money everywhere. I should have gone out for some of it, found backing, kept my gang together, and gone on about my business. There was no law against my making pictures, and I would have got distribution, all right. *Because the public wanted me.* If the public wants you, there's always a way. And I would have been doing what Chaplin had been doing: making the money myself instead of a salary. I'm sure that's what they figured me to do.

"But, instead, I went out, had three drinks, and called on Nick Schenck all softened up. Walk in and lead with my right. 'What *is* this thing? Am I with MGM?' 'That's right,' he says. 'Your studio is a little place; our big new plant will give you bigger production, relieve you of producing. You just have to be funny. We got great writers and directors out there. The best. Experts. Don't worry. Be happy.'

"Then he says, 'Now, money. Three thousand a week and a percentage.' 'No percentage,' I say. I know from nothing about their bookkeeping. 'If I go with you I want bonuses.' 'Bonuses it is. Should we argue?' says Nick Schenck. 'And five thousand a week,' I say. 'Three thousand.' 'No four thousand.' Nick Schenck just smiled. 'Three thousand a week is just right,' he said. 'And now we go to lunch.' "

Buster Keaton returned to Hollywood to find himself the hero in the last chapter of an Alger book. He had scored a brilliant coup by going wih Metro-Goldwyn-Mayer. What could stop him now?

MGM rolled out the red carpet, assigning the great Thalberg as his producer. Thalberg surprised and nearly disarmed him by his unexpected understanding. "Look," he said, "you don't need a producer, Buster. But we have to go through the motions to satisfy the front office. I'm assigning you Larry Weingarten. A nice boy. Just married my sister. But I'll look out for you. You're my pet."

Uneasy as he was, Keaton still did not fully realize what a tight setup this really was. "They made a big deal out of it," he has since remarked, "but, actually, for Joe to hand me over to Nick was about like transferring change from one pocket to the other."

The big names of that day in management and ownership, such as Marcus Loew, Joseph and Nicholas Schenck, and Louis B. Mayer, all went back to the turn of the century or shortly after. Loew went from a penny amusement arcade on New York's Fourteenth Street (while Buster Keaton was a child vaudeville star on that same street) on to an empty store that—with a sheet and a rented projector and bentwood chairs—became a nickelodeon and then on to a chain of "200 theatres" (to quote, by permission, Edward Lawrence's unpublished *History of MGM*, in the company files) "in key situations throughout the U.S. and Canada, with Metro showcase theatres in 20 countries and on every continent." Marcus Loew's canny thought was this: you can't show movies without a theatre, so the theatre spells control. As history has made all too clear, this sound if not altruistic principle became the guiding motive of Hollywood.

"At approximately the same time," Lawrence's history continues, "two young New York druggists, Nicholas and Joseph Schenck, abandoned the prosaic filling of prescriptions for the more stimulating field of entertainment."

These tactics, which might fairly be called diversionary, paid off, on a borrowed-cash shoestring, with the building of an amusement park at Fort George in upper Manhattan and a still-larger and more lucrative pleasure purlieu across the Hudson at Fort Lee, New Jersey. The latter, Palisades Park, still thrives today, although it and the Fort George Park were sold by the Schenck brothers long ago for the foundation of their fortunes.

Joe and Nick met Marcus, and they hit it off immediately. On Loew's advice the two brothers bought two movie theatres, one in New Rochelle, the other in Hoboken. Now Loew took Nick in as his right-hand man. The time came when there were not enough new films for the swift-hatching Loew theatres—not enough good ones, at any rate. These cinematic landlords, renting films with one hand and five-cent seats to the public with the other, knew exactly what they liked. Their collective sense of responsibility—or, rather, their personal predilection—was strong and clear. Nicholas Schenck, as quoted by Lillian Ross some years ago in *The New Yorker*, delivered an exposition of his aesthetics: "I like . . . clean, wholesome entertainment. . . . I love dramatic, romantic stories. . . . I don't like slapstick."

By 1917 Joe Schenck was producing films starring the Talmadge sisters and Fatty Arbuckle. Then in 1919 Loew (and N. Schenck) bought Metro in Hollywood. Metro had been organized four years earlier, with Louis B. Mayer as its secretary for the first two years, after which Mayer went into production on his own, a staunch independent at that time, vaunting the motto "Inspiration Springs Only from Independence of Thought," sound sentiments for the lower rungs of the ladder.

There are a number of versions of Mayer's background, just as there are wildly varying estimates of the man and his work. One story has him beginning as a junk collector in Nova Scotia. It is certain, anyway, that he bought *his* first nickelodeon in 1917, the Gem in Haverhill, Massachusetts. As Mayer collected more theatres (no one ever stopped with one), he too felt the need of films with an uplift. The very year he bought the Gem, he began producing at Fort Lee with Anita Stewart as his star. Then Mayer moved to Hollywood, eventually got a studio, and added to his roster Renée Adorée, Mildred Harris (later Mrs. Charles Chaplin), and Norma Shearer (soon to become Mrs. Irving Thalberg).

"Irving Thalberg was touched with genius," says the MGM history. His rapid rise was phenomenal, even in Hollywood. "At sixteen he was Carl Laemmle's secretary. Before he was legally old enough to sign the company's checks, he [became] general manager of Universal Pictures." Giving his genius more rein, Thalberg was soon producing very successful pictures: *Foolish Wives* in 1922 (with Erich von Stroheim as star and director); Lon Chaney's famous starring vehicle of 1923, *The Hunchback of Notre Dame*; and, also in 1923, Von Stroheim's *Merry-Go-Round*, which featured Mary Philbin and Norman Kerry.

"Mayer had watched Thalberg's progress with keen interest," our historian continues. "In 1922, Thalberg became Mayer's associate in the Louis B. Mayer Productions." Things had evidently come to some sort of head. "Now all the elements which have made MGM the standard of quality in motion pictures were about to be united. Conversations between Loew, Schenck, and Mayer began. . . . Mayer and Thalberg were signed to a management contract."

Now here, six years later, with both he and Metro-Goldwyn-Mayer firmly established, Thalberg, acknowledged young genius, was extending a friendly hand to a newly hired young genius, Buster Keaton. It was on the level. Thalberg was and remained Keaton's friend.

Work began immediately on the first MGM-produced Keaton

Edward Martin Sedgwick, Jr.,
and Buster Keaton
arrive in New York
to film *The Cameraman*, 1928

comedy, with the working title *Snap Shots*. It was released as *The Cameraman*. It is a fine picture and was very successful. It has remained in the Metro-Goldwyn-Mayer vaults ever since as a model of comedy writing, acting, and directing.

In 1953, when a friend of Buster Keaton asked to see it projected, he was told a surprising thing. "The present print is worn out," an executive said. "It's been our training picture. Ever since 1928 we've made each new comedian study it. From Durante to Abbott and Costello, from Mickey Rooney to Red Skelton and the Marx Brothers."

The MGM man spoke with evident pride. But it is equally evident that he was not thinking of Buster Keaton, a man whom MGM had already long since forgotten. He was thinking, *MGM story, MGM direction, MGM production.* The Machine not the man. That sounds like the story of Buster Keaton, and so it is. At MGM the real history of *The Cameraman* is not remembered: the man, Keaton, fighting The Machine, MGM.

In June, Buster suggested the story idea; it was turned over as a long memo to the writers, who ground away until the end of summer. The script was approved by the front office. The Keaton producing unit was ordered to New York to begin shooting. There—what with the complicated plot and the utter impossibility of publicly photographing the famous Buster Keaton in Manhattan without stopping traffic and attracting a mob—operations ground to a halt.

Buster locked his hotel-room door, got Thalberg on long distance, and told him what had happened. "Now," he said, "for God's sake, authorize me to throw this cockeyed script in the ash can and shoot from the cuff from here on." He could hear Thalberg gasp. Keaton rushed on. "Build the front of the New York City Hall out on Lot Two—we only need the lower floor. I'll shoot backgrounds here and start home in three days."

After a long pause Thalberg replied, "Well, okay, Buster. God knows what will happen up front, but go ahead."

Buster saw Weingarten. "We're shooting a half-dozen backgrounds and then going home."

He knew in advance what the reaction would be. Thalberg had told his brother-in-law when assigning him to Keaton, "Look, Larry, Keaton doesn't really need a producer. Just do the office work and take the screen credit." Weingarten, however, was an activist. "He rushed on the set," Buster has recalled, "overseeing the works. Rode the writers, rode the director, rode me."

Now Weingarten said firmly, "No."

Buster said, "I just talked to Irving."

Looking mortally wounded, Weingarten left the room.

Buster immediately threw away a full three-quarters of the plot. "It was as long as *War and Peace*," he has said. "I took out forty useless characters and a couple of subplots. These guys didn't realize —they *still* don't realize—that the best comedies are simple. Give your comedian room to move around in."

Back at MGM came more trouble. It was the first day on the set in front of the City Hall replica. Buster was in costume: a tintype photographer who snaps pedestrians, develops the pictures under the black camera cloth, and sells them for a dime. The cameras were ready. Director Sedgwick, megaphone in hand, was in his chair. Edward Martin Sedgwick, Jr., was a well-known veteran who had first attained prominence years before through directing the melo-drama-mystery serial *Fantomas*.

Buster still has vivid recollections of the scene, the first in which he had ever stepped in front of MGM cameras. "I walked on," he says, "without a care in the world. Automatically start to work as I have all my life. Started feeling around for bits of business and material. I said, 'I'd like to do something with a drunk and with a fat lady and a kid. Get 'em for me.' I was trying for some establishing shots—and a couple of laughs—before we hit the plot.

"At my studio they would have had the characters I wanted in ten minutes—if they had to go out in the streets and lasso them. But not MGM. You had to requisition a toothpick in triplicate. I just stand there, and everybody is hassling. After twenty minutes, Sedgwick said, 'Let's go over to your bungalow a minute, you and I.' Over there—we had bungalow dressing rooms at MGM—he said, 'I don't think you did it deliberately, but you made a horse's ass out of me in front of my own company.'

"I said I hadn't meant to, I didn't know any other way to work, I was sorry, I wouldn't do it again. 'All right,' he says, 'just so we understand each other.'

"We go back. 'Everybody on the set,' he says. I stand and wait. Forty-five minutes later they bring in the fat lady and the little boy. I wait for him to tell me what to do. For a half hour it goes on. 'Do this! No, do that! Shoot this over. Fat lady *must* you stand in front of Mr. Keaton?'

"Finally Sedgwick says, 'Buster, line these goddamn people up and get this_____shot over with.' 'Me?' I ask. 'You,' he says. That's when we became friends, Sedgwick and I, and I began calling him Junior."

So *The Cameraman* ended up a Keaton picture, not just one with Keaton. It tells of the tintyper's struggles to become a newsreel cameraman. Sally, receptionist of the newsreel company, advises him, half in amusement and half in pity, "Buy a movie camera, take some shots, and submit them."

He trades his tintype box plus his savings for a secondhand movie camera and tripod. Soon he brings in his sample shots, and Sally secures a screening for the company officials. The projection room rings with the merry, lighthearted laughter of the executives. It's the best "in" joke they've seen for years, this gray, fuzzy, out-of-focus, double-exposed, tilted "newsreel" in which automobiles race through pedestrians, trolley cars run backward, and a battleship steams up Fifth Avenue.

He is out before he is in. But he is in with Sally. He asks to see her. She replies, "I'll try to break a date. I'll call you Sunday morning."

On Sunday he is up at dawn, waiting in his tenement room, racing downstairs at each imagined ring of the telephone in the hall, climbing back upstairs to wait again. At last it rings.

Sally says, "My date's off . . ." and he drops the receiver and darts through the hall, down the steps, and through the streets.

She is at her telephone trying to get him to answer. She tosses her head, slams the receiver, turns, and he is standing behind her.

"I'm sorry," he says, "if I'm a little late."

They visit an amusement park (familiar Keaton ground) and are

Buster Keaton and Josephine. Scene from *The Cameraman*, 1928.

having glorious misadventures, when it starts to rain. The tintype boy's rival, Stagg, happens by in his car. He picks them up, quickly dumps the boy, and goes on with Sally. But the tintyper is on the inside track anyway. Next day Sally gives him a hot tip but withholds it from the office, even though Stagg is her company's head cameraman. The tip: "Hurry! There's a tong war starting in Chinatown."

The boy is off. On his way, through an absurd accident, he finds himself owner of an organ-grinder's monkey. As he runs, the monkey sits on his shoulder like a jockey riding sidesaddle. They find the tong brethren shooting and hatcheting away. The boy has just filled a reel as the fighting comes to a halt. He has it all, close up, a scoop. He runs for the newsreel offices. "I've got some great pictures of that tong war."

The projection starts. Nothing happens. The screen is empty. A blank film. No merry big-shot laughter now. "Pretty short war. Why don't you get lost?"

He still won't give up. Next day he is at a regatta with his camera set up on the shore. Stagg and Sally race by in a speedboat. Stagg tries too tight a turn and the pair of them are thrown into the water. The scene fades out on their initial struggles and fades in on the tintyper leaving his camera and running off. The monkey, trained at organ-grinding, begins turning the camera crank.

Then the scene cuts to Sally lying on the shore, Stagg kneeling beside her. She looks up and says, "You're awfully brave to have saved me."

"What else could a fellow do?" asks Stagg modestly.

The tintype boy comes running up with an armful of medicine bottles. His object: to revive Sally. But Sally has just left. That does it. He gives up the battle, turns in the movie camera, and takes back his old equipment.

Sally finds him working in the street and says, "You left your film at the office. Don't you want it?" They go back and find that, by mistake, his reel is just going on in the projection room. They go in.

The boss is leaping to his feet and yelling, "Best camera work I've seen in years. Get that boy here quick!"

The tong war is on the screen! And yet everyone had thought the reel was blank. What is the mystery? In answer, the narration flashes back to the time and the place in which the boy was photographing the Chinese at battle. He has just completed taking a reel and the fighting is over. This much we already knew. He turns from the camera. Then we are shown what we were not shown before: the monkey removing the exposed reel, taking a fresh one, and reloading. Yesterday this new, unexposed reel had been shown. Now, however, it is the exposed reel on the screen.

When it reaches its end, still another reel comes on. Now we see water, a wildly careening speedboat, two people being thrown out. One, Sally, is floundering. The other, Stagg, strikes for shore. Then the tintype boy, close up and to one side, dives in and swims out to Sally. He carries her ashore, lays her down, and runs to the drugstore. Stagg comes over; she revives, then thanks him for saving her. The projection machine plays out the true story, recorded by the fingers of a grind-organ monkey.

The little simian's real name was Josephine, though Buster Keaton might well have renamed her Kismet. He remembers her well. "Josephine," he says, "had been in pictures for years. She enabled an organ-grinder to come in off the streets and retire in comfort."

There was a lot of laughing and backslapping at MGM when the sample print of *The Cameraman* was run off. Even Mayer was there to see it. They knew they had a winner. Then Thalberg spoke up. "Buster," he said, "Mr. Mayer and I want you smiling in that last fade-out."

Here we go again, Buster thought. He knew the riposte. "All right," he said, "we'll do it and use it at the preview. If the public likes it, fine. If they don't, we agree that the smiling deal's a dead duck from now on. Okay?"

Thalberg and Mayer agreed. It was like a fixed fight. It could go but one way. The preview showed, once more, that the public knew what Keaton was all about, even if Hollywood did not.

With *The Cameraman*, Keaton was at the height of his art. He was master of every detail of silent-film making—story and camera work, directing and acting, editing and cutting. He, not MGM, made this picture. He knew it was fine, perhaps his finest. It had taken time and patience, worry and sweat—more than it need have taken. But he had made it at MGM, where Chaplin said it couldn't be done.

He began to seethe with ideas as he had eight years earlier, when Joe Schenck had said, "The Arbuckle company is yours." Stories began pouring into his mind. Whole plot ideas would wake him up at night. He would switch the light on and think them out. He found it as restful as sleep.

He took one of these stories to Thalberg.

Resting between takes. *The Cameraman*, 1928.

THIRTY-ONE

"**S** IT DOWN, Buster," said Thalberg. "So what's new?"
"A story."

"Good."

"I want to team with Marie Dressler."

Thalberg looked perplexed and a little disappointed. Marie Dressler had not set the world on fire at MGM, the extent of her achievement up to then being a picture just as well forgotten, a hoked-up bit with Polly Moran called *The Callahans and the Murphys*.

Buster spoke quickly. "You know I had great luck with Ernest Torrence in *Steamboat Bill Jr.* This would be the same kind of thing."

When Keaton said "luck" he was thinking of artistic results. Thalberg, however, knew the sad story of *Steamboat Bill's* low gross, even though he may not have known the extenuating circumstances of its handling by United Artists. He said, "Go on."

"Well, we start in Dodge City with a wagon train. Marie Dressler's going alone in her own wagon, when she gets word that I—her nephew—am showing up. She waits—I'm a day late—and the wagon train has gone on. Then, when she sees me—ouch!—I'm a real nincompoop. I say, 'Aunty, we can catch them.' 'Think we can?' 'Sure.' "

Buster continued, "So we set out. Terrible equipment, a horse teamed with a mule, a cow at the end of a rope, and me the world's most incompetent man. While I'm being scared by rabbits, she's chopping wood."

"Go on," Thalberg said.

"Well," said Buster, "that's your plot."

Thalberg stared.

"Well, uh," Buster said, "you know—we fill in. I have to make good for Aunty . . ."

"It seems to me . . ." Thalberg began.

Buster spoke up quickly again. "There's lots of stuff. Let's see—we fight Indians, we ford a river, we get detoured from Oregon by taking a wrong fork in the trail. We, well, we get lost on the desert, a sandstorm obliterates the trail"—now he was talking faster—"so we're getting our direction by the sun. Then the Indians close in at night—drums, war cries—and we beat it. Off in the dark and into a fog too—we're sure the Indians are right on our tail. We come to a river so wide you lose it in the fog, too deep to ford. No time to lose —we fell trees and make a raft. Put everything on it—wagon, horse, cow, mule, belongings, and ourselves—and take off. A few hundred yards, and the fog lifts—it's dawn, and there we are on the Pacific Ocean! We go ashore and reconnoiter. And"—he paused trium-phantly—"what do you think we find?"

"What do you find?" Thalberg asked.

"A sleepy little adobe town—we take it from an old print—Los Angeles in 1848!"

Irving Thalberg looked unhappy. He hesitated, shuffled the papers on his desk, sat in thought, and said at last, "Buster, it seems in-sufficient plot for a feature-length picture."

Buster said, a little impatiently, "Insufficient for your writers. They're plot-crazy. Me, I can make eight reels out of it." Then he added, "Oh, and look, I want to do it in sound."

"I'll think it over," Thalberg said, in the "don't call me, I'll call you" tone. A year later he was still thinking it over. Then suddenly Marie Dressler was a top star, with an Oscar for her work with Wally Beery in *Min and Bill.*

In the meantime MGM tossed Keaton into a thirteen-reel extrav-aganza made in sound and partly in color. *Hollywood Revue of 1929* presented the entire star roster—MGM had gone all out for the star system, with the slogan "More Stars Than There Are in Heaven."

Sound was a bombshell. It had been only a year (it had happened on October 23, 1927) since Warner Brothers' *The Jazz Singer,* with Al Jolson, had electrified audiences with its inclusion of sequences with sound. Warners had glommed on to a process and patented it. All the other companies had begun frantically developing their own systems or else sending engineers to be trained in New York at Bell Laboratories, which had developed a new patent. At the moment, even colossal MGM had only one set of sound equipment, weighing two tons, and was making three pictures in round-the-clock shifts on its solitary soundproof stage.

While Keaton had been talking vainly with Thalberg for what might well have been a great picture with Marie Dressler, MGM's writers, without his knowing it, had been busy. In due time the star was let in on the secret. Surprise! Weingarten announced it: a new story for Buster. He even divulged the name: *Spite Marriage*. In a further violation of protocol, Keaton again went over his producer's head and directly to Irving Thalberg. He pleaded for sound in the new picture.

It is extraordinary that he should have done so. Sound was ending the career of many a star—for example, Norma and Constance Talmadge and John Gilbert. Chaplin at that very moment was condemning it as the potential ruin of pantomime and fine comedy. Why should Buster Keaton have wanted sound? His work, indeed, had been so purely and oustandingly visual that, appraising it many years later, James Agee would write in *Life*:

> Keaton's style and nature [were] so much the most deeply "silent" of the silent comedians that even a smile was as deafeningly out of key as a yell.

Keaton's reasoning was valid, nor had his taste gone astray. He saw that sound would win. He already knew, as the majority still did not, that the silent film was doomed. Just as in 1917, on the Roscoe Arbuckle set, he had grasped the scope and essence of the silent film, now in 1929, with equal intuition, he saw the aesthetic problems that sound would bring. He regarded sound objectively. Not for nothing had he been meeting the inevitable over the years in each of his films. Sound was here to stay. He was intrigued, not overwhelmed, by the new gadget.

He also foresaw that sound would be misused by overuse. "It needn't be one long yak-yak," he told Thalberg. "There's nothing wrong with sound that a little silence won't cure."

"Wrong?" Thalberg was astonished.

"I visualize," said Keaton (he even "visualized" sound), "I visualize sound effects. When you fall down and go *boom*, you really go *boom*. But leave the wisecracks and the bad puns and the dirty jokes to the burlesque comedians. No one wants Chaplin or me to do much talking. Better we keep our mouths shut. Let the man say, 'Now you go and do this,' and then we go about our silent business with sound all around us."

The trouble was that Keaton was a comedian, and in the pinch, no one—not even Thalberg—could take a serious comedian seriously. Stereotype stepped in the way. Like the Negro, the thinking clown was an Invisible Man. That particular conference ended with Thalberg's polite no. The public, he said, would stand still for Buster

Keaton in silent films. Perhaps Thalberg boggled at the idea of a Buster Keaton acting away silently in front of Metro-Goldwyn-Mayer's only microphone. Or perhaps the sound stage was too tightly scheduled for even a Thalberg to reschedule one eight-hour daily shift.

Buster returned silently to his silent set. It was becoming clear: MGM was not working for Keaton, but Keaton for MGM. This was the second lesson in a row. A week before, he had taken a comic fall for Lew Cody on his set. Cody's stunt-man double was gumming it up. The director complained, "Either he makes it brutal or he makes it awkward."

"I'll do it," said Buster. Elaborating on the fall as it had been planned, he did a spectacular but very funny fall on his head and shoulders. Though he made it look easy, it was both difficult and dangerous.

The next day he was summoned to the inner inner sanctum, L. B. Mayer's office. Didn't he think, the MGM president asked, that he took enough chances in his own pictures? The conference opened and closed unilaterally. The ultimatum: Keaton was not to do that again.

Then he was assigned a larger bungalow, on the lot and rent-free, to replace the one he himself had rented just across the street.

"Oh no," said Buster. "I'm not Marion Davies."

"You're one of our stars," said Thalberg persuasively.

"No," said Buster.

"Mr. Mayer wants you to have it," Thalberg replied.

Keaton turned, walked to the gate, out, and across the street. "Come on, Carruthers," he called to his handyman-secretary-valet. "Pack up the skillet and the cocktail shaker. We're moving." He named his bungalow, perhaps not without significance, Keaton's Kennel. After twelve years of living in Hollywood, he had found out where he was.

Starting his second MGM picture, he found that the climate had changed overnight. *The Cameraman* was out and coining money, but its star was a forgotten man. Scriptwriters, directors, producers, cutters, editors—all hands were comedy experts.

One morning at the rushes, Weingarten turned to the cutter and said, "Don't bother to tear that sequence down. I don't like that type of thing in *my* pictures."

"I talked like a Dutch uncle to save that scene," Keaton recalls. "It was only the biggest laugh in the film."

The scene in question is the one in which Buster struggles to put his bride to bed, both of them equally full of wedding champagne. The scene made the picture—both because of Keaton's famous way with props and because it was an especially pretty prop. It proved, too, to be a long-lived bit of foolery. Almost twenty-five years later, Gregory Peck tried his hand at it with Audrey Hepburn in *Roman Holiday*.

Along in those same later years, Buster himself was using the sequence with his present wife, Eleanor—likewise a pretty prop—at the Cirque Médrano in Paris. "Lucky I got it into Weingarten's film," says its originator.

All the good sequences in *Spite Marriage* represent battles with one MGM executive or another. One of these, in the early-Keaton parody vein, is a theatre scene in which Buster, as an extra, completely wrecks a serious Civil War drama. The other is the finale, in which, on a yacht, he uncorks the old heroic, breathtaking acrobatics above and in the water, like those on the Truckee and Tahoe in *Our Hospitality* and on the Sacramento in *Steamboat Bill Jr*. Half flight and all speed and accuracy, they still shine, although the acrobat was thirty-four years old when *Spite Marriage* was made.

As the experts grew more expert, the battles became harder, and each victory carried some kind of penalty. "I'm afraid," Buster says today, "that Larry Weingarten was plenty sore, especially when the putting-the-bride-to-bed was such a success. But, God Almighty, I'd fight for the darnest things, that I knew were right, and they'd brush me off." By degrees, Keaton got the reputation for being "uncooperative," and thus he was a convenient guy to blame everything on. As for Larry Weingarten, whatever happened, he was on his way to a seat on the executive board.

It was unbeatable, a situation deeper than mere studio chicanery. By now it was built in. It was the end of an era, not only for Keaton but for Charlie Chaplin, Harold Lloyd, Doug Fairbanks, and even D. W. Griffith, the old master. Improvisation was over. The great improvisers were through. Part of the fault lay with sound and the new techniques. Part was costs—soaring overnight. Big investment called for strong protection; safety lay in the surefire plots, the time-proven clichés.

The comedy of silence had been a divine comedy. It was, indeed, dying in the blare of the loudspeaker. Of all the great pantomimists, Buster Keaton was the likeliest to have saved it, sound or no. He knew how to use silence and still have sound, how to use sound and still have silence. He had always juggled opposites as difficult as that. His instincts were right, but he had passed up his chance to follow them on that morning when, with three strong drinks under his belt, he had called, all but hat in hand, on Nicholas Schenck.

Now, controls began to go. First, his control over his pictures. He could no longer even suggest story ideas; or if he suggested them, they were rejected.

It was the blackest of all the tragedies that can happen to an artist: the murder of his art. He recalls it today with the sorrow scarcely diminished. "No one saw it for four or five pictures, then it got so bad no one could miss it—*What, No Beer?* and *Sidewalks of New York*, oh, they were brutal! I knew before the camera turned on the first scene that we had the perfect foundation for a stinker. And by now, I couldn't tell anyone anything. They had the one answer for it all. 'What's happened to Keaton? Nice guy, but he's slipping.'

"So—I slipped. I did what so many others have done. I started to drink. And that's when I blew it."

THIRTY-TWO

~~~~~~~~~~~~~~~~~~~~~~~~~~

"THERE I was," says Buster Keaton, "sitting on top of the world—on a toboggan."

As if he were actually living the dream sequences of a *Sherlock Jr.*, the real-life scene had cut abruptly from a gilded surfboard on the crest of the wave to a long toboggan slide down an icy slope.

It was quite a toboggan ride, not altogether continuous, slow at first and then gathering speed, until at last the toboggan went out of control completely. Then it hit bottom.

It was not altogether a sad ride—until near the end—nor was it entirely lonely. Noise, laughter, bright lights, popping corks, friends —all the stage dressing and all the actors of a brilliant success—were part of the blurred landscape.

The real stinkers did not begin coming until 1932, with *Sidewalks of New York*. *Spite Marriage*, made in 1929, was followed by an all-out MGM effort. The whole factory went to work on Buster Keaton's first sound picture, *Free and Easy*, which was ready for an April, 1930, release. MGM shot the works: Turk and Ahlert for the music, Trixie Friganza, Anita Page, Robert Montgomery, and Lionel Barrymore to support the star. Even Sam Goldwyn appears in one sequence. *Free and Easy* was both a compliment to Keaton and an institutional ad for Metro-Goldwyn-Mayer. Primarily the studio writers' baby, *Free and Easy* is a hodgepodge of farce, slapstick, burlesque, musical comedy, and sentimental drama. Keaton might have married some of those opposites; the staff geniuses couldn't. The only thing Keaton about it is the central character and what Buster is able to make out of him: a dope called Elmer from Gopher City, Kansas.

But the time was right for this all-palace celebration. Hodgepodge though *Free and Easy* is, it *does* have sound. For a short time, right then, sound pictures could do no wrong. The public ate them up, intrigued by hearing the voices of the so-long silent. Buster passed the test that so many failed: his voice fitted his character. It was like Louis Armstrong's: it had to be as it was. Keaton's was deep, slightly Midwestern and flat, and as uncommunicative as his face.

So *Free and Easy* enjoyed a popular and financial success. The experts were feeling their oats. They were no longer whispering behind Buster's back. They were talking right out in meeting. If Buster Keaton's comedy training and his own story writing had given him anything, it was a sure instinct for that precise moment just before the words "too late." He had only one man to turn to: Irving Thalberg. On the heels of this film's wholly unmerited success, it was not the ideal time—but it was the only time.

Thalberg listened with the close, probing attention he knew how to give. It was intelligent attention, particularly in its picking up of overtones. Besides, Thalberg was genuinely fond of Buster. Certainly he could see the strain in his face, hear the urgency, almost agony, in his voice. In all likelihood they were stronger points than his arguments, cogent as they were, for autonomous control of his own pictures.

Thalberg did not interrupt, did not interpose either answer or question. He heard his star out. When Buster was through, Thalberg finally spoke. "The answer," he said "is yes. I'm going to let you produce your own pictures."

It was like General Motors letting an employee make Thunderbirds.

"Now Buster," Thalberg went on, "you're ahead of schedule. Here is what I want you to do: finish your next picture—and, I repeat, *your* next—then take Natalie to Europe. Have a good time for yourselves."

To the full extent of his power, and in all likelihood stretching it a bit, Thalberg made good his promise. The story for *Doughboys* was Buster's, and although the staff writers got in a few complications and the screen credit went to Boasberg and Lazarus, it is a picture that, even with sound, has the old-time feeling. Partly this is because the sound is so largely that of two twangy voices, Keaton's and Ukulele Ike's. Both performers play doughboys, and Cliff Edwards, or Ukulele Ike, fits well with Keaton both as actor and as singer, with his wild, rhythmic vo-de-o-do scatting and his strummed uke accompaniment. Sally Eilers furnished the feminine graces in this essentially masculine picture. The story is largely based on Buster's war memories as embroidered by imagination. A highlight is the moment Buster fails to about-face and the regiment marches over him, just as the 40th Infantry had done twelve years before at Camp Kearney.

By the end of summer Natalie and he were on their way. They went first to England, with bobbies clearing a path for them through the crowds, then in a rented car to Scotland. Magically, the tensions were gone; they got acquainted again. Buster was continually pointing to ducal land tracts and saying, "Could we build a ranch there!"

In Paris an MGM representative took Buster away from Natalie and on an interminable, mysterious drive in the dark. The company man spoke only French and Keaton only English, so it was not until the reached Brussels that the passenger discovered that he was to make a personal appearance at a theatre showing the film *Buster Se Marie*, the French version of *Spite Marriage*. In those early days before dubbing techniques had been developed, several films were made of the same story, each with a different foreign supporting cast; they were separately filmed in French and German and, often, Italian and Spanish. With Keaton in *Buster Se Marie* were Mona Goya, Françoise Rosay, and other French actors.

Buster returned to Paris in the early hours, to find Natalie, completely bewildered, waiting at the hotel and asking, "Where *have* you been?"

"Brussels," said Buster.

"Why didn't you tell me?"

"Because *they* didn't tell *me*."

Next was Berlin, where *Wir Schalten um auf Hollywood*, the German version of *Hollywood Revue*, was playing and where, Buster predicted, he would know everyone "because all Germans are vaudeville acrobats." They arrived at night during a political celebration that seemed to be in honor of President Hindenburg. The guttural crowd noise frightened Natalie, and she fled to their rooms.

Buster went walking alone and found a policeman following him. He tried to shake him off and failed, so he turned suddenly and said, "Well?"

The cop was only an autograph hunter. "*Bitte*," he said politely, "*Sie sind der berühmte Herr Keaton, nicht war?*

Yes, he was the famous Herr Keaton, and the famous Herr Keaton would be glad to give his autograph.

Next day in an interview with the critic Erwin Gephard, Buster, asked about *die Tonfilme*, said, "I have nothing to say about it: the American people wanted them." Asked, "Don't you believe that the sound picture distorts the art in cinema?" he replied, "I play only in pictures where pantomime instead of speech remains the chief thing."

It was September, then the vacation, almost like the honeymoon they had never had, was interrupted. Norma Talmadge arrived, with her Rolls Royce and Gilbert Roland, she and Joe Schenck having parted. So, Roland being Spanish, it was off to Spain for them all, with *aficionado* Roland, en route, explaining the *mystique* of the *corrida*. In Barcelona, Buster went to the arena with Gilbert.

They were settled into their seats, when the man alongside Buster tapped the shoulder of the man in front, jerked his head sideways, and whispered something. Hands began tapping shoulders, the whispers flew. Faces turned to look, and the shout went up: "Pampliñas!" Pampliñas!" Suddenly Buster found himself lifted up and being handed down from man to man until he ended up in one of the boxes. There he was greeted by four dignitaries.

But the chanting continued with a new refrain, which, translated, ran as follows: "Pampliñas kill the bull! Pampliñas kill the bull!" With no more ado the four men—one of whom Buster now knew was the mayor—picked the comedian up and dropped him into the arena. The matador bowed, handed Buster his cape and weapon, and stepped aside. It was Pampliñas and *el toro*.

Drama and life, here, were unquestionably one, and the frightened slapstick—the stumbling, slipping, and clawing up the fence—was for real.

"You were a wow!" Roland said.

"Thanks," Buster said. "Give me baseball."

In November, Buster and Natalie turned homeward to a Hollywood Thanksgiving. Buster went to the lot to plunge into his second MGM feature as his own producer. He found that the story idea he had left with the writers had been shelved. In his absence, office politics had been at work. As a heretic he was eternally vulnerable. He could do no right because he wanted to do it alone. *Doughboys'* success only prompted whispers that "such slapstick is undignified and unsuited to the modern sound picture." Thalberg—perhaps stung by the implied criticism of him—had bought a story for Buster and had assigned comedienne Charlotte Greenwood as leading lady. It was the 1917 Broadway hit *Parlor, Bedroom and Bath*.

Buster took it well, but with reservations. "It's a farce—not my kind of story," he said frankly. Seeing Thalberg's evident disappointment, he added, "But we'll make a good pic."

He tried hard and made at least a merry film. However, some of the leading critics, American and foreign, questioned MGM's judgment in putting Keaton into farce. This must have nettled Thalberg. Buster was in good spirits, feeling that, little by little, he was winning. His feeling was bolstered by the fact that MGM was now allowing him to play baseball.

At that ill-fated luncheon several years before, Nicholas Schenck had warned him: no baseball on the Metro lot. L. B. Mayer repeated the warning, and it was written into his contract. This was all forgotten later at one of the annual picnics. Softball and bats appeared, and Thalberg and Mayer themselves chose sides. "Let's do this every Sunday," it was decided.

It took a script boy to bring the Sunday softball games to a sudden end. He charged a bunt, scooped it up, and turning to make his peg, found the first baseman standing right in front of him. He had left the bag uncovered and run over to watch the play. "You stupe!" the script boy yelled, with suitable adjectives, and broke up the game.

The offended first baseman, a famous director, tossed his glove down and went home.

Then Buster's director, "Junior" Sedgwick, suggested regular hardball. "Separate the men from the boys," he said. Buster seconded the motion with enthusiasm. Sedgwick rented a vacant lot, passed the kitty, and built a small grandstand, and the MGM Lions were in business. Keaton held down third. They played every Sunday for years.

Baseball, to Buster Keaton, betokened normality. He relaxed still more. Ignoring Mayer's standing orders to him, he again began visiting other sets. One day, dressed in cutaway and top hat for an upcoming scene, he dropped over to a set built around a swimming pool. Director Jack Conway called to him, "Ten dollars if you go in." Without breaking stride, Buster went straight on into the pool, out, and over to Conway with his hand outstretched for the bill.

Two days later he broke out all over with the fungoid skin infection popularly called barber's itch. His doctor was certain he had contracted it from the pool water. He was off work for several days. On his return certain well-wishers took pains to tell him that the delay had cost MGM fifty thousand dollars. Buster went to Sedgwick for verification. "Well, no," said Junior, "not quite that bad. Nearer thirty, I guess." He looked unusually serious.

Keaton had been with MGM a little over three years, fighting every inch of the way for the rights he felt to be self-evident, inherent in his own creativeness. He had more than stayed on schedule, making five features, *The Cameraman, Spite Marriage, Free and Easy, Doughboys,* and *Parlor, Bedroom and Bath,* and had even squeezed in a European holiday. Of the five, *Cameraman* had been all Keaton

and fine; *Doughboys*, 86-proof Keaton and very good. These had
had Keaton stories (the second with a little tampering) and, in
substance, Keaton direction. From the other stories he had salvaged
more than had seemed possible. Perhaps his best idea—the pioneer
Western epic with Marie Dressler—had been vetoed in default of
decision. But on the whole it seemed reasonable for him to feel, as
he did, that he had at least held his own in this David-and-Goliath
duel with The Establishment.

There was no arguing that he had been paid well. A lesser artist
would have, as the saying went, cried all the way to the bank. Adding bonuses to salary, Metro-Goldwyn-Mayer had paid Keaton in the
neighborhood of seven hundred thousand dollars. This was Hollywood, still untouched by the Great Depression, feeding its great
placebo to a sad, harried, deprived country. The excitement that had
ended for the rest of America still gripped the movie capital. There
everyone was making money. Money fueled the off-hours festivities.
There were parties every night at Pickfair, Tom Mix's, Buster's
Italian Villa, or out on the Santa Monica Riviera, where a row of
châteaux—Norma Talmadge's, the Thalbergs', Constance and Town-
send Netcher's, Bebe Daniels and Ben Lyon's—culminated with
Marion Davies' beachside Colonial manor. And nearly four hundred
miles north along the same ocean shore, on the Big Sur cliffs, was
the fabulous Hearst's fabulous barony, San Simeon.

Money and excitement fueled it, and energy was drawn on sight
draft. People too tired to sleep drove themselves around the clock,
from work to play and back again. No wonder that in the memories
of those who survived it, it was the time of the golden smog.

For Buster Keaton it was still the turning wheel, now turning
faster in his two different worlds.

THIRTY-THREE

ALTHOUGH Natalie Keaton too was part of this play world
and in Europe had shared it with Buster, once home again
the two had drifted back into separate ways. It was to have been the
situation Natalie had seemed to want and certainly had reached for:
the house, the motorcars coming and going, the music, and all the
gay, expensive, festive things. But it had become bigger than Natalie,
bigger than the Villa—it was Hollywood. She must have felt that
everything was getting away from her.

Buster's constant companions—almost as if he were a bachelor
again—were more and more becoming just men: Norman Kerry, Lew
Cody, Buster Collier, Doug Fairbanks, Jack Pickford, Tom Mix, Hoot
Gibson. It could have been about then that, womanlike, Natalie began to wonder, *Where are the women?*

Buster was away from home a lot, and when at home, it was always bridge, the game in which Natalie would take no part.

Nor would Buster Collier. "Bridge helped to undermine his life,"
was Collier's opinion, expressed many years later. "Bridge at two
dollars a point—you could lose twenty thousand dollars in an evening.
And he was a whiz, always in demand. It's a strain, anyway, playing
with the Goldwyns and the Schencks—more can ride on a game than
winning or losing. I recall Buster in some of those close matches
taking that deep breath—the acrobat's trick—when he felt himself
getting nervous. Or even going outside for air. Remember too that
Lou Anger, Eddie Mannix, and financier I. C. Freud all had pieces
of Buster. He was as good as syndicated. They bet on him—if he lost,
they lost. I recall once, after a streak of bad cards, they sent him a
picture of a funeral. He laughed, but he was upset.

"Now this," said Collier, "was the man that never had a nerve
in his body—terribly athletic, terribly strong, his own stunt man, and
never a better. Handle his body like a cat—throw him out of a window and he'd land on his feet. Remember, this is a guy I loved from
the old vaudeville days, now shading forty and never stopping to

Left to right:
Buster Collier,
Constance Talmadge,
Buster Keaton,
Natalie Talmadge Keaton
(during filming of *College*, 1927).

think, *I better ease up and get more rest.* Even at the studio, where you work like a dog from seven A.M. to seven P.M., he had to have twelve to sixteen everyday for lunch at his bungalow.

"Buster Keaton," Collier said, "needed excitement. But deeper than that, he loved to make everybody happy, liked his gang around. So it became two drinks in the evening, then four, and then the sky's the limit. Whereupon you move it down into the daytime, and soon you have a bottle beside the alarm clock.

"He was well informed and intelligent. But he was sensitive, almost abnormally so. Most people didn't know that because of the unreadable face. But Buster didn't have that hard shell of ego. As a rule, you came out of vaudeville hard as nails. Take Al Jolson or George Jessel—a sledgehammer wouldn't dent them.

"I saw it begin to happen. I loved and admired the guy too much to stick around and watch it. We drifted apart. I tried to talk to him, but his gang had made a wall around him; he didn't feel like facing anything unpleasant. When he started to go, he really went. It seemed as if it had to happen—like in his pictures—but, of course, it didn't. What do you say about Buster Keaton?" Collier paused. "He was just too good a guy."

Nor, surely, can Natalie have borne seeing it happening. But there had been silence too long between them about the things that mattered. She seemed paralyzed. Of the three Talmadge sisters, Natalie, quite obviously, took marriage the most seriously. She perhaps even foresaw that this would be the only marriage she would ever undertake. She retreated as mothers often retreat, lavishing more and more of her time and affection on their two boys. By this time, 1932, Jimmy was ten and Bobby eight. As sons often do, they become surrogates for the father. In addition, Natalie's sisters were constantly undermining her loyalty and determination.

Even from a distance there is always a deep sadness about all the old, foolish, tragic scenes of the human comedy. Buster Keaton today, piercing the wall of the old, sad memories, can bring reluctantly to mind how Natalie would sometimes protest to him, as if driven, about his drinking. As he tells it, slowly and hesitantly, one can sense *her* slowness, *her* hesitation, and all the remote and curious ineffectiveness. And one senses strongly the effort it must have taken for her to make even this small breach in the tyranny of their silence. And soon the point would come when this too could no longer happen.

Now it was Buster who filled the Villa at all hours with people—his refuge against the loneliness and estrangement that lived there. It was the time that the animals, like refugees from the ranch that never was, began coming too—the quail, the pet raccoons for Jimmy and Bobby, the endless dynasty of dogs, even the inarticulate trout in the brook.

Trotsky had succeeded the police dog Captain when Captain was killed by a car. Trotsky, an Irish wolfhound, in hot weather slept in the ornamental pool entirely submerged except for his head. Next came Barry, the short-haired St. Bernard who snapped his leash and wrecked a dog show at the Ambassador Hotel and then was given to Norman Kerry. Then had come the long-haired St. Bernard, Elmer, named after Buster's part in *Free and Easy*.

"Elmer," says Buster, "did his own shopping. He would look a butcher in the face until the guy couldn't stand it and would throw him a steak, the best in the house, and then charge it to Keaton. Elmer ate three lunches at MGM—the original expense-account dog. He lunched at my bungalow at noon, with Marion Davies at one, and with the executives at two."

Elmer, Keaton relates, was fond of Greta Garbo in a remarkably restrained sort of way, even for a St. Bernard. Elmer was always by her side when, as was her lonely custom, she strolled in the remoter regions of the vast MGM lot. She seemed to look forward to his silent, undemanding company. If she patted him, however, he always growled and moved out of reach without breaking step.

"Elmer isn't looking for love," Buster had said to Kerry. "He wants prestige."

Another endless processional was that of the state cars, the limousines and big sedans for Natalie's use. Even Bobby and Jimmy had cars, given them by Norma, small, battery-propelled roadsters that they drove around the grounds and in the house. Although Buster had once owned a Browniekar (to be sure, he had earned it), he objected to these cars and to all the lavish gifts and the elegant clothes ("like Little Lord Fauntleroys") and the children's parties ("Do *they* have to have a butler?"). The father's antipathy to the situation very likely reflected his own discomfort in the general matriarchal climate (*"Four* mothers for two kids!").

When he had slid two-year-old Bobby across the polished floor, Natalie had been furious. "Joe did it to me," he had replied, and later he began privately teaching both boys to tumble and take falls. The lessons were no longer a secret when they showed off their new tricks at a party. The boys themselves were quite evidently confused as to which parent to follow and alternated between playing Fauntleroy and the Kid.

But these were fleabites compared with the real troubles, the personal impasse between husband and wife. Suspicion sprouts in loneliness and estrangement. With any start at all it can luxuriate in Hollywood.

"I was a star," says Keaton, "and in Hollywood. It's an automatic problem in the best of circumstances. Why even Joe Schenck could have second thoughts seeing a pic that he himself had chosen and produced for Norma. No one could do a love scene better than she, so convincingly that a man has to call himself aside: *Is* all *of that acting?* Everyone said—and I believe—that Clark Gable's love scenes on the screen broke up his first marriage. Like all of us, he was on this spot: look like you're enjoying it and your wife jumps to conclusions; look like you're not and you're out of a job.

"It finally got so that Natalie practically took for granted that I had an affair with every leading lady. There again, you're stuck: keep trying out new ones to get a good actress and you're promiscuous, a chaser; get a good one and put her on the payroll and it's 'Where are you keeping her?' I was accused every picture. *She* knew I was chasing them, and *I* knew I wasn't.

"Then"—Buster drew in his breath sharply in the way that Collier remembered—"then I was *really* in the soup. It could have been in one of my pictures. My God! You would have to know Hollywood. . . ." He hesitated, gave up trying to explain Hollywood, and went on. "Somebody brought a girl, a bit player, to my bungalow for lunch. Late that afternoon Carruthers had gone, and I was there alone. She came back. 'I've decided,' she announced, 'to let you keep me.' 'Just dandy,' I said, 'and now, kid, I've got news for *you*—I'm not keeping you or anybody. Now flag your ass out of here quick.'

"Good Christ! She starts screaming like a Louise Fazenda, whips out a knife, and jumps me. I knocked the knife out of her hand, but

Buster Keaton
with his sons,
Jimmy and Bobby.

she scratched my face and ripped my shirt and undershirt. I finally got her off me and backhanded her with all I had. Her screams brought the studio police. Even they had trouble getting her out.

"One week later she's in bandages, has a crew of doctors and lawyers, and is suing me for ten thousand. It's all in the papers. Reporters go to the Villa. 'What are your views, Mrs. Keaton?' Natalie wouldn't talk to them. *That* helped.

"So there's a big meeting with Mayer and Thalberg. 'Gotta kill this fast. Give her the ten grand. Settle it. Now!' I had no choice. I paid. Natalie had it all figured out: I'd been keeping this floozy; here was the breakup, and she wouldn't stand still for it. Then my canceled check came back—joint account. That did it."

It was trouble everywhere. Buster's precarious control over his picture making was slipping. Thalberg's promise had expired, and he was now either too busy elsewhere or too fed up with the perennial problem of Keaton the individualist in the MGM assembly-line system. Sedgwick was taken off his pictures, and two other directors, Jules White and Zion Myers, were assigned to codirect Keaton in the new feature. This was *Sidewalks of New York*, with Anita Page and Cliff Edwards in the supporting cast. The new directors, says Buster, "alternated telling me how to walk, how to talk, how to stand, and how to fall—where and when, how fast or slow, how loud or soft. I was Trilby with two Svengalis—MGM had gone to the two-platoon with unlimited substitutions. It came out such a complete stinker, such an unbelievable bomb, that they gave Sedgwick back to me."

Events, now completely out of Keaton's hands, were rapidly crystallizing in both his worlds. The toboggan was picking up speed. "So I had Sedgwick, but I also had a story—*The Passionate Plumber*, which was *The Cardboard Lover* on the stage. It was entirely wrong for me. Jimmy Durante was in the cast. He tried hard and I tried hard, but our styles, our timing don't jibe. I could see that MGM was grooming Durante. He knew it too—but he stole no scenes."

Speak Easily, Jimmy Durante's first appearance with Keaton, plus Thelma Todd and Hedda Hopper (in a bit), had been a bad enough picture. In fact it was Jimmy who held it together. The old Keaton —even the more recent Keaton—is not there. Though nominally the star, he was a pale, staring ghost who dragged himself to the studio each morning shaking with a hangover.

Finally, *What, No Beer?* signals the approaching end. Something was going to have to give. The accidents were beginning, not the kind with the capital A that functioned as miracles in Keaton films, but the real and deadly kind. Even Myra Keaton, living on unfashionable Victoria Avenue, began worrying when she discovered what was going on with her son across the railroad tracks. This was in late 1932, right after *What, No Beer?* was finished. Myra heard that Buster had been injured during the Christmas celebrations on the lot. He had attempted a funny (and, of course, dangerous) fall in director James Cruze's bungalow, had "missed," and had struck his head violently. In the general drunkenness, she was told, no one had paid any attention. He was lying on the couch when the party broke up. Early Christmas morning, they said, he had found his way home.

Myra never could completely verify all the details, but she did find out that Buster had been hurt. It was what happened later that chiefly worried her. Years later she told about it. "About six weeks after that," she said, "he had a convulsion. The laundryman told me about it when he came past my house. I rushed up there, but Natalie wouldn't let me see him. I said, 'Natalie, if it was one of your boys, nobody could keep you from him.'

"The cook let me stay in her room until the Talmadges all went to bed. Constance had been entertaining District Attorney Buron Fitts and a lot of friends. Then I got in. He had a high fever and was asleep. A nurse was with him. She didn't want him disturbed. 'Why don't you call Dr. Shuman?' she said. I said, 'Whatever you say, I just wanted to see him,' and got in my car and drove home.

"There were two more convulsions, all in about a year's time. After the second one, Dr. Shuman said to me, 'Ma, I think there's more to these fits than the head injury. I don't buy *all* of this new psychology, but these convulsions look like a frenzy of grief. I think I know enough to know grief when I see it.'"

Now it was 1933. Natalie had moved out after a quarrel. A week later, when she returned, Buster handed her some keys. He had bought a hundred-foot yacht for her. Then another quarrel, and she fled again, even leaving the two boys. They were now eleven and nine. "Come on, we're going to Mexico," said their father. He chartered a plane, and they took off. They landed in San Diego to get tourist entry papers before crossing over.

The sheriff was there. "I have a wire here from MGM that you are kidnapping two children," he said.

"Kidnapping them? They're mine."

The sheriff telephoned the San Diego district attorney. Natalie, the DA said, had asked Metro to send the wire. "I'm sorry, Mr. Keaton, but I'll have to ask you to take them back," he added.

Back they went to the Villa. Natalie was not there, so they packed for camping and drove up to Lone Pine. They ate, they slept, they rode horseback in the sun. Ever since starting for Mexico, Buster had been on the wagon. He steadfastly refused to drink. The fog was clearing. Each day he would telephone from a different place. "Is Mrs. Keaton home? No?" Then finally he called and said, "Tell her we'll be back there tomorrow. If she's not there, we're going on another trip immediately."

He had withdrawn from liquor, had fought off all the cravings. He was going to talk to Natalie cold sober. He would make her see how he felt, get back to happiness. Then he could even whip MGM.

Natalie was cold, unapproachable. Recriminations began. She flung the yacht keys in his face. Keaton fled the Villa, drove to his bungalow at Metro. His only friend was there—the bottle. He pulled the cork.

The nightmare began.

"I heard knocking at the door. It was pitch-dark. I sat up. It made me so dizzy that I put my hand out to steady myself. My open hand landed on something—a naked body. The knocking went on.

"I couldn't find the light. I didn't know where I was or who the owner of that body was. Finally my hand hit a light chain. I pulled it, then I could see. I was in bed, and there was a girl beside me, naked and sound asleep.

"I bent over and looked at her. I didn't even know her. The knocking was getting louder. Then I saw where I was—in bed with some dame I didn't know, in the master stateroom on the yacht I tried to give to Natalie.

"They were hammering now. I got up and got over there someway and opened up. There were four people standing there: the L.A. district attorney, some other man, and Nat and Constance."

Divorce followed immediately. In the property settlement everything went to Natalie: the Italian Villa and its furnishings, the new yacht (which she immediately sold), all the cars, all cash on hand, and, of course, custody of the children. By court order, Keaton was to pay three hundred dollars a month to support his sons. There was no contesting suit, nor, indeed, was there any basis for one.

Buster Collier had correctly sensed the growing crisis that had led to this debacle. "If," he said many years later, "if some strong influence could have taken Buster away for a year—the desert, the mountains, a spa like Carlsbad, anywhere—with that magnificent physique he would have been a new man or, better, the old one. But no one did."

Buster Keaton himself says today, taking that long breath, "I know of no woman in the world who could have taken me from Natalie— except Natalie herself. I tell you truthfully, I may not be a strong character, but I was strong enough for that."

Shortly before she died at seventy-seven in 1955, Myra Keaton was talking about Natalie and her son. "I know my son," she said in her thin, strong little voice, "and I know that he loved Natalie Talmadge."

Then she seemed to be changing the subject. "Did I ever tell you," she asked, "about a racehorse named Buster Keaton? A breeder," she said, "down at the Tia Juana track named him after Buster. This colt looked like a world-beater—a powerful young animal with no nerves, the fastest and longest takeoff at the barrier that anyone had seen. Buster Keaton won nine of his first ten races, one of them, I am told, by what is still a track record.

"Now, he wasn't two years old yet—bones not really set—and they're handicapping him more with each race. Soon he's carrying a hundred and thirty-six pounds. The owner had a world champion in his hands and he's pushing him on local tracks!

"So the eleventh race did it. He pulled up lame and ruined. Never would race again."

"What happened to him?" someone asked.

"They did what they always do," said Myra. "Shot him."

THIRTY-FOUR

HOLLYWOOD called alcoholism "the occupational disease of the movies," as if to imply that its endemic incidence there was due to some microbe or virus peculiarly infecting the studios and lots. Hollywood probably has never dared look closer than this. Thoughts of the Barrymores and Keatons bring on a kind of localized amnesia. Almost overnight, they are forgotten. MGM historian Edward Lawrence omits even the name of Buster Keaton from his detailed eighty-eight-page survey of the studio history, a carefully researched publicity work written in 1952. This is the rule, not the exception.

And yet Keaton came to Metro-Goldwyn-Mayer an established star, and for several years he was an important and much-needed moneymaker for the company. Perhaps MGM could not overlook the fact that, with all its vast resources, it could not make Keaton pictures as good as Keaton's own and, moreover, that Keaton told them and showed them why—and then lacked the final force of character to compel them to do it his way.

Could he actually have done so? When it comes down to it, no one will ever know whether he or anyone else, in that early period of consolidation, could have won the issue of independent production within the big company setup or, for that matter, successful independent production alongside it. It would take years, government antitrust prosecution, and the slow crumbling of the movie monolith with the advent of television before even the latter course would be generally feasible. As for Keaton in the early 1930's, all that can be said is that he might—just might—have pulled it off at that time; and certainly, failing in that, he could have divorced MGM and gone on his own. He might possibly have found himself without distribution— but he never put it to the test.

But Buster Keaton is what he is. Even his breakdown came far more from his character than from a lack of character. He is complex, surely, but on the whole definable, with a sense of fate so ingrained, not only in his acting but in his life, that the real approach of fate paralyzed him. In his direst straits, his one recourse, the shining action, The Miracle, did not come. There was no Joe around—Keaton or Schenck—to make the dispensation.

Eleanor Keaton, Buster's wife since 1940, says, "Buster needs people to come and offer him things. He'd never in the world go out to make contacts; he'd rather die than seem to be pushing himself on anybody."

In the light of all this, the real magnitude of Buster Keaton's fight at MGM, as measured against his character, looms large—indeed, heroic. As to his chances of success, it needs also to be remembered that he is a comedian. Peg Talmadge's view—"You're not an actor, you're a comedian"—was the general view. In addition, he is a comedian of a special sort: the sort that is helpless (at least generally); the sort that stoically accepts fate; and, even worse than stoic, the Slow Thinker. It's a great characterization, but it stigmatized and stereotyped the man.

As Eleanor observes, "He was always playing the dope. So they tabbed him as a dope and figured they could get away with murder—gyp him, put him down, knife him. Too many times he went along rather than make a scene."

The word "scene," actually, is the key word, but in the theatrical rather than the social-etiquette sense, Buster Keaton is first, last, and always a performer. Wherever he is *is* the scene. He plays out the role, and wherever and whenever the familiar lines are assigned to him, he speaks them. His real audience is invisible. Not even he knows who or what it is. He moves in two worlds, exists in only one.

When Natalie divorced him, his reaction was one of almost total, revulsive abandon. To grief—if Dr. John Shuman's diagnosis was correct—was now added rage. The studio struggled through to finish *What, No Beer?* It proceeded haltingly. Sometimes Keaton would show up, sometimes not. For a while he was suspended by the studio, then reinstated to get the picture done.

He was like a man running in a dream. At this very time he bought a costly toy, a land cruiser, a one-of-a-kind supervehicle. He picked it up slightly used but far from cheap. It had been built by the Fifth Avenue Bus Company for the president of the Pullman Company. The land yacht was some thirty-odd feet long, driven by two magnificent twin-eight motors; it could sleep six, had two drawing rooms (one doubling as dining room), a dressing room, shower bath, toilet, kitchen, and pantry—all this aft the driver's cabin.

Buster was admiral and Cody was captain, in uniforms requisitioned from MGM wardrobe. Buster had a variety of hats, including a cocked hat of the Nelson-at-Trafalgar type. Carruthers was crew. While Sedgwick struggled with *What, No Beer?* and felt his own career slipping, half the time his star was off in the land yacht, fishing, duck hunting, visiting San Francisco, or just cruising. One evening they would park in Harold Lloyd's driveway, refuse a dinner invitation, then eat their own in the observation lounge. By next morning they would be in the mountains, on the desert, or along the seashore. Buster Keaton's Machine had become an escape mechanism.

Just as suddenly Buster would be home—he had bought a small house, where he lived alone except for Carruthers—sitting by himself, fighting to calm down and to kick the alcohol. Sometimes, through a night of agony, he would win and would appear for a good day's work. At other times—most times—he would reach at last, blindly and savagely, for the bottle and darkness. And now, too often, the darkness came after only three drinks.

And yet there were days when hope stirred. Near the completion of *What, No Beer?*, Buster took a story idea to Irving Thalberg. He was sober, shaved, and calm. MGM was just finishing the filming of Vicki Baum's best-selling novel *Grand Hotel* with an all-star cast. Keaton's idea was to do an all-star parody, to be released for its first

The land cruiser.
Left to right:
Buster Keaton,
Jimmy Durante,
Lew Cody, about 1932.

run just when *Grand Hotel* would be going into the second-run neighborhood theatres.

However he did it, in those reckless, debauched weeks, Buster had thoroughly thought out the idea. He was taking no chances of a "not enough plot" reaction. To ensure its success, he proposed to produce it and to share the directing with Sedgwick. He felt and frankly said that given this opportunity, he could hit the comeback trail and restore himself both personally and professionally.

Buster proposed to set his story in New York City's famous old Mills Hotel near the Bowery, a municipal hostelry for bums and near bums. His title, in fact, was *Grand Mills Hotel*. "I want," he said, "to play Lionel Barrymore's part: the man given only a few weeks to live and trying to see life before he dies. He's dying of consumption—I'm dying of the hiccups and have only thirty years to live. In your original, Wally Beery is a manufacturer trying to make some giant merger. I want to use Laurel and Hardy—both collar-button manufacturers, but Oliver Hardy makes only front collar buttons and Stan Laurel makes only back buttons. *They* want to merge.

"Now Marie Dressler"—Buster laughed—"will do Garbo's part. Marie will be a superannuated ballet dancer. She has the opening scene. She leaves the theatre in a huff, throws a fur coat over her costume, and comes home in a limousine. All alone, she takes off the coat and poses before a full-length cheval glass. 'The public thinks I am too old to dance. The fools!'

"Jimmy Durante will play the Count, John Barrymore's part. The love interest will be between Durante and Dressler. Here's the rest of the cast. Polly Moran in Joan Crawford's part of the hotel secretary and Henry Armetta in Jean Hersholt's role of the hotel clerk. You know that Heidelberg dueling scar that Lewis Stone has on his cheek in *Grand Hotel*? Well, in my *Grand Mills Hotel*, Edward Everett Horton has a Band-Aid—cut himself while shaving. And where the wife in your original is going to have a baby, Armetta's cat is expecting kittens in the cellar. That's *his* problem. Just as in the Grand Hotel, we all have our problems at the Mills Hotel."

It would be the kind of travesty at which Keaton was the acknowledged master, but on a scale worthy of MGM. However, it proposed that MGM laugh at itself. Thalberg listened very carefully. He did not speak until Buster was through. Then he said, "It seems a little fantastic. But I don't want to say no. Give me a few days."

Keaton looked badly disappointed.

"Look, Buster," Thalberg said, "depend upon it—I'll call you."

*   *   *

After *What, No Beer?* was shown in the studio projection room, only Sedgwick walked away with Buster. The executives hurried into one-man "conferences," preparing alibis. Thalberg, however, came over to join the star and the director. But there was little to say. After a few awkward moments they parted. Keaton sailed off, minus even Cody, in the land yacht.

He was not seen for a week. On Friday he came back. He looked awful. Sedgwick said, "L. B. Mayer has been looking for you. Better see him."

Mayer made no reference to the new film, seemed not to notice the bad shape Buster was in. He had wanted to tell him, Mayer said, that he was expected to run through a scene with Durante the following day. A teachers' convention would be visiting the lot. The custom in such cases was to do a dry run in front of unloaded cameras but to give the impression of real shooting. As Keaton well knew, this onerous duty was spread out fairly among the various stars. Greta Garbo, Mayer said, would be doing a scene too.

Buster said, "Wait, tomorrow Saturday?"

Mayer said it was.

"I can't do it," Buster said. "I promised the St. Mary's College team to sit on the bench with them as mascot."

Mayer did not take this well. He repeated his request, this time as a command.

"I won't," Buster said, and he walked out.

On Monday, Sedgwick handed him an envelope. He looked as if he were going to cry. Buster tore the envelope open and read the message: "As of this date, Buster Keaton is no longer with Metro-Goldwyn-Mayer," signed, "Louis B. Mayer."

Buster went home to the little house in Cheviot Hills that had cost less than the land yacht and that he was buying on monthly payments of a hundred and fifty dollars. "Take a couple of days off," he told Carruthers, handing him a twenty-dollar bill. Then he carefully got out all the liquor, carefully poured all the contents into the toilet bowl, carefully flushed it after each bottleful. When all were empty he carried the bottles out behind the house and smashed each one separately into the garbage can. He went back in and pulled down all the shades. He called no one, let the telephone ring, ignored the doorbell. He sat in a straight wooden chair. When he trembled, he gritted his teeth and clamped his arms rigidly along his sides. When the trembling spread to his legs, he crossed them and then caught the toe of one shoe behind the heel of the other. Then he sat, as if in an invisible straitjacket, shaking in convulsive spells, quieting, then shaking again. He bit his lips and blood ran down unheeded over his chin and stained his shirt collar.

He would doze and then awaken, sodden with sweat, and the trembling would begin all over again. He foraged for food, emptied a few cans, then munched soda crackers. The crackers gave out. Then the cigarettes gave out. And still he would not leave the house.

There was no time in the room, in the house. There was no time, for nothing happened except this endless cycle: tremble and sleep, awaken and retch, tremble again, sleep again.

Then came the squirrels—ravening, rabid squirrels where his head had been, racing around in a cage resting midway on his shoulders; horrible, gibbering little animals that bit the tails and haunches of those in front of them until he could feel their blood inside his collar.

He stood up, stamped his tingling feet, and went into the bedroom. In the dresser mirror he could see cage and all, where his head had been. He retched, went to the bathroom, but could not vomit. He stretched out on the bed in the darkened room.

Then came the ants. They crawled up onto the bed. They were fast, but he was faster. He reached out and pushed them back with the palms of his hands. They kept coming. He kept pushing them back into a pile that rolled up like a dark blanket to the edge of the bed and then over. He heard them dropping on the floor with a soft, thick sound.

There was a shadow in the room darker than the darkness. A voice—*Sedgwick?* Sudden light exploded like a silent bomb. He turned to the wall. A strong hand was pulling at him, turning him around. It *was* Sedgwick. He was talking. The voice kept thinning into silence, then bursting into a roar.

". . . and Thalberg said," the voice was saying, "have Buster see me."

Suddenly the mild Sedgwick slapped him hard and square across the face. "*Listen* to me!" he shouted. "Thalberg has squared it with Mayer. He wants you to do the *Grand Mills Hotel*."

Here it was at last, the thing he had hoped for. He was trying to speak. His swollen tongue seemed to fill his mouth. His lips were wood. There were no words. Then something boiled up in him, raging, burning, grieving, crying. "Tell the goddamned bastard to go to hell," Buster said, then leaned over and vomited.

Next morning Myra Keaton and Harry found him lying on the living-room floor with wreckage all around him—smashed chairs and lamps, broken bottles, and the reek of whiskey and vomit.

"Don't just stand there!" Myra barked. "Get the land yacht out!"

Forty minutes later they were on their way, Harry at the wheel and Buster, who had been bathed by Harry, asleep in a bunk. Harry had stocked the larder and had set the destination: Kingman, Arizona, where he had been, eight years before, when Buster was filming Go West. It was about four hundred and fifty miles away. They figured to make it there late that night. Then, Myra said, they would just stay in the clean desert air until Buster was all right.

At Barstow in midafternoon, Buster took and retained some hot chicken broth. At Needles, around half-past eight, he was sitting up in the observation lounge at the rear and managing a supper of poached eggs, toast, and tea. By the time they reached Kingman, an hour short of midnight, he had been sleeping for hours. Harry was tired, Myra was exhausted. When a parking place was found, they slept too.

Just before dawn, Myra arose. She put up water for tea, then looked into Buster's room. He was gone. She roused Harry, and they began to search the sleeping town. The all-night cafés had only a yawning customer or two. At sunup they roused the sheriff at his home. He quickly gathered deputies. By now Kingman was stirring, and the words "We're hunting Buster Keaton" brought a score of volunteers. The sheriff sent groups east and west along Highway 66, and he himself took a group, including Harry, to the Santa Fe tracks. There they split into eastbound and westbound detachments. Harry, the sheriff, and three Kingmanites went east. When they were well past the outskirts, they saw a campfire a half mile ahead.

"There's Buster," Harry said, breaking into a run. Around the fire, which had been built on the right-of-way in the lee of a gully, was a seated circle of tramps. At the center Buster Keaton was performing a slapstick pantomime, executing neck rolls and pratfalls, and even doing diving Boranis over the open fire. The tramps were laughing and applauding, and after each fall, one or another would hand a wine bottle to their entertainer.

Harry called from fifty paces away. Buster turned, saw them, scrambled up the bank, and was off down the tracks like a deer.

Slowly they were able to overtake him, and Harry brought him down with a flying tackle.

Buster was mumbling. Harry leaned over to hear. He was saying, "Jus' goin' to Muskegon . . ." Then he passed out. They carried him all the way back to Kingman.

"Not *jail!*" Myra said.

"The hospital, then," the sheriff replied. "And get him out of town by tomorrow."

THIRTY-FIVE

⌇⌇⌇⌇⌇⌇⌇⌇⌇⌇⌇⌇⌇⌇⌇⌇⌇⌇⌇⌇⌇⌇⌇⌇⌇⌇

K EATON'S rage, after being blindly directed at Thalberg, had turned inward again. But it was still working. Buster's drinking became uncontrollable, and he with it. His mother moved into the little Cheviot Hills house with her son and strove to get him straightened out.

At last the seemingly irreversible pace of his self-destruction became clear even to her. She tried to reach Dr. Shuman. He was out. Buster was becoming more violent. Finally, in despair, she picked a physician's name at random from the telephone book. The doctor came, saw the situation, but hesitated at hospitalization; at the same time, since it was acute alcoholism and not irrationality in a clinical sense, commitment was out of the question. He solved the problem by calling in a practical nurse who, he said, was trained in such cases. She would be on the case in residence, not on a shift but to watch him round the clock.

The nurse arrived and took charge. Myra, worn out, returned to her own home. When she telephoned next day, Buster had signally improved, the nurse said. But when she drove out that evening to see her son the house was dark and deserted.

He had gone off the deep end again. While his nurse was napping, he had slipped out of the house and across the way to the bar of the Cheviot Hills Country Club. When he reeled home, the nurse wasted no time. Drawing on her experience, she bundled her patient, now unconscious, into an ambulance and off to one of the so-called quick-cure sanitariums with which southern California abounds. Then or later, she told no one—not even Myra or the doctor who had called her—where Buster was.

Thus began a brand-new nightmare, an almost incredible three or four weeks that have to be pieced together mainly out of Keaton's own intermittent memories, as recalled from his more lucid, sober moments.

It is certain that he was in and out of three or four of these shady institutions and that part of the time he was kept full of whiskey dosed with emetine $(C_{29}H_{40}N_2O_4)$, the active ingredient of ipecac, so that he constantly shuttled from intoxication to rabid nausea, with unconsciousness between. The rest of the time, he was dazed with morphia, apparently after fits of violent rage and attempts to escape. He recalls episodes of rough handling by male attendants who were either interns or (more likely) nurses.

It is certain too that during this phantasmagoria, he entered into civil marriage with the nurse who had come on the case as the result of Myra Keaton's telephone call to a strange doctor. Keaton has never been able to recall the ceremony, but it did take place.

It is certain too that after an interim of unconsciousness following the civil marriage, he awoke on an airplane bound with his bride for Mexico City. There he recalls meeting the nation's president "on a balcony somewhere, probably a hotel," although it may well have been the presidential palace. Proof of this visit was a black, silver-encrusted charro jacket that the president had presented him.

And certain it is too that upon returning to the United States, he went back—or, rather, was taken back—to the sanitarium circuit. Then he himself broke out of the whole hideous entrapment. Once again, as so often in the past, an older man helped him, although *in absentia*—in fact, from beyond the grave.

Keaton came back to consciousness and found himself in bed in the dark, his arms crossed and pinioned inside a straitjacket. It was here that his godfather, Harry Houdini, dead since 1926, came to his rescue. It was in 1903 that Houdini had taught the eight-year-old Kid of vaudeville his own escape method. Sworn to keep mum, Buster had never revealed the secret. Now, at this juncture, it got him out of restraint. Having freed himself, he discovered that he was locked in on the fourth floor of another sanitarium. From there on—down the outside drainpipe to the grounds, over a wall, and out—it was not Houdini but what was left of Keaton's own acrobatism that carried him through.

Then, that same incredible, black, rainy night, in a hospital nightgown on a public street, he hailed a taxi, the driver recognized him, and was persuaded to take him home.

The door was unlocked. His nurse-wife looked up when he walked in, laid her newspaper down, and casually said hello.

He needed reminding again that he was married. "Yes, honey," she said. "It was two weeks ago in Ventura." She produced the certificate. She volunteered other information. "Your ex-wife," she said, "has had your sons' name changed from Keaton to Talmadge. It's here in this paper."

While Buster, still in nightgown, was digesting this, she went on, "And tomorrow, honey, we're driving to Florida."

All the information was true. He was married to his nurse, whom we might as well call Susie, although that is not her name. Natalie had had the boys' surname legally changed. And he and Susie *were* going to Florida, Buster decided immediately, because he had been offered a new picture. Lou Lipton, an MGM writer, had arranged for his friend Buster to star in an independent production to be directed by Marshall "Mickey" Neilan.

The fantasy had not lessened, but it was less grim than it had been in recent weeks. It was evidently the right kind of fantasy: Keaton went right on the wagon and stayed on, and the grief and rage seemed to evaporate. Here was work, and work was where he lived. This was something to put your teeth into: an independent production with a major director and money—here was a check for six thousand dollars, two weeks' salary in advance.

Harry would drive. With no more ado they were off, St. Petersburg-bound. Florida had launched a promotion to bring movie making to the Sunshine State. St. Petersburg was to be the East Coast Hollywood. A Floridian angel's cash was bankrolling the Neilan picture.

They arrived. Neilan and company were there, ready. They went on location. The mosquitoes went too—in force. Over and above the pernicious personnel-biting was their settling on the camera lenses. Take after take was being ruined. Spray equipment was brought in. There was armistice while the mosquitoes were calling up reinforcements. Then came excessive heat, and the emulsion on the film began melting. The cameras were packed in ice. What proved to be the biggest problem, however, was the total lack of facilities—costumes, props, settings, and, worst of all, extras and bit players. There were long delays as the company waited for actors and matériel to come down from New York. The production dragged on into the tenth week. Exasperation and frustration became acute.

Though he had already drawn thirty thousand dollars, Buster was the unhappiest of the lot. His acute needs—money and a revived career—could not match his chronic need—to make good pictures. His intrinsic honesty, sometimes his ally, was here his foe. He saw another bad picture coming up. He brooded, then finally went to their Florida backer and convinced him to pull out. It averted a bad film. It also alienated everyone on the project.

"Why," Keaton asked himself afterward, "why could I be such a good salesman *then*?"

However, he had seen that opportunity could still come. He went back to California sober. And he remained sober even while financial troubles piled up. The breakup with Natalie had left him with an unpaid current income tax of nearly thirty-five thousand dollars. Also, the sanitariums were threatening to sue. He paid them. Then suddenly he had a new, current liability, a beauty shop on Hollywood Boulevard opened by Susie and called the Buster Keaton Beauty Parlor. Finally, she consented to put a "Mrs." at the front.

Buster held off the Treasury Department with five thousand dollars. Then Natalie's attorneys began pressing for thirty-five hundred dollars in arrears on the support payments for the boys. There was no money coming in. After the MGM fiasco, not a studio in Hollywood would touch Buster. His opportunity for a breakthrough had been Florida.

Then, out of the blue, came an offer from Pathé in Paris. By now there was not even money for train and steamer tickets. Buster remembered some World War I Liberty bonds in a safe-deposit box. Having been forgotten, they had escaped being scooped up in the property settlement. On the four hundred dollars they realized, he and Susie started to Europe by freighter to Scotland. He had been powerless to keep her at home. They were three weeks at sea. At Glasgow, the purser brought Keaton a cablegram. It was payable for a thousand dollars and carried the message "Good luck, Buster." It was signed "Joe Schenck."

It was late autumn, 1934. The filming of the Pathé picture took them over into early 1935. Buster was paid fifteen thousand dollars for starring in this comedy, called *Le Roi des Champs-Elysées*, alliteratively rendered into the multilingual pun *The Champ of the Champs-Elysées*. Language difficulties, strange surroundings, different film methods, and a weak story added up to a poor picture. But Keaton, harried, had made a truce with conscience. It was sink or swim, not with an Alger guarantee, but plain sink or swim. To curtail Susie's shopping he greatly misrepresented his salary and instructed Pathé to send the balance to his Hollywood account. Producer Sam Spiegel, meanwhile, had cabled from London. He wanted Buster to star in a film to be called *An Old Spanish Custom*. This little lemon paid Keaton only a small drawing account—his large percentage never materialized.

Back home, before the money could disappear, Buster paid Uncle Sam twelve thousand dollars more, reducing the tax bill to eighteen thousand dollars. He was lucky enough to sell the land yacht to the Union Oil Company as an executive plaything. Then he set about regaining his single status. This proved surprisingly easy and inexpensive. Susie had found Buster Keaton to be no gold mine—and with rather dim prospects of becoming one.

Now Hollywood began to open just a crack. That fall, shelving his habitual reluctance, Keaton went to Earle Hammons, head of Educational Comedies. He wanted work and was still, in the scriptural term, agreeing with his adversary, being still in the way with him. Educational Comedies, known in the trade as "cheaters," were two-reelers shot in three days at an average cost of twenty thousand dollars.

"Yes," said Hammons, and Buster went right to work with alternate directors Charles Lamont and Raymond Kane. As star, Keaton was paid one-fourth of the budget. Sorely as he needed immediate cash, he took the longer view: to take a step back to major-picture work. He became Hollywood's grimmest teetotaler. He concentrated furiously, trying to cheat the cheating, calling upon every resource of skill and experience to do as well as possible the old-time six weeks' work in three days and at a fraction of the old-time cost. Keaton's Educationals are at least good. One or two are almost fine. Out of the eight he made over a period running into 1937, the one called *Grand Slam Opera* comes close to hitting the mark. It uses George M. Cohan's "So Long, Mary" as musical theme, with parody verses and titles ("So Long, Elmer") by Keaton. Rather than exceed the budget to get the rights to the Cohan song, the star himself paid the needed three hundred dollars from his own pocket.

He was free of marital entanglements. He had paid off the last of the tax arrears. While broke, busted, and washed up (by Hollywood standards), he had made and paid thirty-five thousand dollars. He seemed drained of energy, and no doubt was. He was bone tired, but there was no time for a vacation, not even a Lone Pine weekend. He had conquered alcohol. Now, at least, he could take one drink, relax, and go to sleep. He had learned at last when to stop. . . .

Myra Keaton was at Buster's house. Poor woman, now nearing sixty, she once again was facing grim emergency. She succeeded in getting Dr. Shuman on the telephone. She wanted Shuman back as doctor for her son, and she wanted him now.

Over the years, from the early Italian Villa days, Jack Shuman had been both physician and friend to Buster. For most of that time he had

Buster Keaton with Educational Comedies staff, about 1936.

not been seriously needed in the professional capacity. But until more recently, when another doctor (with Susie in his wake) had taken over, Shuman had done the necessary. He had cured Buster of the "barber's itch" contracted in the MGM pool. And it was Shuman who (at L. B. Mayer's request) had certified Keaton as "Aryan and uncircumcised" to get the Nazi permit for his films to enter Germany.

Myra was repeating her periodic plea to Shuman to take care of her son.

"I told you, Ma," Shuman said patiently, "that I won't come until Buster asks for me himself."

"He did," Myra said, "while he still could talk."

"Why can't he talk?"

"He's choking to death on his own blood."

Shuman came to the house immediately. Buster must have had a severe fall. Myra did not know how. Apparently it had happened just before she dropped by. She had found him lying on the floor, his tongue nearly bitten in two and his forehead laid open in a long gash. Shuman asked no questions. He worked swiftly, first injecting a sedative, then repairing the damage. This done, he hoisted Keaton to his shoulder (Shuman was more than six feet tall). "Hold his head up, Ma," he said. "He's going in the back seat of my car. Come on, I'm taking him to Sawtelle."

Sawtelle, so called, is the U.S. Veterans General Hospital (formerly Wadsworth General) in West Los Angeles on Sawtelle Boulevard. Arriving there, Shuman, a retired lieutenant colonel, spoke with authority. "Cut the red tape," he said. "This is Sergeant Joseph

Frank Keaton. Forget the Buster business. To you he's a vet. Put him in a closed ward under a detention sheet."

"Is he nuts?"

"As sane as you are, goddamn it, but when he drinks he can be violent. He's strong, I'm telling you. Handle him, but don't man-handle him. I'm warning you on both counts."

Keaton's recuperative powers still verged on the miraculous. With-in two days he was up and had the run of the hospital.

Shuman ordered exhaustive tests. "Don't worry, Bus," he said. "Uncle Sam is paying for this."

The examinations revealed nothing of consequence in Keaton's current condition—he was fundamentally sound physically and men-tally. Only one thing showed up. "When did you break your neck?" a technician asked, showing him an X ray that revealed cracked vertebrae.

Buster decided that it must have happened years before during the filming of *Sherlock Jr.* An accident occurred in a scene that called for Buster to be swept off the roof of a freight caboose by the spout of a water tank. By Buster's instructions, Gabouri concealed a rope in the stream of water issuing from the spout. Buster was to grab the rope and slide down to the track when the train had moved on. His hands slipped on the wet rope and he crashed to the track, falling backward as he landed, his neck hitting a rail. He recalled details of the mishap—fainting and being brought to by cold water, blinding headaches for weeks afterward.

After five days Shuman allowed the Keatons to visit Buster. He tried, however, to keep Susie away. Nevertheless, she got as far as the hospital steps and talked Myra into posing for a press photo with her. Myra left, and Susie gave out an interview. The resulting headline read:

MOTHER-IN-LAW WAS CAUSE OF IT ALL

Shuman saw the article and the picture and exploded. "For Christ's sake, Ma," he said, "why did you let her fake that scene and kiss you?"

"What should I have done?" Myra asked. "Slug her?"

"Natch," said Shuman.

After a stay of eleven days, Buster Keaton was released. He took a taxi home. Then, instead of going in, he first walked across the street to the Cheviot Hills Country Club, up to the clubhouse, and into the bar.

"Two double Manhattans," he said. "I'm swearing off." He drank them and went to his house. It was stripped. He whistled for Elmer. Even the big St. Bernard was gone. He sat down and laughed: it was all in the old Keaton script.

Buster Keaton did not touch a drop of liquor for six full years.

Next day he went back to Educational to make some more cheaters. He climbed up out of yesterday's sodden despair like a younger Keaton, so long ago, climbing up the paddle wheel in that old three-reeler called *Daydreams*.

And he kept climbing. As his own faith in Buster Keaton returned, others began to have faith. He made several shorts with stories by Clyde Bruckman, among them, *Mooching Through Georgia, Pest from the West,* and *Nothing But Pleasure.*

Before this, however, he had got a personal agent and had even returned, after a fashion, to Metro-Goldwyn-Mayer. His agent was an old friend, theatrical agent Leo Morrison. As early as 1936, Morrison began working on Keaton's professional rehabilitation. That year, with Thalberg's help, Morrison negotiated in Buster's behalf with MGM. Then, suddenly and prematurely, Irving Thalberg died. An old, forgiving friend was gone. Even so, Leo Morrison got his client in as writer and part-time director, starting at one hundred dollars a week, occasionally reaching three hundred and fifty dollars. Employment was intermittent—sometimes for a year or more, sometimes for a few weeks—from his initial employment in June, 1937, to his last, which terminated in September, 1950.

Throughout Buster Keaton's long, shifting battle with fate, or with himself, Morrison was patient. He was by way of making a crusade out of this man and artist. He sat out the ups and downs of Keaton's own behavior. Morrison perhaps realized the kind of personal treadmill his client was on: fleeing or fighting reality and then facing it, dragged under by whiskey and despair, then painfully climbing back up the slippery, whirling rungs to hope.

So at last the prodigal was back. And what did it mean? By now, he and Morrison were fighting not Hollywood but its myths. It had been almost ten years since his last great film, *The Cameraman*— ten times ten in Hollywood. He was too old, they said—as if *they* could ever grasp the timelessness of the art, if not the man. And even the man was Keaton, "whom only God will finally defeat," as Leo Morrison once said. But the thought of Keaton would interrupt Hollywood's long erotic dream of youth, a romantic fantasy that was the most unreal of all. When Buster Keaton *had* been young and (as James Agee wrote) beautiful, his comedy had almost mercilessly destroyed the romantic. But there was time again: now his deep-lined face alone could destroy romance.

Now Hollywood needed its own myth as much as Keaton had thought he needed whiskey. Hollywood too was beginning to grow old and tired. Its long day alone in the sun was all but over.

Though supposedly Buster was forever banned, it was said, from acting for MGM, Morrison got him bit parts and minor roles in a number of important films. The first one came in Twentieth Century-Fox's long extravaganza of 1939, *Hollywood Cavalcade*. They let him throw a custard pie at Alice Faye. It was an arching throw of sheer artistry by the one older comedian who had hardly ever thrown a pie. Mack Sennett was in that *Cavalcade* sequence too. So one legend was perpetuated and another one was born: that Keaton was a survivor of slapstick's real swaddling days and, further, that he had worked for Sennett. Neither is true.

Morrison worked. There is no question of that. He got Buster a chance with Columbia Pictures that resulted in ten shorts over the period 1939 to 1941. Keaton was paid twenty-five hundred dollars a picture, one-half the amount that Educational had paid, and the Columbias are not half so good. They are cheaters in the full sense and are a contributing factor in the lack of appreciation of Buster Keaton's true artistic stature. For up to the present, they and the Educationals (plus a host of specially made commercials) have constituted the most of Keaton films to be seen on television.

In those hard and troubled years from 1937 to 1939, at least Buster Keaton's hunger for creative work was being in part allayed. Whatever their depth or scope, their length or cost, their shaping by his or other hands, films were at least being made. But he still lived alone in the little Cheviot Hills house. Much of his time there was more like the solitude and silence of a widower than the life of a bachelor. Card playing filled the empty hours—solitaire and elaborate games that Keaton himself devised. At other times, visitors came to play bridge, now at modest stakes—and with no career even conceivably hanging on the winning or on the losing.

THIRTY-SIX

E LEANOR NORRIS met Buster Keaton in 1938, when she was nineteen. She was blonde and willowy, blue-eyed and exceedingly pretty, a native of Hollywood and on the make, not to get into the movies (she was already in them), not to get a boyfriend (she already had one), not to meet Keaton (she hardly knew who he was), but to learn to play bridge. Eleanor was taken to the Cheviot Hills house by a dancing partner, Art Whitney, who was also a friend of Harry Keaton.

To Eleanor Norris, Buster Keaton was only a name. She had never seen him on the screen. The name actually signified to her, mainly, certain goings-on she had heard about at five years of age. Eleanor had gone to a kindergarten that ran through from Vine to Lillian Way, where the Keaton Studio was first located. She could dimly remember hearing noisy shouts and laughter that seemed to indicate that there was a lot of fun going on over there, behind a bungalow, and wishing she were there.

Only five years later, when she was ten, Eleanor's father, who was an electrician at Warner Brothers, was accidentally electrocuted at the studio. Ironically, it happened, not at work but in putting up lights on the day before Christmas for the studio festivities. However, a studio pension was forthcoming, and for some years Eleanor, her mother, and her younger sister June lived on the hundred dollars it brought in every month. Eleanor was even able to study dancing, such were the wonders of the Depression dollar. Before she was fifteen, she was one of the Albertina Rasch dancers, dancing in the movies, doing bit parts, and supporting herself.

When she decided she wanted to learn to play bridge and mentioned it to her boyfriend, he promptly said, "Come to Buster Keaton's. You'll learn more in ten minutes than I can teach you the rest of my life."

Eleanor Norris' first glimpse of Buster was a shock. She had thought he was a funny man—instead, he looked old and sad and forbidding.

But she quickly found out that he was kind. He and Myra beat Art and her badly, but he was extraordinarily gentle and patient, and he explained everything slowly and in the simplest terms.

She kept going there. Soon she was going by herself. Then Buster was teaching her baseball. "Before long," as Norman Kerry discovered, "she could heave a ball you couldn't hold onto." After almost a year, Eleanor said with a sort of tentative firmness, "What's the law against our having a date?"

None, it seemed. They went to the wrestling matches. The bachelor thought the pretty little blonde seemed vaguely dissatisfied.

"All right," he said, "get gussied up tomorrow night, because we're going to Earl Carroll's *Vanities*."

The old, sad, forbidding man, she thought, looked exceedingly handsome and distinguished in tux and black tie.

It was a year and a half later when Eleanor Norris finally said, "What's the law against our getting—"

"—married," Buster said, and thus saved her face. With no more ado they were married and drove away in his station wagon. As to where, Eleanor had not the faintest idea. It was dark, and she was

Eleanor Norris Keaton.

asleep, curled up in the seat, long before they got there. The sun, coming level through the windshield, awakened her. Buster was not in the car. Then she saw him, shading his eyes with a hand, scanning the far horizons. All around them were the trackless desert, Joshua trees, and the pallid ghost bushes. There was not a road in sight.

"Where are we?" she called.

"Lost," he said.

Then he was back in the car, laughing and hugging her. "Twenty minutes from the best breakfast you ever ate," he said. "Then we're going fishing in the mountains. Did I scare you?"

"No," said Eleanor. "I was kind of glad."

Ten days of fishing and campfire meals and mountain air, and then they were home in Cheviot Hills. At that moment Buster had no work, but there were savings. Myra had seen to that, managing to put away a few thousand dollars out of the eighty thousand dollars her son had made at Educational. Buster now made one of his retreats into his private world—only partially shared by Eleanor, although they were very happy—and was building a so-called Bourbon Railway in the den. This was constructed in the main out of Erector-set parts. There was a small flatcar that carried a two-ounce tin bucket suspended like a Ferris-wheel seat in order always to remain upright. At the push of a button, the car started along a track laid across the library table, then went toward an endless chain that moved straight up the wall. The car hooked on, and the chain carried it, roller-coaster style, up to and on the plate rack that was part of the woodwork of the room. The car proceeded along the plate rack to a miniature oak keg and stopped. A little pump drew out bourbon and filled the bucket. The car then made the return journey, running backward along the rack, down the wall, and back to its starting point. A music box under the car started up, playing "How Dry I Am," and Buster would say, "Lunch is being served in the diner."

The Bourbon Railway was for the exclusive use of Myra when she came visiting or to stay a spell. A single neat shot with an accompanying cigarette, morning and night, had been her ritual since the medicine-show days fifty years before. She would take the "makings" from her purse, roll and light her homemade Bull Durham cigarette, then push the button and have her shot. "The railway runs only for you," Buster had said, and he himself never even pushed the button.

Soon he was back at Columbia for more shorts, with Bruckman continuing to write most of the stories and the direction usually by Jules White. During 1940, there were five films, three for Columbia and two for RKO, including a *Li'l Abner* (by arrangement with Al Capp). The following year Keaton made an additional four at Columbia.

In the eight years after the MGM debacle—with all the drinking and all the cures, the despair and the hope, the grave physical accidents and the hospitalization, not to mention what Keaton himself calls "my marriage of inconvenience"—he had managed to appear in some thirty-two pictures here and abroad and to make a guest appearance in *Hollywood Cavalcade*.

Now, in addition, he was happy, in a new marriage that would last. Their first-anniversary summer, Buster and Eleanor went east for stock work. They drove back, making a detour to see Lake Muskegon and to "taste Bullhead Pasco's fried perch." Bullhead was still alive, the perch as good as ever. The actors' colony, however, was only a memory, along with so many who had summered there. The dunes seemed haunted by Ed Gray, Big Joe, and Beanie, the hermit. For several days following their stop there, Buster was silent and indrawn. Then his summer-theatre tour began, with a play called *The Gorilla*, filling out the season.

Back in California, Buster quite suddenly went off the deep end again. Driving home, he had become depressed again. Suddenly he was violently, ravingly drunk. Eleanor all but went into shock. She had never seen Buster at any time take a drink. She telephoned Myra. Myra, Harry, and Dr. Shuman bundled him off to a hospital. In a week he was home. For eight more years he did not drink. But it had brought Eleanor Keaton up short. She examined their marriage. If she could judge human happiness, she had brought it to this man. But there were depths of sadness in this sad-looking man, Eleanor realized, that love would never be able to reach again. But she loved him.

At the time of Pearl Harbor, Keaton was again at MGM. The MGM employment was a peculiar thing. Most of the time he would be called and then would have to sit around without an assignment. One of his fellow writers, Lewis Jacobs, who has since become a producer of educational films, remembers Buster as "a sad and lonely figure stuck in a writer's cell. He had a ukulele and sat strumming and singing all day long—one sad little song, over and over: 'If you're through, say you're through.' " This was from the Turk and Ahlert song "You Never Did That Before," from the last really good comedy Keaton had made, *Doughboys*, on that same lot a dozen years before.

Something about the whole Keaton thing appalled Jacobs. "It

seemed to me," he said recently, "that they were buying off their own consciences—at a hundred bucks a week. He was one of the skeletons in the MGM closet. The older writers said that Buster Keaton saved Metro in the critical days. Made millions for them.

"Metro," Jacobs continued, "sold glamour, a streetwalker in lingerie made out of hundred-dollar bills. No crueler industry exists, and no company crueler than Metro-Goldwyn-Mayer. No feeling for art, no feeling for artists, no feeling even for people as such. The moment they stop earning money—and the experts see to *that*—out they go. You watch it and still can't believe it. Buster Keaton is a genius—and MGM can't use him! The older and sadder he got, the more touching and compelling became the clown. That's what you call aborting art. Take Clark Gable. They let his contract run out—'Clark's getting old'—and then no one—not even the guards at the gate—said good-bye. Thank God, Gable went on to show them up. But not Greta Garbo. They ended her career."

The Garbo incident to which Jacobs is referring took place in 1941. John Bainbridge, writing in *Life* in 1955, told how the "Metro executives . . . decided that Garbo must be transformed into a fun-loving American glamour girl. The picture selected for . . . this new incarnation was called *Two-Faced Woman*. It was . . . her last." The Garbo who had played Camille was now displayed in a bathing suit, even in the "flimsy finery" of intimate lingerie. MGM succeeded on two separate counts: the picture was banned (pending a purifying) by the League of Decency, and a great actress gave up acting forever. "They've dug my grave," Bainbridge quoted her as having said to a friend. Nor was the Bainbridge-*Life* point of view necessarily a retrospective judgment. *Time* had reviewed *Two-Faced Woman* at the time of release and flayed MGM for "a trick played on a beautiful, shy, profoundly feminine actress—Sarah Bernhardt swatted with a bladder."

Becoming restless in his paid idleness at MGM, Buster Keaton began hanging around with another pair of "has-beens on salary," Edward Sedgwick and Lucille Ball. The brass had decided that Sedgwick was "incurably old-fashioned" and Lucille "washed up." The discarded trio began meeting in Sedgwick's office and building fantastic machines dreamed up by Keaton.

Lewis Jacobs has called these inventions "whole logical continuities of mad activity. The engineers from Consolidated Aircraft actually came over to MGM to see them. They called them 'mechanical wizardry.' *Popular Mechanics* ran articles about them."

There were three machines all told: the Cigarette Lighter, the Nutcracker, and the Venetian Blind Raiser. The Lighter was two feet high. An elevator carried a steel ball up a tower, the ball spiraled down a track and set off a lighter shaped like a cannon. As the lighter flamed, an American flag went up on a mast at the top of the tower and a concealed cap pistol went off. A box of safety matches had already been pushed out for use "just in case."

The Nutcracker was larger and more complex, filling half the office. A three-foot crane supplied one walnut at a time, and a pile driver cracked it. But woven through, before, and after these two essential performances was a bewildering maze of utterly useless mechanical happenings. While it operated, more spectators stood silent than laughed. It raised the operation of machinery (long before the Neo-Dada of a Jean Tinguely) to the level of abstract art, investing it with a kind of bitter poetry. It is a pity that no one seems to have asked Keaton what the walnut cracker really signified to him. He might not or perhaps could not have answered, but a good case might be argued for this: the Nutcracker equaled MGM; the nut equaled Buster Keaton.

All the stars, directors, and producers came to see it. Bandleader Tommy Dorsey had a hundred-pound sack of walnuts delivered to Sedgwick's office.

Then came a machine to raise Sedgwick's blinds, another poem of movement and clearly the coda or afterword to the Nutcracker. There are a dozen accounts of its intricate operation. After a long mechanical churning by this colossus came a one-minute explosion of events: the venetian blinds flew up, a .32-caliber pistol shot off a blank cartridge, and while an Edison phonograph played John Philip Sousa's "Hail to the Chief," up from behind the sofa, on wires, shot a large picture of Louis B. Mayer. Mayer finally came to see it, and the following day witnessed its dismantlement.

As American war participation stepped up, Keaton and Sedgwick dropped their gadgetry. They conceived a sequel to *Doughboys*. Though it had been made twelve years before, they discovered that every member of the original cast was alive and living in the Los Angeles area.

"We've got it. It's perfect," said Buster. "Without any makeup, we've all aged."

They replotted the original World War I story to make everyone's reappearance in this new war plausible. They planned to use actual sequences from the original *Doughboys* as flashbacks in the opening scenes of the new film, then show that everyone was still saddled with the same old problems. "The topkick would still have trouble getting me to do an about-face without my getting marched over," Keaton said.

When they had it all set—plot, gags, and all—they went to the top brass. They got a quick answer: "You can't kid the war."

"Chaplin did it in 1918 with *Shoulder Arms*," Buster said.

"That war and this war are two different things," was the reply.

Nevertheless and notwithstanding, MGM was soon filming *Buck Privates*—full of updated episodes drawn from *Doughboys*—with Abbott and Costello, in their biggest hit, kidding the war. In a sequel they spoofed the U.S. Navy. The war ended before they reached the Marine Corps.

No one bothered to ask Keaton and Sedgwick to help. They were back in Siberia with Lucille Ball building those machines.

THIRTY-SEVEN

≈≈≈≈≈≈≈≈≈≈≈≈≈≈≈≈≈≈≈≈

BY THE 1940's it was becoming evident that the creative continuity of Buster Keaton's career had been too often ruptured. It wasn't tracking any more. The momentum was gone. It had become a kind of intermittent vaudeville of writing, supporting roles, and occasional directing. Given half a chance and half a role, he could do unforgettable things, as he did in Universal's *San Diego I Love You* (1944) or as he would do still later (1952) in Chaplin's American valedictory, *Limelight*. In the earlier film he is a bus driver who, tiring of the same old route, takes his passengers on a joyride and, through a miracle of disassociation, brings happiness and a solution of their problems to all of them, while his own remain unsolved. A writer of evident discernment wrote that part for Buster Keaton.

He shines—if only for a few minutes—with all the old brilliance in *Limelight*. During that *pas de deux* of the two masters—Chaplin fighting an implacable violin and Keaton fighting to keep the slippery sheet music on the piano without missing a note—the old mimed magic is unloosed, evoking the tribute of gusty laughter, like a wind from the past, from all who see it.

Keaton's fine early work—the shorts and features made with his own company and long since retired from projection—loomed as the most feasible means of restoring the artist's fame, stimulating new opportunities, and bringing in needed income. Their comedy was fresh; only sound would be needed, which could be dubbed in—music, sound effects, and, here and there, actual speech. Although Keaton had released all rights, some arrangement might be made. During this period before the coming of television, Leo Morrison and Buster Collier independently attempted to get these early masterpieces, which dated from 1920 to 1928, rereleased under some new arrangement. Finally, Joe Schenck gave his substantially disinterested consent, provided Keaton would finance the project. Once under way, the bulk of the profits would then go, as in the past, to Schenck and,

Scene from
San Diego I Love You, 1944.
Left to right:
Buster Keaton,
Jon Hall,
Louise Albritton.

presumably, the old stockholders, though this point was not clarified. However, it was not entirely this far from equitable arrangement that stymied the project but the unavailability on the one hand of cash and on the other of films. For the shocking fact was uncovered that the Keaton films had been destroyed, original negatives and all. They had been put in storage in 1928 and 1939. During the mid-1930's many were ruined by a failure of the cooling system in the vaults. Shortly afterward the others were deliberately destroyed, it was claimed, because of the failure of Schenck or the stockholders to pay the storage bills. Even though many might be found in foreign prints as well as in prints in private collections, the financing problem, in the upshot, proved insurmountable. All attempts to raise capital failed. The many people to whom Buster in the past had lent so much were all looking the other way. All felt that the present Keaton was through and that the public did not want the old one.

Myra's comment on this score was pointed. "You don't *need* to borrow; you only need to be *paid* back." Myra once estimated Buster's unrepaid loans to others (not including the virtual gifts to the destitute Fatty Arbuckle) as "damned close to seventy-five thousand dollars."

On through the 1940's the substance of Keaton's return to the movies had been small chores. A deceptive handyman, he did his tasks so well and so easily that even the small salaries seemed large. He didn't groan like a producer, throw tantrums like a director, or tear his hair like a writer. Being truly competent, he was virtually invisible.

At MGM's request he tried to remake some of his old films with new stars—*Free and Easy* with Lou Costello, *The Cameraman* (retitled *Watch the Birdie*) with Red Skelton. He was given full responsibility and no real authority. MGM's writers, directors, editors, and cutters "improved and modernized" his work, which is Metroese for "sabotaged and wrecked" it—in practice, at least, even if not in intent. Upon request of management, Buster tried to do gags for the Marx Brothers. Groucho would say, "Is this supposed to be funny?" and Buster could only reply, "I'm only doing what Mr. Mayer asked me to do." Then he would add, truthfully, "*You* guys don't need help."

He liked Red Skelton personally, saw his comic possibilities, and went to bat for him as if he were his own son—or an extension of himself from the disastrous past into a restored future. He went straight to Mayer. There was no Thalberg now. In the inner sanctum he surprised himself with an eloquence he had never been able to summon in his own behalf. "Let me take Skelton," he said, "and work as a small company within Metro—do our stories, our gags, our production, our directing. Use your resources but do it our way— the way I did my best pictures. I'll guarantee you hits," he said. "I won't take a cent of salary until they have proved themselves at the box office."

It was no go. As a sop, Buster got a spot of directing. He was responsible for some of the best of the Pete Smith shorts, particularly *Life in Sometown, U.S.A.*, which he also wrote, centering the idea around forgotten but unrepealed laws in statute books all over the country. "One in Kansas says, 'When two railroad trains both approach a crossing, they shall both stop and neither will proceed until the other has gone ahead,' and Los Angeles, 'It is forbidden to shoot rabbits from the rear platform of a streetcar,' and Maine, 'It is against the law for women to go to church unless accompanied by a man with a gun.'"

Keaton placed Pete Smith's dry spoken commentary against the silent acting of the characters on the screen, the pantomime-against-sound technique for which he had pleaded ten years before. It would be ten more years before his concept would be accepted by others. The Pete Smith shorts were shown with other short subjects when the new vogue for the double feature came in.

Joe Schenck had earlier tried in two instances to get directing assignments for his old protégé. He sent for him to take charge of the Ritz Brothers' first picture. "Tell Zanuck," said Schenck just as he left on one of his ceaseless trips. "Right," said Buster, then vainly sought out Zanuck. The producer was never in. Then a week later Zanuck announced that Allan Dwan would direct the picture.

Schenck, returning after the picture was done, asked whether Buster had ever seen Zanuck. "No," said Buster without amplification. Perhaps he was tired of explaining the obvious. Besides, Dwan was his friend, and Keaton's idea of friendship is not Hollywood's. Even Zanuck did not know that as a favor to Dwan, Keaton had studied the Ritz script at home, spotting weaknesses and suggesting improvements. Buster Collier's description still remains as good as any: "He was just too good a guy."

Once again, Schenck tried to help. Again on the eve of a safari, he asked Buster to direct the new Eddie Cantor picture. "I can do a lot for him," Buster said, and meant it. "I can relax him, show him how to go before a camera and not try to be funny every second. Not teach him anything new—only to act in a movie as he always did on the stage."

"See Darryl right away," said Schenck, following his suitcases out the door.

Zanuck was still out to Buster Keaton. Restaurateur Mike Romanoff, who had been around, ticked it off for Keaton. "You'll *never* see Zanuck," said Romanoff. "It's a good idea, and he didn't think of it. Schenck is only the president of Fox; Zanuck is the guy he put in complete charge, with a guarantee never to interfere with him."

Whatever Schenck's true motives may have been, the gestures, certainly, cost nothing. Equally certainly, they accomplished nothing. At home, at least, things were vastly better. The young bride was bringing some practical order to the Keaton life. Eleanor assumed the financial responsibility that Buster's mother had sporadically been allowed to exercise. Eleanor Keaton's love was real. It was also factual. Her feet were always on the ground. She and Myra hit it off from the start.

In 1942 Buster and Eleanor sold the Cheviot Hills place and moved in with Myra in the Victoria Avenue bungalow Buster had bought so many years ago. Myra was alone: Harry and Louise were working in a war plant a Las Vegas, and Myra and Joe had amicably separated. He was now living in a small Los Angeles hotel. Just two years later, a columnist wrote:

JOE AND MYRA KEATON'S
GOLDEN WEDDING DAY

Myra didn't think the children would remember it. She was working that evening as a baby-sitter, and she took clothes along, dressed afterwards, and took a bus downtown to Joe's hotel to take him to dinner. He told her the kids had called that they were preparing a dinner, so they

Eleanor and
Buster Keaton
at the Médrano.
Buster's fifty-eighth
birthday, 1953.

went back to the Victoria Avenue bungalow. To each of them Buster and
Eleanor gave two gold frames: in one a picture of Joe and Myra and in
the other Jimmy Talmadge, their first grandchild.

Two years later still, on January 10, 1946, Joe Keaton died at the
age of seventy-nine. He had recently broken a hip and had recovered,
only to be struck down by a car. Until she herself died, nine years
later, Myra loved to show the marks at the top of the frame of the
breakfast-room door. "Joe kicked those there," she would say, "just
limbering up a bit, when he was seventy-five."

At war's end, when Louise and Jingles returned, four of the old
Five Keatons were back under the same roof. The house, with its
nine rooms all on one floor, was big enough for them all plus a troupe
of cats. Eleanor put the money from the Cheviot Hills house together
with what she had been saving from Buster's varied movie chores. By
1946 they felt ready for a house of their own. They found four acres
near Culver City. They were going to buy it for cash at ten thousand
dollars, then wait and save some more before building. Then a friend
(whom we shall call Fred Jacks) asked to be allowed to buy one-half

of the acreage. Jacks was a radio executive they had known for some time. The land, he said, was big enough for two houses. His idea gave them a way to buy enough land and to start building immediately. They agreed. "My money is tied up for the moment," said Jacks. "I'll have lots of cash in thirty days." His frankness impressed Eleanor. They made a one-half payment on the ground, with the balance due on a short-term agreement. Jacks signed all the necessary agreements to protect them.

Both houses were started. Now at last Buster would have his ranch house. He and Eleanor began planting fruit trees. Then came an offer to make a picture in Mexico City. The story, *El Moderno Barba Azul (The Modern Bluebeard)*, was acceptable, and one of Mexico's leading directors, Jaime Salvador, would be in charge. The money would be a windfall toward the ranch house. As the Keatons were ready to leave, Jacks said, "I'll have a check tomorrow and will square everything."

"Don't do that yet," Buster said. "Take care of the bills on my house as they come along, up to the amount you owe us. And keep both houses moving." Then, as an afterthought, he added, "I'm going to leave you a few thousand besides. We might be delayed down there, and we want to get this house finished. We'll settle all accounts when we get back."

By now the rest of the story—being a Keaton script—is all too plain. It is hardly necessary to read the last page: return; real estate sold at a sheriff's sale; Jacks suddenly dead of a heart attack, leaving only debts; Buster and Eleanor wiped out.

Eleanor Keaton faced that squarely. But her husband's reaction was in doubt. Would it happen again now? But Buster did not drink. Amazingly, he too took the blow well. Then an offer came: twelve weeks in the East in the play *Three Men on a Horse*. That took up the summer, and in the fall there was a cable from Paris. Malec— Le Keaton—was wanted by the Cirque Médrano, the historic indoor circus (originally the Cirque Fernando) near Place Pigalle that had been the haunt long ago of Degas and Lautrec and, a little later, Picasso. It was a place where, as Paul Gallico once wrote in *Esquire*, "you find yourself practically taking part in the performance; the clowns sit next to you . . . the trained dogs or monkeys will stop for a sniff of you if you smell interesting . . . and . . . should the beautiful aerial artist slip, you might well be able to break her fall with your own person and thus earn her undying gratitude. . . ."

The pantomime-loving Parisians know that Malec belongs with the

At the Cirque Médrano,
Paris, 1953.

Behind-the-scenes card game at the Médrano, 1953.

Buster Keaton outside the Médrano.

classic clowns—Orlando, Antonet, the Fratellinis, Groc, and the rest. So, in this fragment of an older Paris, they awaited him with pleasure. There came on, as Gallico wrote, "a sad-faced little fellow wearing a flat, pork-pie hat, string tie, too-big clothes, and flap shoes. He was carrying a mouldy looking dress suit on a hanger, obviously looking for a cleaners. Before he had done, the suit was a wreck on the arena floor and the audience was in hysterics.

"Then a window box of flowers was produced. When he bent over to pick one he found a policeman standing next to him. The policeman became his menace for the rest of the turn."

Then Gallico traced the sad little man's troubles—the stolen balloon, his attempts to read a newspaper eight feet square, and the final chase, with cops, ushers, and attendants all taking part. Through it all "he never once spoke a word, nor ever changed the expression of his face, for his name was Buster Keaton . . . the Buster Keaton of my youth, who sixty-ish, could still fall backwards off a bench, or trip on the ring's edge and end up in a flying forward somersault. This was my dead-pan boy, hero of a hundred movies, Frustration's Mime, pursued, put-upon, persecuted by humans as well as objects suddenly possessed of a malevolent life and will of their own.

"This," Gallico said, was "what he had been and what he is."

THIRTY-EIGHT

〜〜〜〜〜〜〜〜〜〜〜〜〜〜

IT HAS continued ever since, the incomplete vaudeville of starts and stops—the unfounded hopes and half-realizations, the memories half-revived, the shuttle between past and present, here and Europe. The world will never know what to do with its living legends. More than mere anachronisms, they upset everyone—bitter rue for the old; insult, enigma, or will-o'-the-wisp for the young.

Eleanor Norris, though barely twenty-one when she married Buster Keaton, must essentially have grasped all this. It was her first marriage. With all her admirers, she married a man of forty-five who, if anything, looked nearer sixty. No one, in 1940, was marrying Keaton for his money (he had none) or for his prospects (he seemed to have none) or for his fame (that had already withered). Eleanor Norris Keaton proceeded immediately to go through hard times with her husband, hard times that soon amounted to near disaster. She weathered them out; she has seen Buster Keaton through a long period of painful adjustment, relapse, and readjustment and a dozen partial comebacks. She has carried him, content and at times happy, across the threshold of his seventies. She has lived with that most difficult and tragic of human beings, the exiled and estranged artist. Through it all she has retained both love and admiration for him.

Eleanor Keaton says, "I don't understand Buster Keaton. No one ever will—even Buster himself." Yet she gives evidence of understanding him, or his needs, better than Hollywood ever has. She has a sense of fate equal to but quite unlike his. Eleanor Keaton's fate is not cruel, senseless, or arbitrary, nor is it benign, paternal, and forgiving—it is simply just. She believes in justice and is content to wait for it, believes that "truth crushed to earth will rise again."

When Eleanor married Buster Keaton she had to look past a ravaged crag of a face and through dark, brooding eyes in order to find the man, the unerodable core, hidden behind his wall. Finding at the end that he could not live in both the theatre world and the real world—or even understand the latter—he had retreated into the

Portrait of
the artist
as an old man.

Keaton and Chaplin. Scene from *Limelight*, 1952.

CC-8
P-456

former or, at least, into his memories of it. He was a marooned Martian, but he was determined to survive.

When they married, Buster had been in Hollywood for twenty-three years, longer than his young wife had been in the world. After three years he had had his own film company; and a whole decade, 1920 to 1930, had been a brilliant time when he wrote, directed, and starred in more than a score of motion pictures, both short and long, that can fairly be called masterpieces.

His technical and artistic innovations have enriched the cinema. His native genius for physical action no one else, not even Fairbanks, has ever approached. His pantomime places him with Chaplin alone. The depth, irony, and mordant vision of his comedy are all but unique. It bids fair to be timeless. Even Chaplin had a dozen imitators, but Keaton's characterization was so wholly his own that no one ever tried to copy it. His was the only unsmiling mask. The term "genius" fits Buster Keaton as it fits Charles Chaplin, with no seams to take in. There are not many geniuses anywhere, not even in Hollywood. Opportunity, money, equipment cannot make one, but in Hollywood their lack can blight one.

Buster Keaton was (and has always continued to be) master of the great illusion of light and shadow, the magic myth that either lies or tells the truth. His mastery was not taken away, only his means.

His latter years have been phenomenally, even if not always significantly, busy. Activity and, more recently, unwonted financial rewards have masked the essential creative emptiness. They have been years, notwithstanding, that have brought certain fulfillments, even finishing a piece or two of unfinished business—for example, bringing at last the longed-for ranch. He has had a profusion of bit and supporting parts. To name a few, he has had comic or straight roles in *Forever and a Day* (1943), *That Night with You* and *That's the Spirit* (1945), *God's Country* (1946), *Un Duel à Mort* (1948), *You're My Everything* (1949), *Sunset Boulevard* (1950), Mike Todd's *Around the World in Eighty Days* (1956), *The Adventures of Huckleberry Finn* (1960), and *It's a Mad, Mad, Mad, Mad World* (1963).

He has made a few movies on his own under unexpected non-Hollywood auspices. One was a hilarious solo performance on an imaginary farm done for a salesmen's convention of the John Deere Plow Company. Another, done in 1955 with Zasu Pitts for television use on NBC's *Screen Directors' Playhouse*, was a virtuoso re-creation of pristine slapstick, acrobatics and all. More recently (1965) he did

Scene from *Sunset Boulevard*, 1950. Left to right: Anna Q. Nilsson, Gloria Swanson, Buster Keaton, William Holden, Erich von Stroheim, H. B. Warner.

a solo opus for the National Film Board of Canada, a two-and-a-half-reel color short called *The Railrodder*. It traces the web of mischance to be expected with Buster alone on a sidecar along the endless tracks of the Canadian National Railway. The magic is still there, as it would beyond doubt be even if Buster should be filmed in a spaceship. With all the machines, Buster Keaton—that is to say, man —survives.

The National Film Board, perhaps more conscious of values than Hollywood is, also did a biographical film profile, with interviews, entitled *Keaton Rides Again* (1965).

Hollywood, however, tried. In 1957, Paramount did *The Buster Keaton Story*, with Rhonda Fleming, Ann Blyth, Peter Lorre, and, starring as Keaton, the young comedian Donald O'Connor. Despite on-the-set coaching by Keaton himself, O'Connor could not become Keaton. No one ever has. And the story was not Keaton at all but a bit of protective Hollywood hokum.

The Buster Keaton Story did, however, buy the Buster Keaton Ranch. It is only an acre and a half in the San Fernando Valley, where he had wanted to settle so long ago, but it is not measured by Keaton in acreage. Measured by his hopes, it is large indeed. William Butler Yeats had "nine bean rows" on his lake isle of Innisfree; Keaton has nine walnut trees, a new St. Bernard (Elmer III), and a one-man tractor.

Television's *This Is Your Life* gave Buster the tractor as a gift when he came as guest and subject of the program, to see again the people who had been important in his life. It came a little late. Mother and father (two members of the Three Keatons) were gone. So too was the first movie partner, Roscoe Arbuckle, who had died in that disastrous year for them both, 1933, to be displayed, with no one caring, in the same New York funeral parlor where Valentino had been laid out. The first wife, and first love, could not be invited, nor could the two sons of that union—they were no longer even Keatons in the eyes of the law. That old crew "who ate and slept comedy," Gabouri, Havez, Sedgwick, and Bruckman, were all gone. The most tragic end of all was Bruckman's. "The former movie director and writer," the newspapers said, "borrowed a pistol from comedian Buster Keaton and killed himself in a restaurant restroom." Clyde had asked to borrow the gun, so he had said, for a little target practice. His last words, on a neatly typewritten note were: "I have no money to pay for a funeral."

So Keaton came and was greeted by peripheral people (Red Skelton and Louise Dresser) and one former cohort, Eddie Cline.

When Keaton and Eleanor moved into the ranch house, their little community gave him a further gift, electing him mayor for several terms.

Just as television made the movies move over, it has been a major outlet for Buster Keaton even though he has never had a show of his own on network. In fact, he was one of the West Coast live-television pioneers. He and Ed Wynn did more than a dozen local shows together that were very successful. Following this, Keaton did seventeen shows for the Studebaker dealers of southern California. They were talked about, even raved about in the trade journals, but the kinescope films of the live performances (this was before the coaxial cable was built or audio-video tape perfected) were too faulty for station use in the East.

When NBC announced plans to build the big television center in southern California, Buster Keaton was ready. He designed a com-

Scene from *The Railrodder*, 1965.

plete television plant and built a quarter-inch scale model. It had theatres that could shrink to small, intimate sets or expand into great stages that revolved and moved up and down hydraulically. It employed every trick of mechanics, lighting, and sound, of multiple utilization of space, and of camera manipulation that Buster Keaton had learned or, in many cases, invented. It was far more complicated than the Nutcracker—and far more serious.

Buster flew with the model to New York and showed it to the top NBC officials and the architect. They were polite (Keaton had once been a great name), but they went ahead and built the plant their own way. It had, according to Eleanor Keaton, at least one omission glaring enough to be noticed by all. "If you had to go," she said, "you could go to the gas station a block away."

From 1950 through 1964, Buster Keaton made some seventy or more guest-star appearances on television, with no fewer than five with Ed Sullivan and twelve with Garry Moore, as well as turns with many other television lights, from Rosemary Clooney and Kate Smith to Jack Webb and Jack Paar.

If television has brought Keaton no great creative opportunities, it has far more than amply provided for his financial security. His television commercials, with all the accruing residuals from replays, have made him a fortune while at the same time making his face one of the most familiar on the home screens. Few turn off the set when the Great Stone Face makes his silent plea for Colgate, Alka-Seltzer, U.S. Steel, 7 Up, RCA Victor, Phillips 66, Milky Way, Ford Motors, Minute Rub, Budweiser—you name it. He is a blast. He even turns on the young.

Onstage he has, over these years, enlivened the proceedings in *Merton of the Movies* and *Once Upon a Mattress,* as well as playing three months in English theatres. He has entertained the home folks at the state fairs in Michigan, Iowa, Minnesota, Kansas, Tennessee, and Alabama; brightened expense-account evenings in nightclubs in Las Vegas, Los Angeles, and Miami; twisted for the rock 'n' roll set in movies like *Pajama Party* and *Beach Blanket Bingo;* and returned

Buster Keaton and Ed Wynn re-create *The Butcher Boy* on CBS television.

The train that ran through a landscape of memory.

to the sawdust ring at Médrano and at other circuses in Brussels and Milan.

It is vaudeville—the Buster Keaton Circuit. In between these activities, he farms his ranch, plays bridge. At one time he built a miniature railroad that ran on schedule through a landscape of memory: from Perry, Oklahoma, to Lake Muskegon, and on through a town or two where vaudeville once brightened the nights, ending up at a station on the old Third Avenue Elevated in Manhattan.

The Italian Villa has gone through many hands. Natalie Keaton sold it in 1933. Fanchon and Marco lived there, Barbara Hutton, a millionaire glass manufacturer, and, during a more recent period, James and Pamela Mason. It was Mason who, in 1955, happened on the secret panel to a film-storage vault behind the private projection room of the Villa. There, untouched for twenty-two years, was a cache of films—all of Keaton's own features, from the first, *The Three Ages*, to the last, *Steamboat Bill Jr.*, plus a good number of the shorts.

All the available films have been assembled, and a business firm has been set up for Keaton by Raymond Rohauer, who had headed a film-appreciation society in southern California. Rohauer has bought films—prints or negatives—wherever he could find them, restoring them and making fresh negatives. Rohauer got *The General*, with added sound track, exhibited in central Europe, with Buster himself piloting a replica of the old locomotive (albeit on standard-gauge track) from Germany to Austria. Rohauer now is trying to untangle the complicated legal maze surrounding the pre-MGM Keaton work.

But it all now begins to assume the aspects of a race with time. It is late, late evening. Walter Kerr, the New York *Herald Tribune* drama critic, sensed it ten years ago, when he wrote what he called "a love letter, some years late." His was an article full of a vast nostalgia and an imminent apprehension of loss. "Better hurry," Kerr wrote, "a great man is slipping away from us."

Yet he is still alive, needing only one more miracle, a simple request: "Buster, make us laugh again."

For that, he will never be too old, too tired, too sad.

*   *   *

RESHOOTING THE LAST SCENE

In 1965 the Final Miracle, at long last, began. It had started in 1955, when Raymond Rohauer, then head of the Society of Cinema Arts in Los Angeles and a longtime admirer of the art of Buster Keaton, met the artist himself. And precisely that: met not a businessman but an artist, one totally unaware of even his elementary rights in his own creative work.

Appalled, Rohauer began what was at first a virtually unaided crusade to secure justice, recognition, and a new chance for the great comedian. In the ensuing decade, Rohauer began collecting and restoring prints of Keaton's own films wherever they might be found, here and in Europe. He set up a corporation for Buster and then, through all possible means—locating old contracts, purchasing rights, buying off claimants of all shades of legitimacy, using persuasion and even litigation—Rohauer began to give the corporation assets, power, and meaning. It is a full turn, indeed, of the Hollywood wheel: Keaton, the nonorganization man, is now the center of an organization framed not to exploit but to restore his rights.

Along the way others joined the effort: Leopold Friedman, formerly with Metro-Goldwyn-Mayer, and in France, a famous disciple of Keaton's art, Jacques Tati. The long single-minded effort is now near completion. The corporation now owns all of Keaton's work, beginning with *The Butcher Boy* of 1917 made with Roscoe Arbuckle, through all of Buster's own silent two-reelers and features from 1920 to 1928, on to the cream of his MGM work from 1928 to 1933, and even including all of his Educational Comedies from 1935 to 1937. Literally rescued from the edge of destruction, the art of the great deadpan boy is now being restored to public view.

It is a timely restoration, with the public tiring of stand-up, one-line comedy and sick comedians, and turning back eagerly to the visual gag and the timeless silent art of the mime. But it still is late, late evening for the mime himself. His race with time quickens. For Buster Keaton it has become the Final Chase.

* * *

HOLLYWOOD, Feb. 1, 1966—Buster Keaton died today at his home in Woodland Hills.

This is the last take of the last scene. The Chase has ended.

Story conference. *Film*, 1965. Left to right: Alan Schneider, Buster Keaton, Samuel Beckett. *Film*, only completed part of a Samuel Beckett trilogy, was made by Evergreen Theatre. A silent Keaton *pas de seul*, it was presented as an entity in October, 1965, at the Venice Film Festival. It and its star received, as the New York *Times* reported, "a five-minute standing ovation. Fighting back tears, Mr. Keaton told a correspondent: 'This is the first time I've been invited to a film festival, but I hope it won't be the last.'" But it was. Three months later, Buster Keaton was dead.

LIST OF FILMS (1917-1966)

(*Compiled by* RAYMOND ROHAUER *and* RUDI BLESH)

Arbuckle Period

(TWO-REELERS BY COMIQUE FILM CORPORATION)

1917   1. *The Butcher Boy.* Directed by Arbuckle. With Roscoe Arbuckle, Al St. John, Buster Keaton, Josephine Stevens. (New York)

1917   2. *Rough House.* Directed by Arbuckle. With Arbuckle, Keaton, St. John. (New York)

1917   3. *His Wedding Night.* Directed by Arbuckle. With Arbuckle, Keaton, St. John, Alice Lake. (New York)

1917   4. *Fatty at Coney Island.* Directed by Arbuckle. With Arbuckle, Keaton, St. John. (New York)

1917   5. *Oh, Doctor!* Directed by Arbuckle. With Arbuckle, Keaton, St. John, Lake. (New York)

1917   6. *Out West* (alternate title: *The Sheriff*). Directed by Arbuckle. With Arbuckle, Keaton, St. John, Lake. Released 1918. (California)

1918   7. *The Bell Boy.* Directed by Arbuckle. With Arbuckle, Keaton, St. John, Lake. (California)

1918   8. *Goodnight Nurse.* Directed by Arbuckle. With Arbuckle, Keaton, Lake, St. John. (California)

1918   9. *Moonshine.* Directed by Arbuckle. With Arbuckle, Keaton, Lake, St. John. (California)

1918   10. *The Cook.* Directed by Arbuckle. With Arbuckle, Keaton, Lake, St. John. (California)

1919   11. *A Desert Hero.* Directed by Arbuckle. With Arbuckle, Keaton, Lake, St. John. (California)

1919   12. *Backstage.* Directed by Arbuckle. With Arbuckle, Keaton, Lake, St. John. (California)

1919   13. *A Country Hero.* Directed by Arbuckle. With Arbuckle, Keaton, Lake, St. John. Released 1920. (California)

1919   14. *The Garage.* Directed by Arbuckle. With Arbuckle, Keaton, Lake, St. John. Released 1920. (California)

Feature Film Starring Buster Keaton

1920   15. *The Saphead.* Based on the play *The New Henrietta.* Directed by Winchell Smith. Released October. Metro Corp.

Comedies Produced by and Starring Buster Keaton
(TWO- AND THREE-REELERS)

1920   16. *The High Sign.* Written and directed by Buster Keaton and Eddie Cline. With St. John. Released March 11, 1921. Metro Corp.

1920   17. *One Week.* Written and directed by Keaton and Cline. Released September. Metro Corp.

1920   18. *Convict 13.* Written and directed by Keaton and Cline. With Joe, Myra, Louise, and Harry Keaton. Released October 4, 1920, by Metro Corp.

1920   19. *The Scarecrow.* Written and directed by Keaton and Cline. Released December. Metro release.

1920   20. *Neighbors.* Written and directed by Keaton and Cline. Released January, 1921. Metro release.

1921   21. *The Haunted House.* Written and directed by Keaton and Cline. Released February 7, 1921. Metro release.

1921   22. *Hard Luck.* Written and directed by Keaton and Cline. Released March 14, 1921. Metro release.

1921   23. *The Goat.* Written and directed by Keaton and Malcolm St. Clair. Released May 17, 1921. Metro release.

1921   24. *The Electric House* (incomplete first version, destroyed).

1921   25. *The Playhouse.* Written and directed by Keaton and Cline. Released in October, 1921. First National release.

1921   26. *The Boat.* Written and directed by Keaton and Cline.

1921   27. *The Paleface.* Written and directed by Keaton and Cline.

1922   28. *Cops.* Written and directed by Keaton and Cline.

1922   29. *My Wife's Relations.* Written and directed by Keaton and Cline.

1922   30. *The Blacksmith.* Written and directed by Keaton and St. Clair.

1922   31. *The Frozen North.* Written and directed by Keaton and Cline.

1922   32. *The Electric House* (Second and complete version). Written and directed by Keaton and Cline.

1922   33. *Daydreams* (3 reels). Written and directed by Keaton and Cline.

1922   34. *Balloonatics.* Written and directed by Keaton and Cline. With Phyllis Haver. Released 1923.

1923   35. *The Love Nest.* Directed by Buster Keaton.

Feature Comedies Produced by and Starring Buster Keaton

1923   36. *The Three Ages* (6 reels). Written by Clyde Bruckman, Joseph Mitchell, and Jean Havez. Directed by Keaton and

Cline. With Wallace Beery, Margaret Leahy. Released
August 24, 1923. Metro Pictures.

1923   37. *Our Hospitality* (7 reels). Written by Bruckman, Mitchell,
and Havez. Directed by Keaton and Jack Blystone. With
Natalie Talmadge Keaton, Joe Keaton, Joseph Keaton Talmadge, Big Joe Roberts. Released November 20, 1923.
Metro Pictures.

1924   38. *Sherlock Jr.* (4½–5 reels). Written by Bruckman, Mitchell,
and Havez. Directed by Keaton. With Ward Crane, Kathryn
McGuire, Joe Keaton. Released April 21, 1924. Metro
Pictures.

1924   39. *The Navigator* (6 reels). Written by Bruckman, Mitchell, and
Havez. Directed by Keaton and Donald Crisp. With Kath-
ryn McGuire. Released October 13, 1924. Metro-Goldwyn.

1925   40. *Seven Chances* (6 reels). Written by Bruckman, Mitchell, and
Havez. Based on a play by Roi Cooper Megrue. Directed
by Keaton. Released March 16, 1925. Metro-Goldwyn.

1925   41. *Go West* (7 reels). Story by Keaton. Screenplay by Raymond
Cannon. Directed by Keaton. With Kathleen Myers,
Howard Truesdale, Brown Eyes. Released November 1,
1925. Metro-Goldwyn.

1926   42. *Battling Butler* (7 reels). Written by Al Boasberg, Paul Gerard
Smith, Charles Smith, and Lex Neal. Directed by Keaton.
With Sally O'Neill, Snitz Edwards. Released August 30,
1926. Metro-Goldwyn-Mayer.

1926   43. *The General* (8 reels). Story by and directed by Keaton and
Bruckman. Screenplay by Boasberg and Charles Smith. With
Marian Mack, Joe Keaton. Released February, 1927. United
Artists.

1927   44. *College* (6 reels). Written by Carl Harbaugh and Bryan Foy.
Directed by James Horne. With Florence Turner. Released
August 9, 1927. United Artists.

1927   45. *Steamboat Bill Jr.* (7 reels). Written by Harbaugh. Directed
by Charles "Chuck" Reisner. With Ernest Torrence. Released May 12, 1928. United Artists.

Metro-Goldwyn-Mayer Period, 1928–1933

1928   46. *The Cameraman* (8 reels). Produced by Keaton. Story by
Bruckman and Lou Lipton. Screenplay by Richard Schayer.
Directed by Edward Sedgwick, Jr. With Marceline Day,
Harry Gribbon. Released August 15, 1928.

1929   47. *Spite Marriage* (7 reels). Story by Lou Lipton. Screenplay by
Schayer and Ernest Pagano. Directed by Sedgwick. With
Dorothy Sebastian, Leila Hyams.

1929   48. *Buster Se Marie* (French version of *Spite Marriage*). Directed by Claude Autant-Lara. With Mona Goya, Françoise Rosay, André Luguet.

1929   49. *Hollywood Review of 1929* (13 reels). Directed by Reisner. All-star cast, including Lionel Barrymore, Joan Crawford, Laurel and Hardy. (Sound picture)

1929   50. *Wir Schalten um auf Hollywood* (German version of *Hollywood Review of 1929*). Directed by Frank Reicher.

1930(?) 51. *Spite Marriage* (with added sound track, length expanded to 9 reels).

1930   52. *Free and Easy* (10 reels). Story by Paul Dickey. Screenplay by Boasberg and Schayer. Directed by Sedgwick. With Anita Page, Robert Montgomery, Lionel Barrymore, Trixie Friganza, Karl Dane, Fred Niblo. (Sound picture)

1930   53. *Estrellados* (Spanish version of *Free and Easy*). With Raquel Torres, Don Alvarado, Maria Calvo, Emile Chautard.

1930   54. *Doughboys* (8 reels). Produced by Keaton. Story by Boasberg and Sidney Lazarus. Screenplay by Schayer. Directed by Sedgwick. With Sally Eilers, Cliff Edwards, Edward Brophy, Victor Potel. (Sound picture)

1930   55. (Spanish version, title unknown, of *Doughboys*.)

1931   56. *Speak Easily* (8 reels). Screenplay by Laurence Johnson and Ralph Spence. Based on the play *Footlights* by Clarence Budington Kelland. Directed by Sedgwick. With Jimmy Durante, Ruth Selwyn, Thelma Todd, Hedda Hopper, Sidney Toler, Henry Armetta, Edward Brophy. (Sound picture)

1931   57. *Sidewalks of New York* (8 reels). Written by George Landy and Paul Gerard Smith, with dialogue by Robert E. Hopkins and Eric Hatch. Directed by Jules White and Zion Myers. With Anita Page, Cliff Edwards. Not released until 1933. (Sound picture)

1931   58. (French version, title unknown, of *Sidewalks of New York*.)

1932   59. *Parlor, Bedroom and Bath* (8 reels). Story by Charles Bell and Mark Swann. Screenplay by Schayer, with dialogue by Schayer and Hopkins. Directed by Sedgwick. With Charlotte Greenwood, Reginald Denny, Cliff Edwards, Dorothy Christie, Sally Eilers, Edward Brophy. (Sound picture)

1932   60. *Casanova wider Willen* (German version of *Parlor, Bedroom and Bath*). Directed by Brophy. With Marion Lessing, Françoise Rosay, Wolfgang Zilzer. (Sound picture)

1932   61. *The Passionate Plumber* (8 reels). Screenplay by Johnson, with dialogue by Spence. Based on the play *The Cardboard Lover* by Jacques Deval. Directed by Sedgwick. With Jimmy

Durante, Irene Purcell, Polly Moran, Gilbert Roland, Mona Maris, Henry Armetta. (Sound picture)

1932   62. *Le Plombier Amoureux* (French version of *The Passionate Plumber*). Directed by Claude Autant-Lara. With Jeanette Ferney, Douglas Fairbanks, Jr.

1933   63. *What, No Beer?* (7 reels). Story by Hopkins. Screenplay by Carey Wilson and Jack Cluett. Directed by Sedgwick. With Jimmy Durante, Phyllis Barry, Roscoe Ates, Henry Armetta, Edward Brophy. (Sound picture)

Miscellaneous Features Starring Keaton, 1934–1935

1934   64. *Le Roi des Champs-Elysées* (*The Champ of the Champs-Elysées*). Written by Arnold Lipp, with dialogue by Yves Mirande. Directed by Max Nosseck. With Paulette Dubost, Colette Darfeuil, Pierade, Lucien Gallemand, Gaston Dupray, Madeleine Guitty, Jacques Dumesnil. Nero Film production, released by Paramount. (France)

1935   65. *An Old Spanish Custom* (alternate title: *The Invaders*). Directed by Adrian Brunel. With Lupita Tovar, Esme Percy, Lyn Harding, Hilda Moreno. (England)

Educational Comedies Starring Keaton, 1934–1937

1935   66. *Allez Oop*.
1935   67. *The Gold Ghost*.
1935   68. *Palooka from Paducah*. With Joe, Myra, and Louise Keaton.
1935   69. *Tars and Stripes*.
1935   70. *Hayseed Romance*.
1935   71. *E-Flat Man*.
1935   72. *One Run Elmer*.
1936   73. *Timid Young Man*.
1936   74. *The Chemist*. Produced by Al Christie. Written by David Freeman. With Marilyn Stuart, Earl Gilbert, Don McBride. Herman Lieb.
1936   75. *Three on a Limb*. Directed by Charles Lamont.
1936   76. *Grand Slam Opera*. Written by Keaton and Lamont. Directed by Lamont.
1936   77. *Blue Blazes*. Written by Freeman. Directed by Raymond Kane.
1936   78. *Mixed Magic*. Written by Arthur Jarrett and Marcy Klauber. Directed by Kane.
1937   79. *Ditto*. Written by Paul Gerard Smith. Directed by Lamont.
1937   80. *Jail Bait*. Written by Paul Gerard Smith. Directed by Lamont.
1937   81. *Love Nest on Wheels*. Story by William Hazlett Upson. Screenplay by Paul Gerard Smith. Directed by Lamont.

Miscellaneous Films Featuring or Starring Keaton, 1939–1940

1939   82. *Hollywood Cavalcade* (10 reels). Story by Hilary Lynn and Brown Holmes. Screenplay by Ernest Pascal. Slapstick sequences directed by Malcolm St. Clair. Directed by Irving Cummings. With Don Ameche, Alice Faye, Ben Turpin, Chester Conklin. 20th Century-Fox.

1939   83. *The Jones Family in Hollywood.* Story by Keaton and Hoffman. Screenplay by Hoffman and Stanley Rauh. Directed by St. Clair. With Prouty, Byington. 20th Century-Fox.

1939   84. *The Jones Family in Quick Millions.* Story by Keaton and Hoffman. Screenplay by Hoffman and Rauh. Directed by St. Clair. With Prouty, Byington. 20th Century-Fox.

1940   85. *The Villain Still Pursued Her.* Written by Elbert Franklin. Directed by Cline. With Anita Louise, Richard Cromwell, Alan Mowbray. RKO Pictures.

1940   86. *Li'l Abner.* Story by Ben Oakland and Milton Berle. Screenplay by Charles Kerr and Tyler Johnson. Based on characters created by Al Capp. Directed by Albert S. Rogell. RKO Pictures.

Columbia Comedies Starring Keaton, 1939–1941

1939   87. *Mooching Through Georgia.* Written by Bruckman. Directed by Jules White. With Monte Collins, Bud Jamison.

1939   88. *Pest from the West.* Written by Bruckman. Directed by Del Lord.

1939   89. *Nothing But Pleasure.* Written by Bruckman. Directed by White.

1940   90. *Pardon My Berth Marks.* Written by Bruckman. Directed by White.

1940   91. *The Spook Speaks.* Written by Bruckman and Ewart Adamson. Directed by White. With Elsie Ames.

1940   92. *Taming of the Snood.* Written by Bruckman and Adamson. Directed by White.

1941   93. *So You Won't Squawk.* Written by Ellwood Ullman. Directed by Lord.

1941   94. *His Ex Marks the Spot.* Written by Felix Adler. Directed by White.

1941   95. *General Nuisance.* Written by Adler and Bruckman. Directed by White.

1941   96. *She's Oil Mine.* Written by Adler. Directed by White. With Elsie Ames, Monte Collins.

Films with Casts Including or Starring Keaton, 1943–1965
(WITH ONE EXCEPTION, FILMS MADE FOR TELEVISION NOT INCLUDED)

1943   97. *Forever and a Day* (10 reels). A film of short sketches. Keaton was in one sketch. Directed by René Clair, Edmund Goulding, Cedric Hardwicke, and others. RKO Radio.

1944   98. *San Diego I Love You* (8 reels). Story by Ruth McKenny and Richard Bransten. Screenplay by Michael Fessier and Ernest Pagano. Directed by Reginald LeBorg. With Jon Hall, Louise Albritton, Edward Everett Horton, Eric Blore. Universal Pictures.

1945   99. *That's the Spirit* (9 reels). Written by Fessier and Pagano. Directed by Lamont. With Jack Oakie, Peggy Ryan, June Vincent, Arthur Treacher, Gene Lockhart, Johnny Coy, Andy Devine. Universal.

1945   100. *That Night with You* (8 reels). Story by Arnold Belgard. Screenplay by Fessier and Pagano. Directed by William Seiter. With Franchot Tone, Susanna Foster, David Bruce, Louise Albritton. Universal.

1946   101. *El Moderno Barba Azul.* Directed by Jaime Salvador. (Mexico)

1946   102. *God's Country.* Screenplay by Robert Tansey. Based on a novel by James Oliver Curwood. Directed by Tansey. With Robert Lowry, Helen Gilbert, William Farnum. Screen Guild.

1948   103. *Un Duel à Mort.* With Berval. (France)

1949   104. *You're My Everything* (9 reels). Story by George Jessel. Screenplay by Lamar Trotti and Will H. Hays, Jr. Directed by Walter Lang. With Dan Dailey, Anne Baxter, Shari Robinson, Anne Revere, Alan Mowbray. 20th Century-Fox.

1949   105. *In the Good Old Summertime* (10 reels). Directed by Robert Z. Leonard. With Judy Garland, Van Johnson. Metro-Goldwyn-Mayer.

1949   106. *The Lovable Cheat* (7 reels). Directed by Richard Oswald. With Charles Ruggles, Alan Mowbray, Peggy Ann Garner. Film Classics production, released by United Artists.

1950   107. *Sunset Boulevard* (11 reels). Written by Charles Brackett, Billy Wilder, and D. M. Marshman, Jr. Directed by Wilder. With Gloria Swanson, William Holden, Erich von Stroheim, Jack Webb, Cecil B. DeMille, H. B. Warner, Anna Q. Nilsson. Paramount.

1952   108. *Limelight* (11 reels). Written and directed by Charles Chaplin. With Chaplin, Claire Bloom, Sydney Chaplin, Charles Chaplin, Jr. United Artists.

1953   109. *The Awakening.* Based on Gogol's "The Overcoat." Produced by Douglas Fairbanks, Jr., for television. (England)

1953   110. *Paradise for Buster*. Produced by Wilding Picture Productions, Inc., for Deere & Company, for private showings. Never released commercially. (Chicago)

1956   111. *Around the World in Eighty Days* (15 reels). Screenplay by S. J. Perelman, James Poe, and John Farrow. Based on a novel by Jules Verne. Directed by Michael Anderson. All-star cast, including David Niven, Cantinflas, Shirley MacLaine, Robert Newton. Mike Todd independent production, released by United Artists.

1960   112. *The Adventures of Huckleberry Finn* (10 reels). Produced by Samuel Goldwyn, Jr. Directed by Michael Curtiz. With Eddie Hodges, Archie Moore, Judy Canova. Metro-Goldwyn-Mayer.

1962   113. *Ten Girls Ago*. With Bert Lahr, Eddie Foy, Jr., Jan Minor, Jennifer Billingsley. Am-Can Productions. (Canada)

1963   114. *It's a Mad, Mad, Mad, Mad World*. Produced and directed by Stanley Kramer. All-star cast, including Sid Caesar, Milton Berle, Buddy Hackett, Dorothy Provine, Jonathan Winters, Ethel Merman, Mickey Rooney, Spencer Tracy. United Artists.

1963   115. *The Triumph of Lester Snapwell*. Directed by James Cahoun, starring Buster Keaton. Eastman Kodak Co.

1965   116. *The Railrodder* (2½ reels). Directed by Gerald Potterton. National Film Board. (Canada)

1965   117. *Keaton Rides Again* (2 reels). Profile of Buster Keaton's career. Directed by John Spotton. National Film Board. (Canada)

1965   118. *Film*. Silent-film story written by Samuel Beckett for solo performance by Keaton (one part of a trilogy). Produced by Evergreen Theatre. Directed by Alan Schneider.

1965   119. *Pajama Party*. American International Productions. (California)

1965   120. *Beach Blanket Bingo*. American International Productions. (California)

1965   121. *How to Stuff a Wild Bikini*. American International. (California)

1965   122. *2 Marines e un General*. Directed by Luigi Scattini, starring Franco Franchi, Ciccio Ingrassia and Buster Keaton. Italian International Film. (Italy)

1966   123. *A Funny Thing Happened on the Way to the Forum*. Directed by Richard Lester. With Zero Mostel, Phil Silvers, Jack Gilford. (Spain)

1966   124. *The Scribe* (3 reels, filmed Oct. 3–15, 1965). Directed by John Sebert. Co-producers Ann and Kenneth Heeley-Ray. Film-Tele Productions. (Canada)

Miscellany

1944   *Bathing Beauty* (10 reels). Starring Red Skelton and Esther
Williams, with special gags (without screen credit) by Keaton. Metro-Goldwyn-Mayer.

1949   *Neptune's Daughter.* Starring Red Skelton and Esther Williams, with special gags (without screen credit) by Keaton.
Metro-Goldwyn-Mayer.

1949   *A Southern Yankee.* Directed by Sedgwick. Starring Red
Skelton and Arlene Dahl, with special gags by Keaton.
Metro-Goldwyn-Mayer.

1957   *The Buster Keaton Story* (9 reels). Written by Robert Smith
and Sidney Sheldon. Directed by Sheldon. Starring Donald
O'Connor (as Keaton), Rhonda Fleming, Ann Blyth, Peter
Lorre. Paramount.

1963   *Thirty Years of Fun.* (Assemblage from old films.) Produced
by Robert Youngson, starring Charlie Chaplin, Buster Keaton, Laurel and Hardy, Syd Chaplin, Charlie Chase, Harry
Langdon. 20th Century-Fox.

Photographic Credits

INDEX